The Child Language Reader

Edited by

Kate Trott, Sushie Dobbinson and Patrick Griffiths

Routledge
Taylor & Francis Group

LONDON AND NEW YORK

First published 2004
by Routledge
11 New Fetter Lane, London EC4P 4EE

Simultaneously published in the USA and Canada
by Routledge
29 West 35th Street, New York, NY 10001

Routledge is an imprint of the Taylor and Francis Group

Typeset in Perpetua and Bell Gothic by
Florence Production Ltd, Stoodleigh, Devon
Printed and bound in Great Britain by
TJ International Ltd, Padstow, Cornwall

British Library Cataloguing in Publication Data
A catalogue record for this book is available from the British Library

Library of Congress Cataloging in Publication Data
Trott, Kate, 1963–
    The child language reader/Kate Trott, Sushie Dobbinson, and Patrick
    Griffiths.
        p. cm.
    1. Language acquisition.   I. Dobbinson, Sushie, 1965–   II. Griffiths,
    Patrick, 1942–   III. Title.
    P118.T755 2004
    401'.93–dc21   2003012736

ISBN 0–415–28100–8 (hbk)
ISBN 0–415–28101–6 (pbk)

Contents

Contributors

Priscilla Alderson, Childhood Studies, Social Science Research Unit, Institute of Education, University of London.

Melissa Bowerman, Max Planck Institute for Psycholinguistics, Nijmegen, and Free University of Amsterdam.

Joan Chasin, Royal Holloway, University of London.

Jennifer Coates, English Language and Linguistics, School of English and Modern Languages, Roehampton, University of Surrey.

E. Jane Fee, formerly of Dalhousie University.

Jane Gillette, formerly of the University of Pennsylvania.

Lila Gleitman, Linguistics, Department of Psychology, University of Pennsylvania.

Alison Gopnik, Department of Psychology, University of California at Berkeley.

Margaret Harris, Developmental Psychology, Department of Psychology, Royal Holloway, University of London.

Nina Hyams, Department of Linguistics, University of California at Los Angeles.

Elena Lieven, Department of Developmental and Comparative Psychology, Max Planck Institute for Evolutionary Anthropology, Leipzig, and Department of Psychology, University of Manchester.

Brian MacWhinney, Department of Psychology, Carnegie Mellon University.

David Malvern, Institute of Education, University of Reading.

William Merriman, Department of Psychology, Kent State University.

Yvonne Oakley, formerly of Royal Holloway, University of London.

Ann Peters, Department of Linguistics, University of Hawai'i.

Brian Richards, Section for Language and Literacy, Institute of Education, University of Reading.

Suzanne Romaine, Merton College, University of Oxford.

Colleen Stevenson, Department of Psychology, Muskingum College.

Carol Stoel-Gammon, Department of Speech and Hearing Sciences, University of Washington.

Deanne Swan, formerly of Georgia State University.

Caroline Yeeles, formerly of Royal Holloway, University of London.

Preface

The study of children's language acquisition and development is pivotal to research in a number of related disciplines. It is a major branch of psycholinguistics and a central theme in the research of linguists and psychologists. It is also of natural interest to educationalists, speech and language therapists and figures increasingly in sociolinguistic research. The fact that research on child language is published in such a range of disciplines can make accessing appropriate texts difficult for students. *The Child Language Reader* is designed to help students overcome some of these difficulties, while offering opportunities for critical engagement with original research, ideas and findings.

We anticipate that this *Reader* will meet the needs of many students interested in child language acquisition and development, and their teachers. In practice this will include students following second or third level undergraduate courses in linguistics and psychology departments, plus those on taught postgraduate programmes in linguistics, applied linguistics, psychology and language pathology/speech and language therapy. It may also be of use to the large and varied category of TEFL/TESOL-related students, which includes teachers on in-service courses. The book presents a significant and carefully chosen set of papers suitable for assigned reading, browsing and research projects, whether primarily theoretical or practical. It is designed for child language students in universities and colleges throughout the world, wherever English is used as the medium of learning. The inclusion of some cross-linguistic consideration in the book as a whole should make it of interest and relevance to a wider readership as well.

In a number of ways this *Reader* offers something different from the valuable resource represented by handbooks on child language. Handbooks present summaries and 'state of the art' accounts of the branches of the subject. Their material is usually comprehensive and thoroughly organised, but this diminishes opportunities for students to be creators of their own understanding. The selection of articles and chapters in our *Reader* comes mainly from major, refereed journals and specialist collections, which means that they often exemplify original research 'in the raw' and reading them enables students to gain practice in searching for, judging and integrating ideas, findings and theoretical stances. The Part introductions of the *Reader* provide contextual information and explanations to facilitate access to the substantive papers. For users who may be unfamiliar with statistical analysis there is a short, non-technical introduction in an appendix. The inclusion among the articles of first-hand accounts of fieldwork and experiments will also encourage students to probe and assimilate detail relevant to doing research. Finally, we anticipate that by virtue of size alone, this *Reader* may prove less daunting than the usually much bulkier handbooks.

In the preparation of the book, we compiled a shortlist of over 130 journal articles and chapters. The final selection contains 17 papers. We dearly wanted to include more but the hard facts of wordage meant that, very regretfully, we could not. In selecting items for inclusion, the objectives were to produce a reader which satisfied several criteria.

First, the editors identified the need for a reader which provides a reflection of recent research. Classics such as Lieven (Chapter 1.1) are included because they are felt to represent a particularly interesting or important contribution.

Our second criterion was to include articles illustrative of research practice and representative of original research.

Our third consideration reflects the multi-faceted nature of contemporary child language research. The approaches of psycholinguistics, psychology, linguistics and, to some extent, sociolinguistics and education are represented in the text, as is a range of theoretical standpoints.

Fourth, we have made a selection which aims at some breadth of coverage within the constraints of volume size. The concentration of the book is on first language acquisition and development during the pre-school years but articles on bilingualism, plus some linked to older children's language development, are included. Besides the traditional levels of linguistic patterning – phonology, word and sentence structure (syntax and morphology), meanings (semantics) – there are sections on explanations of language development (including theoretical approaches) and the social matrix of language development. Methodology (Part 2) and statistical analysis (Appendix) are under-represented in many child language texts and it is hoped that students will find them highly useful here.

Finally, while we have included a number of seminal works that have appeared in other collections or which have been written by key names in the field, in general the articles presented have been chosen because they are interesting. We hope readers will find them clear and accessible. Where it is felt that students might need additional support this has been addressed through editing and the editorial introductions.

The *Reader* is made up of individual parts which provide a clear indication of focused coverage on specific issues. All the parts follow a common organisation, comprising an editorial introduction followed by a selection of papers. The editorial introductions to parts explain essential terminology and background assumptions required to ensure that the material accessibly meets a broad spectrum of needs. Cross-referencing between introductions highlights material elsewhere in the book on related contexts, language structures, research questions, methodologies or age ranges.

A note on the editing of papers

We have endeavoured to reproduce all original papers and chapters as faithfully and as fully as possible, bearing in mind length restrictions. The writing conventions used by the authors have been maintained (including spelling and referencing systems). [. . .] in the text indicates where material from the originals has been shortened. Any editorial comments within the papers appear within square brackets: [ ].

Kate Trott, Sushie Dobbinson, Patrick Griffiths

B. MacWhinney, 'Emergent language', in M. Darnell, E. Moravcsik, F. Newmeyer, M. Noonan and K. Wheatley (eds), *Functionalism and Formalism in Linguistics, Volume 1: General Papers*, 1998, pp. 361–86. Reproduced by permission of John Benjamins Publishing Co.

B. MacWhinney, 'Introduction', in *The CHILDES Project: tools for analysing talk; transcription format and programs, Volume 1*, 3rd edition, 2000, pp. 1–9. Reproduced by permission of Lawrence Erlbaum Associates.

W.E. Merriman and C.M. Stevenson, 'Restricting a familiar name in response to learning a new one: evidence for the mutual exclusivity bias in young two-year-olds', *Child Development*, 68(2), 1997: 211–28. Adapted by permission of the Society of Research in Child Development.

A.M. Peters, 'Filler syllables: what is their status in emerging grammar?', *Journal of Child Language*, 28: 229–42. © Cambridge University Press 2001.

B.J. Richards and D.D. Malvern, 'Investigating the validity of a new measure of lexical diversity for root and inflected forms'. Specially commissioned paper, 2004.

S. Romaine, 'Bilingual language development', in M. Barrett (ed.), *The Development of Language*, Psychology Press, 1999, Taylor & Francis Books, pp. 251–75.

C. Stoel-Gammon, 'On the acquisition of velars in English', in B. Bernhardt, J. Gilbert and D. Ingram (eds), *Proceedings of the UBC International Conference on Phonological Acquisition*, 1996, pp. 201–15. Reproduced by permission of Cascadilla Press.

D.W. Swan, 'How to build a lexicon: a case study of lexical errors and innovations', *First Language*, 20, 2000: 187–204. Reproduced by permission of Alpha Academic.

Every effort has been made to obtain permission to reproduce copyright material. If any proper acknowledgement has not been made, or permission not received, we invite copyright holders to inform us of the oversight.

Part 1

The Social Matrix of Language Development

> The limitations of the [Chomskyan] perspective appear when the image
> of the unfolding, mastering, fluent child is set beside the real children
> in our schools. [. . .] To cope with the realities of children as commun-
> icating beings requires a theory within which socio-cultural factors have
> an explicit and constitutive role; [. . .]. We have then to account for the
> fact that a normal child acquires knowledge of sentences, not only as
> grammatical, but also as appropriate. He or she acquires competence
> as to when to speak, when not, and as to what to talk about with whom,
> when, where, in what manner.
>
> (Hymes 1972: 270–7 passim)

Though many researchers of child language have accepted the idea behind Hymes'
broader notion of communicative competence – that children do far more than
acquire rules of grammar (in the sense of pure linguistic structure) – there can still
be strong tensions amongst them regarding what the child is bringing to the process,
through inherited predispositions, etc., as opposed to factors shaped by social influences. That there is undoubtedly an interplay between these two rather crudely
grouped issues makes the examination of any individual child's language development a very complex task.

So, what is meant in this section by 'social matrix'? The term 'social' appears
to be straightforward enough as a descriptor of issues important to child language
development which can be related to a child's interactions with parents, immediate
and broader family, peers and their wider community or communities. 'Matrix' has
been chosen to give a sense of the direct, shaping influence which social factors can
be argued to wield. The term also suggests the structure, patterns, trends or norms
which can emerge in children's language use and language development as a result
of these influences. From research and comparison of findings, it is possible to make
generalisations about the way social factors tend to affect the developing language
of children in diverse communities. This knowledge can allow similarities to be
charted between individual children, family types, communities and cultures and how
language develops in and is used by them. It can be used to explore differences too,
in terms of variation between individual children, groups and so on, and why this
variation might exist.

In a useful and in many ways ground-breaking account, Wells (1986) attempted
to formulate an explicit description of the types and sources of variation in child
language use and development. He listed 'social background' ('family structure,
social group affiliation, cultural environment'); 'style of linguistic interaction'
('interpersonal relations, parental child-rearing methods') and 'situation' ('setting,
activity, number and status of participants') as social matrix-type influences
(p. 112). Interestingly, he suggested that situation and style of linguistic interaction both have a direct influence on the child's linguistic behaviour but that
social background has only an indirect influence. He represents quite a complex
co-variation between social matrix influences, or what sociolinguists would call
extralinguistic or **independent variables**. These concepts will be revisited later in
this introduction.

The papers

The two papers which are reproduced in Part 1 have been selected from a very wide pool; only constraints on space prevented more being included. However, these papers are not the only ones in this volume to be concerned with social issues. They are related to two others in this collection, Romaine (Chapter 7.1) and Gopnik (Chapter 7.2) Part 7 on Bilingualism and Cross-cultural Comparisons.

The papers discussed below have been chosen because they represent quite specific yet linked social matrix themes: the significance of carers, interaction and conversation in children's language acquisition and the role of gender in that process. These are areas which continue to be both important and popular in the field of child language research.

Elena Lieven (Chapter 1.1) explores the relationship between the language used with children by their primary carers (here, mothers) and the language used by the children themselves. In response to Chomsky's early claims that the language heard by children was poorly structured, detailed research into the characteristics of language addressed to babies and young children followed, with the 1970s seeing a wave of publications from key figures such as Catherine Snow and Charles Ferguson. Much of the research to date has indicated that adults (males as well as females) and older children tend to make modifications in their language when they address young children. These modifications are now commonly referred to as caregiver speech or **child-directed speech** (CDS). Commonly identified features of CDS are outlined in Lieven's paper; a useful summary of features can also be found in Snow (1995), along with an overview of the development of CDS studies.

The role of conversation in both language development and the mother–child relationship is strongly emphasised by Lieven and she makes the point that many CDS features are 'implicitly' conversational ones. There are clear links between her views and those of Wells (1981) and French and Woll (1981), who argued that conversation has a 'constitutive' role in language development (that is, the context of interaction and the language used actually create each other; there is close interdependency). This view has much in common with the theoretical standpoint of Bruner (1983). His theory of cognitive growth identifies the typical carer–child routines of social interaction, many of which are rooted in conversation, as a central feature of his explanation of language development. Lieven notes Snow's (1975) observation that:

> as [. . .] children grew older, the mothers became more stringent in their criterion of what was an acceptable utterance on the part of the child, although they were willing to accept 'almost any conversational opening on the part of the child and to fill in for the child whenever necessary'.
> (Snow 1975)

Lieven's paper takes the examination of the nature and effects of CDS further. It suggests that individual differences between children can elicit different types of CDS from mothers. Note that, as a result, CDS does not emerge here as an unvarying primarily responsible for shaping gendered behaviour. 'Nature'-linked ones (those linked to biological sex) emerge in her account as less powerful in determining differences between girls' and boys' language development. However, they may be responsible for girls' faster maturation, which in turn can seem to give girls an advantage in language acquisition at certain stages of development. Bornstein and Haynes (1998) is one example of a study which has produced evidence of girls' faster language development. Their research, based on a large sample of children (184), showed female precocity in language learning at 20 months.

It is worth noting that there has been a fairly recent resurgence of interest in the biological underpinning of gender differences in language. Neurological evidence that different areas of male and female brains are activated during specific tasks (such as verbally based and spatially based ones) has revived the debate, as has evidence from people with congenital adrenal hyperplasia (CAH) – a condition caused by exposure to large quantities of the male hormone testosterone whilst in the womb. Women with CAH have been observed to show more masculine traits, including enhanced spatial skills compared with verbal ones (see Hampson 1998). Kimura (1996: 259) notes:

> Scientific evidence for consistent sex differences in cognitive function between men and women has accumulated for well over fifty years. A solid body of research, carried out primarily in North America and Western Europe, has established that men, on average, excel on spatial tasks [. . .], mathematical reasoning and spatio-motor targeting ability. Women, on average, excel on tasks of verbal fluency [. . .], perceptual speed [. . .] verbal and item memory, and some fine motor skills. [. . .] Women have larger colour vocabularies [. . .].

Kimura defends this stance that male and female brains are differently endowed and organised, and that this causes differences in development and learning, arguing that:

> It has been fashionable to insist that these differences are minimal, the consequences of variations in experience during development. The bulk of evidence suggests, however, that the effects of sex hormones on brain organization occur so early in life that from the start the environment is acting on differently wired brains in girls and boys.
>
> (Kimura 1992: 119)

'Nature' versus 'nurture' arguments on this topic of gender, as on others linked to child language, are likely to roll on for some time. These themes are picked up again in Part 6 (Explanations of Language Development). Useful introductory further reading on issues related to gender and language acquisition, including educational issues, can be found in Swann (1992) and Graddol and Swann (1989). The website www.literacytrust.org.uk also affords interesting insights into gender, language and educational performance, especially from a UK perspective. There are many sites focusing on similar issues in other regions. Examples include: www.edc. org for US perspectives and sites such as www.education.qld.gov.au or www.schools. nsw.edu.au for Australian ones.

What should already be clear from this introduction and the papers discussed herein is the diversity and complexity of issues surrounding the social matrix of language development, only some of which can be touched on here.

Readers who wish to read accounts of other research linked to the notion of the social matrix, in addition to those references mentioned earlier in this intro- duction, might find the following interesting. Several of the studies centre on children of school age, emphasising the continuation of language development into middle and later childhood:

- Axia (1996) investigates 'How to persuade mum to buy a toy'. As in Lieven (Chapter 1.1), the context of her research is interaction (conversation) between individual children (aged 4, 6 and 8 years) and a close family member, usually the mother, but sometimes the father or one of the child's grandpar- ents. The setting is an Italian department store. Axia's stated aim is to discover whether there are grounds for proposing a sequence of development in the strategies children use to influence other people's behaviour during sponta- neous interaction. This focus places the research in the domain of **pragmatic development**: how children learn to communicate meanings in particular contexts or social settings.
- Ely and Gleason (1995) explore children's socialisation through language and context. They probe the roles of specific influences such as carers, the peer group, school and mass media.
- Fowles and Glanz (1977) outline the development of children's joke-telling skills and appreciation, when the jokes rely on linguistic factors. The paper explores the cognitive and social/pragmatic influences on this growing com- petence.
- Kerswill and Williams (2000) suggest not only how socialisation enforces linguistic norms (through social networks, for example) but also the key role children and their language can play in language change. It studies children aged between 4 and 12 years, focusing on accent features in a UK town (Milton Keynes).
- Maybin (1996) provides an analysis of children's spontaneous narratives (using the framework developed by William Labov) and shows how the 10–12- year-old subjects make connections with stories and conversations from other contexts to construct their meanings.

example: considerable discussion has centred around the very high proportion of questions in adults' speech to young children relative to their normal speech (Remick, 197[6]; Sachs, Brown and Salerno, 1976). Questions, at least in speech among adults, presuppose answers and are, according to Sac[k]s, Schegloff and Jefferson (1974), a device for ensuring continued turn-taking in conversation.

If it is the case then, that certain features of the adults' speech to the child are both important to language learning and dependent on conversation-like interactions between adult and child, it would be interesting to re-examine protocols in terms of the conversational skills of the participants. Catherine Snow (1975) has argued that the interactions between the two children in her study and their mothers gave the impression, at 18 months, of being 'proper' conversations. This was in part due to the mothers' effectiveness in keeping the conversation going despite the inadequacies of the children (i.e. interrupting, failing to answer) but also because the children *were* reasonably adequate turn-takers by this age although in other respects their language was not particularly advanced. Looking at conversations between these mothers and their children from 3 to 18 months, she showed how the mothers treated their children as partners from a very early age and how initially they would accept almost anything (e.g. a burp) as constituting the baby's turn. As the children grew older, the mothers became more stringent in their criterion of what was an acceptable utterance on the part of the child, although they were still willing to accept 'almost any conversational opening on the part of the child and to fill in for the child whenever necessary' (Snow, 1975).

In analyzing the data from two of the children whose language development was being studied, a very marked degree of individual difference both between the two children's speech and between that of the two mothers to them became obvious. On looking more closely, it was clear that the child–mother pairs were

Table 1.1.1 Summary description of sessions.

Session	Age (months, weeks)	MLU	Total number of comprehensible utterances	Type/ token ratio	Comprehensible utterances/ minute
Kate					
1	18.2	1.07	65	.59	1.7
2	19.1	1.10	66	.66	4.3
3	20.3	1.14	195	.46	6.4
4	22.3	1.54	201	.44	7.8
5	24.3	1.98	263	.46	6.9
Beth					
1	20.0	1.16	72	.33	2.8
2	22.1	1.22	163	.26	5.2
3	24.0	1.30	163	.26	5.3
4	25.1	1.76	170	.27	9.3
5	26.1	2.23	342	.12	9.3

Note:
A comprehensible utterance was defined as an utterance containing only one or more lexical items of English but including items which the child used idiosyncratically but systematically as lexical items if these were agreed to be such by the mother and the investigator.

also very different in terms of the conversational skills described by Snow. One child–mother pair conformed to Snow's description of conversational interaction between the two pairs in her study when the children were 18 months old, but the other mother–child pair in my study appeared to be interacting very differently and, at least on the surface, not to be having conversations at all.

Data to illustrate these points is taken from a study of these two mother–child pairs over a six-month period for each child. The children were seen in their homes with their mothers. Recordings were made at approximately fortnightly intervals but the data presented here are taken from sessions when only the mother, child and investigator were present.

The investigator behaved, and seemed to be treated, as a familiar visitor by both mothers and children. One child (Beth) was 20 months at the start of the study and the other (Kate) was 18 months. Beth was second-born with a brother who was two years older. Kate was first-born. Both mothers spent all day at home with the children at the time of this study and both fathers had professional occupations. Tape recordings were made with a Uher 2000 Report L and sessions lasted 45 minutes. Summary descriptions of the sessions are presented in Table 1.1.1.

The children's speech

In terms of MLU (measured in words), the children were not very different. At 20 months, Beth's MLU was 1.16 and Kate's was 1.10. By approximately 25 months, Beth's MLU had increased to 1.76 and Kate's to 1.98. Kate therefore appears to be only slightly ahead of Beth at 25 months. In other respects however the children did differ very markedly.

Beth was at least twice as repetitive as Kate in all sessions. Beth said a small number of words over and over again in both her single-word and multiple-word utterances. In all sessions the words *mummy*, *look*, *there* and *Sebastian* (Beth's brother) were the most frequently used. Her multiple-word utterances gave the appearance of lacking word order rules. For instance, in the session at 25.0 there were nine occurrences of *Sebastian there*, four of *there Sebastian*, two of *there Sebastian there* and one of *Sebastian, Sebastian there Sebastian*, to say nothing of *there Sebastian mummy*, *mummy there Sebastian* etc., etc. To make matters more confusing, Sebastian was *not* present at the time and Beth was not pointing to one of his possessions or at pictures in a book. These and nearly all of her utterances were made in a high-pitched excited tone and appeared to be attempts to attract her mother's attention.

The children's spontaneous multiple-word utterances were analyzed into semantic–syntactic categories based largely on those used by Bloom, Hood and Lightbown (1974). Categories were defined as follows:

Notice. Utterances that called attention to the existence of an object and included a notice verb such as 'see' or 'look' or the form 'hello' (changed from 'hi' in Bloom's definition) as in *hello spoon* e.g. *look mummy*.[1]

Locative Action. Utterances that made reference to movement that had the goal of affecting an object by changing its location in space e.g. *hand off*, *stick it there*, *go on self*.

mother's interest. These characteristics relate to features of the mothers' own speech to their children.

The mothers' speech

The speech of both mothers to their children showed many of the features which by now have become familiar (cf. Snow, 1977). In comparison with their speech to the investigator in the same sessions, the MLUs of the mothers' speech were much lower to their children. The MLU to the children, measured in morphemes for sessions 1, 2 and 3 was 7.25 for Kate's mother and 5.61 for Beth's mother. It was considerably more difficult to measure the MLU of the mothers' speech to the investigator, mainly because of the problem of determining the end of an utterance. However, average values of about 14.0 morphemes for Kate's mother and 20.0 morphemes for Beth's mother were obtained after somewhat *ad hoc* decisions on this point had been taken. The mothers used less subordinate clauses and considerably more imperatives and interrogatives to the children. However there were also some differences between these mothers in their speech to their children and this is clearly reflected in an analysis of their responses to the children's utterances. None of the measures in the analysis presented here showed any developmental trend over the five sessions and they have therefore been collapsed into an average percentage for the purposes of this paper. Measures were made of the frequency with which the mother responded to an utterance of the child within two seconds (chosen by inspection as the interval within which virtually all responses fall); and of the outcome in cases where the mother did not appear to respond. This was analyzed into occasions after a child's utterance when there was at least two seconds silence; those during and/or after which the mother was talking to the investigator; and those after which the child spoke again within two seconds. The figures are given in Table 1.1.2. It will be seen that, on average, Kate's mother failed to respond to

Table 1.1.2 Mothers' responses to the children's utterances.

	Kate's mother	Beth's mother
Percentage of comprehensible utterances to which mother did not respond*	19%	54%
*Types of non-response:***		
>2 seconds silence	35%	28%
mother in conversation	25%	34%
child speaks again in <2 secs	40%	38%
Questions in response to child's utterance***	36%	23%

Notes:
*   Percentages are of total number of comprehensible child utterances for sessions 1–5.
**   Percentages are of total number of comprehensible child utterances not responded to by either the mother or the investigator for sessions 1–5.
*** Percentages are of total number of mother's responses to the child's utterances for sessions 1–5.

only 19% of Kate's utterances, while Beth's mother, on average, failed to respond to 54% of Beth's. When we look at what happened when the mother did not respond, we can see that Beth's mother was particularly likely to simply continue her conversation with the investigator. Kate's mother, in contrast, tended to interrupt herself in conversation with the investigator in order to answer Kate.

It is also the case that when the two mothers did respond, Kate's mother was more likely to respond with a question to Kate (see bottom of Table 1.1.2). This would presumably have had the effect of extending the conversation. One could, I think, fairly deduce from these observations that there is less turn-taking in conversations between Beth and her mother than there is between Kate and her mother. Beth's mother made less effort to keep the conversation going and showed less interest in what Beth was saying. This is also demonstrated when we look at the types of responses made by the mothers when they did answer the child within two seconds. In both the case of Beth and Kate, the main category of adult response not included in Table 1.1.3 is a residual category of responses which were judged to be conversationally appropriate to the child's utterance but not to fall into any of the other categories. About 20% of both the mothers' responses fell into this category. A further 13% in Kate's case and 11% in Beth's is accounted for by word-for-word repeats by the mother either of what the child had just said or of what she herself had said just previous to the child's utterance.

Categories of response type are defined as follows (and included here are only those categories on which the two mothers showed some differences):

Expansion. An utterance in which the adult expands the child's utterance to a syntactically correct equivalent without adding any more new semantic information than is required to render the child's utterance syntactically.

Extension. An utterance in which the adult, in addition to expanding the child's utterance, adds new semantic information in excess of that required to render the child's utterance syntactically.

Query. An utterance in which the adult explicitly asks the child what he/she has just said.

Ignore. An utterance in which the adult seems to ignore the content of the child's previous utterance, where this utterance itself was not related to any prior utterance of the adult's.

Table 1.1.3 Types of maternal responses to the children's utterances.

Types of response	Kate's mother	Beth's mother
Extension	33%	9%
Expansion	15%	10%
Query	2%	5%
Ignore	9%	14%
Correct	2%	11%
Ready-mades	4%	21%

Note:
Percentages are of total number of mother's responses to the child's utterances for sessions 1–5. They do not sum to 100 due to utterances in residual categories.

Correct. An utterance in which the adult explicitly corrects the syntactic, semantic or phonological content of the child's previous utterance.

Ready-made. An utterance which does not fall into any grammatical class and which is defined by Lyons (1968) as 'expressions learnt as unanalysable wholes and employed on particular occasions by native speakers'. Examples are: 'yes', 'no', 'please', 'thank you', 'oh dear', 'jolly good'.

From Table 1.1.3, it can be seen that Kate's mother responds to Kate with a high proportion of extensions and expansions relative to Beth's mother. The latter has a higher probability of either responding to Beth with a ready-made word or phrase, or of correcting the child or ignoring her previous utterance in her reply. Where Beth is responded to, therefore, she is less likely to hear an utterance that relates specifically to what she has just said or provides her with new information, but she is also more likely to be explicitly corrected about her actual utterance.

To summarize then, these two children's mothers talked to them very differently. Kate's mother seems highly responsive to what Kate says and her utterances seem to be closely related to it. Beth's mother seems considerably less 'tuned-in' to Beth's speech and less accepting of it. There are also differences in the children's own speech which indicate that the children have learnt to converse in different ways about different things.

The implications of individual differences

Clearly one cannot make any causal statement on the basis of two children. Indeed it is doubtful that causal statements would be at all appropriate however many children were under consideration. Rather than labouring the implication that the speech styles of the two mothers are somehow 'responsible' for the differences in their children's speech, it may be useful briefly to look at the problem from two, perhaps less common, perspectives.

Firstly there will certainly be more or less important effects of the child upon various aspects of the adult's speech to him/her from a very early age and, in particular, the effects of styles of speech may be two-way, even between a two-year-old child and an adult. For instance an analysis of the investigator's (my) speech to the children indicates that the differences in their speech may have influenced the way that the investigator spoke to them. This is shown in Table 1.1.4.

Only in one session with Kate, Session 5, were there enough responses by the investigator to Kate's utterances, to justify an analysis. This was due to two factors. Firstly Beth spoke directly to the investigator considerably more often than Kate did. Secondly, Kate's mother was very highly responsive to Kate's utterances and gave the investigator little opportunity to enter into conversation with Kate even had she wished to. The reverse was true in the sessions with Beth when the investigator often felt constrained to enter into some sort of dialogue with the child. These differences are in themselves very interesting and, apart from their implications for the development of language skills in the children, they very likely reflect important features of the developing social relationships of these children which would bear considerably more analysis.

Table 1.1.4 Types of response by the investigator to the children's utterances.

Types of response	to Kate[*]*** (Session 5)	to Beth[**]*** (Sessions 1–5)
Extension	27%	16%
Expansion	27%	18%
Query	3%	0
Ignore	0	8%
Correct	0	2%
Ready-made	0	10%

Notes:
[*]   Percentages are of total number of responses by the investigator to child's utterances in Session 5.
[**] Percentages are of total number of responses by the investigator to child's utterances in Sessions 1–5.
[***] Percentages do not sum to 100 due to utterances in residual categories. About 26% of the investigator's responses to both Kate and Beth fell into the residual category of utterances judged to be conversationally appropriate but not to fall into any of the other categories. A further 16% in both cases were accounted for by word-for-word repeats of either what the child had just said or of what the investigator herself had said just prior to the child's utterance.

It will be seen from Table 1.1.4 that the way in which the investigator responds to the two children is somewhat different and that furthermore it is, in each case, more similar to that of the mother to whose child she is responding at the time than to the mother of the other child. However, the investigator did not extend Kate's utterances as much as Kate's mother did and she both expanded and extended Beth's utterances more frequently than Beth's mother while ignoring and correcting her less. She also used less ready-made utterances to Beth than Beth's mother did. It would be possible to argue that this was an effect of the mother on the investigator, i.e. that the investigator was imitating each mother's speech style with her child. However, I, as the investigator, found it much easier to carry on a conversation with Kate than I did with Beth. It is difficult to respond informatively, for instance to expand or extend utterances which are extremely repetitive and seem not to relate clearly to anything in the immediate context; in fact it is often very difficult to say anything other than 'yes', 'no' or 'really?'. My impression is that these figures reflect a possible influence of the child's speech on the adult. If this is the case, then however it was that Beth and Kate came to speak the way that they did, it is possible that they would evoke in others who were conversing with them, a speech style similar to that of their mothers. That is to say, a child, by virtue of the way that she/he talks, may be influencing the way in which other people speak to her/him.

Secondly, if it turns out to be the case (1) that many of the features of adult speech that have been noted in the literature as potentially helpful to the language-learning child are dependent for their efficacy on the already acquired conversational skills of the child, and (2) that individual differences in language learning are related to individual differences in conversational interaction between the child and others, then perhaps we shall have to look more closely at the development of pragmatic skills in young children. Amongst other things, this would involve investigating individual differences in the development of turn-taking in infancy and possible manifestations of these during the period of language learning.

One final point is the importance of defining in each case under discussion what the end-point of language learning is considered to be. In superficial terms, Beth and Kate, who are by now at school, are judged to be fluent speakers of English. It may be, however, that there are differences in their conversation styles and, perhaps, skills, that may have more far-reaching implications for their general development than a test of, say, their syntactic or semantic abilities would show. At 25 months, Beth was violating Grice's (1975) conversational maxims of manner and relevance; she was neither brief, relevant nor orderly. Kate, although the same age and not particularly advanced in other aspects of her language development, managed those skills well. On the other hand, within the context of their families, both children succeeded in making their wishes known and both seemed happy, intelligent children with no obvious problems. [. . .]

Notes

* The study [. . .] was supported by a grant for training in research methods from the Medical Research Council, London, England. I am more than grateful to Joanna Ryan for supervising me for the research on which this paper is based, to Catherine Snow and Gerald Gazdar for their criticism and encouragement and to John McShane for help in the final stages.

1   There is a confusion in the analysis here which requires further elaboration. It appears that those utterances of Beth which were placed in this category all had the pragmatic force of demanding the mother's (or investigator's) attention and this was reflected semantically in the fact that they did not, in fact, call attention to the existence of an object linguistically specified in the utterance by the child. The utterances of Kate which were placed in this category did turn out, however, on reinspection, to belong to a genuinely semantic category as defined.

2   Categories not included here which occurred in the children's speech are action-on-affected object; state-location of object; rejection-denial; non-existence (cf. Bloom et al., 1974). A number of multiple-word utterances appeared to be rote-learnt and are also not included in the analysis. Examples are *please mummy* and *thank you* (mainly by Kate) and *what's that* (by Beth).

Jennifer Coates

THE ACQUISITION OF GENDER-DIFFERENTIATED LANGUAGE

1. Children and gender identity

[. . .]

[**W**]**OMEN AND MEN DIFFER** linguistically in a wide variety of ways. In this chapter I shall look at the way these different repertoires are acquired. Work on child language acquisition is relatively recent, and it tends to concentrate on how the (undifferentiated) child acquires his (*sic*) language. Language is often interpreted in the narrow sense of grammar, phonology, and lexicon, with particular emphasis on the development of syntax. Classic studies in this field are Bloom (197[3]), Brown (1973), Dale (1976), Fletcher and Garman (1986), Ingram (1989). More recently, with increased awareness of language as social behaviour, researchers have widened the scope of their enquiries. They still aim to discover how a child becomes linguistically competent, but 'linguistically competent' has been redefined. [. . .] [A] knowledge of grammar, phonology and lexicon is not enough – it does not make the child competent; children need to master not only the formal rules of language, but also rules for the appropriate use of language. Linguistic competence is now taken to include a knowledge of the cultural norms of spoken interaction. The best work using this new framework is Ochs and Schieffelin's (1983) study of children's acquisition of conversational competence.[1]

Works such as the latter are based on the premise that learning to speak is learning to be a member of a particular culture. The social order, in other words,

1993, reprinted with permission from *Women, Men and Language*, London: Longman, 143–67.

is reproduced through speech. This being so, and since it seems to be common to all cultures that women's and men's roles are distinguished, it is reasonable to assume that when children learn to speak, one of the things they learn is the cultural role assigned to them on the basis of their sex. This is a two-way process: in becoming linguistically competent, the child learns to be a fully fledged male or female member of the speech community; conversely, when children adopt linguistic behaviour considered appropriate to their gender they perpetuate the social order which creates gender distinctions.

[. . .] [W]omen and men [represent different] social groups [. . .]. Girls and boys learn during childhood to identify with one group or the other. They demonstrate their membership of the group by their use of gender-appropriate behaviour, and this includes gender-appropriate *linguistic* behaviour. Social psychologists refer to this process of learning how to be a 'proper' girl or a 'proper' boy as the acquisition of gender identity.

In this chapter I shall describe work which demonstrates that gender differences are found in the speech of children. This work is of two kinds. First, there is work which aims to test the belief that girls acquire language at a faster rate than boys; this work will be described briefly. Second, there is work which explores children's acquisition of gender-differentiated language in terms of both formal features and communicative competence; this work will be described in some detail. In this second group I shall include work which analyses the ways in which adults – particularly parents – interact with children, as well as work which analyses the ways in which children interact with each other in same-sex peer groups.

2. Gender differences in early language learning

One of the most well-known and best established generalisations in the area of gender differences is girls' superiority over boys in the acquisition of speech. On measures such as the onset of babbling, the first word, number of words used at 18 months, girls tend to do better than boys. This contrast between girls and boys seems to have been exaggerated in the past, although it has been suggested that differences between male and female children might be diminishing as a reflection of less polarised gender roles and less sexist modes of child care in contemporary societies. However, Maccoby and Jacklin's (1974) authoritative survey of all extant research in the area concluded that the generalisation still holds good. For pre-school children, the research findings indicate that where a gender difference is found, it is nearly always girls who are ahead. Not all these differences achieved statistical significance, but the combined results of all the studies amount to a significant trend. For the early school years, on the other hand, no consistent differences emerge from the research literature, but from the age of 10 or 11, girls again outscore boys on a variety of measures of verbal competence. Some examples of these findings are described below.

Clarke-Stewart (1973) observed American mothers and first-born children for 9 months, from when the children were 9 months until they were 18 months. She found that the language skills of girls in the sample in terms of both comprehension and vocabulary were significantly higher than those of boys; this was paralleled by the girls' more positive involvement with the mother. The girls' mothers differed from the boys' mothers in that they spent more time in the same room as their daughters, had more eye contact with them, used a higher proportion of directive and restrictive behaviours, and a higher ratio of social to referential speech. (Social speech includes greetings, *thank you*, apologies, etc. while referential speech, as its name implies, means speech which refers to things: *What's this?*; *Give me the red brick*, etc.)

Nelson (1973b) studied the acquisition of vocabulary by eighteen children between 1 and 2 years of age (again in the USA). She divided her sample into two groups according to the rate at which they acquired vocabulary (the index was the age at which the child had acquired fifty words). All the boys fell into the group with a slower acquisition rate. The mean age for fifty words was 18.0 months for the girls and 22.1 months for the boys.

Perkins (1983) reports a study of modal expressions (*can, will, have to, probably*, etc.) used in spontaneous speech by children aged between 6 and 12. His subjects were the ninety-six children taking part in the Polytechnic of Wales Language Development project. All the children were monolingual English speakers, and the sample was balanced in terms of age, gender, and social class. Perkins discovered that frequency of use of modal expressions varied in relation to the child's gender, with girls using modal expressions more frequently than boys (though this difference was too small to be statistically significant). Interestingly, Perkins found that social class was significantly correlated with modal usage: children from middle-class homes used modal expressions more frequently. This parallelism between girls and the middle class on one hand and boys and the working class on the other is something that has been noted [elsewhere (see Edwards 1979)]. In fact, linguistic gender differences seem to be more marked in poorer families: two studies of disadvantaged children (Shipman 1971; Stanford Research Institute 1972) found girls clearly ahead on a number of language measures.

These studies are representative of the many that have been carried out on child language and show a general pattern of girls acquiring language faster than boys. This means that at any given age, girls will be found to be superior in terms of comprehension, size of vocabulary, reading ability, handling of complex expressions such as the modals, etc. While such findings are of interest, they are not necessarily relevant to the linguistic differences we find between women and men (many just reflect slower maturation). In the next section, I shall describe work which, it can be argued, shows children developing gender-differentiated language. The linguistic differences described below show girls and boys acquiring the gender-roles prescribed by society.

3. The development of gender-appropriate speech

In this section I shall look first at work which describes gender differences in children's language which anticipate formal differences in adult language [. . .]. Secondly, I shall look at work where children's language usage anticipates adult communicative competence differences [. . .].

3.1 Formal differences

Before puberty, children's vocal tracts differ only in relation to the child's size and not in relation to the child's gender. But work on *pitch* has revealed that gender differences emerge before the onset of puberty. Liebermann's (1967) study suggests that, even before they can talk, babies alter the pitch of their voices depending on the gender of the addressee: their average fundamental frequency is lower when they 'talk' to their fathers than when they 'talk' to their mothers.

Several projects (e.g. Sachs et al 1973; Meditch 1975; Fichtelius et al 1980) have tested the ability of adult judges to identify a child's gender from recorded samples of speech. These projects find that judges identify children correctly as male or female at well above chance level. Further analysis of the child speech samples suggests that it is **formant** patterns which identify speakers as male or female. (A formant is a concentration of acoustic energy, reflecting the way air vibrates in the vocal tract as it changes its shape; most sounds can be described on the basis of three main formants.) 'The child would be learning culturally determined patterns that are viewed as appropriate for each sex. Within the limit of his (*sic*) anatomy, a speaker could change the formant pattern by pronouncing vowels with phonetic variations, or by changing the configuration of the lips' (Sachs et al 1973: 80). So even at an age when their articulatory mechanisms are identical, girls and boys are learning to speak appropriately, that is, to produce higher or lower formants respectively.

Fichtelius et al (1980) showed that both adult and child judges could still guess the gender of a child speaker even when the tapes had been submitted to a process which affects the sound so that individual words and syllables are no longer discernible but rhythmic patterns and intonation are still apparent. Older children were more easily identified than younger ones, since as girls and boys get older, their speech becomes *prosodically* differentiated. Boys begin to employ a more rapid tempo, while girls use a greater variety of intonation patterns.

Children's acquisition of *intonation* has also been investigated by Local (1982) as part of the Tyneside Linguistic Survey. The children were aged between 5¼ and 6 by the end of the study. Taped extracts of their speech were abstracted from a larger corpus collected over a period of about a year. Adults on Tyneside use a system of nuclear tone which differs markedly in its frequency distribution from the system used by adult speakers of Standard English. [. . .]

[. . .] [D]uring the year all the children shifted their speech in the direction of adult Tyneside English. However, the relative frequency of these tones was not the same for all children, and Local identified three different patterns [. . .]. These patterns reveal that the children's speech varies on the basis of speaker's gender. Pattern 3 (more rises than falls or levels) is typical of girls' speech; pattern 1 (falls and levels more frequent than rises) is typical of boys' speech; while pattern 2 [(more falls than rises and more rises than levels)] is ambiguous, being realised by both girls and boys. Patterns 3 and 1 are also found in adult speech on Tyneside, with adult females using more rises than falls or levels and adult males using more falls and levels than rises. Thus Local's analysis reveals children acquiring not just Tyneside intonation, but Tyneside intonation appropriate to their gender.

Work on *phonological variation* in children's speech also confirms that gender differentiation is present from an early age. In the course of a study of child-rearing

Table 1.2.1 Gender differences in the use of
(ing) (based on Fischer 1964: 484).

	More [ɪŋ]	*More* [ɪn]
Girls	10	2
Boys	5	7

in a semi-rural New England village, Fischer (1964) was struck by differences between the pronunciation of girls and boys. Using his tapes of interviews with the twenty-four children in the sample, he carried out a quantitative analysis of the variable (ing). In this community, (ing) has two variants: the standard variant [ɪŋ] and the non-standard variant [ɪn]. The twenty-four children in the sample consisted of two equal age groups (3–6 year olds and 7–10 year olds), each group containing equal numbers of girls and boys. Fischer's analysis of his data revealed that the girls used the standard variant [ɪŋ] more frequently, while the boys preferred the non-standard variant [ɪn] (see Table 1.2.1). These differences are statistically significant. It seems likely that the children have learned that in their speech community [ɪŋ] is a marker of female speech and [ɪn] is a marker of male speech.

[. . .] Romaine's (1978) study of primary school children in Edinburgh [. . .] found that speaker's gender was the single most important factor correlating with use of the phonological variable (r). In a survey of gender differences in the language of children and adolescents, Romaine (1984) compares her results for 10 year olds in Edinburgh with Macaulay's results [(1978)] for 10 year olds in Glasgow [. . .]. Although the scoring procedures used in the two studies were slightly different, the results are very similar. Both Romaine and Macaulay investigated the variables (gs) (the glottal stop), (i), (au), and (a), which occur in words like *butter*, *hit*, *house*, and *bag*. For all these variables, there is clear gender differentiation in both Edinburgh and Glasgow (though for (a) in Glasgow the differences in girls' and boys' scores is not large enough to be significant). In other words, girls obtained lower scores than boys for all these variables; their lower scores reflect less frequent use of non-standard variants.[2] The pattern of gender differentiation found among children in Edinburgh and Glasgow is the same as that found in the adult population: the girls consistently prefer forms which are closer to standard pronunciation, while the boys prefer forms which are more non-standard.

It's even possible that these findings greatly underestimate the variation in children's speech. The results discussed here are for 10 year olds; as children get older and move through primary school, their use of non-standard forms appears to diminish, so 10 year olds have lower scores on average than 6 year olds. If we look at the variable (au) in Edinburgh, as used by three different age groups, we can see how the scores get lower, apparently reflecting diminished use of the stigmatised non-standard variant [uː] (as in *hoos*) and increased use of the standard variant [au] (as in *house*) (see Figure 1.2.1).

At the age of 6, the difference between boys' and girls' use of (au) is very marked – boys are shown to choose the non-standard variant [uː] more than 50 per cent of the time (that is they tend to say *hoos* rather than *house*). Girls at 6, on the

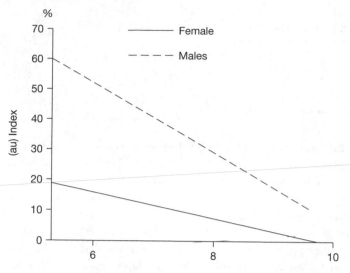

Figure 1.2.1 Percentage of non-standard [uː] in the usage of girls and boys in three age groups in Edinburgh (Romaine 1984: 101).

other hand, use the non-standard variant less than 20 per cent of the time. As the children get older, both girls and boys are recorded as using fewer stigmatised forms, and the difference between girls' and boys' usage gets smaller.

Romaine (1984) suggests that what these figures might actually show is children's growing ability to code-switch, that is, to use different forms in different contexts. She observes that while use of the stigmatised variant certainly decreases in the interview situation as children get older, it is still much in evidence when children are talking among themselves in the playgrounds. So these children can be seen to be acquiring competence in style-shifting (they are learning which styles are appropriate in which contexts), as well as acquiring competence in gender-appropriate linguistic behaviour.

Eisikovits's study (1987; 1988) of adolescent speech in Sydney, Australia, provides very interesting evidence of the way children's usage shifts as they acquire gender-appropriate speech. She obtained data from two groups of working-class adolescents, interviewed in self-selected pairs (to reduce the formality of the situation). The twenty subjects in the first group had an average age of 16 years 1 month; the twenty subjects in the second group had an average age of 13 years 11 months. [. . .] [T]he results for the 16 year olds showed the expected pattern, with male speakers using consistently more non-standard forms than female speakers. But if we compare these results with those for the 13 year olds, we can see that there are significant differences between the two: the younger speakers do not conform to the expected pattern. As Figure 1.2.2 shows, the younger girls use a *higher* proportion of non-standard past tense forms than any other group, while their use of multiple negation is very similar to that of the younger boys. Invariable *don't* is the only non-standard grammatical feature which shows clear gender variation for both age groups; moreover, the boys increase their usage of this feature significantly as they get older.

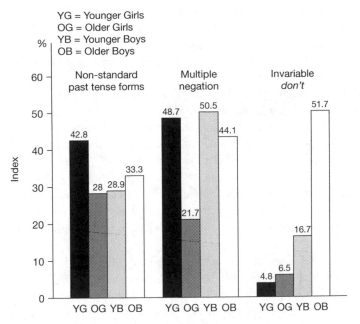

Figure 1.2.2 Age and gender differences in Sydney, Australia, for three non-standard grammatical features (based on Eisikovits 1988).

What we see here is declining usage of non-standard forms among the girls, and stable or increasing usage among the boys. It looks as if many of the non-standard features of Sydney vernacular speech have prestige for young adolescents of both sexes. But as they get older, the girls learn to modify their speech in the direction of the standard, while the boys seem to consolidate their perception of non-standard forms as having positive value. In discussion with the interviewer, the older informants displayed divergent attitudes: the girls became increasingly conservative, the boys increasingly non-conformist. For example, the girls said they didn't like swearing any longer, and objected to their boyfriends swearing, while for the boys swearing is a normal part of everyday life: 'If I swear in front of me mother now, she don't say nothing'. It seems that a growing awareness of gender norms is matched by a shift in linguistic usage so that, by the age of 16, these speakers have adjusted their speech to be more congruent with adult patterns.

3.2 Differences in communicative competence

So far I have looked at work which shows children acquiring the formal features of language. Now I shall examine children's acquisition of gender-differentiated communicative competence. I shall look at work on verbosity and conversational dominance, interruptions and simultaneous speech, question-and-answer sequences, and politeness.

As far as *verbosity* is concerned, Smith and Connolly (1972) conclude that girls are both more talkative and more fluent. They talk more, both to their mothers and to other children, before the age of 4, but after that such quantitative differences disappear. These results could be the product of different expectations on the part of parents. Our culture expects girls and women to talk more and early research in this area, with crude measures and small samples, seemed to confirm the talkativeness of pre-school girls. However, [. . .] work on adult language indicates that women talk *less* than men in mixed company.

Certainly, recent research suggests that boys dominate mixed conversation from an early age. Adelaide Haas (1978) analysed the amount of speech produced by girls and boys aged 4, 8, and 12 in mixed-sex pairs: she found that boys used longer utterances than girls. Joan Swann's (1989) analysis of classroom talk (using 9–11 year olds) showed convincingly that boys talked far more than girls, both in terms of the number of turns taken and the number of words uttered. [. . .] She also demonstrates that *all* participants in the classroom collaborate to achieve male dominance: the teacher by paying more attention to the boys; the boys by using the interactional resources available to contribute more; the girls by using the same resources to contribute less.

This pattern of differential usage of interactional resources can also be seen in the context of the family. Male children are socialised to dominate conversation with the active support of female participants. Frederick Erickson (1990) analysed the dinner-table conversation of a large Italian-American family: mother, father, four sons (aged 7–14 years) and a daughter (aged 9 years). A female researcher was also present at the meal. The conversation consisted of a series of narratives. One set of narratives focused on accidents or near-misses experienced by members of the family when riding their bikes. The initial story was told by the youngest boy. This was followed by stories from the older boys. Finally, the father told a dramatic story about his own experience of nearly crashing his motor-bike, which capped the previous stories. The stories were recounted almost exclusively by the male members of the family (the daughter started one but didn't succeed in sustaining it), and celebrate the bravery and skill of the riders. The mother, daughter and female guest acted as an attentive audience for the story-tellers. These stories not only establish the relative status of male family members; they also function as a display of male dominance which is achieved collaboratively by the whole family.

Research on *interruptions* and *simultaneous speech* has found no significant differences between girls and boys. Parents, however, apparently do differ significantly on both these measures. Greif (1980) studied sixteen middle-class children, aged between 2 and 5, in conversation with (1) their mothers and (2) their fathers. Her results show that fathers interrupted more than mothers (though this difference was not quite large enough to be statistically significant), and that both parents interrupted girls more than boys. In terms of simultaneous speech (that is both speakers starting to speak at the same time), parents were significantly more likely to continue talking than were children, father-and-child pairs were more likely to engage in simultaneous speech than mother-and-child pairs, and finally both fathers and mothers were more likely to engage in simultaneous speech with daughters than with sons.

[. . .] [T]he use of interruptions and simultaneous speech can be interpreted as a way of controlling conversation. It seems that fathers try to control conversation more than mothers (which fits the research results for adult conversations), and both parents try to control conversation more with daughters than with sons. The implicit message to girls is that they are more interruptible and that their right to speak is less than that of boys.

When equals, as opposed to asymmetrical pairs such as father–child, engage in simultaneous speech, then such linguistic behaviour is likely to symbolise solidarity and cooperation rather than dominance. In his study of the gender politics of an elementary school classroom in San Diego, California, Jurgen Streeck (1986) describes an episode where the girls' ability to talk in unison becomes a powerful strategy for demonstrating to the boys the unity of the girls' coalition.

(1)   [The teacher has given the group a task to do]

Leola:	I know y-you gotta make some wo:rds out of these	
Wallace:	you don't	

{
| *Leola*: | *yes* ⌈ you do |
| *Wallace*: | ⌊ you don't |
}

{
| *Leola*: | you see, here it s ⌈ ay-   how man- |
| *Carolyn*: | ⌊ it say- |
}

{
| *Leola*: | ⌈ how many words can you make out of those |
| *Carolyn*: | ⌊ how many words can you make out of those |
}

{
| *Leola*: | five letters |
| *Carolyn*: | five letters |
}

Given that talk in unison is not easy to accomplish, we have to admire the girls' interactive skills, which clearly prefigure women's later skills in contrapuntal talk.

Question-and-answer sequences are the focus of Hasan and Cloran's (1990) research on mother–child interaction. They studied twenty-four Australian mother–child dyads and found that the semantic features of question-and-answer sequences between mother and child differed depending on the social class of the family and the gender of the child.[3] There was overlap between patterns typical of mother–daughter dyads and middle-class dyads, an overlap we have remarked on before (see section [. . .] 2).

Politeness is another dimension of communicative competence where we find gender differences [. . .]. Research on child language has concentrated on the way parents teach polite language, for example, formulae like greetings and *thank you*. Gleason (1980) studied parents and children in both natural and laboratory settings. She was interested in finding out how much *explicit* teaching of such formulae goes on. She found parents very consistent in prompting their children to respond with socially appropriate items, particularly *thank you*. Parents treated girls and boys similarly, but provided different models: the mothers used far more polite speech than the fathers. Thus, while girls and boys are both urged to use polite forms, the children observe that it is predominantly adult females who use them themselves. The one significant difference observed of the children was that the boys were more likely than the girls to greet the researcher spontaneously (41 per cent:18 per cent). This may also result from the children's observation of adults: adult male speakers tend to take the initiative in conversation.

Politeness is a relevant dimension for the speech act of requesting. A request may vary from the blunt imperative *Give me a pound* to the more polite (because sensitive to the face needs of the addressee [. . .]) *Would you lend me a pound?* Walters (1981) observed the requests of thirty-two bilingual children in four different contexts. He found no significant differences in terms of speaker's gender, but the gender of the addressee was significantly correlated with the politeness of the request. The children in the study were more polite when the addressee was female, and less polite when the addressee was male.

It seems that adult interaction with girls and boys may be significantly affected by *context*. In a long-term study of children in Bristol, Wells (1979) examined all conversations occurring when the children were 3¼ years old, and categorised them according to who initiated them (the child or the adult) and according to the context (mealtime, watching television, playing with another child, etc.). 30 per cent of conversation sequences were initiated by an adult (usually the mother), and an analysis of these revealed significant differences in the context in which adults addressed girls or boys. Table 1.2.2 gives the figures. This table shows that over half the sequences initiated with girls were in helping or non-play contexts – a ratio of 2:1 compared with the boys. Sequences initiated with boys, on the other hand, were overwhelmingly in the context of play. 'This suggests that adults emphasise more useful and domestic activities in their interaction with girls, whilst the emphasis with boys is towards a more free-ranging, exploratory manipulation of the physical environment' (Wells 1979: 392).

Children are acquiring not only gender-appropriate behaviour, but also a knowledge of the folklinguistic beliefs of our society. At what age do children learn that in our culture swearing, for example, is considered 'masculine'? Edelsky (1976) tested this by selecting twelve language variables conventionally associated with 'women's language' or with 'men's language' and presenting them, embedded in utterances, to adult and child judges. The judges were asked to rate each sentence as probably made by a woman, probably made by a man, or no preference. Her child judges (aged 7, 9, and 12 years) demonstrated a growing ability to recognise certain linguistic forms as appropriate to speakers of a particular gender. At 7 years, only two variables get a consistent response: *adorable* is judged to be female, and *Damn it!* is judged to be male. At 9 years, this has increased to eight variables:

Table 1.2.2 Proportions of conversations initiated by adults with girls and boys in different contexts (based on Wells 1979: 391).

	Girls (%)	Boys (%)
Helping/non-play activity	56.8	28.8
Talking and reading	19.0	22.5
Playing with adult	5.2	18.1
Dressing, meals, toileting	12.1	14.4
Playing alone	3.4	8.1
Watching TV	0.9	5.4
Playing with another child	2.6	2.7
Total	100	100

adorable, oh dear, my goodness, won't you please are judged to be female, *and damn it!*, *damn* + adjective, *I'll be damned* are judged to be male (tag questions get a neutral response). At 12 years, the child judges agree on assigning every one of the twelve variables to one sex or the other: tag questions, *so, very, just* are added to the female list, and commands to the male list.

We can see that children are gradually acquiring a knowledge of adult norms, and internalising the folklinguistic beliefs of our society (the fact that some of these beliefs are false [. . .] is irrelevant). Edelsky gives a more delicate analysis of her findings to show that there are two clear patterns of acquisition. Variables in her first group – *adorable, oh dear, my goodness, so, just,* tag questions – show a steady increase with age in the number of people able to interpret them as being appropriate to a particular sex. Variables in the second group – *I'll be damned, damn* + adjective, *damnit, won't you please, very,* command as male – show a different pattern: there is an increase in 'correct' answers peaking at 12 years old and decreasing in adulthood. It seems that the variables in this second group are features of language which are explicitly commented on through proverbs or admonishments. Expressions such as 'Little girls don't say that' mean that children are *taught* the gender-appropriateness of some linguistic terms. As happens with other features of child language, when a rule is learned it is frequently over-generalised. Just as children add *-ed* to all verbs to form the past tense, once they've grasped this rule, producing forms like *goed, eated, singed* (even though they earlier used forms like *went, ate, sang* – and of course subsequently do so again), so it seems they over-generalise the rule for gender-appropriate language and treat such differences as *gender-exclusive* rather than *gender-preferential*. As a result, they have to modify their rules later to conform to adult norms.

3.3 Subculture and conversational style

The focus of much recent work on children's communicative competence is child–child talk rather than adult–child talk. It is now widely accepted that the peer group is of vital importance in a child's sociolinguistic development. Girls and boys tend to play in same-sex groups; gender is the organising principle that structures their activities. Streeck, for example, describes the behaviour of the children he observed in primary school: the girls and the boys huddled on opposite sides of the table, their posture and position clearly signifying two separate camps; when joint activity was required, talk between the two groups was antagonistic (Streeck 1986).

One of the chief reasons that girls and boys develop different styles of talk is that the all-girls and all-boys groups to which they belong interact in vastly different ways. Boys play in larger, more hierarchical groups, while girls play in small groups, often in pairs. Boys' friendships tend to be based on joint *activity*, while girls' friendships are based on *talk*. In their seminal article on gender-specific subcultures, Daniel Maltz and Ruth Borker (1982) argue that girls learn to do three things with words:

1.   to create and maintain relationships of closeness and equality
2.   to criticise others in acceptable ways
3.   to interpret accurately the speech of other girls.

Boys, on the other hand, learn to do the following when they speak:

1.   to assert a position of dominance
2.   to attract and maintain an audience
3.   to assert themselves when another speaker has the floor.

Maltz and Borker (1982) characterise girls' talk as **collaboration-oriented**, boys' talk as **competition-oriented**.

These gender-specific patterns of interaction develop very early. Girls and boys deal with conflict, for example, in very different ways. In a study of quarrels between children aged 5–7, Miller et al (1986) found that boys used a more heavy-handed style, their priority being to get their own way, while girls used more mitigating strategies (such as compromise, evasion or acquiescence) and were more concerned to maintain interpersonal harmony. Boys were more likely to resort to physical force to resolve conflicts. Similar findings emerged from a study of talk among 3-year-old friends in same-sex triads, carried out by Amy Sheldon (1990). She analyses in detail two disputes over a plastic pickle which arose when the children were playing in the home corner (with a toy cooker, pots and pans, a sink, and plastic items of food). One of the disputes occurred in a group of girls, the other in a group of boys. The girls succeeded in negotiating a resolution and maintained interconnectedness among members of the group. They also sustained their fantasy play, pretending to prepare food for the dolls. The boys, by contrast, adopted a more adversarial style, and since neither of the main protagonists was prepared to give in, the conflict escalated (and lasted considerably longer than the girls': 5 minutes compared to 1 minute 45 seconds for the girls). Moreover, this conflict disrupted the boys' fantasy play.

Disputes between boys at nursery school in Italy (Corsaro and Rizzo 1990) deal not only with issues of ownership and protection of territory, but also of who is 'il capo', the boss. In the following example, Matteo and Luigi are making a space ship; Nino approaches and tries to join in.

(2)   *Nino*:   Anch'io posso?
                I can also?
        Luigi: si, puoi giocare
                yes, you can play
        Matteo: no, io sono il capo
                no, I'm the boss
        Nino: si, e vero
                yes, it's true
        Luigi (to Matteo):   Lui – puo giocare?
                    him – can he play?
        (Nino reaches over and picks up some building materials near Matteo)
        Matteo: no non puoi, ma, non puoi!
                no you can't, but, you can't!

Girls in this nursery school also get involved in disputes over ownership and in excluding third parties from their play, but they demonstrate an ability to work *together* to achieve their aims. For example, in one incident observed by the researcher, Rosa and Grazia work as a team to get a piece of building material back from an intruder, Sara.

Goodwin's research on Black children's street play [analyses] the way arguments among the children were structured [and] shows that girls and boys use many common strategies (Goodwin and Goodwin 1987). They organise their talk to emphasise disagreement or opposition. This is true both of same-sex and mixed talk.

(3) [talking about Sharon's hair]
     Eddie: wet it!
     Sharon: no, I don't *wanna* wet it

(4) [talking about slings]
     Chopper: I don't want these big thick ones
     Michael: you is crazy boy. I swear to god. You need that – thick like that

However, there was one strategy which was used only by the girls, labelled 'he-said-she-said'. This strategy only indirectly challenges another participant, and opens the dispute to a wider group of participants. Examples (5) and (6) are typical he-said-she-said accusations:

(5) *Darlene*:   and *Ste*phen said that *you* said that *I* was showin off just because I had that *blouse* on

(6) *Pam*:   Terri said you said that. I wasn't gonna go around *Pop*lar no more

Framing accusations in this way allows both the accuser and the accused to save face. The accuser focuses attention on somebody not present (Stephen in example (5); Terri in example (6)). The accused can deny responsibility (*I ain't say anything*), or can blame someone else (*that was Vincent said*), or can blame the third party referred to by the accuser (*well I know that they telling a lie cuz I know I ain't say nothin about you*). The he-said-she-said strategy allows for much more complex talk, involving many speakers and a longer time-span, than the two-party adversarial disputes typical of all-boy and of mixed talk.

Studies of older *male* children have found that most conflict exchanges are not resolved. In fact, resolution does not seem to be a primary goal. Some conflict is highly ritualised: what is most important is the display of verbal skill. The following example comes from Labov's famous study of pre-adolescent and adolescent boys in Harlem (Labov 1972).

(7) C1:   your mother got on sneakers!
     C2:   your mother wear high-heeled sneakers to church!
     C3:   your mother wear high-heeled sneakers to come out and play on the basketball court!

A second function of the exchange of ritual insults such as these is to create and maintain status differences among the boys. Girls are far less likely to engage in ritual exchanges of this kind (see Goodwin 1980). When they do, they seem more concerned with establishing normative behaviour than with status distinctions. Girls aged 10–14 were observed by Donna Eder (1990); in their conflicts they focused on resolving issues such as what does it mean to be someone's best friend, or what constitutes flirting. The trick is to respond to insults with a clever remark or a counter-insult, and not to take them seriously. The girls show some skill at defending themselves against insults from each other, but at other times their inability to joke about certain topics shows how significant such issues are for them.

Goodwin's work on directives [(1980)] showed how boys' strategies for getting someone to do something reinforce the hierarchical organisation of the boys' group. Dominant members use bare imperatives (*Gimme the pliers*), while subordinate members use mitigated requests (*can I be on your side Michael?*). Girls prefer to use forms such as *let's* which minimise status differences between participants and which emphasise joint action. Jacqueline Sachs (1987) looked at similar strategies in the talk of much younger children in a pre-school playgroup. Same-sex dyads were videotaped while they played at doctor-and-patient. Sachs analysed the use of 'Obliges', a category wider than directives which includes any utterance that demands a response from the addressee. The following are different sorts of Obliges:

1.   imperatives   (a) positive, e.g. *bring her to the hospital*
                    (b) negative, e.g. *don't touch it*
2.   declarative directive, e.g. *you have to push it*
3.   pretend directive, e.g. *pretend you had a bad cut*
4.   question directive, e.g. *will you be the patient?*
5.   tag question, e.g. *that's you bed, right?*
6.   joint directive, e.g. *now we'll cover him up*
7.   state question, e.g. *are you sick?*
8.   information question, e.g. *what does she need now?*
9.   attention-getting device, e.g. *lookit*

Sachs used as her data the fantasy play of four 5-year-old girl dyads and four 5-year-old boy dyads. She found that girls and boys used roughly the same number of Obliges, but they varied significantly in terms of which type they preferred. Table 1.2.3 gives the results. Notice the boys' preference for imperative forms, and the girls' for tag questions. Overall, the girls preferred more mitigated strategies than the boys: 65 per cent of the girls' Obliges were mitigated, compared with only 34 per cent of the boys'. These findings are summarised in Table 1.2.4. The girls softened their Obliges, and seemed more concerned to include the other child in planning what they were going to play.

The question of topic is addressed in Haas's (1978) study of child language. Adelaide Haas analysed the speech of 4-, 8-, and 12-year-old children in same-sex and mixed-sex pairs. In same-sex pairs, the main difference between girls and boys was that boys talked significantly more about sports and location, while girls talked significantly more about school, identity, wishes, and needs. Haas's comparison of mixed-sex pairs also found a difference related to topic – the subject of sport was significantly associated with boy speakers. Boys also used more sound effects (e.g. *brrmm brrmm goes the car*) and more direct requests. The girls laughed more and used

Table 1.2.3 Distribution of Obliges by category and gender (Sachs 1987: 182).

Category	Girls (%)	Boys (%)
Imperative	12	36
Declarative directive	5	6
Pretend directive	11	4
Question directive	2	0
Tag question	35	16
Joint directive	15	3
State question	2	11
Information question	16	22
Attentional device	2	2
Total	100	100

Table 1.2.4 Distribution of mitigated and unmitigated Obliges (Sachs 1987: 183).

Category	Girls (%)	Boys (%)
Mitigated	65 ·	34
Unmitigated	17	42
Other	18	24

more compliant forms (e.g. *okay that's a good idea*). The girls' use of laughter was far more prominent in their interaction with boys than in same-sex interaction – they laughed only half as much when talking to each other. Haas comments that boys seemed to be the initiators of humour, and laughter was the girls' response to this. Laughter may also be seen as appropriately deferential behaviour by the girls, and therefore occurs more with the boys.[4] Both girls and boys adapted their linguistic behaviour when in mixed pairs, but girls accommodated to boys more than vice versa.

Tannen (1990a; 1990b) analysed the conversation of pairs of best friends (conversations which had been video-recorded for research purposes by a psychologist, Bruce Dorval). These children were asked by the researcher to talk about something serious or intimate, and were then left alone in front of a video camera. The youngest boys (8 years old) squirmed in their chairs, kicked their feet, made faces at each other and at the camera. Their conversation jumps from topic to topic, and consists of very short turns. They rebel against the researcher's instructions: they tell jokes, fool around in front of the camera, and conduct mock interviews. The following extract is typical of their conversation:[5]

(8)   *Sam*:   did you see Star Wars
      (0.8)
      Jeff: no, hey, guess *what?* (1.1) ahm =
      Sam: = you have HBO? (0.6) do you? =
      Jeff: = no [shakes head]

(0.4)
Sam: neither do we (1.5) you saw Star Track?
(0.3)
Jeff: yeah:: = [enthused tone, head motion]
Sam: = I like the part when they um, .hh when they
           ⎡ were having that:: battle =
Jeff: ⎣ I, I, I,   = at the en', hah
(0.5)
Sam: Un hn
(0.7)
Jeff: that's goo::d

Girls of the same age carried out the researcher's instructions to the letter, and talked seriously for twenty minutes with no sign of discomfort.

(9)   Ellen: Remember what when I told you about my uncle? He went up the
                ladder after my grandpa? And he fell and um cracked his head open?
                He's and you know what? it still hasn't healed
      Jane: one time, my uncle, he was uh he has like this bull ranch? in
                Millworth? and the bull's horns went right through his head
      Ellen: that's serious

Note how Ellen's comment on her friend's anecdote is supportive, and explicitly orients it to the instructions they've been given.

Pairs of male friends at all ages seemed less comfortable with the task assigned to them. They avoided eye contact and sat parallel rather than facing one another. Older pairs were able to sustain topics for longer, but preferred to remain at an abstract level of discussion and avoided personal details. The only pair who became involved in a personal discussion (16 year olds) did not respond to each other's revelation of anxiety or unhappiness with support, but played down the significance of what the other had said.

(10) [talking about who to take to the dance]
      Tim: I don't want to ask Bar-, I just don't feel like asking anyone, and I
                don't know why, and I don't want to ask Janet, and I felt so bad
                when she came over and started talking to me last night
      (0.1)
      Robert: why?
      (0.9)
      Tim: I don't know, I felt uncomfortable I guess
      (2.3)
      Robert: I'll never understand that [laughs]
      (0.7)
      Tim: why?
      (1.1)
      Robert: ((x)) well I can't seem to just do that, ah, I mean, I know that's
                what you do, but I mean, I just could never do that

The girls, on the other hand, sit closer to each other and look at each other directly. They talk about serious topics and self-disclose that about feelings. Even the youngest girls can sustain a topic over several turns. Individual turns are longer, as the following example shows. It is taken from the conversation of the pair of 12-year-old friends.

(11) *Susan*: too bad you and Lesley are not good good friends anymore
    Jane: I know. God, it's- she's so *mean* sometimes because .h I mean-she/jus'gets you sta:rted in something nice, she says, um, she's so *ni:ce* today, that's why I wanted to be her best friend, I mean, I wasn't tryin' to to take her away from you or anything, .h but I mean she's so ⌈ *ni:ce*=
    Susan: ⌊ *ni:ce*=
    Jane: =like I just couldn't (let) her down or anything, .h an' so I just wanted to BE her friend, I mean- I wanted to be ⌈ her best friend
    Susan: ⌊ (I know)
    Jane: .h and then- what was so sad she just gets mad at you all of a sudden .h an like if she does somethin *I* don't like (0.3) I mean, I jist (0.5) I don't *li:ke* it, I mean I don't get *ma:d* at her!
    (0.7)
    Susan: she tries to upset people
    (0.5)
    Jane: she *doe:s*, and she just sees me crying an everything (0.5) she just lets me suffer=
    Susan: =and she loves it
    Jane: I know

Note how the girls work together to try to understand a problem. Their talk involves longer turns than that of boys of the same age, and their turns follow very closely one after the other, with only occasional pauses. Moreover, when a girl told a story like this, her friend invariably responded with concern, rather than belittling the problem (compare Tim and Robert in example 10). The girls' body posture, their patterns of eye contact, and the topics they choose, all emphasise closeness. The boys, on the other hand, choose patterns of physical alignment and eye contact which symbolise separateness, and their choice of impersonal topics and lack of engagement in each other's problems reinforce the impression of separateness.

    All the studies referred to in this section demonstrate significant differences in the conversational strategies of girls and boys. Girls prefer a more mitigated style; they use linguistic forms which minimise differences between participants and which are sensitive to speaker's and hearer's face needs. Boys, on the other hand, prefer a more adversarial style and pursue their own agenda without reference to other participants. For boys, winning is all-important. Girls, by contrast, seem aware that where there are winners there are also losers; they prefer jointly negotiated outcomes. However, several of these studies show that, both when interacting with boys, or when taking on roles such as mother in pretend play, girls are perfectly competent at the more adversarial style typical of boys (see Goodwin 1980; 1988;

1990; Maynard 1986; Miller et al 1986; Goodwin and Goodwin 1987; Sheldon 1992). Girls, in other words, can style-shift to suit the sociolinguistic context; boys, on the other hand, tend to be mono-stylistic.

These studies encompass children as young as 3 years old, and include both Black children and white children, working-class children and middle-class children, in both natural and experimental situations. This research is unanimous in showing that the gender-specific subcultures which children belong to generate different linguistic subcultures. These anticipate the gender-differentiated talk of adult women and men.

4. Conclusion

As we have seen, various studies show differences in male and female children in a wide range of linguistic forms. What emerges is a picture of girls acquiring linguistic skills at a faster rate than boys (though this superiority is not as marked as was claimed in the past), and acquiring patterns which differentiate them from boys. In the past, researchers believed that such differences arose from innate biological differences, but now differences in linguistic usage are explained by differences in the linguistic environment of girls and boys. Work on the development of differential communicative competence illustrates particularly clearly the crucial role played by environmental factors.

Language is an important part of the socialisation process, and children are socialised into culturally approved gender roles largely through language. Learning to be male or female in our society means among other things learning to use gender-appropriate language. This survey of work on children's acquisition of language suggests that socialisation is achieved in a variety of ways:

1.   through explicit comment on certain aspects of linguistic behaviour (e.g. swearing, taboo language, verbosity, politeness);
2.   through adults providing different linguistic models for children to identify with [. . .];
3.   through adults talking to children differently depending on the sex of the child (e.g. adults are more likely to interrupt girls, and lisp more when talking to little girls);
4.   through adults having different preconceptions of male and female children (e.g. adults expect female infants to be more verbally able than male infants);
5.   through adults responding differently to girls and boys using the same linguistic strategy (e.g. boys arguing or talking assertively are more likely to get a positive response than girls);
6.   perhaps most importantly, through children's participation in gender-specific subcultures which create and maintain distinct male and female styles of interaction.

[. . .]

Notes

1   Other good work using this framework includes Ochs and Schieffelin 1979; McTear 1985; Foster 1990; Schieffelin 1990.

2   Both Romaine and Macaulay adopted scoring procedures which represent RP with a score of 0.

3   Hasan and Cloran (1990) assigned class position according to the autonomy experienced by the main breadwinner of the family in his (*sic*) profession (all main breadwinners in the sample were male). Families were assigned to one of two groups: LAP (Lower Autonomy Profession) or HAP (Higher Autonomy Profession).

4   See Pizzini (1991) for an analysis of the way humour is used to reinforce existing power relationships between women and men in the obstetrical/gynaecological setting.

5   Examples (8), (10), and (11) are taken from transcripts given in the Appendix of Dorval (1990). Example (9) comes from Tannen (1990a).

Part 2

Methodology

INTRODUCTION

M ETHODOLOGY IS CONCERNED with how research is done, focusing on the working principles of researchers and the methods they employ. Child language study is **empirical**, which means that its theories are tested against observation; theories are expected to fit what is known about real children's language development. Theoretical explanations are the theme of Part 6. The present part concerns the ways generally regarded by child language researchers as appropriate for collecting evidence on which to build and test theories.

Theory guides the investigator regarding what kinds of data to look for, what methods to use and how to interpret data (see the Introduction to Part 6 for further discussion). There are some differences, in emphasis at least, between the several academic disciplines with interests in child language (psychology, linguistics, sociology, education) regarding sources of evidence. Instructive comparisons could be made between articles in the *Reader*.

The topics of the three chapters in Part 2 are:

2.1: the responsibilities of researchers in relation to the rights of children and the community;
2.2: an integrated set of computational tools for analysing child language data and making data accessible to other researchers;
2.3: quantifying vocabulary usage (illustrating questions about the representativeness of data samples).

In the course of providing background for these chapters, attention will be drawn to related points in the methodology of other studies in the *Reader*. There are many books on methodology, but one that can be recommended as accessible, thought-provoking and practical is Robson (2001).

Longitudinal and cross-sectional studies

Studying development involves comparisons between children at different ages or stages. Researchers wanting to understand the changes in children's language between the ages of, say, 1 year, 1½ years and 2 years, can take two approaches:

1   The same children can be studied as they become more skilled in the use of language. This is the **longitudinal** way, which can yield important insights. It sometimes allows researchers to observe key transitions and perhaps notice what prompted change. However, it takes time: there is a whole year of waiting as a child grows from 1 to 2 years old. The longitudinal study of a child with Down's syndrome reported by Fowler *et al.* (1994) was based on data collected over more than 3 years.
2   In a **cross-sectional** investigation a group of children of different ages is studied together. For example there might be some aged 1;0, some aged 1;6 and some aged 2;0. No individual subject undergoes a year's development during the study, but there is 'apparent development' across the group. The subjects can all be tested in the same week or month on the researcher's schedule; so there does not have to be a long wait. This saving often makes it possible to include many more children in a cross-sectional study. Larger samples increase our confidence that the findings represent children more generally. The drawback is that the age differences are tied to individual differences. We cannot be sure that the younger individuals are on the same trajectory as the older ones they are compared with.

Patient longitudinal studies can provide rich, fine-grained data, as illustrated by the following papers in the *Reader*: Lieven (Chapter 1.1), Harris *et al.* (Chapter 3.1), Bowerman (Chapter 3.3), Swan (Chapter 4.2), Peters (Chapter 6.1) and Hyams (Chapter 6.2). Several *Reader* papers show how a combination of longitudinal and cross-sectional data collection can be used to good effect: Stoel-Gammon (Chapter 5.1), Fee (Chapter 5.2) and Gopnik (Chapter 7.2). Gopnik undertook cross-sectional studies to check the generalisability of results from longitudinal work. Both kinds of data are drawn on in the survey articles by Coates (Chapter 1.2) and Romaine (Chapter 7.1).

Data sources

In child language research, the two main sources of data are experiments and records of children talking. Two others are questionnaires answered by the child's caregivers and studies of comprehension. There is cross-cutting between these: for example comprehension may be the focus of an experiment, comprehension can be observed in conversation, and some questionnaires ask about comprehension. There are other approaches as well: e.g. MacWhinney (Chapter 6.3) uses computer synthesis as both theory and a method: if software can learn significant parts of human languages and make errors similar to those made by children, then the computer programs are models for how we become language users; and it can be instructive for the development of theory to see what needs to be modified to make the computer's performance more like that of a child.

Diaries and questionnaires

Baby diaries, in which the researcher (often a parent) keeps a careful written record of observations on a child's development, have a long history in the language acquisition field. See Ingram and Le Normand (1996) for an interesting outline of a language development diary dating back to the opening years of the seventeenth century. Leopold's (1939–49) impressive diary-based account of his daughter Hildegard growing up in the US as an English–German bilingual is discussed in Chapter 7.1 (Romaine). The English data in Chapter 3.3 (Bowerman) came mainly from diaries that Bowerman kept on the language development of her two daughters.

Some researchers have asked parents to log their children's language development in structured diaries. In the Harris *et al.* study (Chapter 3.1) parents provided the researchers with lists every two weeks of all new words that their children comprehended and produced. A widely used instrument for collecting child language data from parents/caregivers is the MacArthur Communicative Development Inventory, or CDI (Fenson *et al.* 1993). This comes in two forms: one for infants, up to age 16 months, and one for toddlers, 16–30 months. Both forms of the CDI present hundreds of words that children in the relevant age bracket might know and the adults mark the words that their child knows.

Merriman and Stevenson (Chapter 3.2) present CDI totals as part of their summary of the characteristics of the children in their experiment. Chapter 2.3 (Richards and Malvern) employs an earlier but similar questionnaire devised by the originators of the CDI. Norms are available for the CDI, enabling several aspects of children's vocabularies to be compared with data collected from large, representative samples of children. Versions of the CDI in languages other than English have been constructed and normed, or are under way (see the CDI website http://www.sci.sdsu.edu/cdi).

Transcripts

Diaries continue to provide valuable data, but much child language research in the past half century has been based on audio- or video-recordings of children talking. In the mid twentieth century the weight and price of tape recorders came down sufficiently to make it feasible for a researcher to take a recorder to where children could conveniently be recorded. The possibility of listening again and again to stretches of child talk increased the objectivity and scope of child language study.

Later, the advent of video cameras light enough to be carried around was valuable for child language study in general and stimulated investigations into children's acquisition of Sign Languages too (e.g. Morgan *et al.* 2002).

A prerequisite for analysis is a written/printed version of what has been recorded on an audio- or videotape. A detailed record, on paper or in a computer file, of what was said and done on a tape is a **transcript**. Some basic points about the analysis of transcripts will be illustrated with an excerpt (see box) from the transcript of a conversation between a little boy aged 2½ years (CHI) and an adult researcher (RES). They are talking about pictures in books. The utterances are numbered for reference.

1	CHI:	That one.	
2	CHI:	Want this one.	(CHI picks up another picture book.)
3	CHI:	This is ə very big one.	(CHI is referring to the book.)
4	RES:	Oh yes.	
5	CHI:	Look ə this door.	(CHI looks at picture of steps leading up to a house front door.)
6	CHI:	Ring ə bell.	(CHI is talking about the bell push next to the door in the picture.)
7	RES:	Is it . . .?	
8	CHI:	There's orange.	(CHI has paged over to a picture of an orange.)

Source: From the project described in Griffiths *et al.* (1974).

Types and tokens

As part of the analysis of a transcript, it is very common for researchers to find themselves counting words or morphemes or syllables or phonemes or patterns of interaction or syntactic constructions, etc. What they count depends on whether they are mainly interested in vocabulary learning, morphological development, phonology, syntax, or any of several other aspects of language or language use. Whenever counting is done, an important distinction becomes relevant: between a **token** (a specific occurrence of something) and a **type** (a distinguishable category of things). Tokens can be thought of as items of data, i.e. occurrences that have been observed. Types are elements in an account of what the tokens represent, which means that they are theoretical entities.

The total length of CHI's utterances 1 and 2 is five word tokens (*that* + *one* + *want* + *this* + *one*), but the tokens belong to only four different word types (*that* + *one* + *want* + *this*), because there are two tokens of the type *one*. In CHI's utterances 1, 2, 3, 5, 6 and 8, there are 20 word tokens: *that, one* (×3), *want, this* (×3), *is*, ə (×3), *very*, *big*, *look*, *door*, *ring*, *bell*, *there's* and *orange*, but the number of different words (types) in CHI's vocabulary that this sample apparently gives evidence for is 14 (counting no extras for the multiple tokens of *one*, *this* and ə). There is room for argument, however, about the allocation of tokens to types, regarding at least ə and *there's*.

If CHI had been an adult then a transcriber would quite likely have written *This is a very big one* for utterance 3, *Look at this door* for 5 and *Ring the bell* for 6, associating the pronunciation [ə] (schwa) with three different word types: *a*, *at* and *the*. That would change the count for types in CHI's six utterances: the 20 tokens would be allocated to 16 types, instead of 14. In the project from which this specimen transcript came, it was decided not to presume that young children have adult-like grammatical sophistication. When a schwa was heard in the position of a small grammatical function word it was transcribed as [ə], rather than using the spelling of a function word that could plausibly occur in that position.

In the instances discussed in the previous paragraph, the spoken schwa tokens were part of the data. It amounts to a theoretical claim to suggest that, even though the child just said [ə] each time, schwa represents the indefinite article *a* in utterance 3, but *at* and *the* in 5 and 6, respectively. Swan (Chapter 4.2) notes that her analysis is stated in terms of types, rather than tokens, an important distinction whenever counts are reported.

An interesting chapter by Johnson (1999), in a book on methods for studying language production, presents persuasive examples to support her view that using the ordinary writing system, instead of phonetics, can lead to researchers being unaware of theoretical assumptions they are making in what they might feel is a transparent process of transferring sound (and images when transcribing videotapes) into words on paper or a computer screen. Fee (Chapter 5.2) also stresses the importance of phonetic transcription. Peters (Chapter 6.1) shows that crucial aspects of language development can be uncovered by taking an interest in **fillers**, which are essentially tokens that are very difficult to allocate to types.

Phonetic transcription is valuable, but not a magic solution. Many degrees of transcriptional precision are possible. It might be that a more detailed phonetic transcription would reveal that the three tokens transcribed as [ə] in the sample transcript were three subtly different schwas. That would be evidence for an analysis which associated [ə] with three different words. It would not prove it, because, examined microscopically enough, every spoken token is different from every other, but language users ignore differences that do not count as contrastive in their phonology. Theorising has to be done, with arguments offered to support alternative allocations of tokens to types. No matter how hard the analyst listens to or looks at a given token, of ə for example, there is not going to be certainty about the type it belongs to. It is necessary to consider the bigger picture: in the present case, this could involve seeing whether any of CHI's utterances at this age suggested that he was making a contrast between the articles *a* and *the*, whether he used other prepositions than *at*, whether he sometimes pronounced fuller tokens of *at* and *the*, and so on.

Formulas, productivity and distribution

If utterance 8 had been spoken by an adult, then *there's* would probably be taken as consisting of a sequence of two tokens: *there* and *'s* (where *'s* is a token of *is*). Should we regard the *'s* in CHI's utterance as a token belonging to the type *is*, along with the token *is* in utterance 3? Did CHI construct *there's* by putting together a token of *there* with a token of *is*? And did he, as is common in conversational English, contract *is* to *'s*? Or was *there's* a memorised stretch of language functioning as an unanalysed unit, a **formula** (Hickey 1993) or – another term used for unanalysed wholes – a **frozen form**?

A rule, pattern or process is said to be **productive** for a language user if it is employed to assemble output (and comprehend input), instead of the user having to rely on memorised 'prefabricated' formulae. To begin to judge whether CHI's *there's*, in utterance 8, was a formula or a productive construction, it would be worth looking at the other tokens of *there*, *there's*, *'s* and *is* in the full transcript from which the sample, above, was taken. **Distribution** is the term for statements about where linguistic items are found, perhaps also taking account of how often they appear in particular places.

It turns out that, besides many examples of *there's*, the transcript has occurrences of *here's*, *where's*, *he's*, *the cow's*, *that one's*, *this man's*, *that's*, *what's* and *it's*. These occur in sentences such as *The cow's eating ə flowers*, where they are not plausibly tokens of the possessive *'s*. They all very probably belong to the type *is*. There are also tokens of *there* (and *here*) without *'s*; there are six *is* tokens, all occurring in the sequence *this is*; *this* appears without *is* too; there are no examples of *are*, *was* or *were* in the transcript. Humans have impressively large memories, so they can store many frozen forms. Consequently this quick survey of distribution is not conclusive. However, the fact that the parts of *there's* occur separately and in different combinations does suggest that, at age 2½, CHI had a system that he could have used productively to assemble *there's* from *there + is*.

Distribution is of central importance to six of the papers in the *Reader*:

*   the distribution of verbs, particles, case endings, etc. in Bowerman's account of differences between the acquisition of Korean and English (Chapter 3.3);
*   Gleitman and Gillette's proposal that children can discover important aspects of verb meanings from noticing how verbs affect the distribution of noun phrases (Chapter 4.1);
*   the distribution of morphemes (Swan, Chapter 4.2);
*   the distribution of consonants within words (Stoel-Gammon, Chapter 5.1);
*   the distribution of syllable constituents in words (Fee, Chapter 5.2);
*   the distribution and frequency of inflectional forms (Hyams, Chapter 6.2).

Other papers in the *Reader* involve study of the distribution of various units:

*   speaker turns with various interactional roles (Lieven, Chapter 1.1);
*   sociolinguistic variables and patterns of communication according to gender, age and situation (Coates, Chapter 1.2);

- 'fillers' (Peters, Chapter 6.1);
- bilingual children's languages across situations (Romaine, Chapter 7.1).

Creative errors

Productivity is strongly suggested when a child says something that could not plausibly have been memorised from input. For example a child who appears to treat the spoken word *box* as a plural, creating from it a singular form *bock*, is making an error, but clearly has learnt something about plural formation in English.

Errors which 'although cut to the English pattern, happen not to be the conventional way of expressing the desired meaning . . .' provide Bowerman (Chapter 3.3) with a powerful argument for the conclusion that some English-speaking two-year-olds have begun to use combinatorial principles for packaging meanings. Fee (Chapter 5.2) offers good evidence for her view that young children speak words according to prosodic patterns when she is able to point to cases where 'children produce forms which contain two syllables even when the target contains only one'. Other arguments based on children's systematic errors can be seen in Chapter 4.2 (Swan).

Agreement between transcribers and coders

Subjective judgement is involved in transcription and in deciding which types to allocate tokens to. Testing theories against data often requires researchers to sort into categories children's and adults' conversational turns, utterances, syntactic constructions, or responses in experiments, etc. This can involve marking the utterance or other unit with a coded symbol, as a reminder of which category it has been put into; so the process is called coding. A first important step is to write out a **coding scheme**, a tight specification of criteria for membership in each category, with examples. One of Lieven's (Chapter 1.1) categories was *Recurrence*. She coded an utterance as belonging in this category if it 'made reference to the reappearance of an object or another instance of an object or event, e.g. *more mummy, more car bang*'. Other coding schemes can be seen in Chapters 3.2 and 4.2 (Merriman and Stevenson; Swan).

An important test of a coding scheme in relation to a given set of data is whether, in practice, different people following the scheme agree over the sorting of instances into categories. On at least one issue, Lieven (Chapter 1.1) consulted the children's mothers for a second opinion. Swan (Chapter 4.2) provides a good model for the process of ascertaining and reporting inter-coder agreement.

Lieven based her coding scheme on an earlier one by Bloom *et al.* (1974). Science is a collaborative effort with researchers trying to understand each other's theories, test them and then explain what is still unconvincing. Using someone else's coding scheme is an excellent way of getting a real grasp of how their theory relates to data. Chapter 2.2 (MacWhinney) is about CHILDES, a major undertaking to help child language researchers exchange expertise and data.

Variability

In child language studies, statistical analysis sometimes reveals underlying trends that are masked by the variability of human performance. However, variability can also be an important source of information. Differences between Kate and Beth's language acquisition are the focus of Lieven's study (Chapter 1.1). Peters (Chapter 6.1) gives prominence to findings that not all children follow the same route in language acquisition. Coates (Chapter 1.2) focuses on gender differences, rather than averaging across them. Romaine (Chapter 7.1) discusses how different acquisition environments might favour different patterns of bilingualism. Variation between individual children is noted in several other papers in the *Reader*.

Reliability and validity

In the *Reader* excerpt from MacWhinney's introduction to the Child Language Data Exchange System (Chapter 2.2) he cites one of the goals as enhancing the reliability of transcription. Reliability and validity are central themes in Chapter 2.3 (Richards and Malvern), and they are relevant concepts in all empirical research on language acquisition.

A measurement or classification is **reliable** to the extent that it is stable and repeatable. A measurement or classification is **valid** to the extent that it taps the knowledge or skill that the researcher wants it to represent.

The following sorts of question are ones about reliability. If the same children were recorded or tested next week would the same results be found? If a different researcher did the testing, transcription or coding would the results be the same? If different children from the same population were studied or if different parts of a long transcription had been quantified or coded, would the results have remained the same?

Instruments such as the CDI (discussed under the subheading 'Diaries and questionnaires', above) are said to be **standardised**. This means that they come with detailed instructions and explanations; have been tried out on large, carefully described samples of children, with a view to assessing their reliability and validity; and results from the standardisation sample(s) are provided as **norms**, against which subsequent users of the test can compare the levels of children they test with the instrument.

Correlations (briefly discussed in the *Reader* appendix on statistical analysis) are the usual way of expressing reliability and validity. For what is called **test-retest** reliability, a group of children is tested twice, generally within about a week, and the figure for reliability is the correlation coefficient between the two sets of test results. The reliability coefficient will be high if a group of testees ranked in a particular order by a test is ranked in the same order when retested on the test.

The ranks are more likely to be maintained if the test separates the subjects widely rather than bunching them close together. A test that is too easy will be unreliable because the scores are concentrated near the high end; likewise a test that is too difficult, with most of the sample scoring near zero. A test with few items cannot yield a wide spread of scores. This harmonises with the intuition that taking a measurement repeatedly increases confidence, i.e. enhances reliability. The procedure advocated by Richards and Malvern (Chapter 2.3) for measuring richness of vocabulary use, gains reliability from including all of the available data, rather than only a small proportion.

The logic of trying to ensure that our measurements make it unlikely that members of a sample will overnight switch ranks helps to explain why it is important to keep the testing situation constant and also ensure that all subjects understand the task. If some subjects understand only when retested, or happen to be put off or encouraged by something about the way they are tested on one occasion, then reliability could suffer. These considerations carry over to other methods of data collection, e.g. recording children talking or having them participate in experiments. This is why research reports have a procedure section describing the test situation and stating in detail what was done. Full reporting on how the data were gathered is an element of research ethics too (see comments, below, on Chapter 2.1 by Alderson).

As MacWhinney (Chapter 2.2) explains, the researchers who founded CHILDES wanted to get away from each researcher using 'a project-specific system of transcription and project-specific codes'. Making it easier to document and implement transcription and coding conventions and to share them across the research community could be expected to improve the reliability of data gathering.

Turning now to validity, an example is offered by the use of mean length of utterance (MLU) as an indicator of level of syntactic development. Utterance length is reasonably easy to work out. On the other hand, syntactic development is an intricate concept and assessing it could be time-consuming (see McDaniel *et al.* 1996). Syntactic complexity is more than sentence length. It involves considerations such as the embedding of clauses into other clauses, dependencies between items not adjacent to each other, whether or not constituents appear in canonical order, whether certain constituents are physically present or whether they are merely inferable from their effects. However, more complex sentences tend to be longer; so MLU is sometimes used as an approximate indicator of children's syntactic development. Asking whether it is good enough for the purpose is a question about validity. (There is further discussion of MLU in a later subsection of this introduction.)

When speech and language therapists are considering what to adopt as an economical screening test for children referred to them – instead of booking all comers in for a battery of diagnostic tests and clinical interviews – they have to ask how far the results from a simple test are relevant pointers, and that is a question about the validity of the test.

In the case of reliability, correlation coefficients are calculated between two applications of the same test (or two look-alike versions, or halves, of a test). It is different for validity: here correlations are calculated between test results and measures that are clearly distinct from the instrument being evaluated. For instance, the validity of Richards and Malvern's (Chapter 2.3) lexical diversity index D is supported by its strong correlations with accepted indicators of language development: MLU and the Bristol Scale.

Construct validity, mentioned by Richards and Malvern, has to do with whether a sensible theoretical rationale can be given for regarding a measure as appropriate for a specified purpose – a rationale that must fit with our understanding of the relevant issues.

Experiments

The naturalness of recordings of spontaneous child speech gives them an important claim to validity: this is what language use really is like in the worlds of children. However, natural performances captured on tape could lead us to underestimate children's language knowledge – their **competence** (see the introductions to Parts 1 and 6 of the *Reader* for discussion of the notion of competence). Transcripts of free conversation are also usually no more than suggestive about comprehension.

Careful study of transcripts often provides ideas regarding the causes of particular developments and, when features of observed language use are quantified, interesting correlations are sometimes found. But correlations do not guarantee causality. The natural ecology of language development has so many possible influences in play that it is very difficult to be sure which are the important ones that make changes happen.

Experiments aim to reduce these indeterminacies. In an experiment the focus is deliberately restricted to a very limited number of possibilities. Potential causes are systematically isolated and assessments are done before the operation of a possible cause and again promptly afterwards. This makes data from experiments a respected foundation for arguing that something is a cause of some aspect of development, but the discipline required in an experiment means that naturalness is sacrificed. Experiments and less constrained observation are complementary approaches. An experiment is a bit like a microscope: extremely useful for examining detail, but one also needs wider vision to find interesting things to put on to microscope slides.

Merriman and Stevenson (Chapter 3.2) and Gleitman and Gillette (Chapter 4.1) report on experiments that they carried out. Results from experiments are included in Coates' survey (Chapter 1.2).

Experiments begin with clear hypotheses. A **hypothesis** is more than a guess. It is a motivated guess – one that derives from a theory – even if the theory is rudimentary. The researcher needs to be able to explain why an outcome is expected and what interesting conclusions would follow if that result were found.

An experiment tests hypotheses about effects that may be attributable to a particular cause by systematically letting some participants, but not others, experience it (alternatively, all participants are exposed to the potential cause, but only on some trials) and carefully observing what happens next. Thus, on some trials, children in Merriman and Stevenson's experiment (Chapter 3.2) were given a made-up name for a picture of an atypical member of a category (to see whether this would lead to them excluding it from a category that it might otherwise have belonged to). A deliberate manipulation like this of the experimental situation is called a **treatment**. Observations or measurements relevant to the hypothesis are made straight afterwards. These outcomes are compared with the outcomes in control conditions – trials when the treatment was deliberately not present. In experiments where some participants experience the treatment and others do not, the latter are called a **control group**.

If the experimental treatment does affect the outcome then comparison with the control outcomes should highlight causal relationships claimed by the hypothesis. (But if the hypothesised outcome does not occur, that might be because the theory is wrong, but the possibility always has to be considered that the children did not pay attention to the treatment or that there was too little of it for a noticeable effect on the outcome.)

Experiments have to be designed to rule out other conceivable explanations for differences between treatment and control, such as that the children changed their way of performing during the course of the experiment through becoming more familiar with the task (or through getting tired and bored), or that the subjects in one of the groups were more precocious. For this reason, random numbers are used to assign children to control and treatment groups, and there is careful counterbalancing of sequences of treatments and control conditions; see the statements about orders of presentation in the 'Procedure' section of Chapter 3.2 (Merriman and Stevenson). Other variables reasonably anticipated as contending influences on the outcomes need to be measured and the possibility checked out that they might explain the results.

A good report on a child language experiment gives details of the sample of children tested. This helps readers decide what population the sample could be representative of: children of a particular age range of course, but also with regard to health, birth order, gender, language, ethnic and socio-economic grouping and geographical area. If statistical considerations were the only ones that mattered, then generalisability from sample to population would be maximised by conscripting the sample of children randomly from the population of interest, but in practice and for obvious ethical reasons child language experimenters generally rely on invitations for getting subjects to do their experiments.

Additional methods

Jean Berko Gleason (Berko 1958) devised a way of investigating young children's productive formation of English inflected words. For instance, she showed them a drawing of a somewhat indeterminate creature and labelled it with an invented word *wug*. Then she displayed a drawing of two of the creatures and encouraged the children to complete the sentence 'There are two . . .'. A child who completes this with /wʌgz/ must know something about the formation of English plurals. Berko's **elicited production** method is justly celebrated. For at least some areas of language acquisition, she had solved two of the problems that beset work based on records of conversations: (1) she did not have to wait to see whether children would eventually say the forms she was interested in (and if the forms were absent from transcripts, be uncertain about whether or not the children could have produced them); (2) using made up forms meant that a response such as *wugs* or *wuggisses* was most unlikely to have been memorised as a formula; it is surely the nonsense word plus a suffix. Several chapters in Menn and Ratner's (1999) book contain accounts of work with versions of Berko's method. It is difficult to get children younger than about 3 years old to play along with elicited production, however.

Brown and Fraser (1963) and Slobin and Welsh (1973) presented spoken sentences to children and asked them to 'say what I say'. They argued that children performing this **elicited imitation** task would have to process the sentences in accordance with their current grammatical system for the language, so that mismatches between the input and the response should be indicative of the child's grammar. Elicited imitation studies have been reported from time to time since then; for example the method is used in an experiment by Santelmann *et al.* (2002), who investigated the development of English *yes/no* question structures in children aged 2–5 years. Elicited imitations can raise two sorts of puzzle: (1) when a child's response fully matches the input, this need not testify to control of relevant aspects of grammar; the performance could be an uncomprehending reproduction of the utterance as a sequence of sounds; (2) failure to respond or a response that bears only a vague resemblance to the model is also hard to interpret. Perhaps relevant grammar has not yet been acquired, but perhaps some low-level memory difficulty is to blame.

Preferential looking is an interesting technique for testing comprehension (see Hirsh-Pasek and Golinkoff 1996a). A pair of visual stimuli is displayed on two video monitors in front of the child subject while a recorded sentence is played. One of the video clips better portrays what the sentence describes than the other. The child's gaze is monitored by research assistants who do not know which sentence the child is hearing. It turns out that children often spend significantly more time looking at one of the clips and this can be related to the presented sentence. Varying the way the 'wrong answer' video differs from the target clip allows for subtle comparisons. The method has been used with children as young as 1 year old, though at that age many lose concentration before the end of the experiment. A disadvantage is the amount of preparation and time needed.

The chapters of McDaniel *et al.* (1996) cover a range of other techniques, including comprehension testing by **picture selection** and **act out tasks**. There is a useful description of semi-formal comprehension testing in Harris *et al.* (Chapter 3.1).

When several methods are used together (sometimes referred to as triangulation), convergent results inspire greater confidence and can often be more enlightening. In the *Reader*, a good illustration of this is Chapter 3.1 (Harris *et al.*), which integrated vocabulary check lists, interviews, video-recording and comprehension testing.

Comparing acquisition across languages and speech communities is a strategy that enables some disentangling of the mental complexity of particular meanings from the formal patterns for expressing them and from culture-specific ways of socialising children. Cross-linguistic comparisons are discussed in Part 7 of the Reader.

Lining up for comparisons

Evaluation and development of theories often requires comparison of findings or pooling of data from different studies. The studies will probably have been conducted with different children. They may also differ in the methods used and/or in the languages that were being acquired. The children have to be comparable in relevant respects, otherwise comparison or pooling is likely to be misleading. Some or all of the following could be relevant: ages of the children, languages being acquired, languages used in the environment, linguistic structures already mastered, vocabulary size, sibling birth-order, health, socio-economic standing, rural or urban status, etc.

What it is most important to equate before making comparisons will depend on the goals of the study and on the researcher's theory. For instance, a theoretical argument by Kuczaj (1977) led him to expect that learning of irregular forms (such as *feet* and *went*) should correlate more strongly with child age than would acquisition of rule-governed parts of a language, because irregular forms have to be learnt one by one. (Groups of them cannot suddenly become available through the acquisition of a rule or principle.) Irregulars can only be picked up through exposure to a speech community using those forms, and the longer a child has been in the community the greater the chance of hearing each irregular form in contexts that make it possible to discover what it relates to (e.g. that *feet* is the plural of *foot*). See Swan (Chapter 4.2) for more on this. Thus age could be an important basis for comparison when the focus is on irregular forms.

Age is only a very approximate indicator of other aspects of linguistic development, however. When atypically developing children are being compared with typically developing children age can be entirely inappropriate as a basis for matching.

MLU (mean length of utterance) is a very widely used index. It is a reliable measure (in the technical sense explained earlier in this introduction), but much of its popularity probably comes from its being fairly easy to calculate and from the very fact that it is so often reported in articles and books on child language. The average length of children's utterances should have some relation to the complexity of the grammatical knowledge that lies behind the utterances, but is probably affected by the topic of conversation, the interactional dynamics of the conversational situation and even other factors. Brown (1973) set out the procedure generally used. He specified that the units counted should be morphemes. MLU in morphemes should, to an extent, reflect the level of development of morphology as well as gross aspects of syntax. However, particularly in the earliest stages, it can be very difficult to decide which words are 'frozen' wholes and which should be counted as productively constructed. For instance, if a child of 18 months says *mine's*, should the word be regarded as representing *I* + POSSESSIVE + *is* (3 morphemes) or as *mine* + *is* (2 morphemes) or as a fused 1-morpheme formula *mine's*? Thus, rather than using the number of morphemes, MLU calculations are frequently based on number of words, as in Lieven's report (Chapter 1.1).

Ingram (2002) has proposed a **phonological MLU** that could be useful for matching in phonological studies. The average number of phonological segments correct in a sample of 50 words is counted, with a bonus of 1 added for each consonant that is correct. Standardised instruments, such as the CDI (Fenson *et al.* 1993) for vocabulary measurement, are valuable when making comparisons. The notion of validity (explained earlier in this introduction) has an important bearing on the choice of measures to use as a basis for comparison. Does the indicator reflect aspects of development that are important, given the theories or practical purposes for which it is to be used? Chapter 2.3 contributes towards understanding the validity of measures that comparisons can be based on.

The papers

Chapter 2.1 is from a book by **Priscilla Alderson** about ethics in research with children. Her goal is to offer guidance on 'ways of researching with children rather than on or for children' (Alderson 1995: 9). *With* signals a more cooperative and respectful engagement with the subjects of research. The excerpt reproduced here gives practical advice on implementing ethical standards, but people planning to do research should seek expert advice regarding ethics in their particular situations.

The foundations of ethical concerns are legal (privacy and data protection laws, etc.) and moral (because research involves interactions between people and because there are asymmetries of power and knowledge between adult and child, and between the researcher as expert and members of society not versed in the researcher's field).

Article 12 of the Convention on the Rights of the Child – an international agreement that has been formally accepted by almost every country in the world – includes the obligation to 'assure to the child who is capable of forming his or her own views the right to express those views freely in all matters affecting the child, the views of the child being given due weight in accordance with the age and maturity of the child' (UNICEF 2003). There are other international agreements and national laws relating to research ethics, privacy, data gathering and storage, and the protection of children.

Professional associations that child language researchers belong to, as well as universities and other institutions that employ some of them, also have rules, codes of practice and research ethics committees. Following best practice protects the researchers too: if there are complaints it is a valuable defence to be able show that such issues have been thought about, legislated for, specified in monitored codes of conduct, and that what the researcher was doing was in compliance. Notwithstanding the laws, rules and committees, however, there can be substantial differences of opinion over particular ethical decisions.

It is essential that procedures followed in studies are fully reported, including precautions taken and explanations given to participants. This is not just so that other researchers will understand the science and be able to evaluate its reliability, validity and generality, but also to keep up a flow of relevant information into continuing debate about ethics. Societies differ, societies change and research changes.

No set of ethical guidelines covers all eventualities. Throughout the research process, each researcher must take ethics seriously. Acting in accordance with formalised rules is important, but good researchers also think for themselves about ethics, and aim to be humane and commonsensical in addition to following rules.

It is important to view research not only from the researcher's angle, but also to attempt to see it from the standpoints of the subjects, their acquaintances and the community at large. How would I feel if asked to participate in this sort of research? How would friends and family members of mine who do not have the same incentive for research feel? If the research is done with subjects from a social or cultural group that the researcher is not part of, it would be good to seek advice from people who do belong; even better to work in collaboration with people from that group. Researchers should be able honestly to give assurances that their activities are not 'harmful, unhelpful or unkind', in Alderson's words.

Child language research can provide helpful information to everyone engaged in child development and education. It can yield findings of interest even to people who have little or no involvement with children. It is fair to point these out, but researchers should never overstate their claim to be public benefactors. Of course, participants should be thanked for their cooperation, but responsibility to them does not end there. They are entitled to expect that data they provided will be accorded confidentiality to the appropriate extent and as promised. No disclosures that could humiliate or disadvantage them must occur. Many people enjoy taking part in research and it will generally be appreciated if arrangements can be made to let participants know about the findings later, for example through an invitation to a talk or via a mailed information sheet (perhaps containing an offer to provide more detail if requested) or a press release.

Part of the planning of a research project must include specific consideration of how it will be explained to participants. The motivation for the research can usefully be included in a leaflet. Distributing a concise account of what you are doing, and why, can forestall rumour and misinformation, and be valuable publicity for a worthwhile project. What participants are told must be clear and true and as complete as they have a right to expect. If 'giving the game away' in advance could influence the subjects to the extent where it would not be worth going ahead with the observations, then the researcher should tell subjects that there will be a fuller explanation afterwards – possibly after all of the subjects have been tested/recorded. In cases like this it is important to consider very carefully whether the subsequent debriefing is likely to make anyone regret agreeing to participate.

If there are benefits to be had from participation in a study, for example when a therapy that really does seem to work features in research with language-impaired children, then all subjects should have the opportunity to receive the benefit; for instance, members of a control group who do not get the therapy during the course of an investigation should be offered it afterwards.

Researchers must ensure that subjects, or at any rate their families, know how to get in touch for further information or to complain. If there is a leaflet, the project address and the names of the principal researchers should appear in it. A leaflet can be accompanied by a detachable consent form (though consent forms have the effect of making some people fear that the procedures must be dangerous if a signature is being sought on an official-looking sheet of paper). Merriman and Stevenson (Chapter 3.2) report that parents in their study completed consent forms. There is a helpful discussion and a model form at the website of the TalkBank project: http://www.talkbank.org/share/consent.html. Accessible further discussion of these issues can found via the index entries for ethics in Robson (2001).

Another aspect of research ethics concerns responsibilities to colleagues: those who study, research or professionally apply child language theories and findings. Sources of data and ideas should be acknowledged. Results must be reported accurately and as fully as is needed to ensure that they are not misleading, with all relevant contextual information made available.

Chapter 2.2 by **Brian MacWhinney** is the introduction to the two-volume CHILDES (Child Language Data Exchange System) manual. MacWhinney is the prime mover in CHILDES, but as he explains, the system arose collaboratively and depends on the efforts and cooperation of numerous others. CHILDES comprises CHAT (an acronym for Codes for the Human Analysis of Transcripts), CLAN (Computerized Language Analysis) and a database containing a large collection of tagged and annotated, computer-readable child language transcripts representing quite a number of languages. More information is readily available on the internet: the CHILDES website is at http://childes.psy.cmu.edu/ and there are mirror sites in Belgium at http://atila-www.uia.ac.be/childes/ and in Japan at http://cow.lang. nagoya-u.ac.jp/childes/. Many useful computer programs have been integrated into the system, for instance CLAN includes a routine for computing the measure of lexical diversity explained by Richards and Malvern (Chapter 2.3). CHILDES is continually being upgraded. It now includes software to facilitate the transcription of digital video on a computer.

CHILDES makes it easier to share data and to refine and use coding schemes. Easier transcription and coding generally leads to higher-quality transcripts and greater reliability. Computerisation is a great help in detecting patterns and for logging 'gems' (instructive instances to use in developing theoretical arguments) and for numerical summaries. Easy access to the data of other researchers promotes wider checking of the generalisability of theories, closer scrutiny and better understanding of the ideas and data of other researchers. Collaboration and sharing foster communication and interchange in the research community. The many references to CHILDES in books and journal articles on child language acquisition testify that the system's achievements are greatly appreciated.

Among the papers in the *Reader*, the following make use of data available through CHILDES: Richards and Malvern (Chapter 2.3), Swan (Chapter 4.2) and Hyams (Chapter 6.2).

Chapter 2.3 by **Brian Richards** and **David Malvern** begins with a critique of the **type/token ratio** (**TTR**). TTR has been thought of as a worthwhile indicator of richness in word usage. For instance, Lieven (Chapter 1.1) reports TTRs. If a child repeats and repeats and repeats words (as in the start of the present sentence) then there will be many tokens for a given number of types, and dividing the number of types by the number of tokens (i.e. the type/token ratio) will yield a smaller figure than the same division for a sample from a child who deploys a richer, more diverse and varied vocabulary (as in the previous half-dozen words of this sentence).

However, Richards and others have shown that the TTR is a problematic measure of richness or repetitiveness of vocabulary use. It is affected by how close the speaker comes to running out of new word types to display in utterances. Think of a child with a total vocabulary of 100 word types. In a transcript that has 100 word tokens, the child could display knowledge of a different type for every one of the 100 tokens, giving the theoretical maximum TTR. For transcripts longer than 100 words, a child with only 100 types is obliged to recycle some of the types, pushing down the TTR. In general, larger samples (i.e. samples having more tokens) depress the TTR. Thus TTRs based on different sizes of sample should not be compared.

A valid index of development should correlate with age, i.e. it should be higher for older children (if we ignore paradoxical periods when reorganisation of a child's system leads to apparent backtracking). Richards and Malvern point out that some studies have found TTR remaining constant with age or even decreasing. These unexpected findings arise because older children tend to produce longer utterances and utterances have been the usual basis for matching sample sizes in comparative TTR calculations. Since longer utterances have more tokens, this tends to lower the TTR. The problem could be sidestepped by always using samples with a fixed number of tokens, e.g. 50 or 100. But restricting comparisons of the richness of children's word usage to some preset small number of tokens results in data beyond that number being wasted. The lexical diversity index D that Richards and Malvern have devised is independent of sample size, so it is possible to include all of the available data in the calculations. Independence from sample size also makes it useful for comparisons across different research projects.

Some readers might find it difficult to understand D fully, but a software program to compute it is available through CHILDES (see MacWhinney, Chapter 2.2). The fundamental point to grasp is that bigger values of D indicate more varied (less repetitive) production of words. It also helps to remember that initial results suggest that D averages around 40 or 50 for 2½-year-old children. Some of the approaches to reliability and validity sketched in the present introduction are well illustrated by Richards and Malvern.

Richards and Malvern also outline a neat technique for putting a number on a child's level of development of inflectional morphology. D is computed with each distinct inflected form of a word (e.g. *go*, *goes* and *going*) treated as a different type; then it is recomputed with the inflected forms of a given word lumped together (e.g. *go*, *goes* and *going* counted as all belonging to the type *go*). If the child is producing a variety of inflectional forms of words then the first calculation will give a bigger value than the second, and subtraction yields an indicator of inflectional diversity (ID). ID should be a more specific measure of children's inflectional development than MLU, for instance, because MLU taps morphological complexity only indirectly.

Priscilla Alderson

ETHICAL STANDARDS THROUGH THE RESEARCH PROCESS

T HE FOLLOWING PAGES review standards through the research process, summarise current guidance, and suggest practical ways of applying it.[1] [. . .]

Planning, explaining and assessing research

Is the research harmful, unhelpful or unkind?

Researchers are urged by funding and other bodies to explain their work in clear terms which lay people can understand. The points are mainly set out as questions, and suggested ways of talking to or writing for subjects are included in italics. Simple terms are especially important in research with young people: no one can give consent unless they understand the key issues.

1. The title of the project

Apart from a formal title, does the project have a user-friendly, working title in words anyone can easily use: 'The streetwise teenagers' project' for 'A survey commissioned by the local authority social services department of adolescents without formal accommodation'.

1995, reprinted with permission from *Listening to Children*, Ilford: Barnado's, pp. 15–27.

2. The problem or question addressed; choice of research topic

The first questions are: Is the topic worthwhile? How are the findings likely to benefit children? How will they make an original contribution? (For example)

> Many young people aged under 16 leave home and live on the streets. We hope to learn from them what kinds of help they need.
> Or:
> Each year, many young people are excluded from their school. Why does this happen? We are asking young people, parents and teachers for their views.
> Or:
> Some people in this school have problems with maths. We want to try out a new maths course.
> Or:
> We do research about how children learn to talk. We hope that our work will help children who are slow in learning to talk.

What new questions does this research ask which no other research has yet answered?

3. The request

> Will you help us with our research?
> Will you take part in an interview and fill in three questionnaires?
> Will you help us to try out the new maths course?

How and why have the subjects been chosen, how many will there be? If their names are on confidential lists, such as school rolls, or 'at risk' registers, will researchers ensure that they do not see the lists. Only professionals with access to the list should select the names and approach the clients; if the clients agree, the researchers can then be informed. Are the clients told about means of access to their names?

4. The hoped-for benefits

Issues about benefits include the following.

- The basic questions or problems the project deals with, and why they matter;
- How common the problem is and how severe it is;
- How the research findings might be used;
- Who stands to benefit:
    - what group are they?
    - roughly how many people?
- If methods are being tested or compared:
    - are they new and/or already widely used?
    - what alternative treatments are there?
    - how do the methods differ?
- The planned outcomes, such as new maths materials, or a book, or a film, who they are designed for, and the effects they might have.

Direct or indirect benefit?

In medical research, it is important to make clear whether the research:

a)   involves treatment which *might* directly benefit the subjects (such as by testing a treatment they need);

b)   involves treatment which *might* benefit some subjects, but not others, such as those in the control group;

c)   offers no treatment or direct present benefit ('non-therapeutic' research), such as interviews, observations or other data collection, which it is hoped will benefit other people in the future;

d)   is intended to add to knowledge and is not concerned with practical benefit.

Medical research which does not offer direct benefit to the children involved is expected to carry very low risks and clear benefits to children. Otherwise, researchers have to justify involving children, and not adults, in the research.

Should the same standards apply in social research? Some researchers report benefits, such as when people enjoy having a willing listener and the chance to develop and clarify their own ideas [Acker *et al.* 1983]. Yet this is a bonus and not the purpose of the encounter which is to collect data. Some people argue that it is important for children to be altruistic and able to contribute to knowledge [McCormick 1982]; others say that children are too easily exploited and should not be used in this way [Ramsey 1976]. Another complication is to define benefit. The views of market researchers, media interviewers and other researchers on 'benefit' may be very different from the views of the children affected. Any benefit or disadvantage from a teaching, social work or psychological intervention may only be known in the long term. Alternatively, there may be short term but no long term advantages. It is very hard to show definitely that any benefit is due wholly or partly to the research intervention and not to countless other factors, unless there is a strictly randomised large trial.

Is the need to involve children in the research justified?

Do the researchers make their aims and their definitions of 'benefit' clear?

Do they help children and/or parents to give informed and unpressured consent or refusal?

5. Research practice

What will happen to people during the research?

Timing

- Length of project
- Amount of time each person will be involved
- How many sessions will there be and where
- How often and how long these will or might be

Interventions

- Such as an interview, a survey, a maths programme, counselling sessions or a focus group

Data collecting

- Interviews, questionnaires, diary-keeping
- Tape-recording, videos, photographs
- Any other data collecting or tests

Topics

- What are the main topics areas?
- What will the questions be like, open or closed or both, about experience or opinions, about public or intimately private matters?

Use of data

- How certain is it that each person's data will be used?
- In qualitative reports or documentaries, for example, might some subjects be mentioned only very briefly or not at all?

Confidentiality

- Does the person mind being recorded, or notes being made?
- How will the findings, such as audio and video tapes be stored (in locked cupboards, separate from names and addresses, registered under the current Data Protection Act)?
- Are subjects assured that everything they say will remain confidential (private, secret)?
- Do research subjects want this? Would they rather be named and acknow-ledged? If so, what is the best response?
- In research such as focus groups how is confidentiality for the people present and the people they talk about respected?
- Who will see research records, notes or film?
- Will other people be informed about the research sessions?
- Will the research subject have a copy of any relevant letters to other people (such as if researchers write to teachers, psychologists or social workers about a child)?
- How will the data be published in ways that protect privacy (change of names, and so on)?
- Do the research subjects have any kind of editorial control, such as to say which comments they have made should be omitted from any reports, and which ones they want to ensure cannot be attributed to them?
- Are records registered under the current Data Protection Act?
- Each fairly large research institution should have an officer who informs researchers how to do this.

• Children have the same rights to confidentiality as any other person. No one has an absolute right to confidentiality. In rare cases, a breach may be justified if it is thought that the person describing the danger, or some other person, is at risk of being exploited or abused. If so, the researcher should first try to get the young person to talk to adults who could help, or else to agree that the researcher should talk to them. 'To breach confidentiality without informing the [informant] and in contradiction of the [informant's] refusal may irreparably damage trust . . . and may result in denial by the young person that abuse has taken place' [BMA *et al.* 1993]. When it seems necessary to breach confidentiality, is this clearly discussed with research subjects? Should subjects be warned in advance about the limits of confidentiality?

Harm

• What are the possible harms (intrusion, distress or embarrassment, loss of the standard teaching or care methods, risks of new or untested methods)?
• How likely and severe might the harms be?
• Are attempts made to avoid or reduce harms? Such as rehearsing with children a way of saying 'no' when they do not want to reply, assuring them that this will be respected and they will not be questioned about why they say 'no', or ensuring that children who feel worried or upset about the research can talk to someone about it afterwards? It can be useful to try to find out gently why young people want to refuse. Does the research seem boring or irrelevant? Could it be improved with their help?
• If someone is unhappy about any aspect of the research, and wishes to complain, or to see that this aspect is changed, whom can they contact? What will happen if there is a complaint? Will the researchers review the comments, and possibly change the research plans?

Cost

• How much time will be needed to take part in the research?
• Does the project cover the costs of fares or, for older teenagers or accompanying parents, any time off work?
• Are two fares paid, such as when an adult brings a child?
• Are taxi fares paid if needed, such as by disabled people?
• How can costs be reclaimed and how soon are they repaid?
• Are any other payments made and, if so, when?

6. Research method

Does the research method need to be explained and justified? For example, what is an interview, a focus group or a trial expected to achieve? Why is the chosen method the preferred one? Are any relevant research terms, such as 'randomised' or 'control group', explained? Are children asked each time researchers wish to observe or tape-record them?

7. Naming contacts

The leaflet should include

> the name of the researcher and 'phone number,
> the name and address of the research base,
> the name of the sponsors,
> and of the local ethics committee if relevant.

8. An invitation to ask questions

The information leaflet could state:

> *We would be pleased to talk to you about any other questions you may have.*

Over- or under-informing children

One balance to consider is between over- and under-informing subjects, in either case preventing them from making a well-founded decision. A core of basic information in a leaflet, with suggested questions and further discussion, can help to achieve a reasonable balance. This can combine what the reasonable researcher would tell, what a prudent subject would ask, and what the individual subject wants to know [see Faden and Beauchamp 1986, Kennedy 1988].

9. Consent: making a decision

Many people think that 'consent' means being informed, but it means more than this. The nature of consent as an informed, freely-made choice needs to be made clear. Here are some common questions about making a decision.

Do I have to say yes?

> *No. It is up to you whether you take part in this project. No one should feel forced to agree. You do not have to give a reason for saying 'no', although giving a reason might help the research.*
>
> *Before you agree, you need to feel sure that the project is worthwhile. If you are not sure what to decide, take time to think. You may want to talk to other people before you decide.*
>
> *You can also change your mind, and withdraw from the project at any time. Please tell us if you do so, but again you do not have to say why.*

(When the research is linked to a service such as teaching or social work which the child is already receiving):

> *If you refuse or withdraw we shall still give you the best care / teaching / services that we can.*

The consent form is often separate from the information leaflet. If a consent form is used, a copy of the form could be kept in the leaflet to remind people of what they have agreed to in writing. A consent form is useful but not sufficient evidence to convince a law court that informed and freely-given consent was obtained. The main purpose of the form is to help to ensure that minimal standards are observed, and also to transfer responsibility for risks which have been explained from the researcher to the subject. There could be a space on the form for both parent and child to sign, though some children prefer to give oral but not written consent.

The double standard of consent has been criticised. When children agree to accept medical treatment, their competence is rarely questioned: when they refuse, the questions about their competence begin. However, with research, the opposite approach is generally supported. The refusal of even very young children should be respected. When young children consent, adults such as parents or the carers should be involved to vet the research and to give supporting consent.

Balancing cost and benefit when deciding whether to consent

In medical research with children, the risks must be very low, unless there are great hoped-for direct benefits. In these cases, the child is likely to be at very high risk from untreated disease or injury, and in great need of benefit which the treatment being researched might offer. Social research seldom involves direct benefit, so in theory should incur no or 'negligible' risk. The usual harms in social research, such as inconvenience, time lost, intrusion, anxiety, mental discomfort, may seem slight, but might be serious to the person concerned. Individuals' informed evaluations should be respected. People can feel wronged without being harmed by research, if they feel they have been treated as objects, deceived, humiliated, or that their values or privacy have been disregarded [Cassell 1982].

Besides personal cost and benefit to research subjects, there is the likely impact on children generally, or on certain groups of young people. How might they stand to gain or lose? For example, is research with teenage mothers likely to increase respect and practical support for them, or increase prejudice against them? Although researchers cannot be wholly responsible for the way their findings are used, they can select the aspects they examine, the ways these are interpreted, and the terms they use to explain them.

Opt in or opt out?

To avoid coercion, some people argue against opt-out research, that is, when researchers 'phone or knock on doors or send a letter saying that unless the person cancels the visit a researcher will call. Critics say that only opt-in research should be done, such as by letters which invite people to return cards if they want to take part in the research. Yet this can create barriers which make it harder for researchers to contact certain groups and to include their views in public reviews.

Involving children in decisions

There is much uncertainty about children's consent to treatment, and even more about their consent to research. Young people between 16 and 18 can give their own consent to treatment without their parents being involved (*Family Law Reform Act* 1969) unless they are thought to be not competent, such as if they have severe learning difficulties, though many people with learning difficulties can make decisions about research. With anyone aged over 18, no one else can give consent on their behalf. In the UK, certain children aged from about six years share in making complex, serious decisions about treatment [Alderson 1993]. Yet some doctors and lawyers still think that adults must always decide for children. A few recent court cases have turned against the 1985 *Gillick* ruling, that competent children under 16 can consent. It now seems that if either the child, or any person with parental responsibility, gives consent to *treatment*, doctors can proceed, even if one or more of these people, including the child, disagree (*in re* R 1991; *in re* W 1992). The ruling would not apply to research.

The long debate over whether or not parents can consent to *research* on children continues. No one is sure what the courts would decide if there were a legal case. Would they insist that researchers must have parental consent? Would they support a child who wanted to consent or to refuse against the parents' wishes? The safest course, though it can also be repressive, is to ask for parental consent and also to ask for children's consent, when they are able to understand. When a local authority is looking after a child, and there is a care order on a child, the authority has parental responsibility, and will delegate this in writing to a social worker or foster parent. Guidelines advise respect for foster parents' views. If there is no care order, social workers can only give consent if the people with parental responsibility have agreed this in writing. If the High Court has parental responsibility, it almost certainly has to be informed about proposed research or publicity.

Parents may have to sign the research consent form until their child is 16 or 18,[2] for medical research. Many people believe that non-invasive social and educational research does not need parents to agree, or even to be informed, unless children might be harmed. As psychological harm is so subjective, it is hard for researchers to be certain about potential harm of their work. Social, far more than physical, research depends on the active cooperation of the subject, such as to answer questions. This could be taken as implied consent. Yet subjects can be afraid, or too embarrassed, to refuse or withdraw, unless they are given a respectful chance to express their own view, such as to refuse to sign a form. Some research involves observing or filming people; researchers will only know if children are willing to consent if they ask them first. The onus should be on adults to prove that the child does not have the capacity to decide, if this is in doubt. Even young children's reluctance or refusal should be taken very seriously.

Apart from consent to planned research, children could be much more fully involved in helping to select topics, plan research and advise on monitoring research and resolving problems as they arise. [. . .]

Research information leaflets

Some researchers now use short leaflets which summarise details about their research project. The leaflets can be given to members of the research team, staff in the institutions where research is taking place who might be affected by it or be asked questions about it, to the funders, and to everyone who is asked to help with the project. Ethics committees often require to see such leaflets, as the only means of checking that potential subjects receive at least minimum information.

In research with children, the leaflets need to be written in terms which children can read, or can understand when adults read to them. For some projects, a coloured sheet of A4 is folded to make four small pages. Short columns are much easier to read, as newsprint shows. A project logo might be added. Large dark print on white or pale matt paper helps people with poor eye-sight as well as slow readers. Subheadings or a question-and-answer format also help them, with the message broken up into short sections.

Clearly written information can help everyone concerned:

- to discuss the research more fully and clearly
- to decide what questions to ask the researchers
- to understand and remember researchers' spoken information
- to know about the hoped-for benefits of the research and any risks or costs
- to go over the information with their friends when deciding whether to take part in the research
- to make a more informed choice about whether to take part in the research
- to feel that they are making an informed and committed decision if they choose to support the project
- to know what to expect, and to avoid misunderstandings and the problems that can then arise
- to reduce the risk of complaint or bad feeling from people who feel under-informed about the research process
- and so to avoid waste of time and money over failed projects
- to cooperate more fully when they know how the researchers would like them to help.

Leaflets can help to increase informed public support for efficient research. They help funders and others who assess projects, such as ethics committee members:

- to find out quickly and clearly the essential points about the research
- to assess the value of the project, and the researchers' attitudes towards the subjects (the tone and style of the leaflet often tell a great deal about this – does it seem child-friendly?)

Clear leaflets show that researchers are willing to think and write in terms young people can accept.[3] They also allow for people who read little English. Such leaflets use [Vernon 1980]:

- short lines (the reason for folding the A4 paper);
- short words, sentences and paragraphs;
- only one or two main ideas per sentence;
- requests rather than commands;
- the active voice (we will meet you . . .) rather than the passive voice (appointments will be booked);
- a personal approach (we, you, your mother) rather than the impersonal (they, those, he or she);
- specific details rather than vague ones.

The leaflets avoid repetition, negative remarks (do not . . .), alienating labels (females), jargon and acronyms unless they are explained. Some researchers use Maketon or other sign language to write leaflets for people with learning difficulties [Cambridge 1993]. Braille and taped information can be used for blind people, large print for those with partial vision.

When writing leaflets, it helps to talk with the people they are planned for. What questions do they want raised? What terms do they use? Plain language risks being crude, simplistic, patronising and irritating. These faults have to be balanced against the worse risks of being confusing and intimidating.

The leaflets could be used by care managers, by psychologists doing statements with children with special needs, and in many kinds of social research. They could also be used by journalists and researchers working on media programmes. The leaflets can explain who you are, what you are doing and why, and what kinds of questions you are likely to ask. This helps children to be prepared and to feel more in control over what is happening. Yet it is important not to assume that people read or remember the leaflets. They are an extra resource, and cannot replace discussion.

Leaflets in other languages

Translations need to be checked by two or three readers to see that they are clear and accurate, and for their tone and style. Ask one person to translate the text, and another to translate it back. Leaflets in other languages should be used with a link worker or interpreter, not seen as an end in themselves. Subjects can then share their views with the researchers. Interpreters can block, rather than aid, discussion, unless they are well chosen; age, gender, empathy, respect for clients, skill in listening and some knowledge of the research can be vital. Research with people who speak little or no English should include funds for these services. The local Council for Racial Equality and other community groups may help. People can only consent if they understand.

Notes

1   The section is drawn from medical ethics guidance, including:

Department of Health 1990 *Patient consent to examination or treatment.* HC(90)22;
—— 1991 *Welfare of children and young people in hospital*;
—— 1991 *Local research ethics committees*;
—— Royal College of Physicians 1986 *Research on healthy volunteers*;
—— 1990 *Guidelines on the practice of ethics committees in medical research involving human subjects*;
—— 1990 *Research involving patients*;
UK Central Council for Nursing, Midwifery and Health Visiting 1989 *Exercising accountability*;
Association of British Pharmaceutical Industries 1988 *Guidelines on medical experiments on non-patient human volunteers*;
Standing Joint Committee of British Paediatric Association and Royal College of Obstetricians and Gynaecologists 1991 *A checklist of questions to ask when evaluating proposed research during pregnancy and following birth*;

Medical Research Council 1991 *The ethical conduct of research on children*;

British Paediatric Association 1992 *Guidelines for the ethical conduct of medical research involving children*.

The section also draws on social research and media guidance including:

American Psychological Association 1992 *Ethical principles of psychologists and code of conduct*;

British Broadcasting Corporation 1993 *Producers' guidelines*. London: BBC;

British Education Research Association 1992 *Ethical guidelines for educational research*;

British Psychological Society 1991 *Revised ethical principles for constructing research with human participants*;

British Sociological Association 1993 *Guidelines for good professional conduct and statement of ethical practice*;

CancerLink 1994 Media exposure, *Link Up*, 36: 14–5;

Carers National Association 1993 *Young carers and the media; Directory of Social Research Organisations in the UK*, Appendix B. Social Research Association Ethical Guidelines 1993;

ESRC 1993 *Notes on research ethics and confidentiality*;

Market Research Society 1994 *Code of conduct*;

McCrum S, Bernal P 1994 (draft) *Interviewing children: a training pack for journalists*. Buckfastleigh: Children's Voices;

National AIDS Trust 1994 *Children, HIV and the media*;

National Children's Bureau 1993 *Guidelines for research*;

National Foundation for Education Research (no date) *A code of practice*;

Save the Children (no date) *Focus on images*; with UNICEF (draft 1994) *Interviewing children*;

Scottish Council for research and Education 1993 *Standards of practice for research*;

Who Cares? *Code of practice*.

2   Some of this section is based on work for Alderson P 1994 *Spreading the word on research: notes on writing information for people asked to take part in health research*. 1994, London: CERES. The work included a review of 50 medical research protocols and patient information sheets, many written very obscurely.

3   See note 2.

Brian MacWhinney

INTRODUCTION
[TO THE CHILDES PROJECT]

LANGUAGE ACQUISITION RESEARCH thrives on data collected from spontaneous interactions in naturally occurring situations. You can turn on a tape recorder or videotape, and, before you know it, you will have accumulated a library of dozens or even hundreds of hours of naturalistic interactions. But simply collecting data is only the beginning of a much larger task, because the process of transcribing and analyzing naturalistic samples is extremely time-consuming and often unreliable. In this first volume, we will present a set of computational tools designed to increase the reliability of transcriptions, automate the process of data analysis, and facilitate the sharing of transcript data. These new computational tools have brought about revolutionary changes in the way that research is conducted in the child language field. In addition, they have equally revolutionary potential for the study of second-language learning, adult conversational interactions, sociological content analyses, and language recovery in aphasia. Although the tools are of wide applicability, this volume concentrates on their use in the child language field, in the hope that researchers from other areas can make the necessary analogies to their own topics.

Before turning to a detailed examination of the current system, it may be helpful to take a brief historical tour over some of the major highlights of earlier approaches to the collection of data on language acquisition. These earlier approaches can be grouped into five major historical periods.

2000, reprinted with permission from *The CHILDES Project: tools for analyzing talk*, vol. 1, *Transcription format and programs*, 3rd edn, Mahwah, NJ: Erlbaum, pp. 1–9.

1.1 Impressionistic observation

The first attempt to understand the process of language development appears in a remarkable passage from *The Confessions of St. Augustine* (1952). In this passage, Augustine claims that he remembered how he had learned language:

> This I remember; and have since observed how I learned to speak. It was not that my elders taught me words (as, soon after, other learning) in any set method; but I, longing by cries and broken accents and various motions of my limbs to express my thoughts, that so I might have my will, and yet unable to express all I willed or to whom I willed, did myself, by the understanding which Thou, my God, gavest me, practise the sounds in my memory. When they named anything, and as they spoke turned towards it, I saw and remembered that they called what they would point out by the name they uttered. And that they meant this thing, and no other, was plain from the motion of their body, the natural language, as it were, of all nations, expressed by the countenance, glances of the eye, gestures of the limbs, and tones of the voice, indicating the affections of the mind as it pursues, possesses, rejects, or shuns. And thus by constantly hearing words, as they occurred in various sentences, I collected gradually for what they stood; and, having broken in my mouth to these signs, I thereby gave utterance to my will. Thus I exchanged with those about me these current signs of our wills, and so launched deeper into the stormy intercourse of human life, yet depending on parental authority and the beck of elders.

Augustine's fanciful recollection of his own language acquisition remained the high water mark for child language studies through the Middle Ages and even the Enlightenment. However, Augustine's recollection technique is no longer of much interest to us, as few of us believe in the accuracy of recollections from infancy, even if they come from saints.

1.2 Baby biographies

The second major technique for the study of language production was pioneered by Charles Darwin. Using note cards and field books to track the distribution of hundreds of species and subspecies in places like the Galapagos and Indonesia, Darwin was able to collect an impressive body of naturalistic data in support of his views on natural selection and evolution. In his study of gestural development in his son, Darwin (1877) showed how these same tools for naturalistic observation could be adapted to the study of human development. By taking detailed daily notes, Darwin showed how researchers could build diaries that could then be converted into biographies documenting virtually any aspect of human development. Following Darwin's lead, scholars such as Ament (1899), Preyer (1882), Gvozdev (1949), Szuman (1955), Stern and Stern (1907), Kenyeres (1926), and Leopold (1939; 1947; 1949a; 1949b) created monumental biographies detailing the language development of their own children.

Darwin's biographical technique also had its effects on the study of adult aphasia. Following in this tradition, studies of the language of particular patients have been presented by Low (1931), Pick (1913), Wernicke (1874), and many others.

1.3 Transcripts

The limits of the diary technique were always quite apparent. Even the most highly trained observer could not keep pace with the rapid flow of normal speech production. Anyone who has attempted to follow a child about with a pen and a notebook soon realizes how much detail is missed and how the note-taking process interferes with the ongoing interactions.

The introduction of the tape recorder in the late 1950s provided a way around these limitations and ushered in the third period of observational studies. The effect of the tape recorder on the field of language acquisition was very much like its effect on ethnomusicology, where researchers such as Alan Lomax (Parrish 1996) were suddenly able to produce high quality field recordings using this new technology. This period was characterized by projects in which groups of investigators collected large data sets of tape recordings from several subjects across a period of 2 or 3 years. Much of the excitement in the 1960s regarding new directions in child language research was fueled directly by the great increase in raw data that was possible through use of tape recordings and typed transcripts.

This increase in the amount of raw data had an additional, seldom discussed consequence. In the period of the baby biography, the final published accounts closely resembled the original database of note cards. In this sense, there was no major gap between the observational database and the published database. In the period of typed transcripts, a wider gap emerged. The size of the transcripts produced in the 60s and 70s made it impossible to publish the full unanalyzed corpora. Instead, researchers were forced to publish only high-level analyses based on data that were not available to others. This led to a situation in which the raw empirical database for the field was kept only in private stocks, unavailable for general public examination. Comments and tallies were written into the margins of ditto master copies and new, even less legible copies were then made by thermal production of new ditto masters. Each investigator devised a project-specific system of transcription and project-specific codes. As we began to compare handwritten and typewritten transcripts, problems in transcription methodology, coding schemes, and cross-investigator reliability became more apparent.

Recognizing this problem, Roger Brown took the lead in attempting to share his transcripts from Adam, Eve, and Sarah (Brown 1973) with other researchers. These transcripts were typed onto stencils and mimeographed in multiple copies. The extra copies were lent to and analyzed by a wide variety of researchers. In this model, researchers took their copy of the transcript home, developed their own coding scheme, applied it (usually by making pencil markings directly on the transcript), wrote a paper about the results and, if very polite, sent a copy to Roger. Some of these reports (Moerk 1983) even attempted to disprove the conclusions drawn from those data by Brown himself! The original database remained untouched. The nature of each individual's coding scheme and the relation among any set of different coding schemes could never be fully plumbed.

1.4 Computers

Just as these data analysis problems were coming to light, a major technological opportunity was emerging in the shape of the powerful, affordable microcomputer. Microcomputer word-processing systems and database programs allowed researchers to enter transcript data into computer files which could then be easily duplicated, edited, and analyzed by standard data-processing techniques. In 1981, when the CHILDES Project was first conceived, researchers basically thought of computer systems as large notepads. Although researchers were aware of the ways in which databases could be searched and tabulated, the full analytic and comparative power of the computer systems themselves was not yet fully understood.

Rather than serving only as an "archive" or historical record, a focus on a shared database can lead to advances in methodology and theory. However, to achieve these additional advances, researchers first needed to move beyond the idea of a simple data repository. At first, the possibility of utilizing shared transcription formats, shared codes, and shared analysis programs shone only as a faint glimmer on the horizon, against the fog and gloom of handwritten tallies, fuzzy dittos, and idiosyncratic coding schemes. Slowly, against this backdrop, the idea of a computerized data exchange system began to emerge. It was against this conceptual background that the Child Language Data Exchange System (CHILDES) was conceived. The origin of the system can be traced back to the summer of 1981 when Dan Slobin, Willem Levelt, Susan Ervin-Tripp, and Brian MacWhinney discussed the possibility of creating an archive for typed, handwritten, and computerized transcripts to be located at the Max Planck Institut für Psycholinguistik in Nijmegen. In 1983, the MacArthur Foundation funded meetings of developmental researchers in which Elizabeth Bates, Brian MacWhinney, Catherine Snow, and other child language researchers discussed the possibility of soliciting MacArthur funds to support a data exchange system. In January of 1984, the MacArthur Foundation awarded a two-year grant to Brian MacWhinney and Catherine Snow for the establishment of the Child Language Data Exchange System. These funds provided for the entry of data into the system and for the convening of a meeting of an advisory board. Twenty child language researchers met for three days in Concord, Massachusetts and agreed on a basic framework for the CHILDES system, which Catherine Snow and Brian MacWhinney would then proceed to implement.

1.5 Connectivity

Since 1984, when the CHILDES Project began in earnest, the world of computers has gone through a series of remarkable revolutions, each introducing new opportunities and challenges. The processing power of the home computer now dwarfs the power of the mainframe of the 1980s; new machines are now shipped with built-in audiovisual capabilities; and devices such as CD-ROMs and optical disks offer enormous storage capacity at reasonable prices. This new hardware has now opened up the possibility for multimedia access to digitized audio and video from links inside the written transcripts. In effect, a transcript is now the starting point for a new exploratory reality in which the whole interaction is accessible from the transcript. Although researchers have just now begun to make use of these new tools, the current shape of the CHILDES system reflects many of these new realities. In the pages that follow, you will learn about how we are using this new technology to provide rapid access to the database and to permit the linkage of transcripts to digitized audio and video records, even over the Internet. For further ideas regarding the future directions of this type of work, you may wish to connect to this site: http://www.talkbank.org.

1.6 Three tools

The reasons for developing a computerized exchange system for language data are immediately obvious to anyone who has produced or analyzed transcripts. With such a system, we can:

1. automate the process of data analysis,
2. obtain better data in a consistent, fully-documented transcription system, and
3. provide more data for more children from more ages, speaking more languages.

The CHILDES system has addressed each of these goals by developing three separate, but integrated, tools. The first tool is the CHAT transcription and coding format. The second tool is the CLAN analysis program, and the third tool is the database. These three tools are like the legs of a three-legged stool. The transcripts in the database have all been put into the CHAT transcription system. The program is designed to make full use of the CHAT format to facilitate a wide variety of searches and analyses. Many research groups are now using the CHILDES programs to enter new data sets. Eventually, these new data sets will be available to other researchers as a part of the growing CHILDES database. In this way, CHAT, CLAN, and the database function as a coarticulated set of complementary tools.

This book, the first of a two-volume set, is composed of two parts. The first part is the CHAT manual, which describes the conventions and principles of CHAT transcription. The second part of this first volume is the CLAN manual, which describes the use of the program. The second volume describes the data files in the CHILDES database.

1.7 Shaping CHAT

We received a great deal of extremely helpful input during the years between 1984 and 1988 when the CHAT system was being formulated. [. . .] Comments developed in Edwards (1992) were useful in shaping core aspects of CHAT. [. . .] The workers in the LIPPS Group (2000) have developed extensions of CHAT to cover code-switching phenomena. Adaptations of CHAT to deal with data on disfluencies are developed in Bernstein-Ratner, Rooney, and MacWhinney (1996). Rivero, Gràcia, and Fernández-Viader (1998) suggested refinements in the transcription of data for analysis by the MLT (mean length of turn) command. Chapter 11 on sign language transcription was written and contributed by Dan Slobin, Nini Hoiting, Amy Weinberg, and colleagues of the Sign Language Work Group at the University of California at Berkeley. [. . .]

1.8 Building CLAN

The CLAN program is the brain child of Leonid Spektor. Ideas for particular analysis commands came from several sources. Bill Tuthill's HUM package provided ideas about concordance analyses. The SALT system of Miller and Chapman (1983) provided guidelines regarding basic practices in transcription and analysis. Clifton Pye's PAL program provided ideas for the MODREP and PHONFREQ commands.

Darius Clynes ported CLAN to the Macintosh. Jeffrey Sokolov wrote the CHIP program. Mitzi Morris designed the MOR analyzer using specifications provided by Roland Hauser of Erlangen University. Steven Gillis built an initial version of MOR rules for Dutch; Norio Naka developed a MOR rule system for Japanese; and Monica Torent helped develop the MOR system for Spanish. Julia Evans has been instrumental in providing recommendations for improving the design of both the audio and visual capabilities of the editor. Johannes Wagner, Mike Forrester, and Chris Ramsden helped show us how we could modify CLAN to permit transcription in the Conversation Analysis framework. Steven Gillis provided suggestions for aspects of MODREP. Julia Evans helped specify TIMEDUR and worked on the details of DSS. Catherine Snow designed CHAINS, KEYMAP, and STATFREQ. Nan Bernstein Ratner specified aspects of PHONFREQ and plans for additional programs for phonological analysis.

1.9 Constructing the database

The primary reason for the success of the CHILDES database has been the generosity of the nearly 100 researchers who have contributed their corpora. Each of these corpora represents hundreds, sometimes even thousands, of hours spent in careful collection, transcription, and checking of data. All researchers in child language should be proud of the way researchers have generously shared their valuable data with the whole research community. The growing size of the database for language impairments, adult aphasia, and second-language acquisition indicates that these related areas have also begun to understand the value of data sharing.

The database has grown so much that the description of the corpora now constitutes a Volume 2 of this manual. In that volume, each section documents a particular corpus and lists the contributors of that corpus.

Many of the corpora contributed to the system were transcribed before the formulation of CHAT. In order to create a uniform database, we had to reformat these corpora into CHAT. Jane Desimone, Mary MacWhinney, Jane Morrison, Kim Roth, and Gergely Sikuta worked many long hours on this task. Helmut Feldweg, Susan Powers, and Heike Behrens supervised a parallel effort with the German and Dutch data sets.

Because of the continually changing shape of the programs and the database, keeping this manual up to date has been an ongoing activity. In this process, I received help from Mike Blackwell, Julia Evans, Kris Loh, Mary MacWhinney, Lucy Hewson, Kelley Sacco, and Gergely Sikuta. Barbara Pan, Jeff Sokolov, and Pam Rollins also provided a reading of the final draft of the 1995 version of the manual.

1.10 Disseminating CHILDES

Since the beginning of the project, Catherine Snow has continually played a pivotal role in shaping policy, building the database, organizing workshops, and determining the shape of CHAT and CLAN. Catherine Snow collaborated with Jeffrey Sokolov, Pam Rollins, and Barbara Pan to construct a series of tutorial exercises and demonstration analyses that appeared in Sokolov and Snow (1994). Those exercises form the basis for similar tutorial sections in the current manual. Catherine Snow has contributed six major corpora to the database and has conducted CHILDES workshops in a dozen countries.

Several other colleagues have helped disseminate the CHILDES system through workshops, visits, and Internet facilities. Hidetosi Sirai established a CHILDES file server mirror at Chukyo University in Japan and Steven Gillis established a mirror at the University of Antwerp. Steven Gillis, Kim Plunkett, and Sven Strömqvist have helped propagate the CHILDES system at universities in Northern and Central Europe. Yuriko Oshima-Takane has brought together a vital group of child language researchers using CHILDES to study the acquisition of Japanese and has supervised the translation of the current manual into Japanese. In Italy, Elena Pizzuto has organized symposia for developing the CHILDES system and has supervised the translation of the manual into Italian. Magdalena Smoczynska in Krakow and Wolfgang Dressler in Vienna have been helping new researchers who are learning to use CHILDES for languages spoken in Eastern Europe. Miquel Serra has supported a series of CHILDES workshops in Barcelona.

1.11 Funding

From 1984 to 1988, funding for the CHILDES Project was provided by the John D. and Catherine T. MacArthur Foundation. In 1988, the National Science Foundation provided an equipment grant that allowed us to put the database on the Internet and on CD-ROMs. From 1989 to 1999, the project was supported by an ongoing grant from the National Institutes of Health (NICHHD). In 1998, the National Science Foundation Linguistics Program provided additional support to improve the programs for morphosyntactic analysis of the database and for initial work linking the CHILDES Project to the Informedia Project of the National Science Foundation Digital Libraries Initiative.

1.12 How to use this book

This book is Volume 1 of the two volumes that document the three CHILDES tools. Volume 1 is divided into two parts. The first part is the CHAT manual, which describes the conventions and principles of CHAT transcription. The second part is the CLAN manual, which describes the use of the editor, sonic CHAT, and the various analytic commands.

Volume 1 is designed for four types of users. Each group will want to use this manual in a slightly different way.

1. If you are an experienced user, you will want to review each section before beginning work with a specific command or the new features of the editor. There have been major changes to the commands interface, support for non-Roman fonts, inclusion of CA format as an alternative to CHAT, many new editing features, and new facilities for linkage to digitized audio and video. Although the basic features of CHAT have not changed, the description of the use of the conventions has been clarified throughout. The chapter on PHONASCII has been dropped, because we are now supporting direct IPA transcription in the IPAPhon font. The system of UNIBET coding has now adopted the SAMPA standard. The sections on audio and video digitization techniques are also new.

2. If you are a new user, you will want to begin by learning the [. . . minimal transcription system, minCHAT]. Next, you will want to starting reading the CLAN manual, which walks you through a basic tutorial on the use of the programs. After finishing the tutorial, try working a bit with each of the CLAN commands to get a feel for the overall scope of the system. You can then learn more about CHAT by transcribing a small sample of your data in a short test file. Try running the CHECK program at frequent intervals to verify the accuracy of your coding. Once you have finished transcribing a small segment of your data, try out the various analysis programs you plan to use, to make sure that they provide the types of results you need for your work.

3. You may be a new user who is primarily interested in analyzing data already stored in the CHILDES archive. You will still need to learn the basics of installing and running the programs. However, you do not need to learn the CHAT transcription format in much detail and you will only need to use the editor to open and read files. You will want to use Volume 2 to understand the shape of the CHILDES database.

4. If you use the CHILDES tools to teach language analysis to students, you can use the online tutorial resources developed by Yuriko Oshima-Takane and her coworkers at McGill. These lessons provide multiple choice questions and other ways of testing your knowledge of the fundaments of CHAT. They are available at http://childes.psy.cmu.edu/CHAT.html.

5. Teachers will also want to pay particular attention to the sections of the CLAN manual that present a tutorial introduction. Using some of the examples given there, you can construct additional materials to encourage students to explore the database to test out particular hypotheses. At the end of the CLAN manual,

there are also a series of exercises that help students further consolidate their knowledge of CHAT and CLAN.

The CHILDES system was not intended to address all issues in the study of language learning, nor was it intended to be used by all students of spontaneous interactions. The CHAT system is comprehensive, but it is not ideal for all purposes. The programs are powerful, but they cannot solve all analytic problems. It is not the goal of CHILDES to provide facilities for all research endeavors or to force all research into some uniform mold. On the contrary, the programs are designed to offer support for alternative analytic frameworks. For example, the editor now supports transcription in Conversation Analysis (CA) format, as an alternative to CHAT format.

There are many researchers in the fields that study language learning who will never need to use CHILDES. Indeed, we estimate that the three CHILDES tools will never be used by at least half of the researchers in the field of child language. There are three common reasons why individual researchers may not find CHILDES useful:

1.   some researchers may have already committed themselves to use of another analytic system;
2.   some researchers may have collected so much data that they can work for many years without needing to collect more data and without comparing their own data with other researchers' data; and
3.   some researchers may not be interested in studying spontaneous speech data.

Of these three reasons for not needing to use the three CHILDES tools, the third is the most frequent. For example, researchers studying comprehension would only be interested in CHILDES data when they wish to compare findings arising from studies of comprehension with patterns occurring in spontaneous production.

1.13   Changes

The CHILDES tools have been extensively tested for ease of application, accuracy, and reliability. However, change is fundamental to the research enterprise. Researchers are constantly pursuing better ways of coding and analyzing data. It is important that the CHILDES tools keep progress with these changing requirements. For this reason, there will be revisions to CHAT, the programs, and the database as long as the CHILDES Project is active.

Brian Richards and David Malvern

INVESTIGATING THE VALIDITY OF A NEW MEASURE OF LEXICAL DIVERSITY FOR ROOT AND INFLECTED FORMS

THIS CHAPTER INTRODUCES a new measure of lexical diversity, described as D, and software called *vocd*, for its calculation directly from transcripts.[1] We outline the problems associated with some previous approaches to measuring lexical diversity, particularly the way in which measures are dependent on the size of the language sample being assessed, and we show how D addresses these. Finally, we present evidence from an analysis of two early language corpora that supports the validity of our new approach and show how these techniques can be used to develop a new measure of morphological development.

Construct validity and reliability

Researchers in language development frequently make use of measures that indicate the diversity, range, richness, or (conversely) the repetitiveness of vocabulary use (see Richards and Malvern 1997 for an overview). The valid measurement of vocabulary diversity, like any attempt to quantify a range in a behavioural phenomenon, is difficult. This is because of an obvious effect of sample size – the larger the *sample* the greater the *range* that is likely to be sampled.

One measure that has frequently been reported in the child language literature, and is still sometimes assumed to overcome the problem of sample size, is the Type-Token Ratio (TTR). This is the number of different words (Types) divided by the total number of words (Tokens) in a transcript. TTR does *not* overcome the

2004, specially commissioned for this publication.

problem, however. As is well documented (e.g. Hess, Sefton and Landry 1986, Richards 1987), TTRs obtained from large language samples are *lower* than those obtained from a smaller number of words. This is easy to explain: if we were to calculate TTRs for a language sample which steadily increased in size for an individual, the number of word *tokens* in the denominator could increase infinitely, while the pool of available new word *types* in the numerator would steadily diminish. As a result, the constant rate of increase in the denominator is accompanied by a continuing deceleration in the rate of increase in the numerator, causing a fall in TTR as the sample size gets bigger.

One would expect lexical diversity to increase as children matured and increased their vocabulary, but a failure to appreciate that TTRs obtained from different baselines of word tokens cannot be validly compared has led to contrary findings. Richards and Malvern (1997) show how more advanced children's TTRs can be depressed because they speak more or produce longer utterances. For example, Fletcher (1985) reported that TTRs *decreased* as children got older, and for Bates, Bretherton and Snyder (1988) TTRs of 28-month-old children were negatively correlated with MLU and vocabulary. Miller (1981) calculated average TTRs for each of the eight age groups in Templin's (1957) study of 50-utterance samples from 480 children and reported that the ratio was fairly constant across age at just below 0.5.

A TTR of significantly less than 0.5, it was claimed, was '. . . probably indicative of a language specific deficiency' (Miller 1981: 41). As we have shown (Malvern and Richards 1997, Richards and Malvern 1997), any speaker or writer, no matter how gifted, will achieve a TTR of below 0.5 provided that a large enough sample is obtained. Even the plays of William Shakespeare fall well below this, with 'Much ado about nothing' as low as 0.14 (Chen and Leimkuhler 1989: 46). The apparent uniformity across age in Templin's data is an artefact of the way older children produced more words across 50 utterances and the larger samples at the older ages depress their TTRs. Nevertheless, instances can still be found where a TTR of 0.5 is treated as a valid diagnostic of language problems (e.g. McEvoy and Dodd 1992, Stickler 1987).

A number of solutions have been proposed to overcome the dependence of measures of lexical diversity on sample size. These include mathematical transformations of TTR such as corrected TTR (Carroll 1964), root TTR (Guiraud 1960) and bilogarithmic TTR (Herdan 1960) and rank frequency measures such as Yule's Characteristic K (Yule 1944) and Michéa's Constant (Michéa 1969). These and others are reviewed by Tweedie and Baayen (1998), but all can be shown to be dependent on sample size and to have problems with reliability and validity (Hess *et al.* 1986, Malvern and Richards 1997, Ménard 1983, Tweedie and Baayen 1998, Vermeer 2000).

One measure which has gained popularity, particularly where comparisons are being made between children with specific language impairment (SLI) and normally developing children (e.g. Klee 1992, Leonard, Miller and Gerber 1999, Watkins, Kelly, Harbers and Hollis 1995) is the Number of Different Words (NDW) contained in a standard number of utterances (e.g. 50 or 100). Klee (1992) found that NDW correlated with age and reliably discriminated between children developing normally and those with specific language impairment, and Miller (1991) found that it correlated strongly with age and MLU. Watkins *et al.* (1995) found that, unlike TTR, NDW was able to discriminate between children with SLI and age-matched normally developing peers whether it was based on a standard number of tokens or a standard number of utterances. In some cases NDW based on utterances has been extended to separate word classes, such as Number of Different Nouns or Verbs (e.g. Leonard *et al.* 1999). The worry about this approach is that, even though number of utterances is standardized across subjects, those capable of producing longer utterances provide more words and therefore, in all likelihood, a greater NDW. If they are so confounded, it is hardly surprising that NDW is correlated with MLU and other measures of language ability that reflect utterance length. Basing NDW on a fixed number of word tokens, rather than a fixed number of utterances, would avoid this problem. It would be even better, however, if a solution could be found which enabled researchers to use all of the data available rather than reduce all samples to the length of the shortest. It is to such a solution that we turn now.

An alternative approach to measuring lexical diversity

Paradoxically, it is the very 'problem' with TTR that provides a solution. As noted above, TTRs for large samples will be less than TTRs for small samples, and TTR can be treated as a function of sample size (i.e. the number of tokens). When, for any transcript or sample of writing, this relationship is plotted, the result is a curve. It begins at the point (1,1), because a sample of only one token will inevitably be of one type also and the TTR will be 1/1, i.e. 1. Initially, the curve falls steeply and gradually becomes less steep. The probability of new word types being introduced into samples containing more and more tokens can be modelled mathematically, and the model consists of an equation which represents the relationship between TTR and the number of tokens (N) taking account of a parameter D:

$$\text{TTR} = \frac{D}{N} \left[\left(1 + 2\,\frac{N}{D} \right)^{\frac{1}{2}} - 1 \right]$$

This equation is a simplification of Sichel's (1986) type-token characteristic curve and its origin is described in Richards and Malvern (1997). It represents a set of curves that relate TTR to tokens such that a curve for a transcript of greater lexical diversity will be situated above a curve for a transcript with lower lexical diversity – i.e. except for the initial point of (1,1), the TTR on the y-axis is higher at each token point on the x-axis (see Figure 2.3.1). The parameter D in the equation determines the height of the curve and is therefore an index of the lexical diversity of the transcript with higher values of D representing greater diversity.

In order to obtain values for D from a transcript or sample of writing it is first necessary to plot its TTR against the token curve and to compare this *empirical* curve with the *theoretical* curves produced from the equation. A value for lexical diversity is obtained by adjusting D in the equation until the theoretical curve which is the best fit to the empirical curve is found. High Ds represent high diversity. This procedure is carried out using dedicated software called *vocd*. For every transcript,

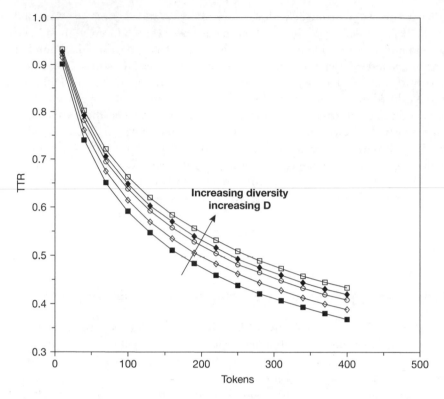

Figure 2.3.1 Family of curves showing increasing diversity with increasing D.

vocd plots a standard segment of the curve from 35 tokens to 50 tokens in incre-ments of one token. This is the segment for which our approximation of Sichel's (1986) original, more complex, model is most appropriate. For the first point on the curve, *vocd* randomly extracts 35 tokens without replacement and calculates a TTR. To increase reliability it does this 100 times and takes the average TTR for the subsamples of 35 tokens. This process is then repeated for 36 tokens and then for each of the remaining 14 points on the curve and a curve-fitting procedure provides the value of D for optimum fit. Because each point on the curve is an average TTR taken from random samples we will obtain a slightly different value for D each time *vocd* is run. These differences are small, but in order to minimize the effect the software processes each transcript three times and outputs the average value. *Vocd* operates on language samples transcribed in the standard transcrip-tion format of the CHILDES Project (Child Language Data Exchange System) (MacWhinney and Snow 1990). It is available as part of the CLAN (Computerized Language Analysis) programs in CHILDES, and allows similar text handling features to other CLAN software (see MacWhinney 2000) including choice of speaker, the exclusion of self-repetition within an utterance, ways of filtering out unwanted items (e.g. pause fillers), and the choice of carrying out the analysis on root forms or inflected forms. *Go*, *go-es*, *go-ing* can thus be treated as either one type or three. A detailed description of the software including a flowchart is contained in McKee, Malvern and Richards (2000).

The measure D has a number of advantages over TTR and its derivatives, and NDW. First, it overcomes the previous problem with sample size (see McKee *et al.* 2000), although sample size effects resulting from changes of context or topics in longer transcripts cannot be ruled out – this points to the need for control of situational and conversational context in obtaining language samples.

The second advantage is that our procedure uses all the words in the sample – even though the segment of the curve on which *vocd* operates is only from 35 to 50 tokens, each point of the curve derives from 100 subsamples extracted at random from the whole transcript. By contrast, indices such as TTR or NDW which overcome the sample size problem by standardizing the number of tokens across subjects waste data by reducing the scope of the analysis to, at best, the length of the shortest sample.

Third, and subject to caveats about comparability of context noted above, values of D obtained by different researchers using different data from the same language can be validly compared. This is not true where researchers have used different baselines for standardizing samples for TTR or NDW.

Fourth, it can be argued that D is a more reliable index of lexical diversity because it represents the *whole* of the TTR versus token curve rather than a single point on it. As far as the reliability of D-scores is concerned, the internal consistency of the procedure has been investigated using the data obtained from a split-half procedure that permits comparison of Ds for the even-numbered and odd-numbered words in a transcript. For 38 children aged 30 months, the D values obtained by McKee *et al.* (2000) from the even-numbered words were correlated with those for the odd-numbered words ($r = .763$; $p < .001$). In a study of the oral language of preschool children, Hess *et al.* (1986) concluded that at least 350 tokens were needed to obtain a reliability coefficient of .70 for lexical diversity. In McKee *et al.* (2000), however, the average number of words in half the transcript was 158 and this suggests that D compares well with previous measures.

Criterion-related validity of D

The introductory sections of this article have discussed the construct validity of D and reported empirical findings relating to reliability. We now turn our attention to the relationship between D and age and other linguistic measures of known validity – including concurrent validity and predictive validity – in two child language corpora. The implications of basing the analysis on root forms versus inflected forms will be addressed, and a comparison between these two versions of D will lead to a suggestion for a measure of inflectional diversity whose validity will also be assessed.

Method (Corpus 1)

The first analysis was conducted on transcripts of the 32 children in the Bristol corpus (Wells 1985) which are available from the CHILDES database. Wells' study was a longitudinal investigation into the language development of equal numbers of boys and girls who were spread across four family background groups. Recordings were made without the presence of an observer, using radio microphones linked to tape recorders pre-programmed to obtain 24 × 90-second samples between 9.00 a.m. and 6.00 p.m. D values were obtained for the children at 30 and 36 months using the command line: vocd +t*ABI -s@excl.txt +r6 abigail.cha, where vocd is the program for calculating D, +t*ABI selects the child speaker tier of the transcript (in this case, Abigail), -s@excl.txt invokes an exclude file containing a list of unwanted items to be filtered out (pause fillers, laughter, exclamations, onomatopoeia with no referential value, and singing), +r6 excludes self-repetitions, and abigail.cha is the child's transcript in CHAT format. Because of one missing transcript at each age, and three transcripts in which the child produced too few word tokens for D to be calculated (a minimum of 50 is required), $n = 29$ at 30 months and $n = 30$ at 36 months.

Results (Corpus 1)

First, the developmental trend over time was tested by comparing the means for D at each age. As would be expected if lexical diversity was sensitive to development, D was lower at 30 months ($M = 46.66$; S.D. $= 20.93$) than at 36 months ($M = 55.61$; S.D. $= 17.18$) and this difference was statistically significant on a Wilcoxon Signed Ranks Test ($Z = -2.62$; $n = 28$; $p < .01$).

Second, concurrent rank order correlations (Spearman's *rho*) at each age were computed between D and mean length of utterance (MLU) in morphemes as calculated by Wells (1985), and scores on the Bristol Scale of Language Development (BLADES) (Gutfreund *et al.* 1989). BLADES assigns children to one of ten levels on the basis of a profile that includes semantics, pragmatics and morpho-syntax. The results, which are shown in Table 2.3.1, show significant correlations with both measures at both ages, with particularly strong effects at 30 months.

Third, we examined the extent to which D scores at 30 months predicted those at 36 months. This also proved to be statistically significant (*rho* = .589; $n = 28$; $p < .001$). Finally, we further tested the validity of D by checking that it replicated any pattern of sex and family background differences, or lack of differences, associated with the other two language measures. Analyses using identical statistical tests found no group differences for sex or family background in D, MLU or the scale scores.

Table 2.3.1 Concurrent Spearman correlations between D and other language measures for the Bristol children at 30 and 36 months.

Measures	30 months			36 months		
	rho	n	p	rho	n	p
MLU	.816	29	< .001	.455	30	< .01
Bristol Scale	.789	29	< .001	.569	30	< .001

Method (Corpus 2)

The second study was carried out on the 38 children in the 32-month directory of the New England Corpus (Snow 1989, Dale *et al*. 1989) in the CHILDES database. The mean age was 30.3 months with a range of 27–33 months. Transcripts contain parent–child interaction involving play with the contents of four boxes presented in succession. There are equal numbers of boys and girls and 21 are described as middle class and 17 as working class.

Ds were obtained using a command line that was analogous to the one used above. However, unlike the Bristol data, transcription of the New England corpus marks boundaries before inflections. This enabled us to run the data through *vocd* twice – first using the standard command line and then adding a switch (+s*-%%) to treat *root* forms as the unit of analysis. The first procedure would therefore treat *go*, *go-es*, *go-ing* as three tokens and three types; the second would treat them as three tokens and one type. Clearly, the first procedure would give higher values for lexical diversity because children who were using a range of inflections would be credited with a greater number of types from the same number of tokens than if the analysis were performed on word roots. This would mean that D was confounding lexical diversity with morphological development, while D based on root forms could be seen as a purer measure of vocabulary development and therefore more useful. However, we predicted that if we subtracted D for word roots from D for inflected forms the resulting values would reflect inflectional diversity and be a valid measure of morphological development in its own right.

Results (Corpus 2)

As expected, the Ds for inflected forms ($M = 46.30$; S.D. $= 17.99$)[2] was higher than those for root forms ($M = 39.51$; S.D. $= 14.12$). This difference is significant on a Wilcoxon Signed Ranks Test ($Z = -5.359$; $n = 38$; $p < .001$). Nevertheless, in spite of the overall difference in the *magnitude* of values it should be noted that the *rank order* of the children is very similar on the two versions (*rho* $= .966$; $n = 38$; $p < .001$). It is also worth noting that the mean for the inflected version at just over 30 months is extremely close to the mean for the Bristol children at 30 months, also based on inflected forms ($M = 46.66$).

Table 2.3.2 Spearman correlations between the two versions of D and age and other language measures for the New England Corpus.

Measures	D-inflected forms			D-root forms		
	rho	n	p	rho	n	p
Age	.376	38	<.01	.372	38	<.05
MLU (morphemes)	.603	38	<.001	.538	38	<.001
CDI productive, 20 months	.327	30	<.05	.248	30	ns
CDI productive, 14 months	.302	34	<.05	.302	34	<.05
CDI receptive, 14 months	.276	34	ns	.285	34	ns

We then correlated the two versions of D with age and concurrent MLU and earlier vocabulary checklists completed by mothers using a forerunner of the MacArthur Communicative Development Inventory (CDI) (Fenson *et al.* 1993) when their children were 14 and 20 months. We were able to obtain scores for productive vocabulary for 30 of the 38 children at 20 months, and at 14 months both the production and receptive scores for 34 children. The full set of correlations is contained in Table 2.3.2.

The concurrent correlations between both versions of D and MLU are highly significant and moderately strong, and, in spite of a restricted range of ages in the sample, they are also significantly correlated with age. The CDI scores at earlier ages are less strongly related with D, and receptive scores are not significantly related at all. Three correlations between D and production scores are statistically significant, but only marginally so. Nevertheless, the overall pattern of results in Table 2.3.2, with the vocabulary *production* scores rather than the comprehension scores correlating with a vocabulary diversity index that measures usage, suggests that D is tapping an important facet of productive language.

Mann-Whitney U tests were used to test for sex and socio-economic status (SES) differences. No sex differences were found for either version of D, but for both versions there was a significant advantage for the middle class group. For inflected forms, the mean for the middle class group was 51.22 compared with 40.22 for the working class children ($U = 108$; $n = 38$; $p < .05$). For root forms the corresponding means were 43.21 and 34.93 ($U = 104$; $n = 38$; $p < .05$). This pattern is replicated for MLU – there were no sex differences but there were higher scores for the children in the middle class group ($U = 102$; $n = 38$; $p < .05$).

Inflectional diversity

Finally, for each child we subtracted the D-score for root forms from the score for inflected forms to obtain the measure of inflectional diversity (ID) proposed above. The values we obtained for ID varied considerably, ranging from zero to 27.97 with a mean of 6.79 and a standard deviation of 5.03. The validity of our interpretation of this measure was tested through correlations with age, MLU, and the mean number of inflections per utterance. All correlations were highly significant with particularly strong correlations with the two other language measures. As one would expect, the correlation with age (*rho* = .405; $n = 38$; $p < .01$) was lower than those with indices that tap grammar, and the correlation with inflections/utterance (*rho* = .846; $n = 38$; $p < .001$), the measure that is most dependent on morphological development, is stronger than the correlation with MLU (*rho* = .733; $n = 38$; $p < .001$).

Conclusions

Previous research has demonstrated the inadequacy of most earlier approaches to assessing lexical diversity in children's language. Measures have been a function of sample size, have been confounded with other aspects of development, have been unable to include all the available data and have lacked reliability.

In this chapter we have outlined a method which overcomes these problems and have tested its validity on two language corpora. We have demonstrated its sensitivity as a developmental measure through its correlation with age. Its relationship with *language* development is shown by concurrent correlations with well validated measures such as MLU and BLADES. The latter are highly significant and strong to moderately strong. Correlations with earlier vocabulary checklist scores are marginally significant and much weaker (as one would expect with measures taken 10–16 months earlier) or non-significant. But even here the pattern is interpretable, with three out of four correlations with *productive* vocabulary being significant, while both those with *receptive* scores are non-significant. In addition, in respect of sex and SES differences the pattern of results for D is the same as for other concurrent language measures across the two corpora. Finally, our interpretation of the difference between D-scores based on inflected forms and root forms, namely that this measures inflectional diversity, is borne out by a highly significant correlation with age, and strong correlations with MLU, and particularly with the mean number of inflections per utterance.

Notes

1   We should like to thank Gerard McKee for writing the *vocd* program and Brian MacWhinney and Leonid Spektor for adding it to CLAN. We are also grateful to Barbara Pan and Steven Reznick for passing on data from the New England children, and Ngoni Chipere and Pilar Durán for their comments on previous versions of this chapter. The research was supported by grants from The University of Reading and the Economic and Social Research Council (R000221995; R000238260).
2   In Malvern and Richards (2000) we reported some pilot analyses of the New England data that quoted lower values for D. This study used an earlier version of *vocd*, and its aim was to make a comparison between sampling tokens sequentially in the transcript and randomly sampling them with replacement. Neither version was free of sample size effects and we have since abandoned both approaches in favour of random sampling *without* replacement.

Part 3

Meanings

INTRODUCTION

SEMANTICS IS THE STUDY OF HOW languages encode meaning. Basically, meaning is the web of connections between words and what we talk about: things, people, actions, events, places, times, relationships, situations, etc. Whatever it is in the world that a word is directly linked to by its meaning constitutes the **extension** of the word. Words **denote** the items in their extension. The extension of the word *tree* is all the things that are correctly called *tree*. The word *tree* denotes any of the things in the extension of *tree*; that is to say, any of the trees that anyone might ever want to talk about.

Most words have an extension made up of a range of different items. (Singular proper names are an exception to this. For instance, there is only one *Hillary Rodham Clinton*, in most people's information about the world.) Think of all the trees there are, have been or could be. The members of this enormous set – the extension of the word *tree* – share similarities, but they are not all the same. There are big trees and little ones, gnarled ones and straight ones, ones that taper to the top and ones that spread; there are leafless wintering trees and ones with needles for leaves, and so on. The individual actions denoted by the verb *jump* are not all the same: there are high jumps and long jumps, record-breaking ones and little ones and so forth. It is clear that processes of generalisation are involved because even toddlers can correctly label instances of trees or jumping that they have not been specifically taught to include in the relevant categories.

Many studies of semantic development have been concerned with how children learn the categories that words denote, that is with how they learn what is and what is not in the extension of each word they know. Two seminal papers in this area are Clark (1973) and Bowerman (1978). Issues researched and discussed in this area over the past 30 years include the following:

- necessary and sufficient conditions: the idea that young children learn the **distinctive semantic features** of the extension of each word that they know (for example, things are called *chair* if and only if they are movable seats for one person);
- the nature of the semantic features that young children most often use (for instance, in a recent survey, Bloom 2001 concludes that the shape of an object is frequently an important characteristic for early noun categories);
- **prototypes**, where the suggestion is that categories are organised around the most typical, central examples. (The extension of *chair* might be centred on plain, upright chairs for sitting at a table, and things are called *chair* if they are more similar to this prototype than to the prototype for any other word known to the speaker.)

Among the three chapters in this part of the *Reader*, Chapters 3.1 and 3.2 focus on the establishment, in the earliest years, of meaning connections between words and the non-linguistic world. The beginning of Chapter 4.1 (Gleitman and Gillette) has further points on early word-to-world links and Chapter 6.3 (MacWhinney) discusses what it takes to get a computer to simulate such learning.

Once we have a start in a language, much of our knowledge of meanings comes to us through the medium of language itself, from the sentence contexts in which words are used and from explanations of meanings given to us linguistically (as when a child is told that '*Huge* is "very big" '). Semantics is thus also about meaning relationships within language. Meaning relationships that hold between words within the vocabulary of a language, such as the one just illustrated (*huge* means 'very big'), are called **sense relations**. Some other examples of sense relations are the sameness in meaning linking the words *garbage*, *trash* and *rubbish*, or the oppositeness between *big* and *small*, or between *huge* and *tiny*; or the inclusion relation that holds between the **superordinate** word *tree* and species terms like *beech*, *cedar* and *oak*. There is a short discussion of the acquisition of sense relations in Griffiths (1986: 303–6).

Children also need to learn that some words are built out of meaningful parts, as with *eggcup* formed from *egg* plus *cup*, or *teacher* from *teach* plus *er*. A representative study of this aspect of meaning development is Chapter 4.2 (Swan). See Clark's (1993) book too.

A further aspect of semantics that children need to develop control over concerns the effects on meanings of putting words into phrases and sentences. A couple of examples are that the meaning of *big* is modified when it is in a phrase such as *very big*; and the meanings of the verb *blow* and the noun phrases *Suzy* and *big bubbles* have to be integrated in a sentence like *Suzy blows big bubbles*. Chapter 4.1 (Gleitman and Gillette) and sections 4.2–5 in Chapter 6.3 (MacWhinney) include proposals about children's handling of meanings encoded by sentence structure. See also Soja (1992).

The grammar of a language encodes information about meaning. For instance the grammar of English requires users of English to indicate tense on verbs, and tense provides information about the timing of events relative to the time of speaking. As young children's control of grammar develops, they can use grammatical cues to gain knowledge about the meaning system of their language. (See Chapter 4.1 by Gleitman and Gillette, for a proposal on how syntax might help children make correct guesses about verb meanings.)

Researchers have wondered whether children growing up with grammatically different languages might develop different semantic systems. It could be that the nature of the particular language infants grow up with influences their construction of reality. Chapter 3.3, discussed below, presents cross-linguistic evidence that, even before 2 years of age, there are parallels between the grammatical patterns of the particular language that children are acquiring and selective emphases in the same children's semantic development.

Opposed to this, or perhaps in some ways a complementary possibility, is the suggestion that a language provides labels for a perceptual and experiential world that young children have come to understand independently of language. Nelson (1973a) suggested that **function** – the uses to which things are put and the actions that they are involved in – is the basis for grouping entities into categories prior to linguistic labelling.

The papers

Infants' comprehension is ahead of their ability to speak. This is seen in the report by **Margaret Harris**, **Caroline Yeeles**, **Joan Chasin** and **Yvonne Oakley** (Chapter 3.1) on lexical development in six subjects up to the age of 2 years. They found intervals of between 2 weeks and 5 months from first comprehended word to first word attested in production. The speed of word learning is impressive too. Hamilton *et al.* (2000) summarise the findings from vocabulary inventories on 669 British children. One of their graphs indicates the median vocabulary sizes shown in Table 3.0.1, at ages from 1 to 2 years. (The statistical term **median** signifies that these are figures for the dividing line between a slower-developing half of the sample and a precocious half of the sample. Of course there were precocious infants with larger numbers of words at each of the ages and there were also infants who were not developing as fast as indicated in Table 3.0.1.)

Over the second year of life, this averages out at 5 new words a week in production ($260 \div 52 = 5$) and around 6 new words a week in comprehension. Estimating the size of a child's vocabulary is not easy. Data obtained with the MacArthur Communicative Development Inventory (discussed in Part 2 of the *Reader*) gives higher figures for English-speaking infants and toddlers in the US (Bates *et al.* 1995). The CDI was the starting point for Hamilton *et al.* when they made the measurements reflected in Table 3.0.1.

The words of infants and toddlers can differ in meaning from the corresponding adult words. For instance, the earliest words are often tied to specific contexts, as when one of the infants reported on by Harris *et al.* (Chapter 3.1) apparently understood *clock* to denote only the clock on the kitchen wall. Flexible use across contexts is the more usual pattern in adult English: a meaning for *clock* that is general enough to also have in its extension alarm clocks, clocks in motorcars and clocks

Table 3.0.1 British children's median vocabulary sizes in production and comprehension between 1 and 2 years old

Age (years;months)	Number of words produced	Number of words comprehended
1;0	none	48
1;6	20	145
2;0	260	around 370

Source: based on data in Hamilton *et al.* (2000).

on public buildings. Harris *et al.* investigated the freeing up of infants' words from the bonds of context, in both comprehension and production, over the age range 6 months to 2 years. On each of the children's first 20 words in production, they found that the status of the word as either contextually flexible or context-bound was overwhelmingly the same in production as in comprehension. They call this 'symmetry'. Only 8 per cent of the words were not 'symmetrical' in this sense. Furthermore, most of the words that were 'symmetrical' were found to have the same range of meanings in production as in comprehension. This suggests that word meanings are part of language competence, neutral between production and comprehension.

Several different attempts to explain the rapidity of child vocabulary acquisition have in common the idea that infants must operate with some time-saving biases. For instance young children appear to have a strong 'whole object' preference to take a noun – such as *bunny* uttered to them by a parent – as denoting a whole object that is at that moment salient in the surroundings (probably a rabbit or a picture of one), instead of treating *bunny* as denoting a part of the object (like one of the rabbit's ears), or a perceptual quality (like its furriness), or an action (hopping that the rabbit might be doing, for instance). Golinkoff *et al.* (1994) surveyed evidence for the 'whole object' bias and five other proposed tendencies that could be helpful to toddlers in the learning of nouns. If early language learning is bound by such **constraints**, the learners could be saved time by a reduction in the number of available hypotheses that their minds have to consider. See also Clark (1987), where a 'principle of contrast' is proposed, a constraint that has been the subject of considerable research.

William Merriman and **Colleen Stevenson** (Chapter 3.2) investigate one of these proposed biases, **mutual exclusivity**. They define the mutual exclusivity bias as 'a tendency to assume that words have no exemplars in common'. (For additional background, see Markman and Wachtel 1988.) In what follows, mutual exclusivity is abbreviated to MEx. Adult English has violations of MEx, for example all the couches in the world form a subset of the extension of the word *seat* (benches, stools and chairs are also in the extension of the superordinate word *seat*), so a couch can be correctly labelled as either *couch* or *seat*. Similarly, a ball is a *ball* and a *toy*. Other counterexamples occur when there is no clear boundary between the extensions of a pair of words, as in the case of *hill* and *mountain*, which share borderline exemplars (big hills or small mountains).

MEx also fails to allow for bilingual children having two labels for the same thing. For instance, in a developmental study of the acquisition of colour terms in Setswana, a Southern African language, Davies *et al.* (1994) report that some of the children had labels in two languages (Setswana and English) for the same colours. Nevertheless, it may be a useful temporary simplification for toddlers to proceed as if the extensions of no two words can overlap. That they eventually learn when to ignore the bias was established by Au and Glusman (1990), who found that 4-year-olds will accept two labels for the same thing if one of the labels is a super-ordinate for the other, for example *animal* is a superordinate for *dog*.

Merriman and Stevenson focus on 'restriction', an occurrence that counts as evidence for the MEx bias. An explanation of their experiment will make clear what is meant by this term. Some 2-year-olds were shown drawings of imaginary crea-tures, for instance of a bear-like creature with a long neck, one that could possibly belong in the extension of the word *bear*. In the experiment, some of the children heard a different label for this candidate 'bear', for example the invented word *mave*. Toddlers who behave in accord with MEx should become reluctant to have the label *bear* applied to the long-necked creature, the extension of the word *bear* having been restricted through long-necked candidate bears going over into a mutu-ally exclusive category of *maves*.

How can we assess whether the long-necked animal would have had a reason-able chance of being counted as a bear if the 2-year-olds had not heard it called *a/the mave*? Merriman and Stevenson addressed this by also testing whether the children would accept *bear* as a name for a similarly strange animal, a bear-like creature with a corkscrew tail and oversized feet. If the children were prepared to regard this creature as a bear, but reluctant to have the label *bear* used for the long-necked animal, then exposure to the competing label *mave* for the long-necked one could be the crucial difference, provided we accept that the long-necked animal and the one with oversized feet and a funny tail are equally non-central in the bear category.

As a check on the comparability of the two atypical 'bears', Merriman and Stevenson exposed half of the children to *mave* as a label for the one with the long neck, but half of them heard this invented word used, instead, for the animal with big feet and a strange tail. In support of the MEx explanation, 'restriction' effects were observed in the experiment: children who had learnt to comprehend *mave* as a label for one of the peripheral 'bears' tended to treat that particular animal as not belonging in the bear category, but remained willing to accept the other atyp-ical 'bear' as belonging in the extension of *bear*. The experiment was run with three other categories in addition to bears.

Merriman and Stevenson carried out a second experiment as a control to see if the mere fact of the experimenter talking about one of the atypical exemplars was what somehow led to it becoming disfavoured for the label *bear*, rather than the crucial experience being the labelling of the picture by means of what was appar-ently a common noun (*a/the mave*). In the second experiment (not reprinted in the version of Merriman and Stevenson's paper reproduced here), the bear was intro-duced as 'an animal called *Jimmy*' and thereafter referred to by means of pronouns, *he, him* and *the one*. Under these conditions no 'restriction' effect was observed. This is evidence that the observed restriction effect was not simply attributable to the particular exemplar having been spoken about by the experimenter. It also confirms an established finding first reported by Katz *et al.* (1974), that 2-year-olds have some sensitivity to the semantic implications of the grammatical distinctions between common nouns and proper names (like *Jimmy*).

An example was cited earlier of an infant having too small an extension for a word: *clock* denoting only the clock on the kitchen wall. Young children have also been widely reported as stretching the application of some words to label a wider range of entities than the corresponding adult word, as when a child uses the word *shoe* to talk about not only shoes, but also socks. Clark (1973) coined the term **overextension** for this phenomenon. By assembling a large collection of instances and discussing possible explanations for overextension and children's eventual recovery from this type of error, she persuaded developmental psycholinguists that it was an important puzzle and a likely source of information about semantic development. Merriman and Stevenson argue in Chapter 3.2 that the MEx bias helps children demarcate the outer edges of the extensions of their words. The 'restriction' effect, for instance, could enable them to avoid incipient overextensions to entities that might be members of another category. Matsumoto (1993: 680) makes the important general point that it is with items on the periphery of a category – ones that are rather different from the category's prototype – that specific exposure to exemplars is needed to establish where the boundaries are.

Melissa Bowerman (Chapter 3.3) presents a cross-linguistic comparison of children's acquisition of ways of talking about directed motion – actions of coming and going. She compares data from children for whom English is the first language with data from children growing up with Korean as their first language. The point is to contrast linguistic input from the environment – Korean or English – with 'unlearned dispositions' for language, which is to say infants' inborn human capacity for developing as language users. Bowerman notes that 'unlearned dispositions for linguistic organization obviously do not provide all the structure, since children in different communities end up speaking different languages' – a truism, but an important one. She argues that cross-linguistic comparisons are indispensable for distinguishing between what comes from the universal foundation and what is attributable to input from the child's speech community.

Early in the acquisition process, the two children who were acquiring English used verbs that included **manner** of motion as part of their meaning, for example *step*, which means 'to move in a stepping manner'. Furthermore, they put these into sequences with words denoting the path of movement, for example *up* in the sequence *step up*. The eight Korean children did not give expression nearly as early to the manner of motion. Instead they used a range of subtly specific verbs that had **path** information as part of their meaning. This difference, and others revealed in Bowerman's comparison, can be related to different tendencies, already noted by other linguists, regarding the ways that the Korean and English languages package meaning in directed motion expressions. Bowerman therefore has a basis for arguing that the nature of different target languages might prompt children to construct distinguishable semantic systems. Bowerman and Choi (2001) is a longer and more recent exposition of these ideas, bolstered by data from comprehension and elicited production. See *Reader* Chapters 4.1 (Gleitman and Gillette) and 7.2 (Gopnik) for related work.

Margaret Harris, Caroline Yeeles, Joan Chasin and Yvonne Oakley

SYMMETRIES AND ASYMMETRIES IN EARLY LEXICAL COMPREHENSION AND PRODUCTION

Introduction[1]

IN THE MID 1980S A CONSENSUS began to emerge in the literature on early lexical development. This was that the first words children produce are not used as the names of objects or actions but are, instead, produced only in one specific situation or context (Bates, Benigni, Bretherton, Camaioni & Volterra, 1979; Dore, 1985; Nelson & Lucariello, 1985; Barrett, 1986). There are many reports of such uses which are commonly described as context-bound. For example, Harris, Barrett, Jones & Brookes (1988) report that James initially used *mummy* only when he was handing a toy to his mother and *there* only when pointing up to a picture on a frieze; and Jenny initially used *bye-bye* only when she was waving goodbye.

Careful inspection of the literature also reveals that, at the same time as the numerous reports of context-bound use were occurring, there were a few reports of very early contextually flexible word use, that is, use of a word in more than one behavioural context (see, for example, Bates *et al.* 1979). The incidence of such reports has greatly increased in the last few years and, in a series of recent papers, a number of authors have argued that children use words in a contextually flexible way right from the outset of vocabulary development (Dromi, 1987; Lucariello, 1987; Harris *et al.*, 1988; Barrett, Harris & Chasin, 1991; Goldfield & Reznick, 1990).

[. . .]

1995, reprinted with permission from *Journal of Child Language*, 22: 1–18.

In the Harris *et al.* (1988) study of the first ten words produced by four children, out of the total of 40 words, 14 were initially used referentially, that is, as object names. A further four words were contextually flexible non-nominals which were used in a variety of different behavioural contexts to express such notions as recurrence and rejection. These two kinds of flexible usage – nominal and non-nominal – contrasted with context-bound word use that was restricted to a single behavioural context.

[. . .]

One question that arises from the growing evidence that children use words both in a context-bound and in a contextually flexible way right from the outset of production is whether these two kinds of word use are mirrored by different patterns in comprehension. In the early stages of lexical development it is common for the onset of comprehension to precede that of production by several months (Benedict, 1977; Bates, Bretherton & Snyder, 1988). Thus, if the contrast between context-bound and contextually flexible word use reflects a significant difference in the child's representation of words, rather than merely some production-specific phenomenon, there should be evidence of corresponding differences in the preceding development of these words in comprehension.

Bates *et al.* (1988) argue that early language production consists of two strands. The first strand, 'analysed production', has a close relationship to comprehension. The second strand, 'unanalysed production', is characterized by an independence from comprehension. Analysed production consists of words that have previously appeared in the child's comprehension vocabulary. According to Bates *et al.* this strand of production is particularly evident in children who build up large comprehension vocabularies before uttering their first word and who subsequently go on to use nouns in a flexible way in production. The second strand of production consists of words and phrases that the child has learned by rote or in fixed routines. By contrast to the words forming part of analysed production, these latter words are not firmly rooted in comprehension. The question that the Bates *et al.* study raises is whether both context-bound words and contextually flexible words are rooted in comprehension or whether, as Bates *et al.* would seem to imply, only the latter have their origin in comprehension.

Another related issue that was addressed in this study concerns the early appearance of nominals in production. If children are capable of using words referentially right from the outset of production, then there should be evidence for the development of an understanding that words can be used to name objects in the period of comprehension development that precedes production. Some preliminary evidence for this comes from Harris (1992), who reports data on the pre-production comprehension of her nephew, Matthew. Extensive testing of Matthew's understanding of object names revealed that, some months before producing his first word, he was aware that words could be used in the context of several different referents. For example, when asked to point out a panda, Matthew was able to point to pictures in books, a picture on a mug, his panda-shaped haversack and to the panda logo of the Worldwide Fund for Nature. When asked 'Where is the clown?', he pointed to several different clowns in a picture of a circus, to a toy clown and to a model of a clown hanging from his bedroom lampshade. His most sophisticated understanding was of the word 'car'. When asked to point out a car on a number of different occasions, he selected real cars on the road, a variety of different pictures of cars (including formula one racing cars), cars on television and an extensive range of model cars. As might be expected, Matthew's first use of the words *panda*, *clown* and *car* was highly contextually flexible and genuinely referential.

It is possible, however, that Matthew's early lexical development represents one extreme. There was a considerable lag between his comprehension and production – Matthew did not begin to speak until he was 1;6 – and he was like the children described by Bates *et al.* (1988) who develop a large comprehension vocabulary and then go on to use words in a contextually flexible fashion in production. It remains an open question as to whether all children show evidence of early contextually flexible comprehension.

The main aim of the present study was to provide a detailed account of the relationship between early lexical comprehension and production in order to answer three specific questions. First, do both context-bound and contextually flexible words in production have a prior history in comprehension? Secondly, is there symmetry or asymmetry between comprehension and production, that is, are words that are context-bound in production similarly context-bound in comprehension and words that are contextually flexible in production also flexible in comprehension? Thirdly, is there evidence for the general development of contextually flexible understanding of object names in the period of comprehension that precedes production?

Method

Subjects

Six children took part in the study. They were recruited through local health visitors and personal contacts. Four were boys (Ben, Andrew, Sebastian and George) and two were girls (Katherine and Katy). The only criteria used for selection, in addition to parental willingness to take part in the study, were that the children be first-born and that English should be the only language spoken in the home. At the time of the first observation the children were six months old (range 0;5.24– 0;6.06). Observation continued until the children were two years old.

Procedure

Identification of words in comprehension. From six months onwards the children were visited at home every two weeks. Initially the home visit had three functions. The first was to collect the diary records which mothers and fathers were asked to keep. These noted down all new words understood by the child and new contexts in which old words were understood. Parents were encouraged to record as much detail as possible about the context in which comprehension occurred. The second purpose of the visit was to carry out an interview in which a researcher discussed the latest instalment of the diary record with the mother in order to clarify and expand the information given. The researcher also observed the child's language comprehension.

From ten months of age, two additional methods of data collection were introduced. At each visit a 15-min videorecording was made of the child. Mothers were also given a comprehension check list of the most commonly understood words organized into categories (e.g. toys, food and drink, people, games, actions). The check list was a modified version of that used by Benedict (1977). Mothers and fathers were asked to record new words as they were understood and, at the home visit, a researcher went through the list with the mother to check that no new words had been omitted and to obtain detailed information about the context in which a new word was understood. The comprehension check list proved to be an invaluable source of additional data especially where parents found it difficult to keep accurate diary records.

These various sources of information were used to provide a detailed picture of each child's developing comprehension vocabulary. Once a new word was identified as appearing in comprehension, controlled testing was carried out to confirm parental reports. Confirmed instances of comprehension were then recorded in a log. Testing was also carried out to determine the range of contexts in which a word was understood. This was to enable a more reliable classification of words as context-bound or contextually flexible. Testing had two specific aims. The first was to confirm initial observation and the second to see whether the child understood a word in a wider range of contexts than was apparent from observation.

For words that referred to actions, testing normally involved saying the word and observing the child's response. For example, when asked about *toes* at 1;2.26, Andrew always responded by looking down and touching his toes. At 1;0.2, Katherine always looked at the speaker and offered the object she was holding or pointed at a nearby object in response to *there*.

In the case of object words, testing explored the range of exemplars to which the child extended the word. Testing of an individual word was often carried out on more than one occasion if there was evidence that understanding had changed with time. Each occasion of testing involved a forced-choice selection task. The testing procedure varied, making use of pictures, toys or other objects as appropriate. However, all testing of object words conformed to certain principles. First, children were presented with at least five items – often more – and asked 'Where is X?'. Secondly, only one of the presented items was a correct exemplar. If it appeared that comprehension was restricted to a single referent, in initial testing the correct exemplar was the one familiar to the child. However, once it was confirmed that a child could select a familiar exemplar, testing with a novel exemplar was introduced.

It will be remembered that the testing was used as a supplement to observation by the mother and the experimenter. Thus, in the case of object words, the main aim of testing, once the report or observation had been confirmed, was to determine whether a word was understood with respect to other exemplars. For example, at 0;10.27, Sebastian was reported as pointing at ducks on the river when asked 'Where is the duck?'. At 0;11.8 testing of *duck* was carried out and, in forced-choice selection tasks, Sebastian chose the family duck nail brush (familiar exemplar) and a novel yellow plastic toy duck. Repeated testing over subsequent months showed that Sebastian's comprehension of *duck*, although contextually flexible, was restricted to yellow ducks. Only at 1;5.3 was he able to select correctly a novel non-yellow duck from an array of model animals.

It is worth noting that, when comprehension testing of object names first began, it was often necessary to rely on changes in facial expression and/or changes in the direction of gaze to decide which exemplar or exemplars a child had selected. When the children became capable of pointing – somewhere between 0;9 and 1;3 – their most common response was to point at an object when asked 'Where is X?'. From 0;10 – covering the majority of instances of comprehension testing – a second experimenter was present during testing to provide an independent observation of the child's response.

The visual similarity between the novel exemplar and the known exemplar varied according to the object concerned. For man-made objects the similarity between the known and new exemplar was often merely a matter of colour and/or size, as in the case of the yellow toy ducks mentioned above. For animate categories there was often a large variation. For example, diary records for Katherine at 0;9.20 noted that she pointed to a dog which visited her home when asked 'Where is the dog?'. At 0;9.23 Katherine was presented with a series of pictures including one of a dog but she failed to select any of the pictures. However, by 0;10.7 she was able to select a dog from among her own toys and also to pick out novel dogs from a selection of pictures. The appropriately selected dogs were of different breeds.

It will be noted that observation and testing of comprehension was a continuing process and was designed to provide a detailed record not only of initial comprehension of a word but also of changes in comprehension. This was a crucial aspect of the methodology because it was not possible to predict when a word in a child's comprehension vocabulary would first appear in production.

Identification of words in production. From 0;10 a second researcher took part in the home visits. She was mainly responsible for observing the child's production of words during the visit and also, where necessary, for testing production.

The procedure for identifying words in production followed that of Harris *et al.* (1988) and made use of the diary records – which later included all new words produced as well as those comprehended – maternal interviews, home observations and fortnightly videorecordings. In order to facilitate the identification of words from the videorecordings, phonetic transcripts were made of all utterances produced by the child. A vocalization was counted as a word only if a diary entry was confirmed either by home observation or from a videorecording. If there was no diary entry, three separate observations were required before a vocalization was treated as being a word. In both cases only spontaneous utterances were counted and imitations were excluded.

If, once a word had been identified in production, the child's use of that word was not clear, controlled testing was carried out to resolve any ambiguity. The most common reason for such ambiguity was that there was some inconsistency between diary entries and observations made either from a videorecording or during a home visit. As in the case of comprehension, testing was directed towards ascertaining whether a word use was context-bound or contextually flexible. For example, at 1;4.20, Andrew's mother reported that he used *hot* when reaching for a cold mug of tea and, at 1;6.3, that he was using *hot* when reaching towards a radiator. At 1;7.13, testing confirmed that Andrew used *hot* when reaching towards both hot and cold objects. This use was therefore classified as context-bound because what was common to each occasion of use was the act of reaching towards a restricted range of objects.

Comparison of comprehension and production. Once a word was identified in production, the comprehension record was inspected to see whether there was an entry for that word. If there was more than one record, the one that occurred nearest in time to the first reliable instance in production was selected. It should be noted that the record of comprehension was designed to keep track of changes in comprehension as well as the initial instance. Thus, it was considered safe to assume that the most recent record of comprehension was an accurate record of comprehension at the time that production occurred.

If there was no record of comprehension – or a word had not been confirmed in comprehension by testing – the word was tested in the home visit immediately following the point at which the word in production was identified. Testing of comprehension aimed to discover whether the context (or range of contexts) in which the word was understood was the same as that in which the word was produced.

The analysis reported in this paper concentrates on the first 20 words produced by each child. Each word in production was classified as context-bound or contextually flexible by one researcher (following the criteria used in Harris *et al.* 1988) and an independent classification was made of comprehension by a second researcher. The classification of each word in the two modalities was then checked by a third researcher and any cases of disagreement, which were infrequent, were resolved by re-examination of diary records, home visit observation notes and video-recordings as appropriate.

Results

Development of comprehension

There was some variation in the age at which the children first began to comprehend words but overall the pattern was remarkably similar. The most precocious child in this respect was Katherine, who showed reliable understanding of *clock* at 0;7.7, and *drink* and *Katherine* at 0;7.21. Ben also showed understanding of his own name at 0;7.25. The two least precocious children were George and Sebastian who responded to their own names at 0;8.16 and 0;8.11 respectively.

Although there was considerable similarity in the age at which the first signs of reliable comprehension appeared – and similarity in the significance of the child's own name – the rate at which comprehension proceeded was much more variable. As can be seen in Table 3.1.1, which summarizes the development of comprehension over the first year of life, Katherine understood 68 words and Katy 37 at 1;0. The four boys all had smaller comprehension vocabularies at the same age. Ben understood only 10 words and Andrew and George only 13. Sebastian understood 22 words.

Table 3.1.2 shows the number of words that the children understood before producing their first word. There was considerable variation both in the size of pre-production vocabularies and in the number of months elapsing between the onset of comprehension and that of production. However, two distinct patterns

Table 3.1.1 Cumulative total number of words comprehended over the first year of life.

Child	Age						
	0;6	*0;7*	*0;8*	*0;9*	*0;10*	*0;11*	*1;0*
Andrew	0	0	4	4	7	11	13
Ben	0	1	3	5	7	8	10
George	0	0	1	1	2	7	13
Katherine	0	3	7	12	20	28	68
Katy	0	0	2	2	9	20	37
Sebastian	0	0	1	4	12	18	22

are evident. Andrew, George and Katherine all had over ten words in their comprehension vocabularies at the point when they produced their first word. They also showed a lag of at least three months between the onset of comprehension and that of production. By contrast, Ben and Katy understood only one and two words, respectively, at the point when they first began production and they showed a lag of less than one month. Sebastian also had a very small pre-production comprehension vocabulary of just four words although just over two months elapsed between the onset of comprehension and production.

Table 3.1.2 also shows that a significant feature of pre-production comprehension vocabularies was that they contained a large proportion of contextually flexible words. Of the total of 54 words that the six children understood before beginning production, 39 were contextually flexible, that is, understood in at least two different behavioural contexts. Many of the words that the children understood in this early period were very clearly nominals. For example, at 0;9.9 Katherine was tested on her understanding of *clock* and she was able to point to several different pictures of clocks as well as to real clocks. At 0;9.27, Sebastian looked towards several different teddy bears when asked 'Where's teddy?' and also pointed to a picture of a teddy bear in a book.

Table 3.1.2 Age at which first word produced in relation to age at onset of comprehension and size of comprehension vocabulary.

Child	Age at first comprehension	Age at first production	Lag	Comprehension vocabulary		
				Total CB	Total CF	Overall
Andrew	0;8.7	1;0.3	3.22	4	8	12
Ben	0;7.25	0;8.9	0.14	0	1	1
George	0;8.16	1;1.11	5.1	2	13	15
Katherine	0;7.7	0;10.23	3.16	6	14	20
Katy	0;8.6	0;8.25	0.19	1	1	2
Sebastian	0;8.11	0;10.22	2.11	2	2	4
Total				15	39	54

Comparison of comprehension and production

The picture that emerged of two distinct patterns in the size of pre-production comprehension vocabularies was in marked contrast to the findings of the main analysis which compared comprehension and production of individual words. Comprehension and production of each word was classified as either context-bound or contextually flexible. There were, therefore, four possible patterns for each word: context-bound in both comprehension and production, context-bound in comprehension but contextually flexible in production, contextually flexible in comprehension but context-bound in production, contextually flexible in both comprehension and production. All four patterns occurred in our data and examples of each are given in Table 3.1.3.

It will be remembered that there were two sources of data about the comprehension of a word at the time of first production. Evidence came either from a prior comprehension record or – where there was either no record of comprehension or a report of comprehension was unconfirmed – from testing at the home visit immediately following production. Of the total of 120 words included in this analysis, there were only 36 (30%) where data on comprehension were collected after production occurred. Thus, in the great majority of cases the comparison is between the child's production of a word and PRIOR comprehension. Table 3.1.4 shows the relationship between comprehension and production in terms of the context-bound/contextually flexible distinction (CB/CF).[2] The data in brackets in Table 3.1.4 show the number of words for each child where comparative comprehension data were collected BEFORE production first occurred. The highest proportion overall (17/20) occurred for Andrew and the lowest (12/20) for Ben.

There are two possible reasons why there was no prior comprehension record for 30% of words. The first is that children did not understand these words when they were first produced. However, another possibility is that comprehension had emerged before production but that this was not detected either by the mother or

Table 3.1.3 Examples of symmetrical and asymmetrical relationships between comprehension and production.

	Word	Comprehension	Production
SYMMETRICAL			
Context-bound	*down*	as C squats down while playing game	as C sits down on floor
Contextually flexible	*cuckoo*	cuckoo-clock wrist-watches clocks	cuckoo-clock wrist-watches clocks
ASYMMETRICAL			
CF in comp CB in prod	*there*	as C offers object held in hand or points at object	as C points
CB in comp CF in prod	*clock*	wall clock in kitchen	carriage-clock wrist-watch wall clock in kitchen

Table 3.1.4 Relationship between comprehension and production for the first 20 words in production (instances where comprehension was assessed before production are shown in brackets).

| | Comprehension | | | | |
| | Context-bound (CB) production | | Contextually flexible (CF) production | | |
	CB	CF	CB	CF	Total
Andrew	3 (2)	4 (4)	0 (0)	13 (11)	20 (17)
Ben	4 (1)	1 (0)	1 (1)	14 (10)	20 (12)
George	3 (0)	0 (0)	0 (0)	17 (14)	20 (14)
Katherine	4 (2)	0 (0)	2 (1)	14 (12)	20 (15)
Katy	3 (1)	0 (0)	0 (0)	17 (12)	20 (13)
Sebastian	3 (1)	1 (0)	0 (0)	16 (12)	20 (13)
Total	20 (7)	6 (4)	3 (2)	91 (71)	120 (84)

in the course of home observation. Such failure to note comprehension would be likely if a child understood a word only very shortly before producing it or if comprehension first occurred at the same time that many other new words were being acquired.

There is no direct way to distinguish between these two possibilities but one way of gaining some insight into their respective merits is to compare the children's production of words in cases where there was a prior record of comprehension with those for which there was no record. If the general pattern of use proved to be similar this would lend support to the view that the absence of a prior comprehension record was the result of observation failure. If the pattern proved to be different this could be taken as indirect evidence that the children did not understand these words.

In order to make a comparison between words with a prior comprehension history and those without, Fisher Exact Tests were performed on the number of words that were either CB or CF in both comprehension and production. The comparison was between the proportion of words in these two categories for cases where there was a prior record of comprehension and the proportions where there was no record of comprehension prior to production. (Cases of asymmetry were excluded as they did not occur sufficiently often to be included in the analysis.)

The Fisher Exact probabilities revealed that, for five of the children, there was no significant difference between the proportions of CB and CF words occurring in the two samples.[3] However, there was a significant difference in George's data. Inspection of Table 3.1.4 reveals that there was no prior comprehension record for any of the initially context-bound words that George produced.

Following Bates *et al.* (1988), one would expect that a child would be less likely to understand a word before producing it where initial production was context-bound. As can be seen in Table 3.1.4, the CB/CB category (context-bound in both comprehension and production) contained the greatest proportion of instances where there was no prior comprehension record. Overall there were only 7/20 cases (35%) where there was a record of comprehension prior to production. This compares with 78% of cases for the CF/CF category. This overall trend, taken together with the data for George, provides some evidence to support the view that words that are initially produced in a context-bound manner are less likely to be understood before being produced than are words that are produced in a contextually flexible way from the outset. However, as the data in Table 3.1.4 show, some context-bound words were understood before being produced and, if this was the case, then production was likely to be a mirror image of comprehension.

Symmetry between comprehension and production is the most striking overall feature of the data in Table 3.1.4. For all six children the number of cases of symmetry between comprehension and production in the first 20 words was considerably greater than the cases of asymmetry, and the most common pattern was for a word to be contextually flexible in both modalities. For two of the children, Katy and George, 17/20 words showed this pattern. Even for George, who produced the smallest number of words that fell into this category, more than half were contextually flexible in both modalities. For all children, the second most frequent pattern was for words to be context-bound in both modalities.

The extent of the overwhelming symmetry between comprehension and production did not lie just at the level of contextual flexibility versus context-boundedness. In the great majority of cases the exact context or range of contexts in which a child produced and understood a word was identical. Two examples – *down* and *cuckoo* – can be seen in Table 3.1.3.

For two of the children, Katy and George, all words were symmetrical. For the other four children some words showed an asymmetrical pattern and, overall, just over 8% of words fell into this category. As Table 3.1.4 shows, there was a slight tendency for asymmetrical words to be context-bound in comprehension and contextually flexible in production rather than the other way round. However, without considering a much larger sample of words it is not possible to say whether this trend has any significance.

Discussion

The main finding to emerge from this study was that there was a very high degree of symmetry between the comprehension and production of early words and this applied equally to words that were context-bound in production and to words that were contextually flexible. If a child's initial production of a word was context-bound then it was highly likely that the child's understanding of that word when production occurred was restricted to the same single behavioural context. If, on the other hand, a child initially produced a word in a contextually flexible way then comprehension was most likely to be similarly contextually flexible.

There was, however, some evidence to support the view that context-bound and contextually flexible words in production differed in their likelihood of having been understood before being produced. For the great majority of contextually flexible word use, children showed evidence of comprehension prior to production. However, fewer than half the context-bound words had a prior history of comprehension. Although this difference could be explicable as a failure to observe the prior comprehension of context-bound words, it is at least plausible, in the light of the present data, to suggest that context-bound words are less firmly grounded in comprehension than words that are produced in a contextually flexible way. This finding provides some support for the distinction drawn by Bates *et al.* (1988) between two strands – analysed and unanalysed production – in early language development and confirms their conclusion that contextually flexible word use is more firmly rooted in comprehension than context-bound production.

The data reveal considerable individual variation both in the number of words that children understand prior to the onset of production and in the time lag between the onset of comprehension and that of production. It is clear even from the small sample studied here that not all children begin production after acquiring 20 or so words in comprehension which is often taken as the norm (Nelson, 1988). Three of the children – Andrew, George and Katherine – showed this typical pattern and several months elapsed between the time that they understood their first word and their own first production. However, this study highlights the existence of another pattern which was shown by two of the children. This is a very small lag between the onset of comprehension and production both in number of days and in the size of the comprehension vocabulary. This pattern of comprehension and production developing very much in tandem can be seen as lying at one end of a continuum, the other end of which is represented by children such as Matthew (Harris, 1992) who acquire a very large number of words in comprehension before producing their first word (Bates [*et al.*], 1988).

In spite of differences in the relative size of comprehension vocabularies at the outset of production, for all six children the majority of their first 20 words were contextually flexible in both modalities. It might have been supposed that the early production of children with larger comprehension vocabularies would have been more sophisticated than that of children with only a small comprehension vocabulary. However, in our sample, even children who understood only one or two words at the outset of production used some words in a contextually flexible fashion right from the outset.

The finding of very early contextually flexible word use confirms that of recent studies (Dromi, 1987; Lucariello, 1987; Harris *et al.*, 1988; Barrett, Harris & Chasin, 1991; Goldfield & Reznick, 1990). What the present study suggests is that the early contextually flexible use of words is underpinned by comprehension that, in the great majority of cases, develops prior to production.

Studies of the development of early lexical comprehension (Benedict, 1977, 1979; Bates *et al.*, 1988; Gunzi, 1993; Harris & Chasin, 1993) have shown that, as comprehension vocabulary increases, children acquire fewer personal names and more object names. However, all studies report that children have a significant number of object names within their first 50 words; and studies that report data on the first 20 words (Bates *et al.*, 1988; Harris & Chasin, 1993) have shown that even at this early stage there are some object names. This suggests that arguments about the child's developing capacity to acquire object names, which have concentrated to date almost exclusively on production (Dore, 1985; Nelson & Lucariello, 1985; Harris *et al.*, 1988; Goldfield & Reznick, 1990), should also consider the possibility of prior developments that have occurred within comprehension.

Given that children show evidence of such early contextually flexible under-standing – and most notably evidence of understanding that words can be used to refer to objects – it becomes less of a surprise to find that they use words as nomi-nals right from the outset of lexical production. What begins to be more of a surprise is that, if children understand that some words can be used as object names, they should, at the same time, use some object words only in a context-bound way in production.

Let us consider each of these issues in turn. First, why might we expect chil-dren to acquire at least some understanding of object names in the first year of life? Two factors would appear to be relevant, one related to the child's own percep-tion of the world and the other to the child's language experience.

One important component of any account of the child's developing under-standing of object names is a consideration of how children perceive objects. In recent years there has been a convergence of evidence towards the view that young infants have a surprisingly sophisticated understanding of objects and some of their properties (see Butterworth, 1989; Slater, 1989 for recent reviews). From the perspective of child language, what is important about recent research on percep-tual development is that it strongly suggests that, by the time children first begin to understand words, they have had considerable experience of perceiving the world as made up of discrete objects that behave in predictable ways.

The other side of the equation lies in the language that the child hears. Maternal speech typically contains a large number of specific object names – as distinct from superordinate terms such as *animal* and *furniture* or general terms such *this* or *it* – which mothers use when the child is focusing attention on the object in question (Harris, Jones & Grant, 1984/5; Harris, Jones, Brookes & Grant, 1986). When children gesture at an object (e.g. by pointing) mothers tend to respond by providing the name of the object, and this practice is significantly associated with the number of different object names that children acquire (Masur, 1982). Ruddy & Bornstein (1982) have shown that there is a significant correlation between vocabulary size at 1;0 and the extent to which mothers encouraged their children to attend to objects at 0;4.

The infant's early knowledge of objects, coupled with the tendency of both adults and infants to pick out objects in the environment which are then labelled by the adult, goes some considerable way to explaining how it is possible for chil-dren's understanding and production of object names (and personal names) to appear so precocious when compared with their acquisition of other types of word. (See Gillis (1990) for a similar argument about why it is considerably easier for the child to acquire nouns than verbs.)

Turning now to the second issue, that of the context-bound use of early words, it is again relevant to consider both child-related and input-related factors. We have shown that children are capable of understanding some object names early on in comprehension and we have argued that both the child's perceptual abilities and the characteristics of adult speech make this achievement possible. However, we also know that early lexical development – at least in the case of production – is very driven by experience. Children's initial use of their first words is extremely closely related to the relative frequency with which they have encountered a particular use of a word in maternal speech. Harris *et al.* (1988) found that, for the first ten words, children's initial production was identical to the most frequent maternal use of that same word in 83% of cases. For example, James's first use of *mummy* only ever occurred when he was holding out a toy for his mother to take. This was identical to the most frequent use of *mummy* by James's mother who would hold out her hand when James proffered a toy and ask *Is that for mummy?*

The effect of frequency, however, operates only over the very initial stage of lexical acquisition so that only the first use of early words, but not subsequent uses, is related to relative input frequency (Barrett *et al.*, 1991). Once children have acquired a significant number of words they are able to discount relative input frequencies and impose more internal structuring on their lexical development.

Combining the findings of the present study with those of Harris *et al.* (1988) and Barrett *et al.* (1991) we would suggest that at the outset of production, having acquired some understanding of object names in comprehension, children are capable of producing a word in a contextually flexible way providing that there are no strong frequency effects in the input that drive them towards a context-bound interpretation. If the child's experience of hearing a word used by an adult is such that there is one use that is much more frequent than any others, context-bound production that mirrors the most frequent adult use will result. However, if the input provides the child with the opportunity to observe a word being used in several different behavioural contexts, a contextually flexible interpretation is most likely.

It is also highly probable that cases of early object name comprehension emerge from a situation where the child hears a word being used in a variety of different contexts. There is good evidence that the child's early experience of words is remarkably consistent over the first eighteen months of life (Harris *et al.*, 1986) so, where comprehension precedes production – as is the case for most contextually flexible words – the child's experience of a word will remain constant over the period of comprehension and production. The contextually flexible production of early words is thus both informed by preceding contextually flexible comprehension and enabled by input that supports such a production pattern. A little later, however, the effects of input frequency cease to influence the child and, from the firm basis of both understanding and being able to produce object names, the child enters a new phase of development where the internal structure of the lexicon becomes increasingly important and the proportion of object names acquired continues to rise.

Notes

1   This paper was written while the first author was on a Social Science Research Fellowship from the Nuffield foundation. The research was supported by grant number R000 23 2037 from the Economic and Social Research Council to the first author. [. . .].

2   In a small number of cases it did not prove possible to obtain reliable data on comprehension. When this occurred, words were excluded from the analysis. Excluded words were as follows: Andrew *hello, ta*; Ben *train, bow-wow*; George *mummy, horse, no, blue*; Katherine *that, woof*; Sebastian *there, yes, woof-woof, what's-that*.

3   The Fisher Exact probabilities obtained were as follows: Andrew $p = 0.49$; Katherine $p = 0.20$; Ben $p = 0.14$; Katy $p = 0.27$; George $p = 0.02$; Sebastian $p = 0.22$.

William Merriman and
Colleen Stevenson

RESTRICTING A FAMILIAR NAME IN
RESPONSE TO LEARNING A NEW ONE
Evidence for the mutual exclusivity bias in young two-year-olds

Introduction

MANY CURRENT ACCOUNTS OF early word learning grant a substantial role to interpretative biases (Clark, 1987; Golinkoff, Mervis, & Hirsh-Pasek, 1994; Landau, Smith, & Jones, 1992; Markman, 1992; Merriman, Marazita, & Jarvis, 1995). One leading proposal is that children have a Mutual Exclusivity bias, which is a tendency to assume that words have no exemplars in common.

The evidence that youngsters who are more than 2½ years old have this bias is quite convincing (see Markman, 1989; Merriman & Bowman, 1989), but the same cannot be said for younger groups. Our goal was to test for the bias in 24-month-olds with a procedure that was not subject to the criticisms that have been leveled against previous studies.

The evidence

Four phenomena have been taken to be evidence for the bias. Two involve the interpretation of novel words (disambiguation and rejection) and two involve the reinterpretation of familiar words (correction and restriction). Children under 2½ years of age have shown only the novel word effects, which may mean that they only operate according to principles that concern solely the interpretation of novel words (e.g., Novel Name-Nameless Category, Golinkoff et al., 1994). On the other hand, methodological flaws may have been responsible for this group's failure to

1997, reprinted with permission from *Child Development*, 68: 211–28.

show the familiar word effects. We shall review how the novel word effects can be explained without the Mutual Exclusivity principle and establish some grounds for skepticism about toddlers' reported tendency to not alter a familiar word's meaning in response to learning a new word for one of its exemplars.

Novel word interpretation. The disambiguation effect is the tendency to select an unfamiliar rather than familiar kind of thing as the referent of a novel word when the intended referent of the word is ambiguous (e.g., to select a painter's palette rather than a cup when asked, "Which one is a pilson?") (Merriman & Bowman, 1989). Children as young as 18 months, as well as older children and adults, tend to select the unfamiliar kind (Golinkoff, Hirsh-Pasek, Bailey, & Wenger, 1992; Hutchinson, 1986; Markman & Wachtel, 1988; Mervis & Bertrand, 1994; Vincent-Smith, Bricker, & Bricker, 1974), which maintains Mutual Exclusivity between the novel label and the label known for the familiar kind.

Merriman and Bowman (1989) suggested an alternative explanation for this effect, however. The children may not be avoiding word overlap so much as filling a lexical gap. That is, whenever they encounter an unfamiliar kind, they may expect to be told its name. Golinkoff et al. (1992) have proposed a similar child expectation, which they call the Novel Name-Nameless Category (N3C) Principle.

The disambiguation effect can also be explained by a principle called Feeling of Novelty, which posits that children expect new names to map onto entities that feel new (Merriman, Marazita, & Jarvis, 1993b, 1995). This principle is not couched in terms of the nameability of candidate referents. How novel an entity feels depends not only on whether it can be named, but also on how recently it or things like it have been encoded.

Finally, two other principles concern both novel and familiar words, but are broader than Mutual Exclusivity. Clark (1983) has argued that the disambiguation effect is evidence for the principle of Contrast, according to which no two words have identical meanings. Although this principle is compatible with the tendency to assume that words will not share exemplars, it does not entail or predict it. The principle does not imply that one way of maintaining Contrast will be preferable to others. In the disambiguation paradigm, for example, the principle would be satisfied just as well by children assigning the new name to the unfamiliar kind as by their making it denote a subcategory of the familiar kind.

MacWhinney (1989) has proposed what might be called the principle of Competition—that words compete with one another for the power to express various concepts. In the Discussion section, we will explain why a semantic retrieval mechanism that abides by this principle necessarily shows a Mutual Exclusivity bias.

The second novel name phenomenon that is compatible with the Mutual Exclusivity bias is the rejection effect, whereby children resist learning a new name for something that they can already label or at least do not learn the name as readily as one introduced for an unfamiliar kind. Although there are anecdotal reports of 2-year-olds openly rejecting second labels (Macnamara, 1982; Markman, 1989; Mervis, 1987), such acts of overt resistance are very infrequent. They are rarely observed in name training studies (see Merriman, 1991).

Regarding more implicit forms of rejection, Banigan and Mervis (1988) found that 24-month-olds only succeeded in learning a name for something that they could already label if a distinctive property of the object was highlighted in training. For example, they did not learn *unicorn* for what they had mistakenly called "horse" unless their attention was drawn to the animal's horn. This finding may not be evidence for implicit rejection, however. It may just be easier to learn associations that involve distinctive elements than to learn ones that do not (Jacoby & Craik, 1979). Also, if highlighting makes an unnamed category salient or feel new (e.g., if pointing out the horn has this effect on the category of horses with horns), then by the Gap Filling, N3C, or Feeling of Novelty principles (i.e., the ones that exclusively concern effects on novel word interpretation), children should learn the name more readily.

Liittschwager and Markman (1994) found that both 16- and 24-month-olds were less likely to learn a novel name for a familiar than for an unfamiliar kind of object, and Merriman, Marazita, and Jarvis (1993a) also observed this effect in 24-month-olds. Here again, the Gap Filling, N3C, or Feeling of Novelty explanations cannot be ruled out. If children expect an unfamiliar kind to be called by a novel name, but have no expectation for or against a familiar kind being called by another name (i.e., no Mutual Exclusivity bias), they may well learn from input compatible with their expectations more easily than from input about which they have no expectation.

Familiar word reinterpretation. Merriman and Bowman (1989) argued that children may preserve Mutual Exclusivity by either correcting or restricting their extension of a familiar name. In the correction effect, a child who believes that something is an exemplar of one name stops believing this after hearing it called by another. In the restriction effect, children who have not previously committed a familiar name to a particular object refrain from doing so because they have heard another name used for the object, or they themselves have generalized another name to it. These effects, which both entail a change in the child's interpretation of a familiar word, may contribute to the decline that begins in the third year of life in overextension errors (Clark, 1973). For example, 2-year-olds may stop calling wolves "doggie," or keep from starting to do so, because they hear them called "wolf." These effects cannot be accounted for by Gap Filling, N3C, or Feeling of Novelty because such principles direct decisions only about as-yet-unnamed categories and novel names; they bear no implications for how familiar names are interpreted.

Although the correction and restriction effects have been documented in children who are 2½ years or older (Gelman, Wilcox, & Clark, 1989; Merriman, 1986; Merriman & Bowman, 1989, Studies 2 and 3; Merriman & Kutlesic, 1993), young 2-year-olds have failed to show them (Banigan & Mervis, 1988; Merriman & Bowman, 1989, Studies 2 and 3; Taylor & Gelman, 1989, Experiments 2 and 3; Waxman & Senghas, 1992). Moreover, in two longitudinal studies of 1- and 2-year-olds' comprehension and production of naturally acquired nouns (Mervis, 1987; Rescorla, 1976), 89%–95% of the children's overextensions were maintained for some period of time after they demonstrated knowledge of the correct name for the object involved.

Markman and colleagues (Liittschwager & Markman, 1994; Markman, 1992; Woodward & Markman, 1991) have criticized the name training assessments of 1- and 2-year-olds for failing to satisfy certain requirements. They noted that the 24-month-olds in Merriman and Bowman's (1989) studies of the correction effect had shown poor memory for name training, and argued that correction of a familiar name would not be expected if the novel name that was supposed to replace it had not been retained. Merriman and Bowman actually acknowledged this problem, but reported that if only trials in which the training object was selected correctly in the posttest were considered, the children's rate of also accepting the familiar name for this object was still very high. However, correct selections in the posttest many not have been based on memory. Most correct selections were of hybrid objects (e.g., a cross between a car and a truck). Because the other objects in the test set were typical exemplars of familiar kinds, the children could have just guessed that the name had been used for the hybrid. Two-year-olds have been observed to favor an atypical exemplar over a typical one as the likely referent of a unfamiliar name (Merriman & Schuster, 1991).

Merriman and Bowman (1989, Studies 2 and 3) also reported that when 24-month-olds were asked to select exemplars of contrastive familiar names from an array (e.g., *spoon* and *fork*), they chose overlapping sets of objects as often as mutually exclusive ones. Woodward and Markman (1991) objected that the children may have been confused about which objects belonged to which name's category and may have had trouble remembering which ones they had chosen for one name when tested on the other.

Experiments 2 and 3 of Taylor and Gelman (1989) are immune to such criticisms because their participants clearly remembered name training. [. . .]

The other name training experiments (Banigan & Mervis, 1988; Waxman & Senghas, 1992) as well as the longitudinal assessments of naturally acquired words (Mervis, 1987; Rescorla, 1976) can be faulted for lacking appropriate controls. Although the children tended to select objects as exemplars of familiar names after acquiring novel names for these objects, their selection tendencies may not have been as great as those of children who had not acquired novel names for them (a between-subjects control) or as great as the same children's own tendencies to select objects for which novel names had not been acquired (a within-subjects control). Thus, restriction or correction effects in young 2-year-olds might be detectable only by a design that includes a control condition.

Goal of the investigation

We reassessed one of the familiar name effects, restriction, in young 2-year-olds. Experiment 1 was a within-subjects assessment. In Experiment 2, a new group of 2-year-olds was administered a no word control procedure, and their selection of referents for familiar names was compared to that of the children in Experiment 1. This comparison constituted a between-subjects assessment of the restriction effect. [The details of Experiment 2 have been edited out of the version of the article reprinted here. Eds.]

Experiment 1

After hearing a story in which a novel word was repeatedly used as a name for an atypical exemplar of a familiar name, children were shown a set of pictures that included the target object (i.e., the one named in the story), another atypical exemplar of the familiar name, a typical exemplar of the familiar name, and an exemplar of a different familiar name. The experimenter asked them to select all referents of the familiar name and all referents of the novel name. The restriction effect was measured by the extent to which the target object was selected less often than the other atypical exemplar as a referent of the familiar name. The particular atypical exemplars that served as target and nontarget objects were counter-balanced over participants. The test of the novel name served as a check on whether the children had learned that the novel name was a label for the target object.

This procedure has two features that recommend it. First, the novel name was introduced for an atypical rather than a typical exemplar. Merriman and Bowman (1989, Studies 2 and 3) found that even older children and adults do not correct or restrict a familiar name for a typical exemplar. Belief that an eighteen-wheeler is a truck, for example, is just too strong to be undermined by hearing it referred to as a pilson. According to Merriman and Bowman, a typical exemplar fits people's representation of the familiar name so well that hearing a novel name for it causes them to override the Mutual Exclusivity default assumption. Second, several aspects of the procedure ought to have promoted the children's acquisition and retention of the belief that the target object was a referent of the novel name, a necessary condition for a test of restriction. The novel name for the target object was presented repeatedly, each time within a meaningful story, and a reminder of this information was delivered immediately before the name tests. The test sets contained only four pictures, and only two names were tested per set.

Method

Participants

The participants were 16 boys and 16 girls ($M = 2,1$, *range* $= 2,0$ to $2,1$) who were located through published birth records and recruited through a mailing with follow-up phone calls. The majority came from middle-class homes (mean SES $= 51$, *range* $= 22$ to 66 on the Hollingshead [1975] index). Their average productive vocabulary score on the toddler form of the CDI (MacArthur Communicative Development Inventory; Fenson et al., 1994) was 381 (*range* $= 45$ to 668). Five children were replaced for not complying with more than half the task instructions.

Materials

Four sets of black-and-white line drawings of objects were developed—bears, horses, spoons, and cars (see Figure 3.2.1). Each set included a typical exemplar of the target category (e.g., an ordinary looking bear), two atypical exemplars (e.g., a bear with a very long neck and one with unusual tail and feet), and a non-exemplar (e.g., a duck). The drawings in each set were positioned in a row on a 28×9 cm strip of laminated cardboard, with the two center items 3–4 cm higher than the end items. Each drawing was approximately 5–7 cm wide and 4–6 cm high. Each of the four types of drawings occurred once in each of the four positions on the strip. The strips were used at the beginning of an experimental trial and in the name comprehension tests.

Typical	Atypical	Atypical	Non-examplar

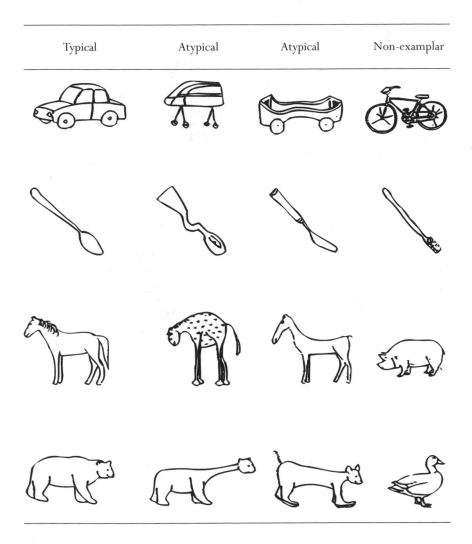

Figure 3.2.1 Pictures used in Experiments 1 and 2.

Eight story books were created, two for each target category. Each book consisted of four black-and-white line drawings on pages that were 27 × 18.5 cm. In the bear and horse stories, the main character was the target object, that is, the one for which the novel name was modeled. In the spoon and car stories, familiar characters (Barney or Bert and Ernie) interacted with the target object. In each story, the target object was one of the atypical exemplars from the comprehension test set. For example, one story was about the bear with the long neck and one was about the bear with unusual feet and tail. The two stories for each category differed only with respect to the atypical exemplar that served as the target object. In every story, the novel name was mentioned six times in reference to the target object. The novel names were *jegger*, *mave*, *pilson*, and *wug*. See Figure 3.2.2 for a sample story.

(1)   Bert has a *jegger*.

(2)   Here comes Ernie. Ernie took the *jegger*.
      Bert's mad, he wasn't finished playing with the *jegger*.

(3)   Look, Ernie gave the *jegger* back.

(4)   Bert's all done playing with the *jegger*.
      Now Ernie can play with the *jegger*.

Figure 3.2.2 A story used in Experiment 1.

Procedure

Parents brought their children to a university-affiliated laboratory room. After the child felt comfortable, the experimenter escorted him or her to a small table in a small room. The parent sat at least a meter away from the child and filled out a consent form, the CDI, and the SES questionnaire.

The child received four experimental trials, then a novel name production test. Each trial consisted of four phases: test strip exposure, story presentation, target object reminder, and name comprehension test. The experimenter began a trial by presenting a test strip (e.g., the four pictures from the bear set) and saying, "Let's look at these pictures. Aren't they neat? Look at all of them. One of these is in a book we're going to read." This procedure was followed to familiarize the child with the set of drawings that would later appear in the name comprehension test, to promote the child's attention to the target object when he or she encountered it in the story, and to help the child realize during the comprehension test that the target object in the test set was the very one he or she had heard called by the novel name in the story.

The strip was removed and the experimenter said, "I'm going to tell you a story about _____." The words that filled in the blank depended on the story: "an animal called a pilson" for the horse story, "an animal called a mave" for the bear story, "a wug Barney finds" for the spoon story, and "a jegger Bert and Ernie play with" for the car story. The experimenter then presented the picture book story.

The book was closed and the test strip was placed next to it on the table. The experimenter said, "We saw one of these [sweeping her hand across the strip] in this book [patting the book]. There's _____ [pointing to the target object]." The blank was filled by "the pilson we saw running" for the horse story, "the mave we saw kissing the bunny" for the bear story, "the wug Barney found" for the spoon story, and "the jegger Bert and Ernie were playing with" for the car story. The experimenter directed the child's attention to the test strip and tested his or her comprehension of both the novel name and the familiar name. For half the children the novel name was tested first, and for the other half it was tested second.

The test procedure will be illustrated with a trial in which the familiar name for the bear was tested first. The experimenter said, "Put your hand on a bear." If the child failed to respond to three repetitions of this request, the experimenter began the test of the other name. Children failed to respond on 5% of the familiar name and 9% of the novel name test trials. On trials in which the child did make a selection, the experimenter followed up with, "Is there another bear?" If the child selected another item, the question was repeated, but if the child said "No" or remained silent, the experimenter asked, "Are there any more bears?" and terminated the familiar name test after the child had an opportunity to respond. Children for whom the question was repeated were given an opportunity to respond to it, and then, regardless of their response, were asked, "Are there any more bears?" Comprehension of the novel name was then tested with the same question format (e.g., it started with the request, "Put your hand on a mave"). To avoid giving unintended cues to the child, the experimenter avoided looking at any particular picture in the test strip and primarily looked at the child during questioning.

Half the children received the trials in one order (horse, spoon, bear, car) and half received them in a different order (car, bear, spoon, horse). After the last trial, the four target objects were placed on the table one at a time for the novel name production test. Regarding the two animate targets, the child was asked, "We saw this animal in a book, what is it called?" For the inanimate targets, the child was asked, "We saw this in a book, what is it called?" This test was included to determine whether it is necessary for children to be able to produce the novel name in order for them to show the restriction effect.

Table 3.2.1 Mean number of trials in which test items were selected in Experiment 1.

Name	Test item × group			
	Target	Atypical	Typical	Nonmember
All participants:				
Familiar	1.25 (1.1)	1.84 (1.2)	3.38 (.8)	.41 (.8)
Novel	2.40 (1.0)	1.44 (1.1)	1.31 (1.2)	.88 (.9)
Learners:				
Familiar	.69 (.7)	1.75 (1.2)	3.68 (.6)	.38 (.8)
Novel	3.00 (.8)	.87 (1.0)	.93 (.9)	.75 (.8)
Nonlearners:				
Familiar	1.81 (1.2)	1.94 (1.3)	3.06 (.9)	.44 (.9)
Novel	1.81 (.8)	2.00 (.9)	1.69 (1.4)	1.00 (1.0)

Note: max = 4; standard deviations are in parentheses.

Results and discussion

Familiar name comprehension test

The average numbers of trials in which the four types of test objects were selected in the familiar and novel name comprehension tests are summarized in the top third of Table 3.2.1. A 2 (gender) × 2 (order of test: novel name first versus familiar name first) × 4 (test item: target versus other atypical versus typical versus nonexemplar) mixed analysis of variance of the number of familiar name trials in which various test items were selected yielded only a significant effect of test item, $F(3, 84) = 62.46$, $p < .001$. (All p values reported in the article are for two-tailed tests, unless otherwise noted.)

The restriction effect was obtained. Children selected the target object less often than the other atypical exemplar as a referent of the familiar name (1.25 versus 1.84 of four trails on average, respectively), matched sample $t(31) = 2.65$, $p < .02$. Thus, at least some young 2-year-olds have a Mutual Exclusivity bias.

An estimate of the number of children who showed the restriction effect was derived by examining the distribution of target object avoidance scores. This score was simply the difference between how often a child chose the other atypical object and how often he or she chose the target object. If the distribution of these scores is assumed to consist of two subgroups, those who showed the restriction effect and those who did not, the average score of the nonrestrictors should be zero. Assuming the distribution of scores for this subgroup is normal, the number who scored below zero should be approximately equal to the number who scored above zero. Because seven children had negative scores (six −1 and one −2), the best estimate is that there are seven children in the subgroup of nonrestrictors who had positive scores (six 1 and one 2); that is, the right side of the nonrestrictors' distribution is estimated to be a reflection of the left side. Thus, this subgroup consisted of these 14 children plus the eight who received zero scores, which leaves 10 restrictors (three with a score of 1, five with 2, and two with 3) (see Figure 3.2.3). Thirty-one percent

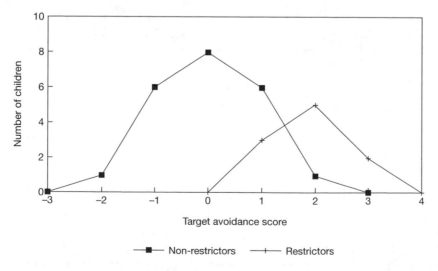

Figure 3.2.3 Distribution of target avoidance scores in Experiment 1.

of the sample is thus estimated to have a Mutual Exclusivity bias strong enough to produce a restriction effect in the current test.

The restriction effect was not limited to one or two items. When the data were collapsed over subject, rather than item, the restriction effect was significant, matched sample $t(3) = 4.97$, $p < .02$. It was, however, about twice as large for the inanimate categories (car and spoon) as for the animate ones (bear and horse). The respective numbers of participants selecting the target object and the other atypical exemplar in the test of the familiar name were 6 and 12 for *car*, 10 and 17 for *spoon*, 11 and 14 for *bear*, and 13 and 16 for *horse*. Sixteen children showed a preference for the nontarget atypical exemplar that was greater in the inanimate than in the animate sets, whereas only six showed the opposite pattern, sign test χ^2 $(1, N = 22) = 4.54$, $p < .05$. (Ten showed equal preference.)

This item difference may reflect children's greater willingness to permit overlap between names for animates than between names for inanimates. However, it may just be an artifact of the atypical exemplars in the animate categories having been less atypical than those in the inanimate categories. Merriman and Bowman's (1989) finding of a restriction effect for atypical but not typical exemplars of familiar names suggests that as typicality increases, the size of the effect may decrease. Analysis of selections in the test of the novel name (next section) as well as selections of a pronoun control group (Study 2) will bear on this issue.

As expected, the typical exemplar of the familiar name was selected ($M = 3.38$ trials) more often than either of the two atypical exemplars, both matched sample $ts(31) > 6.56$, $p < .001$. This finding validates the assumption that children were more certain of the acceptability of the familiar name for the typical exemplar than for the atypical ones.

The target object was selected more often than the nonexemplar of the target category (1.25 versus .41 trials), $t(31) = 4.30$, $p < .001$. For example, the bear with the long neck that had been referred to as a mave in the story was more likely than the duck to be selected as a referent of *bear*. Subsequent analyses will identify two mechanisms as responsible for this effect, namely, some children on some trials failing to accept or retain the information that the novel name is a label for the target object, and thus not restricting the familiar name from it, and some children on some trials simply accepting both names for the target object. Regarding the latter, the partial match of the target object to children's perceptual representations of the familiar name's acceptable exemplars works against their keeping the target out of the extension of the familiar name. Merriman and Bowman (1989) documented a similar limitation in the restriction effect shown by older children and adults.

Novel name comprehension test

Only children who accepted the novel name and remembered that it had been used to label the target object should be expected to inhibit their tendency to accept the familiar name for this object. Analysis of novel name comprehension supported this claim. First, a 2 (gender) $\times$ 2 (order of test) $\times$ 4 (test item) mixed analysis of variance of the number of novel name trials in which various test items were selected yielded significant effects of test item, $F(3, 84) = 16.82$, $p < .001$, and order, $F(1, 28) = 10.97$, $p < .005$. Children selected the target object (2.40 trials) more often than any of the other objects, including the other atypical exemplar (1.44), $t(31) = 3.85$, $p < .001$. Thus, at least some children accepted and retained the information about the novel name that was presented in the story.

Regarding the order effect, children who received the novel name test first selected more items on this test than those given the familiar name test first (1.86 versus 1.14 per trial). This effect did not interact with test item; the differences in frequency between the two orders were nearly identical for the target, atypical, and typical exemplar (.81, .88, and .81, respectively). Children's tendency to assign items to the novel name was inhibited when they had just committed some of the items to the familiar name, but the opposite was not the case (i.e., order did not affect performance on the familiar name test). This asymmetry may derive from our having reminded participants that the target object had been called by the novel name in the story immediately before the comprehension tests. Whether the familiar name was tested first or second, it was always preceded by a procedure that may have caused children to commit the novel name to some of the test items. In contrast, the test of the novel name was preceded only by a procedure that caused the children to commit the familiar name to some of the test items, or at least to remind themselves of which test items could take the familiar name, when the test of novel name came second.

Based on their selections in the test of the novel name, children were identified as either novel name learners or nonlearners. To be considered a learner, a child had to have selected the target object on at least half the trials and more often than any other test item. Sixteen children were classified as learners and 16 as nonlearners. The average frequencies with which the two groups chose the various items in the comprehension tests are summarized in the bottom two-thirds of Table 3.2.1. The nonlearners showed no signs of having accepted and retained the information that the novel name was a label for the target object; this group selected this object on only 1.81 of the novel name test trials, on average, and did not select it more often than the other atypical exemplar.

Only the learners showed the restriction effect. In the test of the familiar name, they selected the target object significantly less often than the other atypical exemplar (.69 versus 1.75), $t(15) = 4.00$, $p < .002$, whereas the nonlearners did not (1.81 versus 1.94), $t(15) < 1$. The learners selected the target object significantly less often than did the nonlearners, $t(30) = 3.12$, $p < .01$. Thus, one reason the restriction effect was not larger was that half the sample never learned, or learned and then forgot, what they had been told about the novel name.

The prospect of finding significant restriction or correction effects decreases as the proportion of participants who fail to retain novel name training increases. Although this proportion cannot be estimated from the retention test used by Merriman and Bowman (1989, Studies 2 and 3), the poor level of performance by their youngest participants on this test suggests that the proportion was very low. Thus, failure to retain training was likely the cause of the null effects reported in their studies.

In the previous section, it was estimated that 10 children showed the restriction effect. Given that 16 children were identified as learners, it is tempting to conclude that six learned the novel name, but did not restrict. However, because our criteria for identifying a child as a learner were rather lenient, there may have been some false positives. We are more confident that any particular child who failed to meet the criteria was a nonlearner than that anyone who met it was a learner. Thus, the number of children who learned the novel name, but did not restrict, cannot be estimated.

The effect of item on restriction

In the discussion of why a smaller restriction effect was found for animate than for inanimate objects, two hypotheses were entertained. First, the Mutual Exclusivity bias may be greater for inanimate than for animate object names. Children know that only animate objects can take proper names (Gelman & Taylor, 1984; Katz, Baker, & Macnamara, 1974), and if they were more likely to make such inter-pretations for the animates and tolerated overlap between a new proper name and a familiar common name, their overall frequency of restriction might be reduced. Children's performance on the novel name test was not consistent with this proposal. If a child made a proper name interpretation, he or she should have selected the story object as the sole exemplar of the novel name. The story object was actually selected as the sole exemplar of the novel name more often in the inanimate sets ($M = .72$ of the two trials) than in the animate ones ($M = .43$). Moreover, when children selected just the story object for the new name, they nearly always avoided selecting it in the test of the familiar name (93% of the animate cases and 87% of the inanimate cases). The novel name was rarely, if ever, inter-preted as a proper name for an animal that could also be given a familiar basic level name.

The second hypothesis, that the animate target objects just happened to be less atypical-looking than the inanimate ones, received support. The proposal implies that the children should have been more resistant to learning the novel name for the animate targets because they should have been less inclined to decide that the familiar name could not be applied to these objects. That is, for animate objects, rejection of the novel name should have been a relatively more appealing option for maintaining Mutual Exclusivity than restriction of the familiar name. In the test of the novel name, the animate target objects were selected less often than the inan-imate target objects ($Ms = 1.06$ and 1.33, respectively), $t(31) = 1.72$, one-tailed, $p < .05$. The nontargets (the typical, atypical, and nonmember) were selected no more often in the animate test sets ($M = .62$) than in the inanimate ones (.58).

Nine children met our criteria for being considered learners of the novel names for the animate objects (i.e., they selected the story object on at least half the test trials and more often than any other test item). Fifteen met these criteria for the [in]animate sets. The two groups showed comparable restriction effects. The animate set learners selected the story object and the other atypical on an average of 0.11 and 0.67 trials, respectively. The corresponding figures for the inanimate set learners were 0.33 and 0.93. Thus, when differences in novel name learning are taken into account, there is no difference between animate and inanimate sets in the size of the restriction effect.

Relations between the novel and familiar names

Children's selections on each test trial were classified according to the relation they imposed between the novel and familiar names. Six codes were used. The first two were consistent with the Mutual Exclusivity bias: refusal (no items were selected for at least one of the names) and restriction (nonempty, nonoverlapping sets were chosen for the names). The others were not consistent with it: coextension (identical sets were chosen), subset (all items chosen for the novel name were also chosen for the familiar name, but not vice versa), superset (all items chosen for the familiar name were also chosen for the novel name, but not vice versa), and overlap (at least one item chosen for one name was also chosen for the other, but unique items were selected for each name as well). Children's selections of the nonexemplar were excluded from this analysis because such selections were more likely due to failure to stay on task or to control an impulse to pick than to a true belief. We doubted whether a 2-year-old who chose a duck when asked for a bear, for example, really believed it was a bear.

All codes except overlap are just estimates from test performance of the relation that the child would maintain between the words with respect to all objects in the world. For example, although a trial in which nonoverlapping sets were selected was coded as restriction, it is possible that an object could be found that the child would accept as an exemplar of both names. The average frequencies of these codes for the learners and nonlearners are summarized in Table 3.2.2.

A 2 (subject: learner versus nonlearner) × 2 (order of test) analysis of variance of the frequency of selections that maintained mutual exclusivity (i.e., refusals plus restrictions) yielded a significant effect of subject, $F(1, 28) = 5.40$, $p < .03$. Learners maintained mutual exclusivity on 66% of the test trials, whereas nonlearners did so on only 44%.

The effect of test order just failed to exceed the conventional significance level, $F(1, 28) = 3.97$, $p = .056$. Children tested on the familiar name first refused to select an exemplar for the novel name more often (mean frequency = .81) than those tested on the novel name first (.25), $t(30) = 2.30$, $p < .05$. These tendencies were offset by the former group's less frequent interpretation of the novel name as superordinate to the familiar name (.06 versus .88, respectively). These findings fit with the significantly narrower generalization of the novel name shown by those

Table 3.2.2 Mean frequency of relations imposed between the familiar and novel names.

| Group and order | Exclusion | | Inclusion | | | |
	Refusal	Restriction	Coextension	Subset	Superset	Overlap
Learners:						
Familiar first	.88	2.25	.00	.50	.00	.38
Novel first	.25	1.88	.38	.62	.75	.12
Nonlearners:						
Familiar first	.75	1.25	.75	1.12	.12	.00
Novel first	.38	1.12	.25	.88	1.00	.38

Note: max = 4; $N = 8$ for each row in the table.

who were tested on the familiar name first, which was reported in the previous section. Children's representation of the familiar name inhibited their generalization of the novel name more when they had just selected exemplars of the familiar name. Their own selections may have served to remind them that they believed certain test items to be exemplars of the familiar name, or to further commit them to this belief, and so promoted their avoiding these items in the test of the novel name.

The relation between the rejection and restriction effects

The rejection effect, which is the tendency to resist or at least have difficulty learning labels for things that can already be labeled, can be explained in a variety of ways (e.g., Mutual Exclusivity, Gap Filling, Feeling of Novelty). Because the restriction effect is an unequivocal sign of the Mutual Exclusivity bias, if the two effects were found to be positively correlated, this would be evidence that the Mutual Exclusivity bias is at least a partial cause of the rejection effect.

It is not appropriate to calculate the correlation between the frequency with which children refused to select a referent for the novel names and the frequency with which they selected nonoverlapping sets for the pair of names tested because these measures are not independent. A child who selected nonoverlapping sets on every trial would necessarily have zero frequency of refusing to select a referent for the novel names, for example. Therefore, a rejection score was created by dividing the number of trials in which the child refused to select a referent for the novel name by the number of trials in which the child either refused or selected overlapping sets for the two names. Similarly, a restriction score was created by dividing the number of trials in which the child selected nonoverlapping sets by the number of trials in which the child selected at least one referent for the novel name (i.e., did not reject the name).

The two scores were strongly related, $r(30) = .57$, $p < .01$. Thus, the claim that children's refusal to select a referent for a novel name that they have heard used for an object they can already label is at least partially motivated by their expectation that the extensions of labels will be mutually exclusive.

Novel name production test

Only two children were able to produce any of the trained names when asked to name the target objects at the end of the experiment. Thus, it is not necessary that toddlers be able to produce a new name for it to cause them to restrict their receptive generalization of a familiar name.

[. . .]

General discussion

In Experiment 1, young 2-year-olds showed the restriction effect in a within-subjects design. When asked to select exemplars of a familiar name, they chose an object that had just been called by a novel name less often than one that had not.

For example, if they had just been read the story in which an atypical-looking bear was referred to as a *mave*, they chose this animal less often in the test of *bear* than a different type of atypical-looking bear. In Experiment 2, the novel names in the stories were replaced by pronouns and proper names, and the children chose the two atypical items equally often in the test of the familiar name. Thus, the restriction effect of Experiment 1 was not likely an artifact of greater exposure to the target object or of the experimenter's reference to this object immediately before the test of the familiar name. The between-subjects restriction effect was also obtained; the children mapped the familiar name onto the target object less often in the first than in the second experiment.

These effects are evidence that at least some young 2-year-olds have a Mutual Exclusivity bias. Based on the distribution of target avoidance scores in Experiment 1, it was estimated that 31% of the sample showed the within-subjects restriction effect. This figure is clearly a lower-bound estimate of the prevalence of the Mutual Exclusivity bias because some children who possessed the bias may have only expressed it by rejecting the novel name. Half of the sample failed to meet our rather lenient criteria for being considered novel name learners. Only those who met these criteria showed the restriction effect.

We had argued that the disambiguation and rejection effects that young 2-year-olds have shown in previous studies might just reflect the operation of principles that concern solely the interpretation of novel words. The finding of a clear manifestation of the Mutual Exclusivity bias, however, strengthens the case for attributing the two novel word effects to the bias. The strong positive correlation between the restriction and rejection effects in Experiment 1 also supports this view.

The results are consistent with a role for the Mutual Exclusivity bias in limiting toddlers' overextension errors. When told that a horselike animal was a *pilson*, for example, 24-month-olds became less likely to accept that it was a horse. It is reasonable to extend this finding to the real world case of toddlers who stop calling wolves "doggie," or refrain from ever doing so, because they hear them called "wolf" (see Merriman & Bowman, 1989, and Hoek, Ingram, & Gibson, 1986, for a list of other factors that might also work to curb errors of this sort).

According to Mervis (1987), children will not respond to hearing a novel name by revising their interpretation of a familiar name until they have come to accept adults' authority in matters of naming and categorization. In our experiments, at least some young 2-year-olds had enough respect for an adult's expertise to revise their beliefs about the meanings of familiar names in response to hearing her use the novel names in a story.

Mervis (1987) also speculated that toddlers might lack the metacognitive ability that the familiar word reinterpretation effects seem to require. Merriman and Bowman (1989) made a similar proposal. [. . .]

[. . .]

Does the mutual exclusivity bias grow stronger during early childhood?

Many studies, although not all, have found the disambiguation, correction, and restriction effects to be stronger in 4- and 5-year-olds than in 2- and 3-year-olds in situations in which little or no evidence regarding the actual relation between two words is given to the child (see Merriman, 1991, for a review). Even though the results of the current investigation indicate that at least some young 2-year-olds have the Mutual Exclusivity bias, it seems reasonable to hypothesize that more older children not only have it, but have a stronger version of it.

This hypothesis could be wrong, however. The trends in correction and restriction may be completely attributable to an increase with age in the general ability to learn new names and to a decrease with age in the rejection effect. As we have emphasized, the correction and restriction effects occur only if children accept and remember name training. Liittschwager and Markman (1994) found 24-month-olds to be less prone to the rejection effect than 16-month-olds. Although no other developmental studies of the rejection effect have been conducted, one would expect it to continue to weaken beyond the second year of life, based on Liittschwager and Markman's hypothesis that the effect occurs only when the resources required to reconcile the violation of Mutual Exclusivity in input and to meet other task demands exceed those available. Because processing efficiency increases with age (Case, 1992; Kail, 1991), older children are more likely than younger ones to have sufficient resources to circumvent the rejection effect.

Second, age-related increases in processing efficiency may also account for the developmental trends in the disambiguation effect. Merriman and Marazita (1995) observed that phonological priming of the unfamiliar word enhanced 2-year-olds' tendency to map it onto the unfamiliar kind, and argued that priming reduced the processing resources that the child needed to establish and maintain the unfamiliar word in working memory while trying to decide how to map it. Also, increasing the number of choice objects in the disambiguation test sets, which presumably increases processing load, has a strong negative impact on young 2-year-olds' tendency to map the novel name into an unfamiliar kind (Evey & Merriman, 1996; Hutchinson, 1986).

One argument in favor of the hypothesis does have some merit, however. Only older preschoolers may have an explicit Mutual Exclusivity principle; that is, they may explicitly reason that because something has one name it is unlikely to have another. This reasoning may itself bolster the unconscious Mutual Exclusivity bias that is an emergent property of the way they associate words with stimulus features. Merriman and Bowman (1989) observed 4-year-olds to be much more likely than 2½-year-olds to justify their choice of the unfamiliar object in the disambiguation paradigm in a manner consistent with the Mutual Exclusivity principle (e.g., when asked why they had selected a garlic press rather than a shoe as the referent of a novel name, to point to the shoe and say, "because this one's a shoe"). Moreover, within groups of 4-year-olds, those who tend to acknowledge their unfamiliarity with a novel name show a stronger disambiguation effect (Marazita & Merriman, 1994; Merriman & Bowman, 1989; Merriman et al., 1993b; Merriman & Schuster, 1991) and a greater tendency to justify their choices in the disambiguation paradigm in terms consistent with the Mutual Exclusivity principle (Marazita & Merriman, 1994; Merriman & Bowman, 1989). When children develop to the point where they tend to encode objects and words spontaneously in terms of whether they know them or not, their tendency to assume Mutual Exclusivity in default situations may become stronger.

Conclusion

The restriction effect shown by the young 2-year-olds is evidence that a fair number of them have a Mutual Exclusivity bias. This conclusion has implications for accounts of why the bias develops and why overextensions decline, as well as for estimates of the age at which the bias has sufficient power to both force a reinterpretation of a familiar word and influence an initial interpretation of a novel word. At least some young 2-year-olds have enough respect for adult authority to both accept a second label for something and revise the meaning of the label they would have used. Such acts of lexical coordination may not reflect the deliberate application of a Mutual Exclusivity rule, however; they may just be unconscious consequences of the competitive nature of category retrieval.

Acknowledgments

This work was supported by an NIH FIRST Award (R29 HD 25958) to the first author. We are grateful to the children and parents of the Akron area for their participation. We thank Julie Evey, Audra Fleisner, and Amy Simeral for their assistance. "In all your ways acknowledge Him . . ." (Prov. 3:6).

Melissa Bowerman

FROM UNIVERSAL TO LANGUAGE-SPECIFIC IN EARLY GRAMMATICAL DEVELOPMENT

Summary

ATTEMPTS TO EXPLAIN CHILDREN'S grammatical development often assume a close initial match between units of meaning and units of form; for example, agents are said to map to sentence-subjects and actions to verbs. The meanings themselves, according to this view, are not influenced by language, but reflect children's universal non-linguistic way of understanding the world. This paper argues that, contrary to this position, meaning as it is expressed in children's early sentences is, from the beginning, organized on the basis of experience with the grammar and lexicon of a particular language. As a case in point, children learning English and Korean are shown to express meanings having to do with directed motion according to language-specific principles of semantic and grammatical structuring from the earliest stages of word combination.

1. Introduction

The acquisition of a first language is a feat of astonishing complexity and speed. Within the first two years of life, children have acquired many words and are putting them together to form simple sentences, and by four years they have mastered most of the syntactic machinery of their language. What makes this achievement possible?

Factors that contribute to language acquisition come from both inside and outside the child. Learners seem to approach language with some sense of what to

1994, reprinted with permission from *Philosophical Transactions B, Royal Society, London*, 346: 37–45.

look for and how to structure what they find. But their unlearned dispositions for linguistic organization obviously do not provide all the structure, since children in different communities end up speaking different languages. In studying language acquisition, it is essential to disentangle the effects of internal and external structuring influences and to determine how they interact. An indispensable tool in this enterprise is the comparison of children learning different languages.

The modern era of cross-linguistic research on language acquisition began about 25 years ago. An important outcome of the first wave of studies, in the early 1970s, was the discovery that all around the world, children's first sentences revolve around a restricted set of meanings to do with agency, action, location, possession, and the existence, recurrence, non-existence, and disappearance of objects. As Dan Slobin (1973b) put it, 'If you ignore word order, and read through transcriptions of two-word utterances in the various languages we have studied, the utterances read like direct translations of one another. There is a great similarity of basic vocabulary and basic meanings conveyed by the word combinations' (p. 177).

These early meanings were strikingly reminiscent of the notions of causality, space, and the enduring object that Piaget (1954) had argued are constructed by children independently of language during the sensorimotor period of development (Brown 1973). This correspondence suggested an intriguing idea: that children's initial step in grammar construction is to discover patterns for positioning words that instantiate relational concepts learned independently of language; e.g. for English, mention the agent before specifying the action he performs (Bowerman 1973; Braine 1976; Brown 1973; Schlesinger 1971).

The idea that the forms of language map fairly directly onto children's pre-linguistic concepts took hold and spread during the 1970s and 1980s. Children were seen as linking not only word-order patterns but also words, inflections, and other grammatical forms to cognitively based categories of meaning and pragmatic function. In a hypothesis that strongly influenced subsequent cross-linguistic research, Slobin (1973a) argued that the non-linguistic notions underlying language emerge in children in the same order and at about the same rate everywhere, regardless of language. Since the linguistic devices languages use to encode these notions vary, children's strategies for language acquisition can be explored, proposed Slobin, by holding meaning constant and comparing the difficulty with which the different devices are learned. In a related proposal, Slobin (1985) argued that children start out with a shared, prestructured 'semantic space' in which meanings and clusters of meanings constitute 'primordial building blocks' onto which functors and grammatical constructions are first mapped. The result of this initial mapping process is a 'universally specifiable "Basic Child Grammar"' (see also Berman 1986).

Of course, not everyone has agreed that children's early grammars should be characterized in terms of a direct mapping between non-linguistic meanings and linguistic forms. Many theorists argue that children are guided from the outset by innate knowledge of (among other things) syntactic categories and relations such as noun, verb, sentence-subject, and predicate. But these investigators too have typically invoked a basic repertoire of privileged non-linguistic meanings to account for language acquisition. Pinker (1984), for example, notes that having innate knowledge of, say, the category 'verb' cannot help learners if they have no way to identify verbs in the speech around them. But if inborn syntactic constructs are initially associated with specific meanings, learners could bootstrap their way into grammar: they could infer, for example, that words naming actions are verbs, words naming concrete objects are nouns, and words naming the agents of actions are subjects. Once children have used this technique (termed 'semantic bootstrapping') to identify instances of formal constructs and register their properties (e.g. nouns may be preceded by *the*), they do not need it any more, and the tight correlation seen in their early grammars between units of meaning and units of form will begin to fade.

But are children's early grammars really semantically so uniform as these views of language acquisition presuppose? In the recent literature there is a new stirring of interest in how children approach language-specific aspects of the grammatical structuring of meaning, and some indications that children learning different languages are in fact less similar than has been thought. In this paper I explore the question of universal vs. language specific in the domain of space, asking how children acquiring very different languages, English and Korean, initially express directed motion.

At first glance, spatial language seems a surprising place to look for evidence of language specificity in children's early grammars, since space has long been cited as a paradigm example of a domain in which language is mapped rather directly onto pre-existing knowledge structures. There is indeed good evidence that non-linguistic spatial cognition is important in the acquisition of spatial morphemes (for reviews, see Bowerman 1996; Johnston 1985). But, as we will see, children turn out to be sensitive to language-specific principles of lexical and grammatical structuring in this domain even before the age of two.

2. Cross-linguistic differences in the expression of motion

An insightful account of cross-linguistic differences in the expression of motion is provided by Talmy (1985). Talmy defines a motion event as 'a situation containing movement of an entity' or – in the limiting case – 'maintenance of an entity at a stationary location' (p. 60). By movement is meant a directed motion that results in a change of location; e.g. going into or out of something, going up or down. Talmy analyses motion events into four basic components: *Motion* (the fact of motion), *Figure* (the moving entity), *Ground* (the reference point object with respect to which the Figure moves), and *Path* (the course followed by the Figure with respect to the Ground). A motion event can also have a *Manner* or a *Cause*, which are analysed as distinct external events.

There are typological differences among languages in how these meanings are characteristically expressed. In English, as in most Indo-European languages, Chinese, and Finnish, the Motion component is typically 'conflated' (combined) with either Manner or Cause (henceforth simply 'Manner') and expressed in the main verb. Path is expressed separately by a 'satellite' to the verb (spatial particle, affix, or preposition). English examples include:

> *The bottle floated INTO/OUT of the cave;*
> *The bottle floated BACK to the bank;*

The balloon floated UP/DOWN the chimney;
John walked/skipped/ran INTO the room.

(The element expressing Path is shown in upper case.) Talmy terms languages of this type 'satellite-framed'.

Analogous sentences are not possible in Romance, Semitic, and Turkish. In languages of this second type, most Path information is conflated with fact of Motion and expressed with the main verb. Manner can be expressed in the clause as well, if desired, but this is done separately, e.g. with an adverbial phrase. Thus, the Spanish equivalents of the English intransitive sentences we just saw are:

La botella ENTRÓ a/SALIÓ de la cueva (flotando)
'The bottle MOVED.IN to/MOVED.OUT from the cave (floating)';

La botella VOLVIÓ a la orilla (flotando)
'The bottle MOVED.BACK to the bank (floating)';

El globo SUBIÓ/BAJÓ por la chimenea (flotando)
'The balloon MOVED.UP/MOVED.DOWN via the chimney (floating)';

Juan ENTRÓ al cuarto (caminando/brincando/corriendo)
'John MOVED.IN to the room (walking/skipping/running)'.

Transitive sentences in English and Spanish show the same typological differences. Compare:

I rolled the keg INTO the storeroom with *METÍ el barril a la bodega (rodandolo)*
'I.MOVED.IN the barrel to the storeroom (rolling it)',

and:

I pulled the cork OUT of the bottle with *SAQUÉ el corcho de la botella (jalandolo)*
'I.MOVED.OUT the cork from the bottle (pulling it)'.

Talmy terms languages of this type 'verb-framed'.[1]

A third basic pattern for expressing motion is represented by Atsugewi, other Hokan languages, and Navajo. Atsugewi lacks verb roots with meanings like 'put', 'give', 'throw', and 'kick' (i.e. English-style conflations of Motion with Manner) or like 'enter', 'ascend', and 'extract' (i.e. Spanish-style conflations of Motion with Path). Instead, it expresses motion events with roots that refer to the movement or location of various kinds of Figures, e.g.:

-lup-   'for a small shiny spherical object (e.g. a candy, a hailstone) to move/be located';

-swal-   'for a limp linear object suspended by one end (e.g. a shirt on clothesline, a hanging dead rabbit) to move/be located';

-qput-   'for loose dirt to move/be located'.

As in English, Path is expressed by a satellite (so Atsugewi is also 'satellite-framed'), but the satellite in this case is not a particle but a verb suffix that combines information about Path with information about the Ground object; e.g.:

-ic't	'into liquid';
-ak	'onto the ground';
-ay	'into someone's grasp';
-wam	'down into a gravitic container (e.g. a pocket, cupped hand, lake basin)'.

Manner is expressed by an instrumental verb prefix such as:

ru-	'by pulling on (it)';
ci-	'by acting on (it) with one's hands';
ca-	'from the wind blowing on (it)';
uh-	'by acting on (it) with a swinging linear object' (such as pounding, batting, or throwing) (Talmy 1982, 1985).

Talmy's analyses show that although languages share a basic inventory of components relevant to motion events – Figure, Ground, Motion, Path, and Manner – they package them differently for linguistic expression. First, there are differences in the semantic categories associated with the components. Second, there is a complex trade-off between lexical and syntactic structure; e.g. if Path is specified in the main verb, Manner will have to [be] specified, if at all, in some other constituent; conversely, if Manner is in the main verb, Path must go elsewhere. Finally, the grammatical differences have consequences for discourse structure (Talmy 1985). For example, information about Manner is backgrounded in satellite-framed languages: in English, it comes 'for free' with the main verb. But in verb-framed languages it is foregrounded, and so it is included much less frequently (Berman & Slobin 1994).

Differences in the linguistic packaging of events raise problems for approaches to language acquisition that assume that children crack into grammar with a uniform inventory of conceptual building blocks. For instance, what portion of a motion event will learners isolate as the 'action'? For a direct mapping to succeed, the child learning English must home in on the manner of the motion, e.g. 'walking' or 'throwing'. The child learning Spanish must pick out motion along a particular Path, e.g. 'entering' or 'ascending'. And the child learning an Atsugewi-style language (Atsugewi itself is alas now defunct) must extract the motion of an object of a particular kind. Further, English learners should construe both 'throwing' and 'giving' as ways of acting on an object, thereby causing it to move, whereas Atsugewi learners must treat them grammatically as different types of meanings: 'throwing' is, as in English, a way of making something move (expressed with an instrumental prefix, although not distinguished from other precursor causal swinging motions made by a linear object), but 'giving' is a Path meaning (expressed with the Path suffix meaning 'into one's grasp').

Knowing how a scene should be conceptually broken up and its elements assigned to different parts of a sentence is, then, a critical part of a fluent speaker's grasp of sentence construction. But, as these examples illustrate, this knowledge cannot flow directly from children's general cognitive understanding of events. To the extent that languages differ, the appropriate segmentation and packaging of events is an aspect of linguistic knowledge that must be learned (see also Gentner 1982). When does this learning begin?

3. Learning to express motion events in English and Korean

To explore this question, Soonja Choi and I have been studying lexical and syntactic development in learners of languages that differ typologically in their expression of motion: English (satellite-framed) and Korean (verb-framed) (Bowerman 1989; Choi & Bowerman 1991). In the present paper, I will compare the way the two sets of children express motion events in the early stages of word combining. The data come from spontaneous speech samples collected longitudinally from two English-speaking children and eight Korean-speaking children between the ages of about one and three years.[2]

On first inspection, the English and Korean learners look remarkably similar (see Choi & Bowerman 1991). They began to talk about motion events at the same time, between 1;2 (one year;two months) and 1;4, and they talked about similar kinds of events; e.g. their own movements, dressing and undressing, and putting objects in, on, or together with other objects and taking them out, off, or apart. These similarities probably reflect correspondences both in the children's level of cognitive development and in their daily activities. Early word combinations expressing motion events also look similar in the two languages, reminding us of Slobin's remark that early two-word utterances 'read like direct translations of one another'. For example:

ENGLISH	1;7	Hat on.	(Wants mother to put her hat on.)
KOREAN	1;8	Moca ss-e.	(Putting on doll's hat.)
		hat put.on-	DECLARATIVE SUFFIX
ENGLISH	1;9	Go in.	(Trying to put peas in cup.)
KOREAN	1;9	An tule ka.	(Struggling to put box in mother's purse.)
		not enter go	

On closer inspection, however, we find not only similarities but also systematic differences.

(a) English-speaking children

Being a fluent speaker of English requires being able to analyse motion events into a Manner portion, which is assigned to the verb, and a Path portion, which is assigned to a spatial particle or prepositional phrase. Learners of English begin to get the hang of this combinatorial system by two years of age or before.

In the speech of our subjects, C and E, motion events were first expressed by Path particles of adult English: *up*, *down*, *in*, *out*, *on*, *off*, *away*, and *back*. These forms appear so early in the speech of English-speaking children, and are so quickly generalized to a wide range of appropriate motion events, that many investigators (e.g. McCune-Nicolich 1981) have proposed that their meanings correspond directly to non-linguistic spatial concepts constructed by all children during the sensorimotor period. For example, a child who says *down* as she climbs down from a lap, sits down, lies down, requests to be put down, drops a toy, or directs mother to put a coffee cup on the table seems to have a notion of 'vertical movement downward', and a child who says *in* as she climbs into the tub, stuffs her hand into her cup, and tries to pour salt back into a salt container seems to have a notion of 'containment'. These meanings might indeed be purely non-linguistic. But in cross-linguistic perspective it is sobering to realize that they are perfectly tuned to the requirements of what is, after all, a language-specific system of expressing Path.

Beyond the one-word stage, Path particles figure prominently in English-speaking children's early word combinations. At first they are combined mostly with nouns naming the Figure, e.g.:

> *Christy down* as the child goes down a flight of stairs;
>
> *socky up* as she picks a sock up off the couch;
>
> *cracker off* as she moves a cracker wrapper off her placemat.

But they also appear increasingly with verbs in the two-part constructions typical of English-style satellite-framed languages, e.g.:

> *step up* as the child steps on a stool;
>
> *pant pull up* as mother pulls up her pants;
>
> *put down* asking mother to put a train on the floor;
>
> *push down* asking mother to push a jack-in-the-box down in its box;
>
> *close in* trying to close the lid on the jack-in-the-box;
>
> *fall off* as a doll balanced on a tiny staircase falls off.

By 24 months our subject E had produced the following combinations, among many others:

get	+ up/down/on/off/away/out/out my suitcase
fall	+ down/off/out/out my coffee cup
run	+ down
step	+ on my bus
pull	+ up/down/out/out my night-night (=bedding)
push	+ down/in/off
pour	+ down there/in/out/on me
drop	+ down there
carry	+ up/out

put   + down/in/on/on your face/back

take   + on/off/outside/upstairs

(See Table 5, Choi & Bowerman 1991, for a complete listing for both children.)[3]

Perhaps this early look of an adult English-style, two-part (Manner + Path) analysis of motion events is an illusion. In adult references to motion events, the verb and the Path marker each make a distinct contribution to the meaning of the whole. But English-speaking children might at first simply memorize each combination as if it were a single verb, comparable to a Path verb in a language like Spanish.

The data argue against this. While some combinations may start out as unanalysed units (e.g. Tomasello 1992, reports that *fall* at first always co-occurred with *down* in his daughter's speech), there is ample evidence that within a short time English-speaking children begin to understand the combinatorial principles according to which the system works. For example:

1.   Children flexibly use the *same* verbs both in isolation and with *different* particles. The verb conveys a constant Manner in which something moves, while the Path varies. This set from E's speech is typical:

      1;7   POUR. (Request to pour pancake batter onto griddle.)

      1;7   POUR. (Trying to pour her juice into father's glass.)

      1;8   POUR *in*. (Watching mother get soap ready to pour into washing machine.)

      1;9   POUR *down* there. (Pointing to place in tub where she wants mother to pour bubble bath.)

      2;0   Deedee POUR water *on* me. (After sister squirts her with water from a bulb baster.)

2.   Conversely, children use the *same* particles with *different* verbs. In this case, Path is held constant while Manner varies, or while different aspects of the same action are highlighted. Examples again from E:

      1;10   *Dip* IN milk. (Dipping noodle into her milk glass.)

      1;10   Lemme *put* IN. (Wants to put toilet paper in toilet.)

      1;9   (E stringing beads. As she pushes thread through holes, she murmurs:)
         'Nother one *get* IN.
         'Nother one *push* IN.
         'Nother one *fit* IN.

3.   For transitive constructions, children show recognition of the independent status of the verb and the particle by beginning to separate them with a noun phrase specifying the direct object (see also Tomasello 1992). These examples are from C's and E's speech between 1;9 and 1;11:

> Want get nipple out,
> take Deedee outside,
> take bottle out,
> brush dirt off,
> take belt off,
> put books away,
> Mommy drop glue down there,
> put socks on me,
> I get my belt on,
> push me off,
> pull my pants up,
> you pull my bear out my night-night (=bedding),
> take your coke upstairs,
> carry me up,
> I put juice in that sink,
> I get sweater on,
> take those out,
> I got papers on those floor.

4. Perhaps most persuasively, children's grasp of the English two-part system for expressing motion is shown by their errors: combinations that, although cut to the English pattern, happen not to be the conventional way of expressing the desired meaning:

> 1;9 *Carry up*. (After mother sets a tipped-over stool upright. Child then goes on to use 'carry up' for many situations in which adults would say 'pick up.')
>
> 2;0 *Catch* me *in*. (Wants mother to chase her and scoop her up in a cardboard carton.)
>
> 2;0 *Blow* it *out*. (Wants mother to deflate a beachball.)
>
> 2;1 Daddy, *pick* me *down*. (Frequent as request to be lifted down from a high place.)
>
> 2;2 *Pick* me *out*. (Wants mother to take her out of her stroller.)

In summary, children learning English acquire a feel for the English-style, Manner + Path packaging of motion events in the early stages of word combining. What about children learning Korean?

(b) *Korean-speaking children*

Korean expresses most Path information with verbs, so it may be considered a verb-framed language, although it deviates from more typical languages of this typological pattern, such as Spanish (Choi & Bowerman 1991). In intransitive clauses expressing spontaneous motion, Korean uses a serial verb construction that usually has as its final (right-most) element a deictic verb like *kata* 'go' or *ota* 'come'. This verb is immediately preceded by a Path verb such as *tule* 'enter', *na* 'exit', *olla* 'ascend', *naylye* 'descend', or *kalocille* 'cross', and this verb may in turn optionally be preceded by a Manner verb. The Ground nominal, if present, is suffixed with a case ending, *-ey* 'at/to' (=LOC), *-lo* 'toward', or *-eyse* 'from'. An example:

> John-i pang-ey (ttwuie) *tule* o-ass-ta.
> J.-SUBJ room-LOC (run) *enter* come-PAST-DECLARATIVE
> 'John came (running) into the room.'

As in other verb-framed languages, information about Manner is foregrounded, so it is included together with a Path verb only if the speaker wants to emphasize the manner in which the motion took place.

In transitive clauses expressing caused motion, no deictic verb follows the Path verb. As in intransitive clauses, a verb specifying manner may optionally precede it. For example:

> John-i kong-ul (kwullye/mile) sangca-ey *neh*-ess-ta.
> J.-SUBJ ball-OBJ (roll/push) box-LOC *put.in*-PAST-DECLARATIVE
> 'John put/(rolled/pushed) the ball into the box.'

Of the transitive Path verbs in Korean, few express 'familiar' Paths corresponding to the meanings of the intransitive Path verbs or to English prepositions and particles: perhaps only *ollita* 'cause to ascend' and *naylita* 'cause to descend'. Most have meanings that seem rather exotic to speakers of English, since they combine information about Path with information about the Ground, Figure, or both; for example:

> 'put clothing onto trunk/head/feet';

> 'pick up and carry on head/on back/on shoulder/in hand/in mouth';

> 'fit or mesh one three-dimensional object with another'.

They also often cross-cut the Path categories associated with English Path markers; e.g, the verb *kkita*, which can be used for:

> 'put these earplugs IN your ears',

cannot be used for:

> 'put these apples IN a bowl'

because it picks out a relationship of tight fit. Unlike *in*, the verb can also be applied to:

> 'put the cap ON the pen'

and:

> 'put these Lego pieces TOGETHER' (see Choi & Bowerman 1991).

Table 3.3.1 Path verbs (shown in citation form, often marked by *-TA*) used by Korean children by age 2;0. (See Choi & Bowerman (1991) for more complete data and a breakdown by age.)

ASCEND/DESCEND:

olla kata/ota	'ascend go/come' (go/come up)
naylye kata/ota	'descend go/come' (go/come down)
ollita/naylita	'cause.ascend/cause.descend'

ENTER/EXIT:

tule kata/ota	'enter go/come' (go/come in)
na kata/ota	'exit go/come' (go/come out)

PUT IN/ON/TOGETHER/AROUND;
TAKE OUT/OFF/APART:

kkita/ppayta	'fit/unfit' (e.g. Lego pieces together/apart, top on/off pen, cassette into/out of case)
nehta/kkenayta	'put in [loose container], put around/take out of [loose container], take from around' (e.g. blocks into/out of box, ring onto/off pole)
pwuthita	'join flat surfaces' (e.g. sticker or magnet on refrigerator, two tables or pieces of paper together)
nohta	'put onto a surface' (e.g. cup on table)
kkacta	'peel/take off covering' (e.g. skin from apple)
kkocta	'put elongated object to base' (e.g. flower in vase, hairpin in hair, book upright on shelf)

DON AND DOFF CLOTHING:

ipta	'put clothing on trunk' (e.g. dress, shirt, pants)
sinta	'put clothing on feet' (e.g. shoes, socks)
ssuta	'put clothing on head' (e.g. hat, glasses, raise umbrella)
pesta	'take clothing off'

PICK UP/CARRY ON OR IN BODY PART:

anta	'pick up/carry in arms'
epta	'pick up/carry on back'
tulta	'pick up/carry in hand'

Like English learners, Korean learners first encode motion events with Path expressions. A list of Path verbs used by many children by the age of two is shown in Table 3.3.1.

As noted earlier, word combinations expressing motion events can look very similar in Korean and English. But when we compare an entire range of utterances produced by the two sets of children, the structural influence of the input language is obvious. For example:

1. English-speaking children use Path markers from their earliest word combinations (and even before) for both spontaneous and caused motion events, e.g.:

   C 1;9   Christy *IN*. (As child is about to climb into bath tub.)

   C 1;8   Letters *IN*. (Putting magnetic letters into a small box.)

> C 1;8   Daddy *OUT*. (Waiting for father to get out of car.)
>
> C 1;7   Balls *OUT*. (Trying to push round pieces out of a puzzle.)

This is, of course, appropriate: the Path particles of English are indifferent to whether a motion is spontaneous or caused.

Korean children, however, are acutely sensitive to this distinction, and consistently use different Path expressions for spontaneous and caused motion, e.g.:

IN: *tule* 'move in, enter' vs. *nehta* 'put loosely in or around':

TJ 2;0   (Wants father to go into shower):
>   Appa *TULE* ka.
>   Daddy *enter* go
>   'Daddy go *in*.'

WJ 2;0   (Wants to put sugar in coffee):
>   Emma, Wonjongi-ika *NEH*-ullay.
>   mother, [child's name]-SUBJ *put.in*-FUTURE
>   'Mother, Wonjongi will put [it] *in*.'

OUT: *na* 'move out, exit' vs. *kkenayta* 'take from loosely in or around':

WJ 2;0   (Remembering owl on Muppet Show):
>   Pwuengi-ka *NA* o-ass-e.
>   owl-SUBJ *exit* come-PAST-DECLARATIVE
>   'Owl came *out*.'

WJ 1;10   (Asking investigator to take things out of her bag):
>   *KKENAY* cwe.
>   *take.out* give
>   'Take *out* for me.'

This is also language-appropriate: the Path markers of Korean are verbs, and, like other Korean verbs, they are strictly distinguished according to transitivity.

2. Many of our English learners' two- and three-word combinations involved both a Path marker and a Manner verb, and before age two the children showed a good understanding of the combinatorial principle that relates them (cf. the discussion of examples given earlier). Our Korean subjects, in contrast, did not combine Path verbs with Manner verbs until many months beyond the stage of early word combinations, and even then did so only rarely. In adult Korean, combinations like 'run enter go' (=go running in) and 'throw put.in' (=throw in) are possible, and our subjects could in principle have produced them since they knew a number of Manner verbs in addition to Path verbs. But, as noted, when Manner information is included along with a Path verb in a Korean sentence, this information is – unlike in a comparable English sentence – foregrounded. This difference in the discourse value and frequency of specifying Manner in conjunction with Path in the two adult languages leads to systematic differences in the composition of learners' early word combinations.

3. The Path expressions of learners of English and Korean pick out different categories of Path meaning. The particles and prepositions of adult English identify highly schematic Paths, i.e. Paths that are abstractly 'the same' across events involving a wide range of Figures and Grounds. But the transitive Path verbs of adult Korean, as noted earlier, distinguish between Paths involving different kinds of Figures and Grounds. English learners appear to associate English particles with broad Path meanings from very early, as judged from their extensions to novel situations. *On* and *off*, for example, are used in connection with all clothing and jewelry items, as well as for many other relationships of contact with or attachment to an external surface in any orientation, e.g.:

E 1;8   *ON* hair. (Wants mother to put her sweat-shirt hood up.)

C 1;9   Want bead *ON*. (Trying to make string of beads stay around her neck.)

E 1;8   *ON* tummy. (Wants a piece of paper stuck on her stomach.)

C 1;11   Can't wow-wow *ON*. (Frustrated when can't put toy dog on moving phonograph record.)

C 1;9   Tail *ON*. (Holding broken tip of toy dog's tail up to dog.)

E 1;6   Baby. *ON* barrette. (Wants mother to put a barrette on her hair.)

C 1;9   Want tie *ON*. (Trying to attach tie to tie holder.)

Korean learners, in contrast, use their Path verbs for different and often more restricted categories of events. For example, our subjects distinguished putting clothing ON the trunk, ON the feet, and ON the head (see Table 3.3.1), and, in contexts similar to those of the seven sentences just given, they used several different Path verbs, e.g.:

Juxtaposing flat surfaces: *PWUTHITA* (cf. third sentence above)
　　　TJ 2;1 Ike *PWUTH*-ye.
　　　this *put.on*-cause
　　　'Put this on.' (Sticking a flat vinyl man on a vinyl road attached to the wall.)

Putting things on a horizontal surface (cf. fourth point above): *NOTHA*
　　　TJ 1;11 Yeki-ta *NOH*-a.
　　　here-LOC *put.on*-IMPERATIVE
　　　'Put (down) on here.' (Asking investigator to put a toy saucer down on the floor.)

Putting a long object into or onto a firm base (cf. sixth sentence above): *KKOCTA*
　　　JS 1;9 Ppin *KKOC-A*.
　　　hairpin *put.on*-IMPERATIVE
　　　'Put on hairpin.' (Wants mother to put a hairpin in her hair.)

The particular Path meanings that English and Korean children express in their early sentences are, then, language specific. The difference in Path schematicity between adult English and Korean is no doubt related to the part of speech in which the two languages characteristically express Path (cf. Talmy 1981): the Path markers of English are members of a closed class of grammatical functors, i.e. particles and prepositions, whereas those of Korean are members of an open class, verbs. The semantic consequences of this syntactic difference are picked up early.

To summarize, although children learning English and Korean combine words into short sentences to express similar kinds of motion events, they do not do so in the same way. English-speaking children associate Path markers with highly schematic Path meanings, and they combine them flexibly with verbs expressing the Manner in which a motion along a Path takes place. Korean children, in contrast, associate Path markers with meanings that are more specific to the movement of particular kinds of Figures with respect to particular kinds of Grounds, and they do not combine them with verbs specifying Manner.

4. Beyond early word combinations in the expression of motion

Choi and I have not compared how learners of English and Korean express motion beyond the stage of early word combinations. But recent work by Berman and Slobin (1994) and their colleagues points to intriguing differences in the development of narrative style by children learning satellite-framed vs. verb-framed languages. Berman and Slobin compared how children aged three, four, five, and nine, and adults, tell the same picture-book story – about a boy looking for his frog – in each of five languages: English and German (both satellite-framed) and Spanish, Hebrew, and Turkish (all verb-framed). Their findings are consistent with the differences Choi and I have observed, and elaborate on them to show early language specificity in the treatment not only of motion but also of temporality, perspective, and connectivity.

Although the children studied by Berman and Slobin grew increasingly skilled over time at the narrative style typical of adult speakers of their language, certain distinguishing characteristics were already present by age three. For example, at all ages, speakers of the satellite-framed languages rarely used a bare verb to describe the Paths followed by the protagonists of the story. Rather, they used a rich array of Manner verbs coupled with Path phrases, such as:

jump down,

jump out the window,

fly out of here,

climb up in the tree,

swim over to the log,

fall off the tree,

throw in the water.

Speakers of the verb-framed languages, in contrast, often used bare verbs, they rarely mentioned Manner in connection with a statement of Path at any age, and they gave much less information overall about Path, often preferring to specify where the protagonist was before and after a change of location, and leaving details of the Path to be inferred. Berman and Slobin were struck by how children as young as three already channel their attention in the way favored by their native language:

> We began the study with an expectation that there was a basic set of semantic notions that all children would try to express by some means or other, whether or not grammatically marked in their language . . . [But] we were repeatedly surprised to discover how closely learners stick to the set of distinctions that they have been given by their language . . . We are left, then, with a new respect for the powerful role of each individual language in shaping its own world of expression, while at the same time representing but one variant of a familiar and universally human pattern.
>
> (1994, p. 641)

This conclusion takes on added weight when we realize that the language-specific properties that so impressed Berman and Slobin in the narratives of three-year-olds can already be observed in the speech of children learning English and Korean more than a year earlier!

5. Conclusions

According to the view of grammatical development reviewed at the beginning of this paper, all children construct their early sentences from the same conceptual building blocks. At a relatively coarse level of analysis, this description is not inaccurate: children learning different languages do talk about similar topics, and their early lexical items and word combinations often look remarkably alike. But when we turn up the power of the microscope, what at first looked like 'the same' building blocks turn out to be shaped in accordance with language-specific principles of lexical and syntactic structuring. In this study we saw that, already by the period of early word combining, children express motion events in the way that is characteristic of the input language. Early language specificity has also recently been documented in the semantic partitioning of modality (Choi 1991; Stephany 1986), tense and aspect (Berman & Slobin 1994; Weist 1986), and agency (Bowerman 1985, 1989).

There is, then, no initial stage in which children's grammars rely exclusively on meanings provided by non-linguistic cognition. From the very beginning, form and meaning are analysed together, and learners are sensitive not only to the formal linguistic devices their language uses to encode meanings, but also to the way the meanings themselves are structured for linguistic expression. We as yet know little about how this subtle, linguistically driven kind of semantic learning takes place (but see Gleitman, this issue [of *Philosophical Transactions B, Royal Society, London,* 346 (1994)], for some ideas). The first step toward coming to understand the process is simply to recognize that it does take place, and this awareness is only recently beginning to dawn.

I thank Soonja Choi, Jurgen Weissenborn, and members of the Max Planck Institute Argument Structure Group for their comments on an earlier version of this paper.

Notes

1   The distinction between satellite-framing and verb-framing captures the most characteristic patterns of a language, but it is not absolute. For example, although Spanish is verb-framed, it allows the English-style pattern in certain contexts (see Aske 1989). And although English is satellite-framed, it does have some Path verbs, e.g. *enter*, *exit*, *ascend*, *descend*, *rise*. Most of these are borrowed from Romance, where they represent the basic pattern; in English they belong to a more formal register than their native counterparts like *go in/out/up/down*. Talmy (1991) argues that satellite-framing and verb-framing are consistent and pervasive patterns that apply not only to the expression of motion events but also to the way languages characteristically express temporal aspect (as in *they talked ON*), state change (*The candle blew OUT*); 'action correlating' (*She sang ALONG*), and 'event realization' (*The police hunted the fugitive DOWN*).

2   The English data come from detailed diary records of my two daughters from the start of the one-word stage, supplemented by an extensive literature on the acquisition of Path words like *in*, *out*, *up*, and *down* by English-speaking children. There were two sets of Korean children:

   (1)   four children videotaped by Choi every 3–4 weeks from 14 to 24–28 months, and
   (2)   four other children taped by Choi, Pat Clancy, and Youngjoo Kim every 2–4 weeks from 19–20 months to 25–34 months.

   Choi and I are grateful to Clancy and Kim for generously sharing their data.

3   Path particles and prepositional phrases were combined even more extensively with the deictic verbs *come* and *go*. But these combinations do not in themselves diagnose language specificity in child English, since their counterparts occur in child and adult Korean as well (see next section).

Part 4

Word and Sentence Structure

INTRODUCTION

THE TWO PAPERS THAT ARE included in this part deal with aspects of word and sentence acquisition that have important theoretical underpinnings. Both papers offer a post-generative perspective on children's language acquisition since each incorporates a view of language as a phenomenon composed of non-discrete levels. Readers should refer to the introduction of Part 5 in this volume for an explanation as to how this view fits into the wider theoretical landscape of child language acquisition.

The papers

Lila Gleitman and Jane Gillette (Chapter 4.1) deal with the issue of mapping in vocabulary acquisition. Mapping is the term used by psycholinguists to refer to the process whereby labels are attached to objects or referents in the real world. At first blush this may seem to be a straightforward activity. As Paul Bloom points out (2000), on the surface, word learning is one of the 'easiest' acquisition tasks. Children do not seem to have to pay attention to patterns that occur across contexts, as they do, for instance, when acquiring pragmatic competence. Further, it is arguably the case that rule extraction during lexical acquisition is less complex than it is for syntax acquisition. Surely attaching labels to objects or activities represents an effort of memory and nothing more.

At the heart of vocabulary acquisition however, lies a puzzle which is most famously associated with the philosopher Quine (1960). Quine highlighted the extent of accomplishment that mapping involves. To begin with, how is it that children manage to associate the correct words with the correct, intended referents? Why is it that when an adult points at a rabbit and says 'Rabbit!' the child understands that the word refers to the whole animal present in front of them; not to its ears or tail, its colour, smell or shape, or even its superordinate term, animal. Neither does the word refer to the hopping or twitching that naturally accompanies rabbits in the real world. Once a word is associated with a referent, the child must then pick out the referents which exist in the world which may also be denoted by that word; that is, the child must learn the correct **extension** of the word. Inevitably on some occasions, the child will **overextend** or **underextend** a label. For example, *rabbit* may be overextended to include all largish rodents such as chinchillas, guinea pigs and even rats. Conversely, *rabbit* may be underextended and used only to refer to a particular rabbit or to a restricted range of rabbits. Part 3 in this volume addresses these issues in more detail.

With regard to nouns, the answer may be seen as relatively straightforward for modern students of language acquisition. In those (predominantly Western) cultures where caregivers pay attention to providing children with names for objects (and may even correct children's labelling errors), the caregiver's label is likely to be contingent on context, concrete and relate to whole objects rather than parts (Bloom 2000). Further, children seem to be predisposed to attach labels to objects in such a way, as well as to abide by other helpful principles (Bates 1979). The earlier chapters in Bloom's (2000) text provide a useful analysis of how children's predisposition to focus on these aspects of the world is capitalised on by the mapping process.

Ostensibly, mapping nouns is a simple, logical activity deriving from two synchronous developments in the child's unfolding mental abilities: first, a cognitive predisposition to notice and pay attention to salient aspects of objects in the environment, and second the child's early forays into language characteristically taking the form of single token utterances. However, Bloom points out that, while mention of noun labels by the more linguistically competent speakers present in a situation often corresponds to objects that are present and salient in the child's environment, in approximately 30 per cent of cases they do not. There still therefore remains a problem that must be explained by accounts of noun mapping. Bloom's text addresses just this problem. His definition of word relates to the Saussurian concept of word, whereby a word (or **sign**) has two components: form and concept. Bloom focuses his discussion on those words for which concept is important; that is, he (deliberately) ignores morphological processes and function words, since here it is **syntagmatic** associations (associations between a word and other items in the same sentence) that are critical rather than the conceptual aspects of a word. Bloom's exposition therefore offers an important account of mapping problems with respect to a subset of words: content nouns. It should be noted by readers that Bloom is first and foremost a psychologist whose interests encompass conceptual development in young children, and it is from this standpoint that his interest in lexical acquisition proceeds. Bloom's viewpoint is compatible with an approach to linguistic enquiry known as Cognitive Linguistics. Cognitive Linguistics is anti-modularist in orientation: explanations of language acquisition make use of cognitive rather than autonomous linguistic factors. This field may be seen as opposed to Generative Linguistics or as a development from it (see the introduction to Part 6, this volume, for a more detailed discussion of theories and explanations of language acquisition). Either way, Cognitive Linguistics offers an approach to the critical issues in language acquisition which represents an important alternative to generative theories.

Nouns are, of course, not the only word classes which must be mapped. Verbs present a different set of problems for young mappers, and it is these issues to which Chapter 4.1 orients. Other studies by the authors Gillette and Gleitman demonstrate that verbs are not accessible to mapping strategies in the same way that nouns are. Verbs are, by definition, intrinsically connected with syntactic processes. They form the predicates of clauses and as such necessitate some awareness of the structural properties of sentences. For language-acquiring infants, mapping verbs requires all the skills that are associated with noun mapping: successfully segmenting the speech stream, paying attention to salient aspects of a situation, correct concept association, and generalisation to appropriate contexts. However, children must also take on additional tasks. Understanding verbs and using them correctly requires the language user to take note of their syntagmatic and morphological properties. Verbs are not related to referents in the same way that nouns are, nor do they figure in conversation in the same way. As Gleitman and Gillette point out, while nouns tend to reflect the here and now of conversational context, caregivers tend to give children far fewer reliable cues as to which is the relevant action denoted by a particular verb. It is simply not possible to draw attention to the correct meaning of a verb in the same way as it is for a noun. How should one point to the activity of *wanting* for instance? The verb mapping challenge is further complicated by the fact that many of the frequently used verbs in caregivers' utterances are abstract rather than concrete. In terms of frequency, it is worth noting that the British National Corpus lists the most frequent verbs occurring in spoken English as *do, have, be, know, get, think* (Leech *et al.* 2001). The two lexical verbs, *know* and *think*, are abstract, while the remainder have a functional component. Researchers describing children's mapping of abstract verbs have noted that to correctly complete their task children must, then, have at least an incipient **theory of mind**: that is, the ability to interpret what an interlocutor is thinking (Bloom 2000).

Unsurprisingly, few verbs occur in children's very first words. Barrett (1996) provides a clear and detailed account of children's first words, their uses and meanings. Very early uses of verbs may be non-referential rather than truly symbolic (Bates 1976). Hence investigators must be careful to ensure that an early usage of a verb accords with an adult interpretation of the same word. In short, the complexity of the verb-learning task is such that their acquisition has been noted by researchers as the likely locus of the onset of syntax (Tomasello 1992; Naigles 1990; Bates *et al.* 1988; Bloom 1981).

Gleitman and Gillette use a carefully designed methodology across a series of related experiments in order to pinpoint the factors which are critical for children learning to associate correct verbs with relevant actions. Their methodology is intended to replicate a 'miniaturised' situation in which a child is faced with a series of verb-learning situations, minus one presumed critical verb-learning ingredient. Each experimental variant has as its focus a different 'ingredient'. The accumulated and statistically worked results allow the authors to determine what it is that enables a child to successfully map verbs. The conclusion is that syntactic knowledge along-side context and contingency are requisite factors, with syntactic ability effectively bootstrapping the child into the process.

This association between syntax and lexis in acquisition is not so surprising when one addresses other issues in acquisition that are otherwise difficult to explain. Gleitman and Gillette present an array of evidence from areas such as atypical acquisition and noted patterns of acquisition from other studies which strongly suggest children do not seem to acquire words then syntax, in that order and in discrete bounded stages. Indeed, the findings seem in accord with a more emer-gentist, less structuralist perspective on language acquisition in which syntax and lexis are intrinsically and inextricably linked. For a more detailed and recent account of investigations into the role verbs play in the acquisition process, interested readers should refer to Gillette *et al.* (1999).

Deanne Swan (Chapter 4.2) deals with lexical innovations and over-regular-isations in children's morphological development. Lexical innovations concern the neologisms that children invent when lacking a conventional word for something. Such innovations depend on rules that exist in the target language, incorrectly applied, so that, for example, a child may say 'cycler' instead of 'cyclist'. Over-regularisations on the other hand concern a child using regular inflectional morphology incorrectly, for example by adding a regular *ed* ending onto an irreg-ular verb such as *think* to make **thinked* or even **thoughted*.

Lexical innovations and over-regularisations are generally considered to derive from different morphological systems, that is, derivational and inflectional morphology respectively. Since the former concerns lexical knowledge and the latter syntactic knowledge it has been presumed that the two are distinct and unrelated. Swan's work however, suggests that the two emerge and follow a developmental course in tandem with one another. Both can be correlated with emergence at a particular chronological age and linguistic stage as determined by MLU; both decrease in incidence after the MLU plateau; neither had completely disappeared by the age of 5;11 in the study subject. Indeed, Swan suggests that, while both belong to apparently different 'compartments' of language, to the language-learning child there are evident similarities. For example, both involve suffixation of roots whether this suffixation denotes grammatical or lexical information. One may wonder if this surface similarity may be enough to give rise to such developmental associations, however.

Since Swan's findings derive from a case study methodology, the generalisa-tions must naturally be treated with wariness. Advantages of a case study approach, of course, are that a fine-grained analysis of the data is facilitated. Such analyses are simply not possible in large-scale studies which rely on quantitative methods alone. As Swan herself indicates, this case study identifies particular foci of poten-tial research from which generalisations may legitimately be made. Further work, particularly in the field of non-error-based morphological development and cross-linguistic morphological acquisition is needed to put the findings into context. Ostensibly at least, however, here is further evidence that syntax and lexis may not be so discrete in acquisition as our adult linguistic categories may suggest.

Lila Gleitman and Jane Gillette

THE ROLE OF SYNTAX IN VERB LEARNING

WE DISCUSS HERE THE MAPPING problem for vocabulary acquisition: how word-level concepts are matched with their phonological realizations in the target language. Traditional approaches to this problem assume that, at least at early stages in the acquisition process, children try to line up the utterance of single words with their contingencies in the world. Thus, their task would be to discover that *elephant* is most often said in the presence of elephants and rarely said in their absence (Locke, 1690, and many modern sources).

Our recent investigations (Gillette [*et al.*, 1999]) show how well such a procedure could work in practice for the case of concrete nouns. Adult subjects are shown videotapes of mothers playing with their infants (aged about 18 months, MLU < 2;0) but with the audio turned off. These film clips are long enough for subjects to pick up the pragmatics of the conversation, e.g. of a mother showing and describing an elephant puppet to the child, who then takes it and manipulates it. The subjects are told that whenever the mother is uttering the target noun, a beep will sound; their task is to identify the word that she uttered. Subjects have no trouble with this task, guessing correctly about 50 percent of the time even on the first video-beep exposure, and improving with the addition of more instances. And if any of the maternal usages are deictic, the subjects are even better in guessing what noun she was saying.

This laboratory situation is radically reduced from the problem that infants face in assigning interpretations to novel words. The subjects are made aware in advance that the target is a noun. These nouns all describe concrete objects that are present

1995, reprinted with permission from P. Fletcher and B. MacWhinney (eds), *The Handbook of Child Language*, Oxford, Blackwell.

in the videotaped scenario, and are foci of the mother–child conversation. In light of the task as set for them, the subjects also know that there exists in English a single common word that will fit their observations of these objects in these scenes. Moreover, they are solving for one target noun at a time; their exposures to this item are not complicated by the intervention of any other novel items, so they have no memory problem. In contrast, a child learner might reencounter the new item only after the passage of considerable time, and mingled with other new words.

One further proviso is even more controversial. No doubt arises that the adult subjects can conceptualize the objects in the scenes (e.g. they can represent the concept "elephant") and can interpret the pragmatics of the mother–child conversation. So built into the claim that these findings are informative for understanding the mapping problem is our assumption that adults and young children are much the same not only in their data-handling procedures, but also in the ways they interpret the everyday world of things, actions, causes, intentions, and so forth (for a recent discussion of this "rationalist perspective," see Bloom, P. [1994]).

Overall, then, the Gillette and Gleitman experiment models the child's vocabulary learning situation in at best a highly idealized fashion. But it does add to a literature demonstrating that maternal usage, at least of highly frequent nouns, is sufficiently faithful to the "here and now" to support learning by inspecting how the sounds of words match up with present scenes (Bruner, 1974/75; Ninio, 1980).

This apparent simplicity of the mapping problem for vocabulary acquisition – once purged of the "concept learning" issues – accounts for why it has been something of a stepchild in recent linguistic inquiry into language learning. The task has seemed devoid of any interesting internal structure: merely a matter of associating single words (*qua* phonological objects) with their standard contexts of use, as in the experiment just described.

The burden of the present discussion is to show that, over the vocabulary at large, this word-to-world pairing procedure is too weak to account fully for mapping. Our claim is that word learning is in general performed by pairing a *sentence* (*qua* syntactic object) with the observed world.

Insufficiency of observation for verb learning

As a first demonstration of the structural requirement in word learning, we now reconsider the Gillette and Gleitman experiment as it pertains to the acquisition of verbs. The manipulation is the same. The subjects are shown silent videotapes of mother–infant interactions, long enough to reveal the pragmatic contexts for the verbs' use. At the moment that the mother was really uttering some target verb, the beep sounds. Again, only the mothers' most frequent child directed verbs are tested, and again the subject receives several beep-scenario pairs (that is, pairings of the utterance of the target verb with its observational contingencies) as the basis for his or her guess. Now the results are entirely different from those of the noun experiments. The subjects correctly identify the verb the mother was actually saying less than 15 percent of the time.

Once again the experiment has various unrealistic elements, notably that the subjects know all these English verbs in advance, and have been told that it is a verb that they are seeking. But this should make their task easier, not harder. One could also object, alluding to the results from a generation of developmental psycholinguists, that children are better language learners (including vocabulary learners) than adults and would therefore do better in this task.

Despite these real contaminants, one effect stands firm: this is the massive *difference* for verbs and nouns in their tractability to this procedure. While the nouns were easily identified from their word (beep) to world (video) contingencies, the verbs were not.

How can we explain the special difficulty of verbs in this manipulation? One factor is that some of the verbs that mothers use *most frequently* to their babies represent concepts that are not straightforwardly observable: *want*, *know*, and *think* are in the top group in usage frequency. Even some of the "more concrete" frequent verbs encode some intentional content rather than solely a property of the perceived world, e.g. *show*, *see*, and *give*. Another factor, evident upon inspection of these videotapes, is the temporal precision with which the environment matches the utterance. When *elephant* is uttered, overwhelmingly often the elephant is being held, waved, even pointed at. But "push" is usually said well before or after the pushing event takes place (Lederer, Gleitman, and Gleitman, [1995]; Tomasello and Kruger, 1992). The verb uses do not line up transparently with their situational contexts, a problem we have called *interleaving*: by the time the mother says *push* ("You pushed the poor elephant down!"), the child is usually *looking* and *smiling* at the consequences of his or her prior pushing action (or the reverse, as when the mother says "Go push the truck"). This makes it hard for the subjects to guess that the beep referred to the pushing act.

If young children are like our adult subjects, they too should have more trouble learning verbs than nouns. And indeed they do. A robust generalization from the vocabulary learning literature is that early vocabularies (the first 50 words) contain few – often no – verbs; and nouns continue to outnumber verbs in productive vocabularies beyond their frequency distribution in maternal speech until the child is past three years of age (Gentner, 1978; 1982).

We have mentioned two usage distinctions that can help explain this learning oddity. The first is merely a pragmatic fact of usage with nothing essential to do with the formal or substantive universals of the word classes: caretakers' most frequent nouns to babies in our corpus are predominantly items that describe observable objects while their verbs are often abstract: they often say "I think . . ." to their babies, but they rarely say "The thought . . ." A second and more important factor is that verb use, as opposed to noun use, is not tightly timelocked with the extralinguistic contexts, and more often refers to the nonpresent. (In fact, in Beckwith, Tinker, and Bloom's (1989) corpus of speech to babies, verbs are used out of context more than a quarter of the time – this includes physical action verbs like *open*.)

But there is a third factor – one that we believe holds the primary key to this lexical-class order effect in vocabulary acquisition: verb acquisition requires access to the phrase structure of the exposure language, and it takes the infant some time to get the structural properties under control.

More power to verb learning

Eric Lenneberg (1967) provided the first evidence suggesting a structure-sensitive model for the learning of verbs (and perhaps all classes of words which do not typically express concrete object concepts): the "explosion" of spoken vocabulary, including sudden increase in the range of lexical types, coincides with the appearance of rudimentary (two word) sentences at approximately the 24th month of life. [. . .]

The idea is that structural information is required by learners – along with the scenario information – to fix the meaning of novel verbs.

Origins and motivation

The first direct demonstration that vocabulary acquisition is sensitive to linguistic context was from Brown (1957), who showed that children would interpret the relation of a novel word to a scene (in this case, a picture) differently depending on available morphological cues: if they heard "the gorp," they pointed to a visible novel object, but if they heard "gorping" they pointed to the implied action, and so forth. The linguistic cues affected the interpretation of the scene in view, to some extent reversing the causal chain suggested by common sense (namely, that the scene in view determines the interpretation of the linguistic object). The findings hint that learners expect there to be a link between formal properties of language (lexical class membership in this case) and semantic interpretation.

Landau and Gleitman (1985) carried this line further, positing that children use linguistic cues in identifying novel word meanings within as well as across the major lexical classes. Their immediate impetus was a quite startling finding: the first verb in a congenitally blind learner's spoken vocabulary was *see*. Although the exposure conditions for learning this word necessarily differ for blind and sighted, both populations acquire the word as a term of achieved perception, and do so at the same developmental moment.

But such exotica are not really required to show that children acquire aspects of word meaning that do not seem to be warranted by perception and pragmatic inference. Consider a sighted child hearing her mother say "I see a bird over there." Often there will be an occluding object between child and bird. Children come to know that *see* means "see" despite the fact that maternal speech is not a faithful running commentary on events in view.

Related problems in learning from observation alone abound. One is that the listener's focus of attention may differ from that of the speaker, as when the adult says "Come take your nap" while the child inspects a cat on a mat. Another is that the scene that accompanies utterance of a verb includes many events, only one of which is encoded by that verb. Consider the plight of the child to whom an adult says "Do you want some ice-cream?" The adult is speaking, smiling, holding, and waving the cone, and perhaps pointing to it; it is observably something good to eat, dripping, pink, an object of present desire, and so forth.[. . .] None of the aspects of the scene just described is irrelevant to the conversational intent, as this might be reconstructed by a sophisticated observer (which we assume the youngster to be). Yet only one of them is correct to map onto the item *want*. A picture is worth a thousand words, but that's the problem: a thousand words describe the varying aspects of any one picture.

Attempts to circumvent these difficulties involve a probabilistic procedure in which the mapping choice is based on the most frequent word–world match across situations (see Pinker, 1984, for discussion). No one can doubt that cross-situational observation plays a role in vocabulary acquisition, but taken alone it seems to be insufficient. One difficulty has to do with the observed rapidity and relative error-lessness of child vocabulary learning. Children are apparently acquiring five or more new words a day beginning at about the fifteenth month of life (Carey, 1978). It strains credulity to suppose that they are lucky enough to hear – within a very short time interval – most such words in the variety of information environments that would be required to parse out the right interpretation.

Form–meaning interactions in verb learning

Inspection of any corpus of natural speech shows that different verbs characteristic-ally occur with different complements, in accord with their differing argument structures. Thus, inalienable actions typically are encoded with intransitive struc-tures (*Pinnochio dances*), acts that affect another's state with transitive structures (*Gepetto kisses the puppet*), and so forth. This form–meaning correlation is usually described by saying that the structure is a projection from (aspects of) the verb's meaning; that is, the surface structures are mapped from the argument structure of the verb. Two complementary views of verb learning have recently been put forward, both taking advantage of such relations between verb meaning and sentence structure.

Bootstrapping complementation privileges from knowledge of verb meaning

If form–meaning correlations are systematic across the languages of the world (quirks aside), we should expect that children can project the complement struc-tures for a verb whose meaning they have acquired via event observation, rather than having to memorize the structures independently (Grimshaw, 1981; Pinker, 1984). One kind of evidence in support of this hypothesis comes from studies of the invention of language by linguistically deprived youngsters (deaf children of hearing parents who are not exposed to sign language; Goldin-Meadow and Feldman, 1977; Feldman, Goldin-Meadow, and Gleitman, 1978). The self-invented gesture systems of these children appear to conform to the theta-criterion (Chomsky, 1981): they gesture one noun in construction with their invented gesture for *dance*, two in construction with *hit*, and three with *give*. Another kind of evidence comes from child errors in complementation; these appear to occur primarily where there are quirks and subtleties in the way the exposure language maps from argu-ment structure to surface structure (Bowerman, 1982c). In short, children use their knowledge of a verb's meaning as a basis for projecting the phrase structure of sentences in which it appears.

Bootstrapping verb meaning from knowledge of verb complementations

A second learning hypothesis also is consistent with the view that verb clause structure is a projection from verb argument structure: hearing some new verb in a
particular structural environment should constrain its interpretation (Landau and
Gleitman, 1985; Gleitman and Gleitman, 1992). Thus, hearing *John gorps* increases
the likelihood that *gorp* means "smile" and decreases the likelihood that it means
"hit." And hearing *John gorps Bill* should imply the reverse. Thus, knowledge of the
semantic implications of the sentence structure in which a novel verb appears can
narrow the search-space for its identification. It is this structurally derived narrowing
of the hypothesis space for verb meaning on which we now concentrate.

The zoom lens hypothesis

According to our hypothesis, the first use of structural information is as an online
procedure for interpreting a novel verb. Though there may be quite a few salient
interpretations of the scene, the learner "zooms in" on one (or at least fewer) of
these by demanding congruence also with the semantic implications of the sentence
form. Thus, the input is

1   the extralinguistic event, as represented by a perceptually and pragmatically
     sophisticated observer,

paired with

2   the linguistic event, represented as a novel verb positioned within the parse
     tree constructed from the adult utterance.

The learner exploits the semantically relevant structural information in (2) to choose
among the several interpretations that may be warranted by (1).

An early demonstration is from Naigles (1990). She investigated responses to
novel verbs as a function of linguistic-introducing circumstances in children under
two years of age, who had no or few verbs in their spoken vocabularies. In the
learning phase of the experiment, the children were shown videotaped action scenes
that had two novel salient interpretations. For example, they saw a rabbit pushing
down on a duck's head, thus forcing the duck to bend over; simultaneously, both
the duck and the rabbit were wheeling their free arm in a broad circle. While
watching this scene, half the babies heard "The rabbit is gorping the duck" while the
other half heard "The rabbit and the duck are gorping." Then "gorping" might
plausibly refer to forcing-to-bend or to arm-wheeling. Subsequently, the scene
disappeared and a voice said "Find gorping now! Where's gorping?" At this point,
new action scenes appeared, one on a videoscreen to the child's left, the other on
a screen to her right. The one on the left showed the rabbit forcing the duck to
bend, but with no arm wheeling. The one on the right showed rabbit and duck
wheeling their arms, but with no forcing to bend. The measure of learning was the
child's visual fixation time on one or the other screen during a six second interval.
Twenty-three of 24 infants tested looked longest at the videoscreen that matched
their syntactic introducing circumstances. Evidently the transitive input biased

subjects toward something like the cause-to-bend interpretation, while the intransitive input biased them toward arm wheeling. Though we cannot know from this manipulation exactly what the children learned about "the meaning of gorp," their interpretation of what they were (relevantly) perceiving during the training phase was clearly affected by the syntax, for the subjects' situations differed in no other way.

More direct evidence of the effect of syntactic context on verb identification comes from studies with three-year-old learners. This age group is the one in which the verb vocabulary (and complex sentence structure) burgeons. These relatively elderly subjects are also useful because they can answer questions about the meanings of novel verbs that they encounter. Fisher, Hall, Rakowitz, and Gleitman (1994) investigated the acquisition of perspective verbs (e.g. *chase/flee*, *lead/follow*) with children of this age.

Principled difficulties for observation-based learning arise for these verbs, for they come in pairs that vary primarily in the speaker perspective on a single action or event, and thus their situational concomitants are virtually always the same. This makes them a good testing ground for proposed learning procedures that rely on word-to-world contingencies only. Consider *give* and *get*. Both these verbs describe the same intentional transfer of possession of an object between two individuals. Disentangling them based on the pragmatics of the conversation would require the listener to gain access to the mental perspective of the speaker – whether she is likely referring to Mary's volitional act of passing the book to John or John's consequent act of getting the book from Mary. [. . .]

But additional information can come from inspecting the structural positioning of (known) nouns in the sentence heard and comparing these against the scene in view, providing that the learner determines the semantic implications of the sentence structure itself. If that scene shows the book moving from Mary to John, then an adult utterance like

(1)   Look! Ziking!

provides no differentiating information, but if she says

(2)   Mary zikes the ball to John

zike likely means *give* (or *throw*, etc.). In contrast, if the sentence is

(3)   John zikes the ball from Mary

then *zike* likely means *get* (or *take*, *receive*, *catch*, etc.). The potential clues for disentangling this pair are the choice of nominal in subject position, and the choice of a goal (*to*) v. source (*from*) preposition.

Fisher et al. (1994) showed such scenes/sentences to young children, in a context where a puppet was uttering the sentence: the children were asked to help the experimenter understand some "puppet words" (e.g. *zike*). The structure of the findings was this: if the input sentence to the child was uninformative of the *give/get* distinction (e.g. example sentence (1)), then child and adult subjects showed a bias in interpreting the scene: they were likely to say that it described something like giving rather than getting. This "agency bias" (whoever was subject of the transitive verb was agent of the action) characterized the set of five scenarios tested, including also chasing in preference to fleeing (running away), and so forth. If the input sentence was (2), which matches the bias as to how to interpret the scene, the tendency to respond with a verb that meant something like *give* was further enhanced; in fact, almost categorical. But if the input sentence was (3), which mismatches the perceptual/conceptual bias toward *give*, subjects' modal response became *get* (or one of its relatives, e.g. *take*).

In sum, structural properties of the sentence heard influence the perception of a single scene even in cases where the bias in event representation, taken alone, leads in the opposite direction. Such findings begin to explain why children rarely confuse the perspective verbs despite the fact that they occur in very similar extralinguistic contexts.

The multiple frames hypothesis

In many cases, a surface-structure/situation pair is insufficient or even misleading about a verb's interpretation. For instance, the phrase structure and the typical situation in adult–child discourse are often the same when the adult says "Did you eat your cookie?" as when he says "Do you want a cookie?" In principle, examination of the further syntactic privileges of *eat* and *want* can cue distinctions in their interpretations. For example, *want* occurs with (tenseless) sentence complements, suggesting a mental component of its meaning.

More generally, the range of syntactic frames can provide convergent evidence on the meaning of a verb. "John is ziking the book to Bill" suggests an active verb of transfer (progressive, ditransitive). This would include a broad range of verbs such as *bring*, *throw*, *explain*, etc. But then "John is ziking that the book is boring" narrows the interpretive range to mental verbs. Taken together – and examined against the accompanying scenes – these structural properties suggest mental transfer, whose local interpretation is communication (e.g. *explain*; Zwicky, 1971; Fisher, Gleitman, and Gleitman, 1991).

There is evidence that the linguistic information provided by mothers to their young children is refined enough to support learning from frame ranges. Lederer, Gleitman, and Gleitman [1995] examined lengthy conversations of mothers with babies (MLU < 2). For the 24 most common verbs in these mothers' speech, a verb by syntactic-environment matrix was developed. Within and across mothers, each verb was found to be unique in its syntactic range. Using a procedure devised by Fisher et al. (1991), it was shown that degree of overlap in syntactic range predicted the verbs' semantic overlap to a striking extent.

The potency of various evidentiary sources

So far we have shown some demonstrations with children and adults suggesting that they can use syntactic evidence to aid in the mastery of new verbs. The question remains how much of the burden of verb identification the structure bears; particularly the multiple-frame evidence. After all, even if syntactic constraints will affect the observer's interpretation in some carefully constructed laboratory situations, in real life the evidence from extralinguistic and other cues may be so decisive that syntactic deductions rarely if ever come into play.

One indirect but suggestive kind of evidence that multiple-frame information is exploited by learners comes from correlational studies (Naigles and Hoff-Ginsberg, 1993). The idea behind such studies is to inquire how well maternal usage at some point in learning ("Time 1") predicts learning, by testing the child's progress after some suitable interval ("Time 2"). Specifically, they investigated the use of common verbs in the speech of mothers to one- and two-year-olds, and then their children's subsequent use of these verbs. The *diversity of syntactic frames* in which verbs appeared in maternal speech at Time 1, with verb frequency in maternal speech partialled out, significantly predicted the frequency with which these verbs appeared in child speech ten weeks later.

Lederer, Gleitman, and Gleitman [1995] have examined the potential information value of various properties of mothers' speech to infants: its (multiple) extralinguistic contexts, nominal cooccurrences, selectional and syntactic properties. Which of these attributes of adult speech, taken singly or in various combinations, provide enough information for solving the mapping problem for verbs?

The method was to provide (adult) subjects with large numbers of instances (usually, about 50) of the use of some target verb by mothers to 18-month-olds, but blocking out one or another potential source of information. For example, some subjects saw 50 or so videotape clips of mothers uttering a single common verb but without audio; the procedure was repeated for the 24 most common verbs in these mothers' child directed speech. Other subjects were told the nouns that occurred with the target verb in each of the 50 maternal sentences. A third group was shown the list of 50 sentences that the mother actually uttered but with all nouns as well as the verb converted to nonsense (e.g. *Rom GORPS that the rivenflak is grum, Can vany GORP the blick?*)

The first finding was that, just as in the Gillette and Gleitman experiment cited earlier, subjects systematically failed to guess the verb from observing its real-world contexts of use (7 percent correct identification). In the second condition, subjects did not see the video but were told the cooccurring nouns for each sentence in which the mother uttered that verb: after all, if a verb regularly occurs with nouns describing edibles, maybe it means *eat*. Subjects identified the verb from this kind of information in about 13 percent of instances.

It is surprising that subjects' mapping performance was so dismal in both the scene and noun conditions. And when new subjects were given both these kinds of information (that is, shown the videos *and* told the cooccurring nouns) they still hit upon the target verbs only 28 percent of the time.

But when subjects were provided with frame-range information – no scenes, no real nouns or verbs, just the set of syntactic structures that the mothers used, with all their content-bearing words converted to nonsense – the subjects identified 52 percent of the verbs correctly. It appears that syntactic range information is highly informative.

A difficulty with interpreting these results onto the child learning situation is that these subjects (when correct) by definition were identifying old verbs that they knew: perhaps they just looked up the frame-ranges for these known verbs in their mental lexicons rather than using the frames to make semantic deductions. Because of this possibility, the pertinence of the findings to the real learning situation is more easily evaluated by inspecting the 48 percent of instances where subjects *failed* in this condition (and the 93 percent of cases where they failed in the scene condition, etc.). The finding is that false guesses given in response to frame-range information were semantically close to the actual verb that the mother had said (as assessed by the Fisher et al. (1991) semantic-similarity procedure), e.g. for *think*, the only false guess was *believe*. In contrast, the false guesses offered in response to looking at the scenes in which *think* was actually said were semantically unrelated to this verb (including *run*, *catch*, *go*, *look*, etc.). The frame-range information put the subjects into the "semantic neighborhood" of the target verb. In contrast, false interpretations of scenes don't get the subject close to the mark at all. This latter result raises puzzles for how a cross-situational learning scheme that is blind to syntax might work in practice.

Note that 52 percent correct identification in the presence of syntactic frame-range information only, while a significant improvement over 7 percent, is not good enough if we want to model the fact that verb learning by three-year-olds is a snap. They do not make 48 percent errors so far as we know, even errors close to the semantic mark. But as we have stressed, our hypothesis is not about a procedure in which the child ignores the scene, or the cooccurring nominals, and attends to syntax alone (as Lederer et al. forced their subjects to do in the experiment just described). We have hypothesized a sentence-to-world pairing procedure for verb vocabulary acquisition. Indeed, adding the real nouns to the frames without video in this experiment led to over 80 percent verb identification; adding back the scene yielded almost perfect performance.

Summarizing these results, scene information and noun contextual information taken alone are quite uninformative (7 percent and 13 percent correct identification, respectively) while frame-range information is highly informative (52 percent correct identification). But when we combine the information sources, the results look quite different. Once the observer is given access to the structure, he or she makes highly efficient use of frame and noun-context information. The reasons why are easy to see. Consider the noun contexts: it doesn't much help to know that one of the words in an utterance was *hamburger*. But if this word is known to surface as direct object, the meaning of the verb might well be "eat." (That is, the structural information converts cooccurrence information to selectional information.) Similarly for the videotapes: once the structure of the sentences uttered in their presence is known, the subject can zoom in on fewer interpretations of the events and states that might be pertinent for the mother to have said of them. So if the child has available – as she does in real life – multiple paired scenes and sentences, we can at last understand why verb learning is easy.

How the structures of sentences can aid vocabulary acquisition

We have suggested that the formal medium of phrase structure constrains the semantic content that the sentence is expressing, thus providing clues to the meaning of its verb. One such clue resides in the number of arguments: a noun-phrase position is assigned to each verb argument; this will differentiate *push* from *fall* when viewing a scene where both actions are taking place. Another concerns the positioning of the arguments: the subject of transitives is the agent, differentiating *chase* from *flee*. The case marking and type of the argument also matters, e.g. spatial verbs which allow expression of paths and locations typically accept prepositional phrases, and verbs that express mental acts and states appear with sentence complements.

Of course, one cannot converge on the unique construal of a verb from syntactic properties alone. Because the subcategorization properties are the syntactic expressions of their arguments, it is only those aspects of a verb's meaning that have consequences for its argument structure that could be represented syntactically. Many – most – semantic distinctions are not formally expressed with this machinery. The role of the syntax is only to narrow the search-space for the meaning, as this latter is revealed by extralinguistic context.

What our experimentation suggests is that this initial narrowing of the hypothesis space by attention to structure is the precondition for using the scene information efficiently to derive the verb's meaning. When babies do not appear to know the phrase structure, they learn few if any verbs (Lenneberg, 1967). When adults and young children are required to identify verbs without phrase structure cues (as when told "Look! Ziking!" or when presented with silent videos of mother–child conversations) again they do not identify target verbs. But the observation of scenes taken together with observation of the structures is sufficient to the task.

Relation of surface syntax to semantics

A well-known view is that there are cross-cutting "verb classes," each defined over some abstract semantic domain (e.g. "mental" or "spatial") and – therefore – licensing certain structural formats, or frames (see Levin, 1993). We suggest instead that verb frames have semantic implications, and verbs have meanings. Neither the frames nor their semantic implications are part of lexical information: any verb can appear grammatically in any structural environment. But owing to the meaning of the verb, it may be semantically implausible, and thus rarely or never uttered, in some syntactic contexts. For example, we do not typically say things like "Barbara looked the ball on the table." Arguably, we do not forbear from such utterances because that verb in that sentence would be ungrammatical. Rather, the interpretation of the sentence structure would imply that some external agent (Barbara) caused the ball to go on the table just by looking at it. The improbability of psychokinesis is what makes this verb in this syntactic context rare. This is shown by the fact that if the rare circumstances do occur, *look* can be used unexceptionally in this structure: the rules of baseball make it possible to say (and sports announcers do say) "The shortstop looked the runner back to third base." In this case, moving is immediately caused by the threatening glance, rendering the sentence plausible.

If the view just sketched is correct, verbs have no "subcategorization privileges." [. . .] If there are no subcategorization privileges for individual verbs, then the child never has to learn them.

What the child *must* know are the semantic implications of these structures. There is considerable evidence from the work of a generation of linguists that these semantic–syntactic linkages are to a useful degree universal (see Grimshaw, 1990, for a review and theoretical perspective) and given by nature to the learner (e.g. the evidence from the isolated deaf that we have cited).

Our suggestion is that learners note the frame environments in which verbs characteristically occur, thus deducing the argument structures with which their meanings typically comport. These ranges of "typical structures" are compatible with only small sets of verb meanings. The phrase structures in turn provide constraints on the interpretation of extralinguistic information, increasing the efficiency of observational learning.

Deanne Swan

HOW TO BUILD A LEXICON
A case study of lexical errors
and innovations

A S CHILDREN ACQUIRE THEIR native language, they uncover regular patterns in language and develop a set of rules or guidelines that govern their early words. In normal speech, successful rule use goes unnoticed. When children's rule use results in an unconventional lexical form, we notice. These novel forms are classified as two different phenomena: grammatical over-regularizations and lexical innovations. Over-regularizations and lexical innovations can provide evidence of children's implicit understanding of linguistic rules (Bowerman 1982a), and both of these phenomena demonstrate aspects of language that capture children's attention. These phenomena create a window through which we can view children's early morphological development.

Over-regularizations are the extension of regular grammatical patterns to irregular words (Marcus, Pinker, Ullman, Hollander, Rosen & Xu 1992), resulting in words like, 'feets' and 'goed'. Over-regularizations are errors related to the rules of inflectional morphology. They occur when a regular rule is over-applied to an irregular stem, and these errors suggest that a pattern has been recognized and extracted from the speech stream. Use of such rules as they are applied to regular stems cannot be differentiated from the use of an unanalysed inflected form that was learned as a whole unit. However, when children learn inflections that mark an aspect of language, such as tense, they sometimes take words such as 'go' and 'teach' and handle them in the same manner as words like 'play' and 'walk' (Berko 1958, Cazden 1968, Kuczaj 1977). The existence of these forms implies that an attempt has been made by the child to inflect a known word for a specific element.

2000, reprinted with permission from *First Language*, 20: 187–204.

Lexical innovations are created through the manipulation of word-formation strategies and thus are related to derivational morphology. Lexical innovations are novel words, coined specifically to refer to an object or event that has no name, or for cases in which the speaker cannot recall a conventional term, such as 'bicycler' and 'candlesmith' (Clark 1993).

The importance of these two phenomena lies in their ability to 'suggest that children are learning the process required in [the] language for creating new words' (Clark 1982: 391). Lexical innovations and over-regularizations are similar because they both demonstrate an understanding of and productivity with morphology. However, as in any comparative analysis, there are important differences to bear in mind. First, the derivational strategies used in the formation of lexical innovations are more heterogeneous than the inflectional strategies of over-regularizations. Second, due to their grammatical function, over-regularizations are dictated by obligatory contexts; there are no obligatory contexts for lexical innovations. Finally, a change in lexical innovation is usually accompanied by a change in referent, but not so for over-regularizations. For example, whether over-regularized into the forms 'eated', 'ated', or 'ate', each of these belongs to the same semantic and grammatical category. However, the addition or omission of a morpheme can have a profound impact on the syntagmatic category of an innovation, as in 'cook + man' and 'cook + thing'.

Lexical innovations and over-regularizations in development

What is the nature of children's early innovations? Clark (1991, 1993) has developed several principles to describe important factors in children's early morphological acquisition. Two of these principles are particularly relevant to the present study: Simplicity and Transparency. According to Clark, children's early morphological development is influenced by simple forms (Simplicity) and easily recognizable elements in the language (Transparency). Hence, children's earliest innovations will be the result of compounding and word-class conversion.

Clark and her colleagues have found empirical support for these principles. Children as young as 2.5 years demonstrate a high level of competence in their comprehension and production of novel compound nouns (Clark & Berman 1984, Clark, Gelman & Lane 1985, Clark & Hecht 1982). Clark (1993) has also found that many of children's spontaneous innovations are compound nouns and denominal verbs (see also Becker 1994). This early reliance on compounding is not because young children are unable to use affixes productively. Clark & Hecht (1982) found that while 3-year-olds preferred compounding, they were also able to use suffixes in their production of novel agentive and instrument terms. This study also indicated a developmental change: 5- and 6-year-olds consistently produced innovations using the -er suffix. Mulford (1983) found a similar pattern of emergence in Icelandic children's use of the suffix -ari, which functions similarly to the agentive -er. Even though English has fewer prefixes than suffixes, evidence suggests that children are creative and flexible in their early use of prefixes as well (for an analysis of un-, see Bowerman 1982a).

There are also developmental trends in the production and comprehension of irregular past tense over-regularizations. Kuczaj (1977) found that in their spontaneous speech, 3-year-olds were more likely to produce a 'base form + -ed' error (e.g., eated), whereas 5-year-olds were more likely to produce an 'irregular past form + -ed' error (e.g., ated). A similar pattern was found in children's comprehension errors (Kuczaj 1978). Because almost all children produce these novel forms, over-regularization is considered to be a robust phenomenon. Even though it is common, it is rare. Contrary to prior assumptions, evidence suggests that the overall rate of production for over-regularizations is infrequent (from 2% to 5%, according to Marcus *et al.* 1992).

The present study

While the existing literature includes both case studies and experimental studies of each of these linguistic phenomena (Becker 1994, Bushnell & Maratsos 1984, Clark 1993, Clark *et al.* 1985, Marcus *et al.* 1992), there has not been a developmental analysis of novel lexical forms from children in naturalistic settings that contrasts production of both lexical innovations and over-regularizations. The present study serves to fill that gap by observing a single child's spontaneous production of these two lexical phenomena as they occur over time. This study also measures the development of these two phenomena in the light of the differential utilization of strategies in the child's productive language and general morpho-syntactic development.

Does the production of these two phenomena change over time, and if so how? Both phenomena should be equally influenced by age and general morpho-syntactic development. Regular patterns and strategies are related to an understanding of morphological complexity and should be correlated with mean length of utterance (MLU); conventional but nonstandard forms (e.g., irregular verbs) are associated with the learning of exceptions to rules and should be correlated with chronological age (i.e., amount of exposure to the language). Both phenomena should emerge between 2 and 3 years (Becker 1994, Clark 1993, Marcus *et al.* 1992). As strategy use becomes more prevalent, indicated by an increase in MLU, there will be an increase in the rate of production for both phenomena. After a peak, between 3 and 4 years of age, there should be a decline and eventual cessation of both phenomena as the child grows older (Cazden 1968, Clark 1993, Kuczaj 1978).

Do the strategies used to produce these creative lexemes change over time, and if so how? Though both forms draw on different strategies, there should be an overall recognizable pattern. Consistent with Clark's principles, there should be a developmental trend from lesser to greater complexity (see also Brown 1973). Early lexical innovations will be the result of compounding and conversion, while later innovations will be the result of suffixation and prefixation. Research (e.g., Bybee & Slobin 1988, Kuczaj 1977) supports a similar pattern for the production of over-regularizations: regular inflection of a bare form will precede both the regular inflection of an inflected irregular and the incorrect use of an irregular inflection.

Method

Participant and materials

The subject of this case study was Ross (henceforth R), a native English speaking, middle-class American boy. He was the first born of two boys. His language development was recorded from 30 to 56 months (ages 2;6.15 to 4;8.7), and additionally, from 63 to 71 months (ages 5;3.15 to 5;11.13). Transcripts were of spontaneous conversations that were audiotaped throughout R's early development. These interactions were recorded in naturalistic settings and situations, usually as the boy was engaged in conversations with his parents and younger brother at the family's home (B. MacWhinney, personal communication). [. . .] There is approximately one hour of spontaneous speech available for each month of observation. The corpus is available on the CHILDES (Child Language Database Exchange System) CD-ROM (April 1998 version, MacWhinney & Snow 1990), listed under the MacWhinney corpus. Comment lines with information concerning context, actions and other background information were used to disambiguate conversations.

Procedure

One observer identified and coded, by hand, spontaneous lexical innovations and over-regularizations in the transcripts of the child's speech. To be considered spontaneous, the novel forms could be neither imitated from another speaker's prior utterance nor explicitly elicited by another speaker (e.g., prompted by a parent to produce an innovation). Creative lexemes were identified in the transcripts by the primary investigator. All examples of creative lexemes were coded for form, strategy (i.e., derivational or inflectional) and grammatical category. Each of these are described in detail below.

Two measures of interobserver agreement were obtained: identification of form and coding of strategy and grammatical category. A trained research assistant re-coded 20% of the transcripts to identify and code each utterance for the presence of a creative lexical form: lexical innovations and over-regularizations. Cohen's Kappa was 0.98 for the identification of form within the transcripts. To obtain a measure of agreement for coding, 20% of each category of the novel word forms were re-coded for strategy and grammatical category by a second trained research assistant. Cohen's Kappa was 0.94 for derivational strategy (innovations), 1.00 for inflectional strategy (over-regularizations), 0.94 for grammatical category (innovations) and 1.00 for grammatical category (over-regularizations).

Coding

Form   Each creative lexeme identified in the transcripts was coded for form: lexical innovation or grammatical over-regularization. For the purpose of this study, lexical innovations were defined as words that are not in the conventional English lexicon and are based on specific word formation strategies of the language. The specific derivational strategies are indicated below. Grammatical over-regularizations were defined as irregular words that have been inflected in a manner different from their

conventional representation in the English language. The possible inflectional strategies are listed below.

Syntactic over-regularizations, which involve the extension of syntactic patterns
to instances where it is inappropriate (e.g., 'I disappeared her', the incorrect use
of an intransitive verb in a causative frame), were not coded in this analysis. For a
further discussion of syntactic overgeneralization, see Bowerman (1982a).

Derivational strategies: lexical innovations   Although it has been shown that children
produce innovations that use a variety of derivational strategies (e.g., reduplication,
blending, see Becker 1994), the present study adopted a strict, homogeneous
definition in order to increase the comparability of lexical innovations to over-
regularizations. Lexical innovations were coded using four different derivational
strategies (taken from Becker 1994, Quirk, Greenbaum, Leach & Svartvik 1985):
conversion (assignment of the base to a different word class with no form change; e.g.,
'a broom' becomes 'to broom'), *compounding* (combination of two bases to one
another; e.g., 'garden + man'), *suffixation* (placement of an affix after the base; e.g.,
'protect + -ment'), and *prefixation* (placement of an affix in front of the base;
e.g., 'un- + polite').

Inflectional strategies: over-regularizations   There were three different inflectional
strategies coded in this study. The three categories included in the analyses were: regular inflection on a bare irregular word or word stem (e.g., eated), regular inflection
on an inflected irregular word (e.g., ated), and irregular inflection on an irregular
word (e.g., droven, tooken).

Grammatical categories   Grammatical categories relate to the syntax of a language,
and thus they are implicated in morpho-syntactic development. The different categories are based on reference to objects and activities in the real world, and these
relationships are fairly stable across languages. Five major classes of grammatical
category were coded in this study. They are defined here with a sensitivity toward
a distributional approach to word classes (Braine 1987, Maratsos & Chalkley 1980):
noun (acts as an argument in a statement), *verb* (acts as a predicate in a statement),
adjective (modifies or describes an argument), *adverb* (modifies a predicate), and
preposition (describes a relationship between one argument and another).

Type vs. token   For each month, the occurrence of novel lexical items detected in
the child's observed spontaneous speech is reported as a frequency count. Because
there was approximately one hour of speech observed per month, this frequency
can also be interpreted as a rate (words per hour). The unit of analysis for this study
was Type. Type refers to the number of lexically different forms; Token refers to
the total number of a specific Type produced within a period of observation. Lexical
innovation research typically uses Type counts, whereas over-regularization research
uses Token counts. To maintain a meaningful comparison, a middle ground was
sought. It was assumed that children create these lexical forms on-line, hence each
new conversation provided a clean start. For instance, if the over-regularized form
'mans' appeared five times within a single conversation, it was coded as 1 type.

General morpho-syntactic development   MLU was calculated for every month of the recorded data as a simple index of morpho-syntactic development. For the purpose of this study, MLU was calculated by averaging the length of 100 consecutive utterances, according to the parameters outlined in Brown (1973: 54). Because of the nature of the transcripts, the 100 utterances were located by date, rather than location in the transcripts. Hence, MLU was calculated using utterances from conversations that were recorded on or near the 25th day of each month of observation (based upon R's date of birth).

Results

R produced a variety of both forms. Table 4.2.1 presents an overall picture of the creative lexemes. More lexical innovations were nouns, whereas more over-regularizations were verbs. Additionally, all of the derivational and inflectional strategies were represented. Over the period of observation, there was an average of 3.4 innovations (SD = 3.1) per month and an average of 2.7 over-regularizations (SD = 2.6) per month.

Does the production of lexical errors and innovations change over time?

Production of lexical innovations and over-regularizations per month were strongly correlated ($r = 0.71$, $p < 0.001$). Figures 4.2.1 and 4.2.2 provide information for overall production of lexical innovations and over-regularizations, respectively,

Table 4.2.1 Production of creative lexemes by form, strategy and grammatical category.

	Noun	Verb	Adjective	Adverb	Total
Lexical innovations					
conversion	10	25	6	–	41 (34%)
compounding	34	–	4	–	38 (31%)
suffixation	18	5	12	1	36 (30%)
prefixation	–	3	3	–	6 (5%)
Total	62 (51%)	33 (27%)	25 (21%)	1 (1%)	N = 121
Over-regularizations					
regular inflection + bare stem	10	71	3	–	84 (87%)
regular inflection + inflected stem	2	7	–	–	9 (9%)
incorrect irregular	–	4	–	–	4 (4%)
Total	12 (12%)	82 (85%)	3 (3%)	–	N = 97

presented in a manner inspired by Tufte (1983). The information presented in both Figs 4.2.1 and 4.2.2 indicates changes in the production of each form over time. Both phenomena evidence an increase in production, a peak at 40 months (3;4), and a gradual decline. At peak production (i.e., 40 months), R produced 14 lexical innovation types (3.5 SD above the mean per month) and 13 over-regularization types (4 SD above the mean per month).

As predicted, there was an increase in MLU during the months preceding the peak in production for lexical innovations and over-regularizations, as shown in Figure 4.2.3. R's MLU trajectory is best represented with two linear functions. The increase in MLU preceding the peak in production of creative lexemes (30 to 40 months) is best modelled by a linear function with a slope of 0.35 ($R^2 = 0.95$, $p < 0.001$); after the peak at 40 months, MLU from 41 to 56 months is best modelled by a linear function with a slope of 0.07 ($R^2 = 0.72$, $p < 0.001$). MLU for the final months of observation, 63 to 71 months, is best modelled by a linear function of 0.02 ($R^2 = 0.45$, $p < 0.04$).

Do the strategies used to produce both phenomena change over time?

R's innovations included examples of all four of the derivational strategies. Table 4.2.2 presents examples of these innovations and the ages at which they were produced. The emergence of lexical innovations based on derivational strategies followed the predicted pattern, as presented in Table 4.2.3. The first strategy used was conversion, in the production of a denominal verb, followed by compounding, suffixation and prefixation. This pattern was replicated when the average age of the first three occurrences of each strategy were observed.

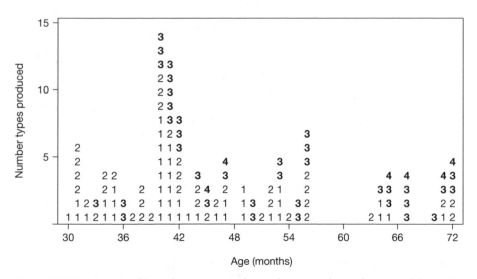

Figure 4.2.1 Frequency of lexical innovations observed per month as a function of derivation strategy: conversion (1), compounding (2), suffixation (**3**), and prefixation (**4**). Bold (**3** and **4**) indicates complex derivational strategies. Because one hour of speech was observed for each month, frequencies can be interpreted as a rate (words per hour).

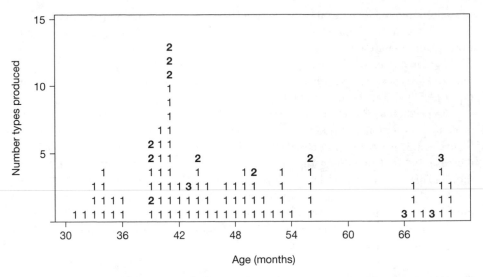

Figure 4.2.2 Frequency of over-regularizations observed per month as a function of inflectional strategy: bare form + regular inflection (1), inflected form + regular inflection (**2**), and incorrect irregular inflection (**3**). Bold (**2** and **3**) indicates complex inflectional strategies. Because one hour of speech was observed for each month, frequencies can be interpreted as a rate (words per hour).

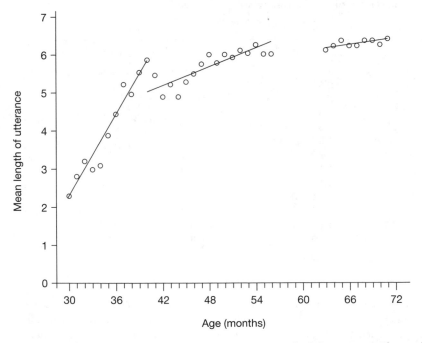

Figure 4.2.3 Mean length of utterance (MLU) over period of observation. Observed MLU is represented by circles. Linear functions are represented by regression lines.

Table 4.2.2 Examples of lexical innovation by derivational
              strategy.

Compounding
    the baker, and the *candlesmith* (2;10.10 [= candlestickmaker]
    thunder + *edge* (5;10.0) [= lightning]

Conversion
    I *magiced* my ball away (3;4.4)
    I *apple-juiced* this shirt (4;0.20) [= spilled apple juice on it]

Suffixation
    You'll make me *vomitate* (5;3.30)
    If you ever want *protectment* . . . (5;5.12) [= protection]

Prefixation
    unpolite boy (3;9.1)
    I got mine *unhardened* (5;6.18)

To test Clark's principles of Simplicity and Transparency, R's use of Simple derivational strategies (i.e., compounding and conversion) was compared to his use of Complex strategies (i.e., suffixation and prefixation). Figure 4.2.1 presents information regarding the derivational strategies used over the period of observation. During the first nine months (30 to 38 months), a higher percentage of the innovations were produced by Simple strategies (88%) than by Complex strategies; during the last nine months (63 to 71), a higher percentage of the innovations were produced by Complex strategies (64%) than by Simple strategies. Figure 4.2.1 also shows a developmental pattern of the increasing use of complex derivational strategies and an accompanying decrease in the preference for simpler strategies.

R's over-regularizations included examples of all three inflectional strategies. Examples of the different types of over-regularizations produced and the ages at which they occurred are presented in Table 4.2.4. There was a predictable pattern of emergence in R's inflectional strategy use, as illustrated by the initial occurrences of each strategy found in Table 4.2.5. The first over-regularized form was the regular inflection of a bare stem, followed by regular inflection of an inflected stem and incorrect irregular inflection. This pattern was replicated when the average age of the first three occurrences of each strategy was observed.

Table 4.2.3 Ages at which earliest examples of lexical
innovations were produced by derivational strategies.

Inflectional strategy	*Age first example produced*	*Mean age of first 3 examples*
Conversion	2;6.12	2;6.23
Compounding	2;6.20	2;6.23
Suffixation	2;8.21	2;10.8
Prefixation	3;9.1	4;3.7

Table 4.2.4 Examples of over-regularizations by
          inflectional strategy.

Regular inflection on bare irregular stem
     We *taked* him to the doctor (2;8.20)
     Little *mouses* don't get mad (3;8.10)
     It *hurted* when I got a shot (4;8.6)

Regular inflection on an inflected irregular stem
     I slept and I *woked* up (3;7.16)
     First the building *blewed* up (4;2.1)

Incorrect irregular inflection on an irregular stem
     . . . because I *tooken* it out (2;7.11)
     I want to be *driven* to school (5;9.6)

Table 4.2.5 Ages at which earliest examples of over-regularizations were produced by
          inflectional strategies.

Inflectional strategy	Age first example produced	Mean age of first 3 examples
Regular inflection on bare irregular stem	2;7.1	2;7.28
Regular inflection on inflected irregular stem	3;2.11	3;2.21
Incorrect irregular inflection	3;7.12	4;11.16

Information regarding the use of specific inflectional strategies is presented in Figure 4.2.2, affording an overall look at the developmental trends for Simple and Complex inflectional strategies. The cross-over pattern from simple to complex strategies was not as apparent for over-regularizations as it was for lexical innovations. Instead, the simple strategy of regular inflection on a bare form dominates throughout the period of observation. However, a closer look at the figure does reveal something of interest. While there is no overall change from Simple to Complex inflectional strategy use, there does appear to be a developmental change within the two Complex strategies. Regular inflection of an inflected word (e.g., ated) is more prevalent in the initial period of observation. However, all the complex over-regularization in the final months of observation (63 to 71 months) were the incorrect irregular inflection (e.g., token). This suggests that there may be development from lesser to greater complexity in inflectional strategies, though it might be more fine-grained than originally hypothesized.

Discussion

Lexical innovations and over-regularizations in this child's spontaneous speech followed a similar path of development. As predicted, both phenomena had remarkably similar rates of production over the period of observation. Also, both forms were influenced by age and MLU. There was an increase in the production of both phenomena, and this increase was accompanied by a concomitant increase in MLU. After the plateau in MLU, the production rate of both phenomena decreased. While there was not a complete cessation of either innovations or over-regularizations, later production rates for both were minimal. As Becker (1994) has suggested, the production of these phenomena is influenced by the lexical knowledge that can aid in the formation of rules and generalizations (i.e., MLU, see also Clark 1982). Furthermore, the learning of conventional nonstandard forms is influenced by exposure to the language (i.e., age, see Kuczaj 1977).

In keeping with Clark's principles, the second hypothesis posits that strategy use will change from lesser to greater complexity. The present results provide partial support for this claim. There was a clear development in the child's use of derivational strategies, changing from simple to complex in the predicted order. For over-regularizations, no such overall change was observed. The simple strategy of regular inflection of a bare stem was the most productive throughout the period of observation. There was, however, a fine-grained change from lesser to greater complexity within the complex inflectional strategies used, demonstrating a sensitivity toward the inflectional treatment of irregular words in English.

General implications

Because immature speakers are likely to have underdifferentiated syntactic categories, Bushnell & Maratsos (1984) have suggested that these novel words are probably examples of incorrect word usage rather than the result of an understanding of derivational strategies within the language. However R continued to produce novel examples of all four derivational strategies even after five years of age. Combined with evidence from similar studies (Becker 1994, Bowerman 1982b), it seems implausible that incorrect usage alone could explain the patterns of strategy use in children's early lexical development.

The comparative differences in the change in strategy use for lexical innovations and over-regularizations raise important points about the developmental relevance of these two lexical phenomena. The change from simple to complex strategy use is more general for innovations than over-regularizations. The strategies for lexical innovations are more heterogeneous and can be applied in more instances than those for over-regularizations. A change in innovative form is usually accompanied by a change in referent, but not so for over-regularizations. Inflectional strategies are dictated by obligatory contexts, and this 'grammatical pressure' is not present for derivational strategies. This restrictive nature of over-regularizations is reflected in the accompanying fine-grained developmental change in complexity of strategy use. Regardless of these differences, the data presented here suggest that there are some underlying similarities producing similar overall patterns of production and compatible patterns of strategy development.

Anglin (1993: 33) suggests that the 'appreciation of derivational morphology . . . begins somewhat later than appreciation of inflectional morphology and compound formation and is associated with a quite gradual development extending throughout the school years . . .' Anglin's study of vocabulary development in the early school years assessed comprehension in the light of children's ability to define a word and in some cases deconstruct the word's meaning based upon knowledge of derivational strategies. The results of the present study suggest that at least an implicit understanding of complex derivational morphology (i.e., affixation) is present even in the earliest stages of language use, and this understanding manifests in creative and productive ways. Furthermore, these results suggest that productive knowledge of both inflectional and derivational morphology emerges at the same time in early language.

Implications for competing theories

The present study shows a relationship between lexical errors and innovations, though the nature of the relationship or presence of mediators is still unclear. Both appear to develop in tandem with one another, which suggests that the definition of morphemes as inflectional or derivational may not serve the same distinction to the nascent language learner as for the adult speaker. Strategies operate in basically the same manner. For example, suffixes are appended to the ends of roots, whether the suffix is used to denote grammatical (e.g., tense) or semantic (e.g., agent) information. There are two dominant theories that have attempted to explain this process of morphological acquisition: Rule-Use and Connectionism.

Rule-Use theorists posit that children are pattern seekers (e.g., MacWhinney 1978). Patterns are recognized in and extracted from the speech stream and lead to the creation of lexical or morphological frames based on derivational strategies. This strategy can be applied both to derivational and inflectional morphological acquisition. Consistent with the Age-MLU dissociation, Rule-Use theories rely on Rote-Memory mechanisms to explain the cessation of novel forms. Thus, memory is equally responsible for learning the distinction between '*cycler-cyclist' and '*eated-ate'.

Problems have been identified in the Rule-Use approach. Predictions for over-regularization rates are too high. A child could apply a rule in all contexts (100% rate) or at the same rate across the board (50% to 75%, the rate of attempted regular inflections in obligatory contexts). However, actual over-regularization rates are low, at about 2% to 5% (Marcus *et al.* 1992). Because there are no obligatory contexts for lexical innovations, it would be difficult to test such a hypothesis contrasting the rate of production of innovative forms with conventional forms. Also, most Rule-Use explanations assume that, even in early production, rules are symbolic. This implication of abstract and broad categories is contrary to the concrete nature of children's early language (Tomasello & Brooks 1999).

Connectionist models are by definition non-symbolic (e.g., Plunkett & Marchman 1993), and thus avoid such difficulties. Connectionist models that have dealt with morphological acquisition have focused on inflectional morphology. In order to claim that the model is truly simulating the morphological acquisition process of children's early language, a model must be able to simulate both inflectional and derivational morphology and must be able to produce the kinds of errors and innovations that occur in early speech.

Connectionist neural networks have had some success in simulating aspects of early phonological and lexical development. Elman (1990) discussed a network designed to simulate parsing of words from a continuous speech stream. Interestingly, the model made segmentation errors, something children do well into early childhood (Chaney 1989). There has also been some success in modelling the vocabulary spurt (Plunkett, Sinha, Moller & Strandsby 1992). Again, the model produced child-like errors, such as over- and under-extension.

A movement toward investigating the difficult questions of morpho-syntax with neural nets is apparent (e.g., Plunkett & Marchman 1993, Plunkett & Schaffer 1999). Although an implicit understanding of and productive use of morphology does not require that they be symbolic, children usually emerge on a symbolic representation of such rules and strategies which operate on a level of conscious accessibility (e.g., Karmiloff-Smith 1992). Children's explanation of words (i.e., Anglin 1993) suggests that at some point in development their morphological knowledge becomes explicit and symbolic. Thus, any successful neural network must be compatible with the growing level of metalinguistic awareness that occurs during the process of language learning. A hybrid model, which incorporates mechanisms to deal with symbolic structure or rule-based processing, might prove fruitful (e.g., Lange 1992, see also Pinker & Prince 1988, for a symbolic system that incorporates aspects of a neural net).

Future directions

Future research should include investigations in three areas. First, the systematic development of morphological competence cannot be fully illustrated by the productivity of two relatively rare phenomena alone. Information concerning the correct use of morphemes should also be included in future analyses. Diary studies can account for the phenomena in question and also afford a look at the development of individual roots and morphemes involved in the creation of novel forms. By tracing the development of individual morphemes as they appear in conventional and novel forms, we can achieve a better understanding of how novel forms are an indication of morphological development overall.

Second, as Becker (1994) encouraged, information regarding the influence of adults' linguistic feedback to these novel forms is needed. Children live in a world rich with feedback. In response to children's creative forms, adults may provide correction, they may give praise or they may even adopt the form for use themselves. Additionally, the model of adult speech in the linguistic environment of children may play an influential role in children's morphological development. Before more can be said about this, empirical studies are needed.

Finally, cross-linguistic studies would yield interesting and beneficial evidence to this line of research. While there has been investigation of lexical innovations in other languages, such as Dutch, German and French (see Clark 1993), there has not yet been a comparison of the relationship between inflectional and derivational morphology in children learning these languages. An investigation of highly inflected or morphologically complex languages, such as Russian, would provide interesting information in the investigation of emerging patterns in morpho-syntactic development. These investigations should not be limited to flectional languages, but also to patterns of acquisition in agglutinating and isolating languages (e.g., Turkish,

Chinese). Is there an impact on morphological acquisition when the form-meaning correspondence is one-to-one? Such studies will provide evidence in the further investigation of children's distinctions between inflectional and derivational morphology in the acquisition process.

Note

* This research was conducted as partial fulfilment for the degree of Master of Science in Educational Psychology at Georgia State University, Atlanta, Georgia. Portions of the lexical innovation data were presented at the 1995 Conference on Human Development, Birmingham, Alabama. Thanks are owed to many people: to Karen Zabrucky, Amy Lederberg and Ann C. Kruger for serving as my thesis committee; to Roger Bakeman for invaluable comments; to Byron Robinson for statistical advice; and to Peter J. Batsakes and Victor Balaban for reliability coding. [. . .]

Part 5

Phonology

INTRODUCTION

THE PAPERS THAT ARE INCLUDED in this part are concerned with different aspects of phonological acquisition and development in children. Both include a substantial proportion of data which work to illustrate the processes discussed. Stoel-Gammon's paper (Chapter 5.1) addresses the process by which velar consonants (k, g, and ŋ) emerge in the phonological representations of words, and hence could be described as both lexically and **segmentally** focused. Segments are vowels and consonants. Fee's paper (Chapter 5.2) is concerned with the **prosodic** features (aspects of pronunciation such as length and rhythm that are 'superimposed' on segments) that influence children's early words. Chapter 5.2 is, then, both **suprasegmentally** (that is, above the level of the segment) and lexically focused. The papers can be allied to different theories in the post-generative tradition (readers should refer to Part 6 for an explanation of recent linguistic theories) and hence offer the student an opportunity to compare modern approaches to phonological acquisition data.

Since post-generative theories owe a great deal to generativism, that theoretical perspective is outlined very briefly here. Interested readers may also refer to Goldsmith (1995; 1999) for more detailed background on this and the phonological theories mentioned below.

Generativism

Generativism in Linguistics is mainly associated with the early work of Noam Chomsky (1965; 1968). Within phonology, the text that really marks the beginning of the generative tradition is Chomsky and Halle's *The Sound Pattern of English*, published in 1968. Here, the move away from earlier, structuralist approaches to phonology is made, and it is to this work that the beginning of the highly influential generative tradition in phonology can be traced. Some important aspects of the structuralist approach to phonology are described below. Interested readers should refer to Matthews (2001) for a fuller account. An important difference between the precursor to generativism, structuralism, and generative approaches to phonology centres on the notion of the phoneme. Generativists rejected the use of the phoneme concept, replacing it instead with the notion of levels of representation. The levels in question are called **phonetic** and **phonological.** The phonological level was tied to the identity of words, and was expected to contain only the significant features of pronunciation that distinguish each word from other words. These features form part of a word's entry in the mental word store (the **lexicon**) just as the lexeme's syntactic and semantic information does. The phonological representation also includes rules which enable it to be mapped onto the phonetic representation. Avoidance of overly abstract representations is desirable in the theory, bringing into play the notion of **value**. Value is determined by relative simplicity in the rules for mapping one representation onto another.

A further important difference between structuralist and generativist approaches relates to the units with which the two are concerned. The generativist considers morphology to be of legitimate phonological interest since many morphological alternations rely on an underlying phonologically motivated alternation. For example, the variation between past tense <ed> forms in the words *passed, buzzed,* and *sorted* (respectively /t/, /d/ and /ɪd/) is determined by the last sound segment of the word stem that the suffix is on. The structuralist, however, assigned such phenomena to the province of morphophonemics and therefore beyond the remit of phonologists. Readers may find the discussion on this topic in Peters' paper (Chapter 6.1) useful.

There are substantial differences between some of the kinds of phonology that developed out of classical generative phonology. For the most part, post-classical generativist theories have diverged in such a way that the formulations of each are not easily compatible. For example, the units of analysis in **autosegmental phonology** and **prosodic morphology** (a branch of phonology despite the name) are distinct and represent discrete ways of approaching phonological analysis. Goldsmith (1999) points out, however, that these theories are united by a common philosophical ideology. While structuralism is underpinned by a notion of a formal arrangement of rules and structures, generativism entails a creativity in the role of the individual in uncovering such rules and structures. The papers below orient to the notion that the language learner does not simply wait to discover the structure of her language, but actively constructs it in some way. Generativist and post-generativist theories are alike, in that phonological processing and the psycholinguistic reality of such processes are issues which cannot be ignored. Perhaps nowhere so much as in phonological acquisition are issues of theory and process so inextricably bound together. In this respect, phonological acquisition represents the vanguard which leads modern phonological theories.

The papers

Chapter 5.1 by **Carol Stoel-Gammon** concentrates on two relatively common phenomena in young children's speech: **velar fronting** and **velar assimilation**. When a velar consonant (k, g or ŋ) is pronounced the tongue touches or comes close to the soft palate in the roof of the mouth. Velar fronting involves the child pronouncing what is supposed to be a velar consonant in the alveolar position instead (i.e. on the ridge immediately behind the upper teeth), as /t, d/ or /n/. Expressed differently this means that a **dorsal articulation** (that is, one made with the back part of the tongue) becomes a **coronal articulation** (that is, one made with the part of the tongue just behind the tip). Velar assimilation involves a non-velar consonant becoming velar under the influence of a velar elsewhere in the target word. It may be either **regressive** (that is, anticipatory, in that the realisation of a sound may be influenced by a later occurring sound) or **progressive** (where the realisation of a sound is affected by an earlier occurring one). Stoel-Gammon uses the data to propose **implicational universals** regarding how velar segments are acquired. An implicational universal is simply a rule which has been deduced from the facts and contexts of occurrence of particular phenomena: in this case, velar fronting and assimilation. The case for implicational universals involving fronting and assimilation is made in a robust way. However, Stoel-Gammon is unable to find enough evidence to posit a clear relationship between velar assimilation and vowels in the same word. Stoel-Gammon's paper is an excellent example of the process of rule induction on the strength of an impressive body of evidence (67 children between 15 and 32 months provide the data). She clearly demonstrates the step-by-step processes which lead to the construction of a universal, presenting her arguments in a transparent manner.

Whilst not ascribing overtly to a particular theory of phonology, Stoel-Gammon's analysis is in accordance with an **autosegmental** theoretical framework (Goldsmith 1976). Autosegmental theory is concerned with the relationships between segments in phonetic representation. Productions of an individual segment can be understood in terms of the features of other co-occuring (or **associated**) segments. Associations between segments are represented in the theory by association lines which determine how co-articulation effects (that is, influences on neighbouring sounds) will show up in the affected segments. The theory has a firm basis in articulatory requirements, and hence can be related to the assimilation and fronting phenomena discussed in Chapter 5.1.

E. **Jane Fee**'s paper (Chapter 5.2) is an example of work carried out in the field of prosodic morphology (McCarthy and Prince 1986). In it she introduces the concept of **mora** (syllable weight). Syllables are described as heavy if they contain two morae (bimoraic), and light if they contain only one (monomoraic). Heavy (bimoraic) syllables are those which contain (besides an optional onset consonant) both a vowel and either a **coda** consonant, (that is, one at the end of the syllable) or a long vowel or a diphthong. Morae are part of the prosodic hierarchy: one or more morae make a syllable, one or more syllables make a foot, and one or more feet make a word. The prosodic hierarchy can be utilised to explain certain aspects of development in children's early word productions.

As suggested above, Fee's theoretical stance is distinct from that of Stoel-Gammon (Chapter 5.1). Stoel-Gammon focuses on the process of segmental acquisition, while Fee addresses acquisition of prosodically defined word shapes. Both agree however, that the units of interest in phonological acquisition lie beyond the segment, and that processes of acquisition are most realistically explained by theories which place such structures at their centre.

In Fee's paper children are shown as progressing through four stages of prosodic development: core syllables, minimal words, stress-feet, prosodic words. Since minimal words are the focus of interest in her paper, this stage is further broken down into three sub-stages: bisyllabic core syllables, bimoraic syllables (with coda consonants), bimoraic syllables (with vowel length). The critical fact about minimal words is that they have to contain binary feet. A foot can be binary either because it has two syllables (bisyllabic) or two morae (bimoraic). Children begin by acting as if this binary state can only be accomplished with two syllables. As they grow, they gradually begin also to produce binary feet with two morae. En route to bimoraicity, children pass through a stage where they will produce only a vowel plus coda consonant, before arriving at a point where a bimoraic syllable can also be realised by a long vowel.

Prosody (the study of features such as length, rhythm and intonation) is somewhat neglected in developmental phonology, possibly due to the difficulty of transcribing it accurately (readers interested in methodological issues are referred to Part 2 of this volume). This difficulty is compounded in the speech of young children, for whom the production target may not always be clear to adult listeners. However, the prosodic hierarchy is able to account rather neatly for the observed patterns of development as outlined by Fee. Her paper has the additional attraction of including cross-linguistic evidence from Hungarian, which adds further weight to her argument. Further to this, prosody has long been cited as the aspect of pronunciation that infants first latch on to (**bootstrapping**) and therefore takes an important role in many accounts of language acquisition. If these accounts are to be accepted, then in the interests of theoretical parsimony, prosody should be incorporated into accounts of children's early language. Fee's paper introduces the reader to a way of considering children's early productions at a level beyond (or, more accurately, beneath) the syllable, and in so doing allows us to account for productions that would otherwise appear perplexing. For instance, few if any children progress neatly from a stage of monosyllabic utterances by adding segments in order of their acquisition. If prosodic explanations are neglected, then researchers are left with little option but to somewhat unsatisfactorily explain children's production choices as arising because certain sounds have more salient properties than others, the question of salience of course needing further definition.

The papers included here represent new and exciting developments in phonological acquisition theory. Far more dynamic and with greater explanatory power than pre-generative theories, they exemplify how a field can be invigorated once it moves beyond a rigidly systematic units and structure-based account. As such, the maturity of the field begins to make itself felt. Structuralism can be seen as both a stage that was necessary in order to lay the foundations of modern theory, and equally as a stage that must necessarily be superseded. In the theoretical under-pinnings of these papers, the systematicity with which phonology has always been concerned is no longer defined by rigidity, but is both fluid and flexible.

Carol Stoel-Gammon

ON THE ACQUISITION OF VELARS
IN ENGLISH

THIS CHAPTER FOCUSES ON THE productions of velar consonants in the speech of children acquiring English. Previous research has shown that velars are less frequent than Labial and Coronal consonants in late babbling, and are generally acquired later than other places of articulation during the period of meaningful speech (Stoel-Gammon, 1985). The study focuses on two common production patterns that involve velars: Velar Fronting and Velar Assimilation; for each pattern, effects of word and syllable position and segmental interactions are examined.

The data are drawn from published and unpublished sources and include longitudinal and cross sectional data from 67 normally developing children aged 15–32 months. With the exception of NE (see section 4.1 [this chapter]), all subjects had normally developing phonological systems. Findings reveal the presence of clear subpatterns in the occurrence of the two processes in question. These subpatterns, conditioned by particular phonological contexts, serve as the basis for positing implicational universals regarding the occurrence of velars and for a proposed set of hypotheses regarding stages of acquisition of velars by children acquiring English.

1 Velar Fronting and Velar Assimilation

Velar Fronting is a relatively common error pattern in early child speech wherein velar consonants in the target word are produced as alveolars in the child's form.

1996, reprinted with permission from B. Bernhardt, J. Gilbert and D. Ingram (eds), *Proceedings of the UBC International Conference on Phonological Acquisition*, pp. 201–15.

Stoel-Gammon and Stemberger (1994) reported that 24 of the 51 subjects in their study produced words in which Velar Fronting was present. Examples of this phenomenon, along with subject's identification and age at time of production are shown below.

go	[do]	(RW, 18 mos)
big	[bɪd]	(KW, 18 mos)
cup	[tʌp]	(TE, 24 mos)
duck	[dʌt]	(LP, 24 mos)
OK	[otʰeɪ]	(MC, 24 mos)

(Note: Transcriptions in examples are from the original sources, thus varying somewhat in format. In some cases, non-essential diacritics have been omitted.)

Velar Assimilation (also called Velar Harmony) is a process whereby Labial and Coronal consonants in the target word are produced as velars when another velar consonant is present in the target form. In the Stoel-Gammon and Stemberger data set, 19 children (of 51) produced forms in which Coronal targets assimilated to velars: 5 of the 19 subjects also produced forms in which Labial targets assimilated to velars. Examples include:

coffee	[kaki]	(DG, 16 mos)
pocket	[gak]	(DM, 24 mos)
fork	[gɔk]	(Cl, 18 mos)
truck	[gʌk]	(KG, 24 mos)
chicken	[kɪkən]	(KW, 18 mos)
doggie	[gagi]	(HM, 18 mos)

When the processes of Velar Fronting and Velar Assimilation are examined on a subject-by-subject basis, it becomes apparent that use of these processes is not uniform. Although some children produce velar targets as alveolars in all contexts, many produce velars correctly in some words while rendering them as alveolars in others. In like fashion, Velar Assimilation is present in some, but not all, words where it might occur. One explanation for these differences is that they are lexically determined; i.e., that a child learns to say a particular word with or without Velar Fronting (or Velar Assimilation) on a word-by-word basis. An alternative explanation, and one that seems more likely, is that these differences are the result of phonological features of the target word, or perhaps of phonological characteristics of the child's production of that word.

The goal of this chapter is to examine the occurrences of the two phonological patterns in question using a data base large enough to allow for the identification of commonly occurring sub-patterns. Previous research has indicated that word and/or syllable position and intrasegmental influences play a role in determining occurrences of both Velar Fronting and Velar Assimilation. These variables are examined in the next sections.

2 Velar Fronting: the influence of word and syllable position

The great majority of children acquiring English produce some velar consonants in the early stages of acquisition, although a few normally developing children have no velar consonants in their phonetic inventories at 24–30 months. (Lack of velar consonants after the age of about three years can serve as an indicator of a phonological disorder.) Stoel-Gammon (1993; Bernhardt and Stoel-Gammon, 1996) examined the phonology of the first 10 words produced by 52 normally developing subjects and reported that, in spite of the limited lexicon size, 46% of them produced velar consonants in at least 2 (of the 10) words. In an earlier study, Stoel-Gammon (1985) found that only 2 of 32 subjects failed to produce velar consonants at 24 months. The data from these studies reveal that if a child produces velars correctly in some, but not all, words, *position* of the target velar in the word is the factor that determines whether the targets are produced accurately or are fronted to alveolars. Subject LP, below, is an example of a child who produced alveolars for target velars in all word positions.

2.0.1 Subject LP (Stoel-Gammon, unpublished data)

Kit	[dɪt]	(24 mos)
key	[tʰi]	(24 mos)
cookie	[tʊdi]	(24 mos)
car	[taː]	(24 mos)
goose	[dus]	(24 mos)
grows	[doz]	(24 mos)
gone	[dan]	(24 mos)
doggy	[dadi]	(24 mos)
piggy	[pɪdi]	(24 mos)
duck	[dʌt]	(24 mos)
book	[bʊt]	(24 mos)
bug	[bʌd]	(24 mos)
frogs	[hadz]	(24 mos)

In contrast to Subject LP, the following subjects exhibited clear differences for the productions of velar targets in word-initial and word-final positions.

2.0.2 Subject MK (Stoel-Gammon, 1985)

2.0.2.1 INITIAL VELARS

cup	[tʌp]	(18 mos)
cut-it	[tʌdɪt]	(21 mos)
climb	[twaɪm]	(24 mos)
cook	[tʊk]	(24 mos)
get-up	[dɪdʌp]	(24 mos)

2.0.2.2 FINAL VELARS

fork	[fok]	(18 mos)
block	[bwak]	(18 mos)
back	[bæk]	(24 mos)
cook	[tʊk]	(24 mos)
take	[teɪk]	(24 mos)

2.0.3 Subject ML (Stoel-Gammon, 1994)

2.0.3.1 INITIAL VELARS

cup	[tʌp]	(30 mos)
kid	[tɪd]	(30 mos)
good	[dʊd]	(30 mos)
game	[deɪm]	(30 mos)
golf	[daʊf]	(30 mos)

2.0.3.2 FINAL VELARS

lock	[jak]	(30 mos)
stuck	[sʌk]	(30 mos)
cook	[tʊk]	(30 mos)
take	[teɪk]	(30 mos)
kick	[tɪk]	(30 mos)

2.0.4 Subject Kylie (Bleile, 1991)

2.0.4.1 INITIAL VELARS

keys	[tiz]	(24 mos)
candy	[tæni]	(24 mos)
Ken	[tɛn]	(24 mos)
go	[do]	(24 mos)
girl	[dʊ]	(24 mos)

2.0.4.2 FINAL VELARS

cake	[teɪk]	(24 mos)
Mark	[mʌk]	(24 mos)
sock	[sak]	(24 mos)
frog	[fɔg]	(24 mos)
bug	[bʌg]	(24 mos)

Productions of target velars in these three subjects exhibit the same pattern in terms of word position: /k/ and /g/ are produced as velars in word-final position, but as alveolars in initial position. In intervocalic position, velars in the productions of these subjects behave like final consonants, as shown in the following examples:

2.0.5 Subject MK: intervocalic velars (cf. 2.0.2 above)

cooking	[tʊkɪŋ]	(24 mos)
dinghy	[dɪɲi]	(24 mos)
motorcycle	[mosaɪko]	(24 mos)

2.0.6 Subject ML: intervocalic velars (cf. 2.0.3 above)

crocodile	[twakədaɪjo]	(30 mos)
tickle	[tɪko]	(30 mos)
cracker	[twækʊ]	(30 mos)
kangaroo	[tæŋgəru]	(30 mos)

2.0.7 Subject Kylie: intervocalic velars (cf. 2.0.4 above)

mackerel	[mæko]	(24 mos)
broken	[boʊkɪn]	(24 mos)
doggie	[dɔgi]	(24 mos)
chicken	[tɪkɪn]	(24 mos)

In terms of the effects of word position, the examples from MK, ML, and Kylie in 2.0.2–2.0.7 are representative of the data from all 67 children in the sample. For subjects who produced target velars in some contexts, velar targets were produced as alveolars in word-initial position, but not in intervocalic or final position. The only exceptions occurred when the intervocalic velar preceded a stressed vowel. In these cases, productions conformed to the pattern documented for word-initial position, and the velar was fronted to an alveolar. The examples from ML (the child cited in 2.0.3 and 2.0.5 above) and KG (Stoel-Gammon, unpublished data), below, illustrate the effects of stress on velar productions:

2.1 Intervocalic velar targets following a stressed vowel

tickle	[tɪko]	(ML, 30 mos)
cracker	[twækʊ]	(ML, 30 mos)
finger	[pʌŋgo]	(KG, 24 mos)
sugar	[ʊgə]	(KG, 24 mos)

2.2 Intervocalic velar targets preceding a stressed vowel

because	[bitʌz]	(ML, 30 mos)
OK	[otʰeɪ]	(ML, 30 mos)
racoon	[wətun]	(ML, 30 mos)
OK	[otʰeɪ	(KG, 24 mos)
again	[ədɛn]	(KG, 24 mos)

In these examples, intervocalic velar consonants following a stressed vowel behave like word-final velars, and thus appear to be codas rather than onsets. In contrast, intervocalic velars preceding a stressed vowel conform to the pattern of word-initial velars. Chiat (1989) reported similar patterning in the production of fricatives in the subject she studied.[. . .]

2.3 Summary

The data at hand can be summarized in a set of general statements regarding the occurrence of Velar Fronting in the 67 children involved in this study. They also serve as the basis for an implicational universal regarding velar consonants in children's productions and for a prediction regarding order of acquisition:

Summary (1) In the productions of some children, Velar Fronting occurred in all word positions. (2) In the productions of some children, Velar Fronting occurred only in word-initial and intervocalic position preceding a stressed vowel; velar targets were produced accurately in other positions. (3) No child in the study exhibited a pattern of Velar Fronting only in word-final position.

These observations allow us to posit an *implicational universal* regarding the occurrence of Velar Fronting in a given child's speech. Implicational universals are statements regarding the occurrence of phonological patterns: The presence of the pattern in one environment (context A) implies its presence in another (context B). The universal pattern is not reversible; thus, presence of the pattern in context B predicts nothing about its presence in context A.

Implicational universal for Velar Fronting: The presence of Velar Fronting in word-final position position implies its presence in word-initial position.

Based on the implicational universal, the following hypothesis can be made regarding the acquisition of velar consonants:

Order of acquisition hypothesis: 1. At the earliest stage, velar targets are fronted to alveolars in all word/syllable position. 2. At the next stage, velar targets in coda position are produced correctly; velar targets in onset position are produced as alveolars when they occur in onset position. 3. Velar targets are produced correctly in all positions.

Children may enter this developmental sequence at any of the three stages. Thus, some children may produce velars accurately in all word positions from the onset of speech; others may produce velars accurately only at the ends of words or syllables. The important aspect of the hypothesis is that it is unidirectional. A child may move from Stage 1 to Stage 2, or Stage 2 to Stage 3, but may not move from a later stage to an earlier one.

3 Velar Assimilation

As stated previously, Velar Assimilation is a phonological pattern in which a non-velar consonant is assimilated to a velar consonant within the same word, yielding forms in which a Labial or Coronal target is produced as a velar. Published studies and preliminary analysis of the data from the children in this study suggests the presence of three sub-patterns in the occurrence of Velar Assimilation: (1) asymmetries in the *direction* of the assimilation; (2) asymmetries in the *scope* of the assimilation; and (3) the influence of neighbouring vowels. The first two variables are discussed in this section; the third is treated in the following section on consonant-vowel interactions.

3.1 The direction of Velar Assimilation

Assimilations can either be progressive or regressive. Progressive Velar Assimilation occurs when a velar consonant influences a following non-velar consonant in the word, as in *cup* pronounced as [kʌk]. Regressive Velar Assimilation occurs when a velar consonant influences a preceding non-velar consonant as in *bug* pronounced as [gʌg] or *tick* as [kɪk]. Data from the present study show that a relatively small number of subjects exhibited both progressive and regressive Velar Assimilation patterns. AS (Smith, 1973) is one of these children:

3.1.1 Subject AS: Progressive and regressive Velar Assimilation

coach	[guːk]	(26 mos)
kiss	[gik]	(26 mos)
kitchen	[gigən]	(26 mos)
glasses	[gagi]	(26 mos)
good	[gug]	(26 mos)
biscuit	[bigik]	(26 mos)
take	[geːk]	(26 mos)
talk	[gɔːk]	(26 mos)
taxi	[gægi]	(26 mos)
tickle	[gigu]	(26 mos)
dark	[gaːk]	(26 mos)
drink	[gik]	(26 mos)

The data for many children in the study contain words in which regressive, but not progressive, Velar Assimilation was present; data from DM (Menn, 1971) illustrate this pattern:

3.1.2 Subject DM

3.1.2.1 OCCURRENCES OF REGRESSIVE VELAR ASSIMILATION

pocket	[gak]	(24 mos)
truck	[gʌk]	(24 mos)
dog	[gɔg]	(25 mos)
stick	[gik]	(25 mos)
tongue	[gʌŋ]	(25 mos)
drink	[giŋk]	(25 mos)

In each of the words in 3.1.2.1, the initial consonant was produced as a velar conforming to the pattern of regressive assimilation. The following set of examples show that, in spite of the presence of regressive Velar Assimilation, progressive Velar Assimilation did not occur in DM's speech at this age.

3.1.2.2 NON-OCCURRENCE OF PROGRESSIVE VELAR ASSIMILATION

glasses	[gæs]	(24 mos)
good	[gʊb]	(25 mos)
cat	[gæt]	(25 mos)
squeeze	[gɪz]	(25 mos)
clover	[gov]	(25 mos)
gone	[gɔn]	(25 mos)

The second example of asymmetrical application of Velar Assimilation comes from AS (cited in 3.1.1 above), whose speech was characterized by both progressive and regressive assimilation at 26 months. One month later, his use of regressive Velar Assimilation remained unchanged, but words that had undergone progressive Velar Assimilation (see 3.1.1) were now produced without it, as shown in 3.1.3.2 below.

3.1.3 Subject AS (Smith, 1973)

3.1.3.1 OCCURRENCES OF REGRESSIVE VELAR ASSIMILATIONS (CF. 3.1.1 ABOVE)

take	[ge:k]	(26–31 mos)
talk	[gɔ:k]	(26–32 mos)
taxi	[gægi]	(26–32 mos)
tickle	[gigu]	(26–31 mos)
dark	[ga:k]	(26–31 mos)
choke	[go:k]	(26–31 mos)
jog	[gɔk]	(26–30 mos)

3.1.3.2 NON-OCCURRENCE OF PROGRESSIVE VELAR ASSIMILATION

cart	[gaːt]	(27 mos)
cat	[gæt]	(27 mos)
coat	[goːt]	(27 mos)
God	[gɔt]	(27 mos)
get	[gɛt]	(27 mos)
kitchen	[gɪtən]	(28 mos)
kiss	[git]	(29 mos)

3.2 Summary

Occurrences of regressive and progressive Velar Assimilation in the data from this study can be summarized as follows: (1) Both progressive and regressive Velar Assimilation were present in the productions of some children. (2) Only regressive Velar Assimilation was present in the productions of some children. (3) No child exhibited only progressive Velar Assimilation. The summary serves as the basis of an implicational universal and a hypothesis regarding stages of acquisition:

Implicational universal: The presence of progressive Velar Assimilation in a child's speech implies the presence of regressive Velar Assimilation.

Stages of acquisition: 1. In the earliest stage, both regressive and progressive Velar Assimilation will be present. 2. In the next stage, only regressive Velar Assimilation will be present. 3. In the final stage, neither progressive nor regressive Velar Assimilation will be present.

As with the previous hypothesis, the sequence of proposed stages is unidirectional, and children may enter the sequence at any of the three stages.

3.3 The scope of Velar Assimilation

In addition to the asymmetry observed in the occurrence of progressive and regressive Velar Assimilation, an asymmetry in the scope of the assimilation pattern was also apparent in the data. For the majority of children, Velar Assimilation only applied to target Coronal consonants; in a limited number of children, both Labial and Coronal consonants affected by Velar Assimilation. Stoel-Gammon and Stemberger (1994) reported that 19 (of 51) subjects produced words in which Velar Assimilation applied to target Coronals; of these 19 subjects, 5 subjects produced forms in which Labial targets were also affected. The wider application of Velar Assimilation is apparent in data from DG (Stoel-Gammon & Cooper, 1984) and DM (Menn, 1971), below.

3.3.1 Assimilation of Labial targets

coffee	[gaki]	(DG, 16 mos)
milk	[gak]	(DG, 16 mos)
block	[gak]	(DG, 16 mos)
book	[gʊk]	(DM, 23 mos)
bug	[gʌg]	(DM, 23 mos)
pig	[gig]	(DM, 24 mos)
mug	[ŋʌŋ]	(DM, 24 mos)

3.3.2 Assimilation of Coronal targets

talk	[gak]	(DG, 16 mos)
duckie	[gʌki]	(DG, 16 mos)
doggie	[gagi]	(DG, 16 mos)

chalk	[gak]	(DM, 24 mos)
stick	[gik]	(DM, 24 mos)
tongue	[gʌŋ]	(DM, 24 mos)
dog	[gɔg]	(DM, 24 mos)

Data from Subject AS (Smith, 1973) illustrate the more restricted use of the assimilatory pattern. Labial consonants do not assimilate to following velars, while Coronal consonants undergo assimilation:

3.3.3 Non-assimilation of Labial targets

black	[bæk]	(AS, 26 mos)
fork	[wɔːk]	(AS, 27 mos)
milk	[mik]	(AS, 27 mos)
pig	[bik]	(AS, 27 mos)
big	[bɪk]	(AS, 28 mos)

3.3.4 Assimilation of Coronal targets

tickle	[gigu]	(AS, 26 mos)
chicken	[gikin]	(AS, 26 mos)
dog	[gɔg]	(AS, 27 mos)
take	[geːk]	(AS, 27 mos)
desk	[gɛk]	(AS, 28 mos)

It is possible that, prior to 26 months. Velar Assimilations in AS's speech affected both Labial and Coronal targets. Unfortunately the data needed to test this possibility (i.e., data from younger ages) are not available.

3.4 Summary

Patterns of occurrence of Velar Assimilation in the data from this study can be summarized as follows: (1) Velar Assimilation affecting both Labial and Coronal consonants was present in the productions of some children. (2) Velar Assimilation affecting only Coronal consonants was present in the productions of some children. (3) No child exhibited a pattern in which Velar Assimilation affected only Labial consonants. The summary serves as the basis of an implicational universal and a hypothesis regarding a unidirectional sequence of stages of acquisition:

Implicational universal: The application of Velar Assimilation to Labial targets implies its application to Coronal targets.

Stages of acquisition: 1. In the earliest stage, Velar Assimilation applies to both Labial and Coronal consonants. 2. In the next stage, Velar Assimilation applies only to Coronal consonants. 3. In the final stage, Velar Assimilation does not occur.

4 Consonant–vowel interactions

Investigations of the relationships between adjacent consonants and vowels in the acquisition of English indicate the presence of consonant–vowel (CV) interactions in both babble and speech. In canonical babble, work by Davis and MacNeilage (1995) shows a greater than chance occurrence of CV syllables in which alveolar consonants precede front vowels, suggesting a coarticulatory pattern between tongue-front consonants and front vowels. The same type of co-occurrence was found by Stoel-Gammon (1983) who examined early word productions of children who produced target Labial consonants as Coronals when the following vowel was front (e.g., in the words *baby*, "*b*", *big*), but produced Labials before back vowels accurately (e.g., in *ball* and *bottle*). The link between alveolar consonants and front vowels has also been documented for some children with disordered phonologies (Gierut, Cho and Dinnsen, 1993: see 4.1 below). For Dorsal consonants, greater than chance co-occurrence of Dorsals and back vowels occurs in babble (Davis & MacNeilage, 1995) and disordered speech (Gierut et al. 1993), but appears to be infrequent among normally developing children.

Given the link between alveolar consonants and front vowels in both babble and early words, one could predict that Velar Fronting would be more likely to occur when the velar target preceded a front as opposed to a back vowel. This possibility was examined in the data on hand and was not supported. If Velar Fronting [. . .] occurred in a child's corpus, it was present in the context of both front and back vowels with no apparent influence of vowel place.

Support for CV interactions between alveolars and front vowels and Dorsals and back vowels can be seen in the speech of NE, a child with a speech disorder. As shown in 4.1 below, he produced alveolar targets correctly when they preceded front vowels, but rendered them as velars when they occurred before back vowels; in contrast, target velars were accurately produced when preceding back vowels, but were fronted to alveolars preceding front vowels:

4.1 NE, age 4 years, 6 months (Gierut et al. 1993)

4.1.1 CV interactions with front vowels

dress	[dɛ]
deer	[diʊ]
cage	[tɛ]
catching	[tɛi]

4.1.2 CV interactions with back vowels

comb	[ko]
cough	[kaʰ]
goat	[goʰ]
Tom	[ka]
tooth	[guʰ]
dog	[ga]

CV patterns like these were rare in the data from this study (but see Levelt, [1996] for an extended discussion of this phenomena in the acquisition of Dutch). However, CV interactions of a slightly different nature were found. The productions of DG at 15–17 months, illustrate one type of interaction:

4.2 Subject DG (Stoel-Gammon & Cooper, 1984)

rock	[gak]	(15 mos)
yogurt	[gogu]	(15 mos)
froggie	[gagi]	(15 mos)
duckie	[gʌki]	(16 mos)
whack	[gak]	(17 mos)
milk	[gak]	(17 mos)

Velar Assimilation was common in DG's speech. In his productions in which this pattern was present, back vowels from the target word maintained their place of articulation. whereas the front vowels in *milk* and *whack* appear to have assimilated to the place of articulation of the velar consonant, becoming back vowels. Elsewhere, front vowels were produced accurately. By comparison, the examples from NE (above) and ML (below) illustrate cases in which consonant place is assimilated to vowel place.

4.3 Subject ML (Stoel-Gammon, 1994)

ML exhibited a consistent pattern of Velar Fronting: Velar targets in word-initial position were produced as alveolars; velars in intervocalic and final position were produced as velars (except when the intervocalic target preceded a stressed vowel (see 2.0.3, 2.0.5 above). In addition, regressive Velar Assimilation was present in a small set of words, yielding forms in which Coronal targets were produced as velars. As shown in 4.3.2, Velar Assimilation occurred *only* when the Coronal target preceded a back vowel:

4.3.1 Coronal C preceding a front V

tickle	[tɪko]	(30 mos)
dig	[dɪg]	(30 mos)
take	[teɪk]	(30 mos)
tick	[tɪk]	(30 mos)

4.3.2 Coronal C preceding a non-front V and a Velar consonant

doctor	[gaktə]	(30 mos)
duck	[gʌk]	(30 mos)
talk	[kak]	(30 mos)
dark	[gak]	(30 mos)
doggie	[gagi]	(30 mos)

The examples in 4.3.2 show that Coronal consonants were produced as velars when the VC rhyme contained a non-front vowel followed by a velar consonant. When the rhyme was composed of a front vowel and velar consonant, as in 4.3.1, no assimilation occurred. It could be hypothesized that the forms in 4.3.2 represent cases in which the non-front vowel alone serves as the trigger for alveolar targets being produced as velars. However, ML's productions in 4.3.3 do not provide support for this explanation.

4.3.3 Coronal C preceding a non-front V (and no velar consonant)

top	[tap]	(30 mos)
doll	[da]	(30 mos)
door	[dɔ]	(30 mos)

(Note: ML's production of *took* was [tʊk], suggesting that the assimilation pattern is limited to non-high, non-front vowels followed by a velar consonant.)

4.4 Summary

Example of CV interactions were infrequent in the data from the 67 children in the study, making it difficult to posit universals and hypotheses regarding order of acquisition. The data presented in 4.1–4.3 provide limited support for previous studies of CV interactions by showing a co-occurrence pattern between velar consonants and back vowels. In the case of DG (4.2), the place of the consonant affected the vowel; in the case of ML (4.3), place of the vowel influenced the consonant. The data from the 33 subjects in Stoel-Gammon's study (1985) did not include additional examples of consonants affecting vowels, but did contain limited support for the pattern seen in ML's speech: Over 90% of the instances of Velar Assimilation in the study occurred in words in which the non-velar consonant preceded a back vowel. This finding suggests a possible implicational universal: The presence of Velar Assimilation in the context of front vowels implies its presence in the context of back vowels. At this point, however, additional data are needed to test the universal.

The same study contained a few instances of (apparent) Velar Assimilation in which the triggering velar consonant was deleted; in these cases, words such as *duck* and *dog* were produced as [gʌ] and [ga] respectively. Such productions could represent instances of rule ordering in which Velar Assimilation occurs prior to the deletion of the final velar consonant. Alternatively, they could represent CV assimilations in which Coronal targets preceding non-front vowels take on place of articulation of the vowel. Support for this explanation was lacking; words such as *doll* or *door* were consistently produced with an alveolar, rather than a velar, onset in spite of the presence of a non-front vowel. In sum, the status of CV interactions in the speech of normally developing children acquiring English remains unclear.

5 Conclusions

This chapter has summarized data regarding the presence of Velar Fronting and Velar Assimilation in the speech of 67 children acquiring English. Both processes were shown to exhibit asymmetrical patterns of occurrence conditioned by phonological context: Velar Fronting occurred more frequently when the velar target was in word-initial position; Velar Assimilation occurred more often when the velar was in final position. Taken together, these two findings suggest an affinity between velar place and coda position.

The proposed implicational universals summarizing the observed patterns and the hypothesized sequences of acquisition can be tested against other subjects acquiring English and compared with data from children acquiring other languages. If verified by further research, the order of acquisition hypotheses may serve as indicators of atypical phonological development: Children who do not adhere to these patterns would be identified as having phonological systems that diverge from the path of normal development.

Acknowledgements

Preparation of this chapter was supported by grants from the Royalty Research Fund of the University of Washington and the National Institutes of Health (NICHD – R01– 32065) "Phonetic and phonological studies of child speech" to the author.

E. Jane Fee

SYLLABLE STRUCTURE AND MINIMAL WORDS

THE LITERATURE ON EARLY phonological development shows that the words used by very young children are restricted in both size and shape and that they frequently vary in segmental content from one realization to the next (cf. Waterson 1971, Ingram 1976, Menn 1983). Demuth and Fee (1995) propose that these characteristics follow if we assume that children's early words take the shape of prosodically well-formed units of the prosodic hierarchy. The authors propose a series of prosodic stages which children pass through as the prosodic hierarchy develops. In this paper I examine the developments which take place within Demuth and Fee's Stage II, the Minimal Word stage, using acquisition data from English and Hungarian. It is shown that children acquiring both these languages demonstrate remarkably similar word patterns during this period of development as the possibilities for producing minimal words become more complex. Further it is shown that prosodic restrictions on children's early words help create much of the phonetic variability seen during this period of phonological development. This research attempts to reverse the trend, which has long characterized the field of phonological development, to focus primarily upon segmental acquisition. By bringing prosodic acquisition into the spotlight, many previously unanswered aspects of early phonological development begin to make sense.

1996, reprinted with permission from B. Bernhardt, J. Gilbert and D. Ingram (eds), *Proceedings of the UBC International Conference on Phonological Acquisition*, pp. 85–98.

1. Prosodic theory

Authors such as Selkirk (1984) and Nespor and Vogel (1986) demonstrate that a prosodic level of structure, above the segmental level of the phonology, is composed of a series of hierarchical units as shown in (1).

(1)   The Prosodic Hierarchy

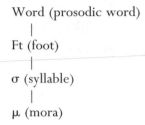

The mora is the lowest level in the hierarchy, representing the notion of syllable weight. Syllables are maximally bimoraic, with 'heavy' syllables containing two moras and 'light' syllables containing only one. Languages differ in which rhymal constituents can be associated to a second mora: Some languages (such as Sierra Miwok) treat syllables containing a vowel and a coda consonant or a long vowel as bimoraic, while other languages (such as Huassteco) treat only rhymes containing long vowels as bimoraic (see Blevins 1995 for a typology of languages based on syllable weight). For the purposes of this paper I assume that both English and Hungarian are similar to Sierra Miwok in their treatment of bimoraic syllables.

Moras are associated to syllables, and syllables to feet. Feet are binary, either at the moraic or syllabic level (McCarthy & Prince 1986, 1995). Single, unfooted syllables occurring at word edges will be associated directly to the prosodic word. Feet may be iambic, where a heavy syllable is the rightmost member of a foot, or trochaic, where the heavy syllable is the leftmost member of a foot. Feet are associated to prosodic words, which represent the highest prosodic unit that will be discussed in this paper (see Selkirk 1984 or Nespor & Vogel 1986 for a discussion of prosodic structure above the word level).

An important body of research (e.g., Broselow 1982, McCarthy & Prince 1986) has shown the importance of the *MINIMAL WORD*, which exists by virtue of the fact that every prosodic word must contain at least one foot (by (1)), and that every foot is binary. A prosodic word will therefore minimally contain two syllables, as shown in (2) or two moras, as shown in (3).

(2)   Bisyllabic minimal word

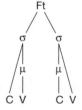

(3)   Bimoraic minimal words

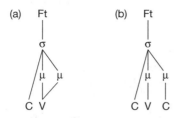

In languages which permit only monomoraic syllables, minimal words will be bisyllabic, as in (2). In languages which permit bimoraic syllables, word minimality will be fulfilled by either the structures in (2) or (3).

Recent work in phonological acquisition (e.g., Fee 1992, Fikkert 1994, Gerken 1994, Demuth 1995, Demuth & Fee 1995) argues that prosodic restrictions play a major role in determining the size and shape of children's early words (and sentences). This research suggests that although children perceive most of the segmental and syllabic content of target words, they are severely restricted in their output forms by immaturities of the prosodic system. Demuth and Fee (1995) argue that four stages of prosodic development can be identified, as the prosodic hierarchy in (1) becomes fully differentiated:

(4)   Stage I – Core syllables
      Stage II – Minimal words
      Stage III – Stress-Feet
      Stage IV – Prosodic words

In Stage I children's words are composed of a single syllable which as yet has no contrast based on mora count. At Stage II children's words are minimal words, composed of binary feet, as in (2) or (3). At Stage III children's words begin to show evidence of the stress-foot, first with one stress-foot per word, and later expanding to include more than a single stress-foot per word. By Stage IV children's words may contain unfooted syllables, and the prosodic structure of multisyllabic words is correctly reproduced.

The notion of *stage* used in (4) is one where at each period of prosodic development the predominant prosodic shape used by the child differs. As is pointed out in Fikkert (1994), this does not mean that prosodic forms characteristic of an earlier or later stage may not be used. However, the majority of forms used at any period will be representative of the prosodic stage the child is in, and over time the child will move forward in the sequence of stages. Frequency criteria are used to determine what the predominant prosodic forms are. Vowel length is considered contrastive when the child is able to match the vowel length contrasts of the language at least 50% of the time (in English, where both tense vowels and diphthongs are phonologically long or bimoraic, the child had to show at least one tense/lax contrast and have a diphthong; in Hungarian the child had to match the vowel length contrast more than 50% of the time). Likewise, a coda consonant had to be used in a majority of the child's forms before CVC forms were considered part of the child's prosodic repertoire.

Demuth and Fee further argue that there are three possible substages within Stage II, the Minimal Word stage. These substages are given in (5).

(5)   Stages of Minimal Word Acquisition
       Substage IIa – Bisyllabic Core Syllables
       Substage IIb – Bimoraic Syllables – coda consonants
       Substage IIc – Bimoraic Syllables – vowel length

In Section 2 the developments within Stage II are outlined for children learning both Hungarian and English. It is shown that during this period some children first acquire the knowledge that feet may be binary at the syllabic level and only later learn that branching may also occur at the moraic level. Children first learn that the second mora in a bimoraic syllable may be associated to a coda consonant and later discover that this second mora may also be associated to a vowel (producing a long or complex vowel). Further, because the restrictions at this stage are primarily prosodic, children frequently have a choice of target segments which can be used within any given form.

2. The acquisition of minimal words

2.1 Acquisition data

The English data used in this study are outlined in (6) and the Hungarian data in (7).

(6)   English acquisition data

Child	Sex	Type of data	Age (range)	Lexical items analyzed	Author (if secondary data)
PJ	F	longitudinal	1;8–2;0	199	
JV	F	longitudinal	0;11–2;0	330	Velten (1943)
AS	M	longitudinal	2;2–2;10	2,037	Smith (1973)
EW	M	single sample	1;4	46	
MH	M	single sample	1;7	84	

(7)   Hungarian acquisition data

Child	Sex	Type of data	Age (range)	Lexical items analyzed	Author
TA	M	Two samples	1;5, 1;10	150	Gosy (1978)
J	F	single sample	1;5	26	Endrei (1913)
L	M	single sample	1;3	26	Balassa (1893)
M	F	single sample	1;11	144	Meggyes (1971)

Two of the English samples are from secondary sources: the longitudinal samples from JV and AS are from Velten (1943) and Smith (1973), respectively. All other English samples were collected by the author. The Hungarian data all come from secondary sources. In each sample phonetic transcriptions of the child's words are provided, although the secondary sources vary as to the amount of phonetic detail given.

2.2 Substage IIa – bisyllabic core syllables

As argued in Fee (1992) and Demuth and Fee (1995) the first minimal word used by many children is a bisyllabic word, containing two monomoraic syllables (i.e. the structure in (2)). Prior to this stage children's words are subminimal, or mono-moraic CV forms (Stage I in (4)). At Stage I vowel length is not yet contrastive and coda consonants are very infrequent. Words and syllables are therefore not distinct, differentiated prosodic elements yet for the child. Subminimal forms were found in the early samples from children such as EW, JV and PJ, acquiring English, and from TA, acquiring Hungarian. PJ, for example, produced six forms for *juice* at 1;8: [du], [duː], [gu], [guː], [gus] and [dʊs]. At this time PJ was not yet systematic in her use of vowel length, as shown by the fact that the vowel in *juice* could be tense ([u]) or lax ([ʊ]), or phonetically long ([uː]) or short ([u]). These forms for *juice* also demonstrate that PJ more frequently omitted coda consonants than attached them at this time. Most of these forms are therefore subminimal words or words which do not meet the requirement of being a binary branching foot, since they contain neither two syllables nor two moras.

Bisyllabic minimal words were used by all children in the data set and were the predominant word structure used by a number of these children. Examples of English bisyllabic forms are given in (8) and examples of Hungarian forms in (9).

(8)   Bisyllabic word forms – English

Target	Child's phonetic form	Sample
cookie	gugi	PJ (1;9)
banana	nana	JV (1;6)
diaper	dʌtə	EW (1;4)

(9)   Bisyllabic word forms – Hungarian

Target	English gloss	Child's phonetic form	Sample
cipő	shoes	poːpoː	TA (1;5)
mama	mother	mɑmɑ	J (1;5)
katona	soldier	tato	L (1;3)

(10) shows several bisyllabic forms used by PJ, one of the English-speaking children at 1;10:

(10)   Examples of PJ's bisyllabic forms at 1;10

Target	Child's phonetic form(s)
candy	gɛdi, kɛni
monster	bɑnə, modə
Patricia	pɪsæ

PJ's forms for *candy* show that this child cannot yet reliably produce the voicing distinction in word initial velar stops, nor can she consistently produce coda consonants. Moreover, the forms for *candy* and *monster* suggest that PJ has more knowledge of adult targets than is apparent in her output forms. In some forms the target coda consonant is realized as the onset of the second syllable (e.g., [kɛni] and [banə]) while in other forms it is the target onset consonant which becomes the onset of the second syllable in PJ's forms (e.g., [modə], [gɛdi]). In the form [pɪsa] for *Patricia* segments from all three target syllables become part of PJ's two-syllable realization. Thus while each of these forms is restricted to two monomoraic syllables, there is some choice in the segmental composition of each syllable.

From a prosodic perspective the most interesting bisyllabic forms are those produced for monosyllabic targets. English examples are shown in (11) and Hungarian examples in (12).

(11) Bisyllabic forms for target monosyllables – English

Target	Child's phonetic form(s)	Sample
box	bæpʌ	EW (1;4)
straw	fowə	PJ (1;10)
juice	čusː, jusiː	PJ (1;11)

(12) Bisyllabic forms for target monosyllables – Hungarian

Target	English gloss	Child's phonetic form	Sample
kész	ready	keze	L (1;3)
tej	milk	teje	L (1;3)
kulcs	key	kuku	L (1;3)

Bisyllabic renditions of target monosyllables were found in the data from English-speaking EW and PJ (until 1;10), and Hungarian-speaking L. Each of these children used very few coda consonants at this time. For this subset of children minimal words initially consisted of two CV syllables, suggesting that foot binarity had to be fulfilled by branching at the level of the syllable. The fact that not all children used bisyllabic forms for monosyllabic targets suggests that Stage IIa may be 'skipped' by some children. This does not mean that the sequence of stages outlined in (4) is variable, but rather that one substage of Stage II may be optional.

In order for a child to produce a bisyllabic form from a target monosyllable a vowel will either have to be epenthesized to the word (as is probably the case in EW's form for *box* and PJ's form for *straw*), or the vowel from the target will be duplicated (as is probably the case in all three Hungarian forms). The fact that children produce forms which contain two syllables even when the target contains only one is strong evidence that prosodic factors are a driving force for them at this point in development.

2.3 Substage IIb – bimoraic syllables with coda consonants

Monosyllabic forms containing coda consonants were also found in the samples from all children, as shown in (13) and (14).

(13) CVC forms — English

Target	Child's phonetic form(s)	Sample
walk	raʔ	MH (1;7)
dog	dʌ, dʌʔ	MH (1;7)
juice	duːs, dus, dʊš, sus	PJ (1;10. 1;11)
beads	biːs, bis, bes, beː, biː	PJ (1;11)

(14) CVC forms — Hungarian

Target	English gloss	Child's phonetic form	Sample
mert	because	met	M (1;11)
szép	beautiful	teːb	M (1;11)
sír	grave	šiːl	TA (1;10)

As the English forms show, children were not always consistent in whether or not a coda consonant was used, and if a coda was used it was often a glottal stop. As PJ's forms for *beads* show, at this stage the vowel was frequently lengthened if the coda consonant was omitted. Vowel length and glottal stops are frequently ignored in phonetic transcription of children's speech: What these data show is that very careful transcriptions are required if we are to arrive at a clear picture of how prosodic structures change over time.

CVC productions were also found in both languages for multisyllabic targets, as shown in (15) and (16).

(15) CVC forms for multisyllabic targets — English

Target	Child's phonetic form(s)	Sample
pocket	bɑt	JV (1;6)
cereal	ɑm	JV (1;6)
berry	bɛʔ	MH (1;7)
again	gɛn, gɛŋ	MH (1;7)

(16) CVC forms for multisyllabic targets – Hungarian

Target	English gloss	Child's phonetic form	Sample
kerék	wheel	kɛk	TA (1;10)
lapát	shovel	pɑːt	TA (1;5)
bácsi	uncle	beš	TA (1;10)

Some of these monosyllabic forms contain phonetic material from a single syllable of the target (e.g., AS's [gɛn] and [gɛŋ], TA's [pɑːt]), while in others phonetic material from more than one target syllable is found in the child's form (e.g., JV's [bat], TA's [kɛk]). The latter forms again demonstrate that the child's knowledge of targets is more complete than it would at first appear.

For PJ, these CVC forms did not become frequent until after 1;10, suggesting that this CVC stage follows the earlier bisyllabic stage. No evidence of a progression from bisyllabic CVCV forms to CVC forms was available from any of the other children for whom longitudinal samples were available (TV, AS and TA). It may be that such a progression actually occurred but was not captured by the sampling method, or that substage IIa, the bisyllabic core syllable stage, is an optional stage for some children.

2.4 Substage IIc – bimoraic syllables with long or complex vowels

The final substage in the development of minimal words is the use of bimoraic syllables containing long or complex vowels. Hungarian has a fourteen vowel system, containing 7 long vowels and 7 short vowels (Ringen 1988). This language therefore has a clear contrast between bimoraic (long) vowels and monomoraic (short) vowels. English has both monophthongs and diphthongs and a further contrast between tense and lax vowels. Both tense vowels and diphthongs behave as bimoraic vowels, while the lax monophthongs behave as monomoraic (Hayes 1989, Jensen 1991).

At 1;5 TA's words were mostly bisyllables or monosyllables containing coda consonants. The few CV forms he produced showed no evidence of vowel lengthening to compensate for a missing coda consonant:

(17) TA's CV forms at (1;5)

Target	English gloss	Child's phonetic form
hal	fish	hɑ
keksz	biscuit	ke
banán	banana	bɑ

However, by 1;10 all TA's CV forms contained a long vowel:

(18) Examples of TA's CV forms at (1;10)

Target	English gloss	Child's phonetic form
orr	nose	o:
szól	is	so:
fűző	lace	zö:

Two of the forms in (18) were produced for targets containing long vowels ([sö:] and [zö:]), while the target vowel in the third form ([o:]) was short. TA was therefore probably using vowel length either for target long vowels or as compensatory lengthening for an omitted coda consonant. By 1;10, TA's output forms could take any of the shapes shown in (2) or (3), although the prosodic shape of the target was not always faithfully reproduced.

All other children showed evidence of bimoraic vowels at some point in their data, with the exception of JV. (19) presents the only CV forms used by AS at 2;2.

(19) CVV forms

Target	Child's phonetic form	Sample
cheese	di	AS (2;2)
nose	nu	AS (2;2)
please	pi	AS (2;2)

Although the coda consonant of the target has been deleted in each of these three forms (and in each case the target coda is [z]), each form is a minimal word because it contains a tense, bimoraic vowel. By 2;2 AS therefore understands that word minimality can be met by bimoraic forms containing either coda consonants or long vowels. (Unfortunately, earlier data from AS, which could document a stage when bimoraic syllables were not present, is not available.)

MH, another English-speaking child, produced four renditions of the target *egg* at 1;7:

(20) MH's forms for *egg* at 1;7

Target	Child's phonetic form
egg	ɛg, ɪʔ, ɛʔ, ʔe

Three of these four forms contain a lax vowel and a coda consonant (either the appropriate target coda [g] or a glottal stop). The only form which does not contain a coda consonant is also the only form with a tense vowel, suggesting that MH understands that monosyllabic words must be bimoraic, and that the bimoraic requirement in English can be fulfilled either by a coda consonant or a tense vowel.

The forms from J in (21) show similar knowledge on the part of a Hungarian child.

(21) J's CV forms at 1;5

Target	English gloss	Child's phonetic form	Sample
virág	flower	viː	J (1;5)
párna	pillow	pɑː	J (1;5)
ló	horse	loː	J (1;5)

Each of J's forms in (21) contains a long vowel. In two of these forms the target vowel is bimoraic, while in the third form ([viː] for *virág*) the target vowel is monomoraic. In the forms [viː] and [pɑː] the child produces a form which is monosyllabic but bimoraic, perhaps in order to avoid a difficult consonant of the target (the following consonant in each case is [r]). In all cases a minimal word is maintained, although in two of the forms the prosodic structure differs from that of the target.

3. Summary

This paper documents several substages children follow in the development of minimal prosodic words. As argued in Demuth and Fee (1995) minimal words first appear (between 1;0 and 2;0) when children realize that words and syllables are contrastive elements in the prosodic hierarchy, and that feet must be binary. Acquisition data presented from children acquiring both English and Hungarian demonstrate that the first type of minimal word some children use is a bisyllabic form, consisting of two monomoraic syllables. It is unclear whether other children skip this substage altogether, or whether it is simply difficult to document its existence. The next type of minimal word appears when children begin to produce monosyllabic, bimoraic words, containing coda consonants. The final type of minimal word appears when children realize that vowels in these two languages may be either monomoraic or bimoraic, with the result that the minimal word may be fulfilled by a monosyllabic form containing a long or complex vowel.

One of the consequences of having to adhere to a minimal word shape is that the segmental and prosodic content of a given form may not match. One type of mismatch will arise when the target has more segmental content than is permitted by the prosodic restrictions, in which case the child has some choices in which segments of the target will be reproduced. The segments chosen may be different in each distinct production of a target, giving rise to the phonetic variability which is so prevalent at this stage of development. Another type of mismatch will occur when the child may be forced to use a greater number of syllables than is found in the target (i.e. at substage IIa), in which case the child's form will contain a copied or epenthesized vowel. Once children move beyond the minimal word stage and are able to produce complex and unfooted syllables within the prosodic word, the segmental content of words will become more consistent and will more faithfully match the segmental content of the target.

The prosodic stages outlined in this research must be tested using longitudinal data from a larger number of children, from a variety of linguistic backgrounds. Data from languages with substantially different prosodic possibilities (from English and Hungarian) will be particularly relevant. In investigating the prosodic shapes of children's early words very careful attention must be paid to phonetic transcription. The amount of phonetic detail must include vowel length and final glottal stops, since these features are crucial to the determination of moraic structure.

Note

* This work was supported in part by Dalhousie University Research Development Fund grant #D-3210. Thanks to audiences at the 1995 Stanford Child Language Research Forum and the 1995 UBC International Conference on Phonological Acquisition, and Katherine Demuth for helpful comments.

Part 6

Explanations of Language Development

INTRODUCTION

THE EXPLANATION OF LANGUAGE development is certainly not a topic which should normally be viewed as self-contained within child language study. How researchers see language development being accounted for – what is often referred to as their **theoretical** standpoint – usually affects their writings and general approach to the study of language structure and processes. Students need to be aware that, whenever they open a book or journal article addressing child language at more than an introductory level, they are likely to be dealing not just with a description and analysis of language. The author's allegiance to certain theoretical standpoints will almost always be embodied in their work, either explicitly or implicitly.

This sounds a very obvious point to make, but in curricula for some fields of study, such theoretical considerations only emerge clearly at more advanced levels. It may therefore take students by surprise that a situation not unlike the rivalry between editors of newspapers, who hold different political standpoints, exists in the world of child language study. Often fiercely defended and seemingly contrasting professional convictions on the reasons why language develops as it does underpin the approaches taken by writers and researchers in this field. Each of the papers included not just in this part but also in the rest of the volume will therefore be rooted to a greater or lesser extent in a particular set of convictions about how and why language develops as it does.

At this point, a clearer distinction should be made between the term 'explanation', on the one hand, and 'theory' on the other. The term 'explanation' has been selected for the title of this part since not all papers included within it are devoted to defending theoretical stances (see, for example, Chapter 6.1 (Peters)). In the context of child language, a **theory** is an attempt to account for processes and language structures which culminate in the adult target language. As such, many theories have a substantial remit to fulfil in explaining how the complexities of a language come about. In constructing theories, many researchers make use of **models**, which are basic or simplified representations of how children arrive at the target language.

'Explanations', on the other hand, may be confined to trying to account for more specific aspects of structure and this is the case in Peters' paper (Chapter 6.1) on filler syllables. However, as was noted earlier, researchers' work is usually motivated by their underlying theoretical leanings too, and Peters is no exception, as will be seen below.

The purpose of this introduction is to summarise the major theoretical themes and standpoints which have been, and are currently, influential in the field. Since theoretical issues are important, cutting across all aspects of child language development, this introduction will be longer than some of the others in the volume. In such an introduction, some bold generalisations will be needed, since the array of theoretical positions is wide and often complex. Once this has been done, discussion will turn to the papers in the selection.

The foundations of current explanations: 'nature' and 'nurture'

The debates surrounding explanations for child language acquisition and development have loomed large in linguistics, various branches of psychology and, in rather different ways perhaps, sociology and education for many decades, with intense activity since the 1960s. The rise and fall of theories cannot be charted in detail here, but a pivotal moment in their history was without doubt linguist Noam Chomsky's publication (1959) of his review of the psychologist Burrhus F. Skinner's book, *Verbal Behavior* (1957). Skinner was researching in the Behaviourist tradition which had links with American Structuralism. Chomsky's early work on language in the 1960s was, in part, a reaction against such Behaviourist theories. This sequence of events helped to kick-start the most fundamental opposition in the history and development of child language theories; what has become known as the 'nature' versus 'nurture' debate.

Behaviourists like Skinner rejected the study of the human mind as unscientific. They asserted that language was one of many human behaviours and as such could be learnt in much the same way as any other behaviour. From the position of a more or less 'blank mind' (often referred to as a *tabula rasa*), Behaviourists believed children learned language through trial and error and imitation. By a process of operant (or language) conditioning, in which desirable behaviour (structures of the target language) occurred initially by chance and were subsequently reinforced by 'rewards' (psychological or material) from the environment (in practice, parents), children were ultimately thought to develop language. Thus, Behaviourism was an early exemplar of a 'nurture' stance, stressing the role of **environmental** stimuli, reinforcement and **learning**. For these reasons, Behaviourism has been seen as an example of an **empiricist** approach and is sometimes referred to as a 'mechanistic' theory. Though it has long ceased to have any significant specific influence in modern theories of language acquisition, some of its over-arching themes still find resonance in current approaches, as will be seen below.

Chomsky's reaction, then, to Behaviourism promoted the 'nature' side of the debate. He failed to see how the complex system of human language could possibly be learned so quickly, with the basics of major language structures in place before school age, simply through a process of trial and error. Furthermore, how could complex structures be learned at all using such a model? Given that adult language is full of false starts, ungrammatical strings, and so forth, how could any child learn the rules of language from such 'degenerate' input, which may not contain all the structures that children need to know to possess linguistic competence in their native languages anyway (see fuller explanation of linguistic competence below, and the introduction to Part 1 for linked discussion)? This last point has become known as the **poverty of stimulus** argument and is related to the **learnability** or **logical problem**, a question implicit in Chomsky's work: how, logically, do children develop language without enough information provided externally to do so?

Chomsky's alternative model or explanation was that in fact language is unique to humans. It is also an autonomous system in that it is distinct from other types of human behaviour, knowledge and cognition. Crucially, Chomsky argued that there has to be an **innate** basis to human language. As his work developed, the notion of **Universal Grammar** (UG) gained importance. UG represents the innate core knowledge about human language and its possible structures which is available to every child. It is separate from general intelligence. All the child needs to acquire language is input from the target language to trigger the process of acquisition, and for the child to recognise from the input what kind of language and language rules it is dealing with. Significantly, this whole process is focused in the child rather than the surrounding environmental influences. In short, it is an innate predisposition to learn language and the innate knowledge about language which allow children to master language quickly via limited and degenerate input from the native language. These themes characterised the 'nature' stance.

Chomsky's writings on language acted as a powerful catalyst for the burgeoning field of linguistics (and not just branches focused on child language) during the 1960s. They also had strong repercussions in psychology and other linked disciplines. Many later researchers define their own work in relation to his **innatist** position (also known as **nativist**, **rationalist** or **mentalist**). Chomsky's theories have undergone several substantial reformulations since his earliest models from the 1960s. These include the placing of greater emphasis on UG; the development of a **Principles-and-Parameters** approach (which has links to **Government-Binding Theory** (G-B) – see Chomsky 1981; 1986) and the more recent **Minimalist Program** (Chomsky 1995), which sweeps away some of the earlier frameworks of G-B in favour of a much broader and less cluttered model, focusing on hypotheses about the very basics of language. (Short, accessible summaries of these models appear in Newmeyer (1998) and Ritchie and Bhatia (1999).) Through all of this, though, it should be stressed that Chomsky is still most concerned with specifying the *nature* of the human language system rather than narrowly focusing on just the acquisition of language, or with full description of any single language.

Chomsky's approach is essentially one of **formalism;** it concentrates on defining the formal relationships between elements in grammar without reference to their semantic and pragmatic dimensions. Some useful definitions and discussion of formalism are provided by Newmeyer (1998) and by Rispoli (1999), whose accounts explain the relationship of formalism with **functionalism**, which is generally seen as a contrasting approach. Newmeyer describes functionalism as a term which is most properly

> reserved for those who believe that in some profound way form is so beholden to meaning, discourse, and processing that it is wrong-headed to specify the distribution of the formal elements of language by means of an independent set of rules or principles.
>
> (Newmeyer 1998: 10)

Integral to Chomsky's early work were his seminal notions of **linguistic competence** (a speaker's abstract knowledge of the rules of his or her native language) and **linguistic performance** (actual utterances produced by speakers of a language which will contain material like unfinished sentences and hesitations that are irrelevant to the underlying rule system) – see Chomsky (1965). Linguistic competence is also referred to in the introduction to Part 1, where it is contrasted with the concept of communicative competence associated with Hymes (1972). In his more recent work, Chomsky has introduced a new opposition: **I-language** and **E-language.** Language in the mind of a person who knows it (as a set of language rules or principles) is referred to as 'I-' or 'internalised' language. This shares some common ground with the older concept of linguistic competence. 'E-' or 'externalised' language, on the other hand, is presented as a set of possible sentences understood independently of the properties of the mind, but this E-language is a construct and does not refer to actual utterances. Chomsky explains that:

> the child is presented with specimens of behavior in particular circumstances and acquires I-language in some manner to be determined. The I-Language is a state of the mind/brain. It has a certain structure (i.e. strongly generates a set of SDs [structural descriptions]). It may or may not also weakly generate an E-language, a highly abstract object remote from mechanisms and behavior.
>
> (Chomsky 1995: 17)

Chomsky notes that '[i]n a highly idealized picture of language acquisition, UG is taken to be a characterization of the child's pre-linguistic initial state' (Chomsky 1981: 7). Lust outlines the significance of the I-/E-language distinction for child language, highlighting the links with UG and the **generative** approaches inspired by Chomsky, which set out to establish a set of formal rules of language that could be used to generate sentences:

> It may be true that the most intense and precise study of UG lies in [*sic*] test of its predictions as a model of the initial state [. . .]. This is because UG is a 'theory of human I-languages' (Chomsky, 1984, p. 8). [. . .] Adult language [. . .] always reflects not only UG but also both specific internal grammatical systems in the mind of those who know a specific language and the acoustic, physical data that are spoken and heard. A profound question persists as to the degree UG remains distinct from the specific language grammar of an adult language. [. . .] Child language also reflects an integration of I- and E-language, but we assume that the closer to the initial state this child language is, the less it is mediated by specific language grammar, and thus the more closely its grammar will reflect UG.
>
> (Lust 1999: 113)

Two further developments from the pivotal debates on language acquisition which began in the 1960s will be touched on briefly here, in order to provide context for the next part of this introduction.

The first theme is a rather crude grouping of issues under the banner 'social influence and social interaction'. These can be seen as offering broad support to a nurture stance. Chomsky's claims about the 'degenerate' input, in the shape of adult language, to which children are exposed prompted empirical study into the nature of that input. Researchers such as Snow (1977 – see also the introduction to Part 1) recorded adults talking to infants and produced evidence suggesting that the input to children was not so ill-formed as Chomsky had suggested because adults in many cultures appeared to make systematic modifications to their language when addressing children. Initially, these modifications were called 'motherese' and later 'carer language' or **child-directed speech**. Speculation and research then ensued on whether the characteristics of this special input were in any sense beneficial or even an essential requirement for children's successful development of language (see, for example, Gleitman *et al*. 1984 and Snow 1995). The broader role of the inter-actions in which children take part also developed as a focus in research, particularly with respect to the development of pragmatics or functions in child language (see, for example, Halliday 1975; Dore 1975; Karmiloff-Smith 1979 and reference to functionalism, above).

The second theme links to the rise of **cognitive** explanations. Initially these came to prominence in association with the work of the Swiss psychologist, Jean Piaget, which was especially influential In the 1970s and 1980s (see Piaget 1954; Piaget and Inhelder 1969 or, for a short summary, Cohen 2002). Piaget proposed stages of cognitive growth, and language development was seen very much in the context of this broader cognitive development and maturation. This clearly differs from Chomsky's view of language as an autonomous system, largely independent from other cognitive systems. In this explanation, language structures will only emerge if other psychological and intellectual conditions are right. For Piaget, language developed following the development of an awareness of reality and it is only *part* of the 'symbolic' function, other examples of that system being symbolic play and artistic expression. Language was not seen as essential for early cognitive growth but, once it develops along with a sense of reality, it was seen as helping children to think, and of course talk, about that reality.

Social Interactive theories such as Bruner's theory of cognitive growth (e.g. Bruner 1975; 1983) combine elements of cognitive theories with social interaction and innatism. They owe much to the work of the psychologist Vygotsky (1978). Bruner's approach is discussed further in the introduction to Part 1 and is especially interesting for its attempts to encompass the development of literacy skills in educational settings, as well as the development of oral language in the domestic settings of early childhood. See Gopnik (Chapter 7.2, this volume) for a more recent theory along these lines.

Current themes and debates in theories and explanations of language acquisition

This section aims to demonstrate further how the legacy of the nature–nurture argument and early theoretical stances lives on in current theories and debates.

There are some general issues which emerge from current explanations and theories and they can help to classify theories into broad groupings. It is important to note that not all theories or explanations address each of these issues, and indeed some researchers feel certain ones are unimportant. However, if an argument is proposing itself as a full-blown theory of child language development, rather than merely as an explanation of a particular aspect of it, then some or all of these criteria might be used to help determine the **explanatory power** of a particular theory. In other words, they could be used to assess how thoroughly any theory addresses the realities of children actually learning language:

- Language structure. It seems obvious to suggest that a theory with explanatory power should be able to account for the development of language structures. However, in practice, some theories focus on certain aspects of structure or give fuller or better accounts of some aspects of it than others.
- What is the goal or end point of language development? Knowledge of the structural rules of the native language (akin to Chomsky's linguistic competence)? The knowledge of those structural rules, plus the ability to use language appropriate to the social and cultural context (akin to Hymes' communicative competence – see introduction to Part 1)? Should competence in reading and writing be embraced, since this is arguably a key part of competence in literate societies (see Garton and Pratt 1998)?
- When does language development end? Some researchers focus on development up until 3;0, others track it into adolescence.
- The role of data as opposed to theory. Where do proposers of explanations start? Do they look at child language data and, on the basis of patterns observed, suggest theories and explanations for what they see, using a **bottom-up** approach? Or do they employ a **top-down** approach where hypotheses or

theories drive their research? The latter is an approach that has been firmly linked to Chomsky's explorations of the nature of human language, including child language, through **language universals** (properties shared by all human languages) and UG. Linked methodological issues are explored in some detail in the introduction to Part 2 of the *Reader*.

- The role of innate as opposed to non-innate influences. This issue was introduced earlier and is still a key theme in current theories. What is the contribution from the child to the process of language development, in terms of innate endowment or effort in practising and learning? Is the child broadly an active participant or a more passive one? How important is the role of carers (parents, older siblings, extended family, guardians, teachers) in providing appropriate input and interaction for the child and in shaping the child's individual language development? The role of the 'social matrix' is the topic of Part 1 of this book.

- The role of learning. Further to the last point, how much does a particular theory depend on the child learning: imitating, practising, observing patterns or being receptive to instruction?

- How far is language development represented in a particular theory as a process which is the same for each child – the elusive 'normal child'? Many researchers find generalisations useful, even essential, for establishing a baseline sense of how language development tends to proceed. This generalising approach is, once again, clearly demonstrated in Chomsky's notion of UG, though his Principles-and-Parameters Theory takes some account of structural *differences* between languages (language-specific parameters) too. See the introduction to Part 7 for some discussion of cross-linguistic studies of language acquisition.

  There is further discussion of the theme of variability in the introductions to Parts 1 and 2, where influences such as social background and gender are aired. Furthermore, many of the world's children grow up in bilingual or multilingual contexts and there is an argument that any theory should account for how language develops in bilingual as well as monolingual children. Bilingualism is one of the topics in Part 7 of this volume. Finally, not all children develop language according to a normative pattern; should theories therefore account for atypical language development in children with developmental disorders, and those who are deaf, or who have suffered some trauma affecting language centres in the brain? For insights into atypical language development see, for example, the relevant papers in Barrett (1999b) and Fletcher and MacWhinney (1995).

It could be argued that if theories addressed all of these questions, and others not mentioned here simply on account of limitations of space, they might get closer to achieving worthwhile **explanatory power**. However, one problem which theorists often note is that the more factors which are taken into consideration, the weaker a theory becomes, precisely because it gets harder to make powerful generalisations.

Table 6.0.1 Distinctions among the major theories

	Theory type	
	Inside-out	Outside-in
Initial structure	Linguistic	Cognitive or social
Mechanism	Domain-specific	Domain-general
Source of structure	Innate	Learning procedures

Source: from Hirsh-Pasek and Golinkoff (1996b: 17).

Hirsh-Pasek and Golinkoff (1996b) and Barrett (1999a) provide complementary summaries of themes and issues in contemporary child language study, whilst at the same time stressing the generalisations which have to be made to do so. Barrett (1999a) suggests that, to some extent, each researcher or writer holds a unique position on the development of language. Hirsh-Pasek and Golinkoff note that ' "shoehorning" a theory into a family may do some violence to the details of that theory' (1996b: 16), but there are clear benefits from assaulting theories in this way. Theoretical standpoints are now so numerous and complex that this can be a necessary step in understanding the range.

A useful diagrammatic representation of the major themes represented in current theories, and how they relate to each other, is provided by Hirsh-Pasek and Golinkoff (1996b). This has been adapted here as Table 6.0.1. (Barrett (1999a: 22) presents a similar pattern of oppositions in a diagram.)

Table 6.0.1 raises several important themes. First, it reflects differences between theorists concerning what the child contributes to language development. It highlights the opposition between an emphasis on the innate basis for language development, on the one hand, and an emphasis on learning on the other. However, in contemporary study, most researchers locate themselves somewhere on a continuum between 'innate' and 'acquired', rather than occupying an extreme 'either-or' position at one of the ends. As Bates (1999: 195) suggests: 'All reasonable scholars today agree that genes and environment interact to determine complex cognitive outcomes'.

A second feature of the summary represented in Table 6.0.1 is the inclusion of **domain-specific** and **domain-general** as criteria. These terms are gaining increased currency in the field. Hirsh-Pasek and Golinkoff (1996b: 16) indicate that the terms are linked to the 'mechanism' or the processes used by the child to acquire language. Barrett (1999a: 19) notes that even key terms such as these, which are commonly used in theories, can be employed with slightly different meanings by different writers or 'camps'. Generally speaking, though, 'domain-specific' is a term applied to cognitive information processing systems which specialise in one kind of information, such as language. However, Barrett (1999a: 21) stresses that 'there is little consensus amongst domain-specificity theorists concerning the level at which domains exist; for example, whether there is just a single domain of language, or whether language processing is performed by several, more specific, sub-systems which operate relatively independently of each other'. An example of a domain-specific standpoint is that of Chomsky (1981) in his Principles-and-Parameters theory, where he not only stresses the possession of an innate bias but also of domain-specific linguistic knowledge. From Table 6.0.1, it is clear that domain-specific theories are more likely to stress innateness.

Domain-general is a term applied to cognitive processes which are not specialised but which are more general and linkable to information in many different domains. Table 6.0.1 indicates that such a position is more likely with theories stressing learning rather than innate endowment. Examples of domain-general approaches are those taken by MacWhinney (Chapter 6.3) and Bates (1999).

Rather than making reference to domain-specificity, some researchers focus on the notion of **modularity**, which has become prominent in cognitive science and linguistics since the 1980s. Following this view, language can again be seen as a self-contained system which is largely independent from other cognitive systems. From this description, it is possible to see why some researchers use the terms 'domain-specificity' and 'modularity' in a closely related sense or even inter-changeably; Bates and Goodman (1999: 31–2) refer to a 'doctrine that goes under various names including *domain specificity, autonomy* and *modularity*'.

Fodor (1983) proposed that the mind itself is modular and comprises several different modules or specialised systems. Modules such as the language system and the vision system exist and operate independently, each having its own distinctive characteristics (though the modules are linked in a systematic and restricted way). This is similar to Chomsky's view of language as a 'mental organ', the growth of which is already preconfigured and which is distinct from other mental organs, though it interacts with them. The alternative view is that the mind has general purpose processing capacities to deal with not only language but other cognitive tasks too.

Further to this, though, language systems (the human **language faculty** – see, for example, Pinker 1984; Chomsky 1986: 24) can themselves be viewed as operating a number of semi-autonomous sub-systems which may be separately wired in the brain. Each sub-system is responsible for particular aspects of linguistic competence. So, for example, the existence of a separate phonetic sub-system with several modules dealing with different aspects of the sound signal may be posited, along with a separate one for grammar with a number of specialised modules, each with its own remit. The Case and X-bar systems are examples of Chomskyan modules in syntax. The case module ensures that the right number of appropriately marked noun phrases accompanies a given verb. The X-bar module could be said to oversee the packaging of head constituents and their modifiers in phrases. These sub-systems interact with each other to produce language. This sense of modularity owes much to Government Binding Theory (Chomsky 1981; 1986). It is reflected in **formalist approaches**, such as that taken in Chapter 6.2 by Hyams.

On the other hand, functionalist accounts (mentioned above) maintain that the forms of any language are in some way determined by their communicative function, by features of human cognition, or by both. A key functionalist tenet is that grammar can emerge from discourse. These convictions usually result in opposition to the notion of autonomous modules of language (whereby discourse would be distinct from grammar; semantics from pragmatics, etc.); to the notion that language is somehow separate from general cognition; and to a strong innatist or UG stance. As will be seen from later discussion of Chapter 6.3, the work of Brian MacWhinney is often associated with a functionalist approach.

Evidence from language pathology has provided some support for modularity. For example, some stroke victims can recognise who is speaking to them without being able to understand (or decode) what is being said; others may only respond to tone of voice. This could imply the existence of separate modules, dealing with tone, speaker recognition and message decoding. People with a pattern of atypicality called Williams Syndrome appear to have an intact language faculty while at the same time manifesting serious impairments in other areas of cognition. This has been taken as evidence favouring a modular interpretation of brain function. However, Karmiloff-Smith *et al.* (1997: 246) discuss evidence suggesting that language functioning is itself impaired in Williams Syndrome, which would mean that WS might not be relevant to the argument.

Bates (1999) provides a useful discussion of research on children with focal brain injury. She suggests that the notion of what is innate has to be more circumscribed than a strong innatist model of innate linguistic knowledge would indicate. Her work is relevant to the question of modularity because she asserts that study of the brain indicates that linguistic knowledge is not innate or clearly localised. The brain is highly plastic and types of competition, experience and activity in brain processes have strong effects on brain specialisation. Language should not, therefore, be viewed as a 'mental organ', the growth of which is already preconfigured. On the other hand, the brain is not a tabula rasa at birth; its architecture is already 'highly differentiated', with tendencies towards information processing which are innate and useful to language, but not specific to it. Bates deploys useful analogies with computers (programs need to have the right kind of computer to run them) and with neural networks to illustrate her points and this links her work with that of MacWhinney (Chapter 6.3 – see also Bates and MacWhinney 1989) and connectionism (discussed below).

In Table 6.0.1, Hirsh-Pasek and Golinkoff (1996b: 17) address the issue of the 'initial structure'. This relates to the question of how theories represent the key source of language structure for the child. Some theorists argue that language structure is already present in the child at birth and all children have to do is 'find counterparts for a priori categories' from the target language to which they are exposed: 'It is a process of discovery instead of construction' (Hirsh-Pasek and Golinkoff 1996b: 18). They dub this stance 'Linguistic'. It is the position of Chomsky (1981) and Pinker (1984) and is in line with the broad approach labelled 'nature' in earlier discussion.

At the other end of the spectrum in terms of the source of language structure are theories which focus on what Hirsh-Pasek and Golinkoff (1996b: 17) call 'Cognitive or Social' sources. The broad notion underlying this grouping is that, rather than stressing the innate existence of language structure within the child, such theories stress the environmental sources of language structure. The child constructs language (see later discussion of **constructivism**), on the basis of informa-tion gained from the social context or interaction and/or from inbuilt cognitive abilities. Cognitive or social factors therefore shape or constrain the child's language development. Consequently, these themes have things in common with earlier theo-ries which sought to stress 'nurture', the role of the environment, carer language, social interaction and, in a rather different sense, the development of language within a more general cognitive framework (see earlier discussion of Piaget's work).

From this discussion, it should hopefully be clear that there are several possible criteria which can be used to distinguish theories from each other. Sometimes differences between theories are subtle, at other times marked. Barrett (1999a: 22) suggests that theoretical positions can be coarsely grouped into four types. Limitations of space prevent these being discussed in further detail here, but clearly each grouping depends on a balance of criteria. The days of very clear-cut theo-retical distinctions are perhaps gone.

A combination of the above factors feeds into Hirsh-Pasek and Golinkoff's (1996b: chapter 1) characterisation of theories. 'Outside-in' theories tend to empha-sise looking outside the child for the source of linguistic structure; they therefore tend to focus less on innate linguistic endowment; they tend to take a domain-general or less modular view (so language is not seen as so specialised or autonomous); and they place greater emphasis on the learning process, and on the emergence and construction of language from these factors. 'Inside-out' theories, on the other hand, tend to focus on the child's innate language endowment for the source of language structure and therefore attach less emphasis to social or environmental sources; they are more likely to take a domain-specific or more modular view of language development (so language is seen as a specialised or autonomous system) and they place correspondingly little emphasis on learning.

The prognosis for reconciling some of the apparently disparate theoretical stand-points is not as bleak as might be assumed from this discussion. For example, Hirsh-Pasek and Golinkoff's 'Coalition Model' (1996b) attempts to 'reach a compromise between what have traditionally been called the nativistic and interactionist theories of language acquisition' (p.11). Meltzoff's 'theory-theory' stance (1999) also attempts an intermediate position on cognitive and communicative development. It is neither strongly modular or innatist, nor Piagetian. Chapter 7.2 in this volume (Gopnik) exemplifies the 'theory theory' conception of development.

The papers

The papers included in Part 6 are, as for other parts, drawn from a very large pool. As noted earlier, most child language study is linked to a theoretical stance of some sort and so theoretical issues are aired in papers throughout the *Reader* and discussed in introductions to other parts of the book as well.

A range of the themes introduced above can been seen within the selection, and new ones will be highlighted during the ensuing discussion.

Ann Peters (Chapter 6.1) examines the role of **filler syllables** in child language development. Broadly speaking, filler syllables are 'unglossable syllables', often used in a non-random way and found in the early utterances of some children and in a number of languages. The paper explores their status, including their possible links with developing categories of **functional items** (e.g. articles, pronouns, determiners and tense markers).

Peters acknowledges that her paper is very much an exploratory one. She sets out to ask what is known about fillers, how they can be identified, and what approaches would be beneficial for their future study. The paper was selected as the discussion article for Volume 28 of the *Journal of Child Language* and it generated 11 commentaries, plus a final response from Peters herself, all of which are certainly worthy of further reading.

As noted above, the primary function of the paper is not to defend a particular theoretical viewpoint. However, there has been intense disagreement regarding the importance of filler syllables, and their interpretation seems to be highly dependent on theoretical stance. Peters demonstrates how this can even be seen from the labels used for them by researchers with different theoretical orientations. So far, fillers have tended to be overlooked by many researchers and theorists. However, Peters argues that the existence of fillers in child speech should be integrated into explanations of child language.

Peters makes the point that, in terms of form, filler syllables 'straddle' phonology and morphosyntax and also pragmatics and the lexicon. As a result, they don't easily fit into the notion of modules of language. Peters claims that, in fact, the modular approach taken in much child language study has been a stumbling block to the recognition of their significance.

She explores fillers from several theoretical perspectives: the structuralist view that overlooked fillers since they demand consideration across linguistic strata; more recent **constructivist** views, which most closely reflect her own, that fillers are syntactic elements under construction showing 'development in progress along several simultaneous fronts'; nativist views that fillers are evidence of innate syntactic patterns; and maturationist views that fillers are evidence of maturing linguistic categories. Peters' views receive support in several of the commentaries on her paper: for example Dabrowska (2001: 245) states that the use of generalised fillers such as those observed in the Naomi CHILDES data (see MacWhinney, Chapter 2.2, for details of CHILDES) is a 'unique source of evidence on the emergence of grammatical categories, particularly relevant to discriminating between the nativist and the constructivist position. . .'. In further support of a constructivist view, such fillers suggest that 'grammatical categories are not available *a priori*, but are acquired by generalizing over previously learned instances' (Dabrowska 2001: 245).

The debate on fillers can also be used to illustrate the interplay between data and theory. Peters asserts that the study of fillers provides a clear case for a child-centred approach to language study. Only by focusing on what children are trying to do with fillers (their **function**), rather than by trying to view them as evidence of emerging adult grammatical categories, can we hope to understand their significance.

Fillers pose other interesting dilemmas from a methodological angle (see linked discussion in the introduction to Part 2), and this impacts on any interpretation of data collected. In Chapter 6.1, Peters comments on the lack of phonetic detail in the transcripts for Brown's seminal work with Adam, Eve and Sarah (1973), which makes it hard for any reader to decide whether the children produced fillers or other forms. Johnson (1999) also explores the importance of developing reliable transcription systems that can accommodate fillers, since failure to do so can lead to important information about morphosyntactic development being overlooked or classified erratically or misleadingly. The difficulties of transcribing the language of a one-year-old child, who was making the transition from single word to multi-word utterances, are alluded to in Scollon (1976). When 'Brenda', the child in Scollon's study, started to combine words, single words which had been pronounced quite clearly became unintelligible when combined, or the form of one word was changed in some way, frequently in line with a previous stage of phonological development (p. 151). This instability in the child's renditions highlights the fundamental nature of the challenges facing the transcriber of child language.

Chapters 6.2 and 6.3 were originally published in the same book and form a pair. They were originally written as papers for a conference devoted to exploring similarities and differences between formalist and functionalist theories: the 23rd University of Wisconsin-Milwaukee Linguistics Symposium in 1996.

Nina Hyams' paper (Chapter 6.2) represents a strong **formalist** stance on language acquisition and, as such, her work is aligned with themes of innateness and modularity. Her definition of modularity also makes clear how notions of form and function (see earlier discussion of formalism and its distinction from functionalism) can be seen as separate modules. This is perhaps most telling in the paper's introduction, where she comments: '[. . .] only under a modular view, which separates grammar from pragmatics and, hence form from function, can we account for the basic properties of early language'. She focuses on the omission of *grammatical items* (such as subject pronouns, determiners and verbal inflection/markers of finiteness) at the 'telegraphic stage' and so there are some interesting comparisons to be made with Peters' discussion of the development of 'functors' (items with a grammatical function) in Chapter 6.1. Hyams reviews evidence in support of the view that children in the telegraphic stage, who underuse such items (the 'underspecification' mentioned in the paper's title), nonetheless have considerable syntactic competence with them. This competence is related to children's language-specific parameter values and so is underpinned by innateness and UG. Therefore, her stance on grammatical items contrasts significantly with the constructivist one favoured by Peters (Chapter 6.1) as well as with Scollon 1976 (discussed above in relation to Peters).

Making wide reference to cross-linguistic evidence, Hyams produces figures to suggest that the 'telegraphic stage' is characterised by systematic 'optionality' of functors, rather than by random presence, or by complete absence. She argues that this supports the idea of syntax as a separate module. The low frequency of use of such grammatical markers at this early stage is presented as an indication that children's pragmatic abilities have not yet caught up with their syntactic competence.

(Hyams, in line with many other formalists, refers to inflections, subject pronouns, determiners, etc. as 'functional categories'. This is because they are the items of a language that tie in with pragmatic issues such as time and person reference and definiteness. Use of this term should not lead to confusion with the approaches discussed everywhere else in the present introduction as functionalist. Hyams' approach is not functionalist.)

In her discussion of morphological overgeneralisation, Hyams also touches on the 'logical problem of language acquisition' and the 'poverty of stimulus' themes, both of which she presents as central. Whilst much research has focused on how children *stop* overgeneralising, she notes that overgeneralisation is interesting in terms of where it *fails* to occur. Hyams suggests that this issue is not adequately accounted for by **competition** or **connectionist** models, represented in the work of researchers like MacWhinney (Chapter 6.3). Children may rely on correction from people in their environment (cf. learning) to help them stop overgeneralising, as connectionists suggest, but this doesn't explain the *absence* of overgeneralisation. She claims that **functionalist** accounts (with which MacWhinney's work is also associated) of why elements such as determiners are omitted by children are not supported by the actual evidence from their language; the patterns predicted by functionalist accounts don't actually occur.

Brian MacWhinney (Chapter 6.3) presents an account of child language acquisition from a functionalist perspective. Other terms which should be noted in association with functionalism are emergent(ism), connectionism, competition and neural networks. The paper effectively provides an accessible short summary of connectionist neural network models and how they can offer non-innatist accounts for a range of observations on the course of language development.

Since they have not been introduced in earlier discussion, and since they are relatively recent themes in child language study, some guidance on the meaning of these key terms may be of use here.

Emergentism is the belief that linguistic form *emerges* from the *interaction* of a range of patterns: patterns in input language, social patterns and from constraints in the general cognitive system. Once again, it should be clear that this is not a modular concept, in linguistic or cognitive terms, and that it will depend on pattern recognition and learning.

Connectionism has its roots in the computational modelling of cognitive functions. A connectionist or neural network models the sorts of structures and processes thought to operate in the brain. Each unit in the network is called a 'neuron' or a 'node' and the system involves each 'node' or 'neuron' being stimulated or inhibited by information received from other units which are connected to it. The ensuing pattern of node or neuron activity represents the data being processed by the network. The term **parallel distributed processing** is sometimes applied to the approach as all the processing units compute simultaneously. For a more detailed account, see Plunkett (1995).

In his paper, MacWhinney probes how linguistic form, such as inflectional markings and basic syntactic patterns, emerges from the interaction of different levels of neurolinguistic processing. His aim is to demonstrate how computer simulations (adaptive neural networks) are able to learn from input. The opening analogy of how supermarket queues even out in a self-organising manner is an adept illustration of the idea of 'competition' and 'emergence through constraint satisfaction'. This can be opposed to the notion, enshrined in innatist accounts of language, that there are categorical rules governing patterns. Like Hyams, MacWhinney addresses the logical problem of language acquisition, though with different conclusions. Intriguingly, he hints at the possibility of applying emergentist accounts to social and discourse pressures which shape the grammar and the lexicon. This underlines the attention to social as well as cognitive concerns in his work and provides an interesting link with material in Part 1.

Each of these three papers represents recent work which is relevant to theories and explanations of child language development. Each one has an individual balance of tenets and perspectives and yet links between their themes and those found in early theories are clearly traceable, as are connections of some sort between each paper. It remains to be seen whether the next wave of theoretical work on child language will bring the field to a greater overall consensus.

Ann Peters

FILLER SYLLABLES
What is their status in emerging grammar?[1]

Introduction

SOON AFTER RESEARCHERS began systematically studying language acquisition in young children they began to notice that some children would incorporate unglossable syllables into their utterances (e.g. n down; ə hot; ŋ go), particularly as they moved from the 'one-word' to the 'two-word' stage. At first this phenomenon was either ignored, or remarked on but then left to one side (e.g. Braine, 1963). Depending on researchers' focus, and on the particular children they were observing, they called these syllables 'placeholders' (Bloom, 1970), 'presyntactic devices' (Dore, Franklin, Miller & Ramer, 1976), 'fillers' (Peters, 1977), or 'phonological extensions' (Macken, 1979; Peters, 1986). (See Peters, 1986 for an early review.) Lois Bloom was the major exception: in her 1970 book she carefully described and tried to account for the many schwa 'placeholders' she found in her data on children's early combinations; in her 1973 book she noted Allison's use of a more complex placeholder of the approximate form /wida/. On the whole, however, this phenomenon has not been followed up on until recently.

In the present note I will use the term FILLERS. There are several reasons why it has been difficult to integrate fillers into theories of language acquisition. One problem is that they do not fit neatly into linguists' notions about 'modules' of language because at the very least they straddle preconceived boundaries, such as those between phonology and morphosyntax, and between pragmatics and lexicon.

2001, reprinted with permission from *Journal of Child Language*, 28: 229–42.

A second problem is that the perceptual characteristics of languages that seem to lead children to produce fillers are closely tied to prosody, particularly rhythm and melody, and this is the aspect of language for which we have had the least adequate descriptive and analytical tools. What we have most glaringly lacked are tools for capturing the prosodic qualities both of input speech in different languages and of children's early productions. This lack is neatly summarized by Berman & Slobin: 'Perhaps if standard writing systems reflected prosodic distinctions, as they do phonological ones, linguistics would have long since treated prosody as part of grammar.' (Berman & Slobin, 1994, p. 109). However, Gerken's pioneering research (Gerken, 1987; Gerken, Landau & Remez, 1990) revealed that, at a stage when children are not yet producing functors, they nevertheless are aware of their presence and distribution. In particular, she found that when children with low MLUs are asked to imitate sentences, (i) they are more likely to OMIT functors which surround FAMILIAR content words than when the content words are not familiar; but (ii) they do imitate 'functoids' that are phonetically similar but not identical to the functors of English. [This] suggests that, because of their normal lack of phonetic prominence, functors may at first seem to children like familiar but weakly specified 'frames' which provide 'slots' for the phonologically and semantically more prominent open-class words.

A third problem has to do with lack of uniformity. Since they were first noticed, fillers have been observed in quite an array of languages (currently at least Danish, English, French, German, Greek, Italian, Norwegian, Portuguese, Sesotho, Spanish, Swedish, and possibly Turkish), and yet a 'filler strategy' may be more common among learners of some languages than others (Peters, 1997). Even when language is held constant, children seem to vary immensely as to whether they produce fillers at all. For example, among English-learners, Peters' subject Minh produced a great many (Peters, 1977), as did her subject Seth (Peters, 1983, 1995, 1996), while Menn's son Daniel (Peters & Menn, 1993) produced no syllabic fillers, though possibly consonantal ones (see below). Looking at children studied by a single researcher we find that Bloom's Eric produced many more fillers than did Kathryn or Gia (Bloom, 1970), and that Brown's Adam, Eve and Sarah (Brown, 1973) seem to have produced very few (although the lack of phonetic information in the transcripts makes this inference problematic). It is also surely the case that, because some researchers are more sensitive to the possibility of fillers, their transcripts will reflect prosodic attributes such as stress and rhythm more accurately than will the transcriptions of more syntactically oriented researchers, although I know of no study that has addressed this issue.

A fourth problem is that it now looks as though different children use fillers for different purposes – see the discussion of phonological vs. protomorphological fillers below. Moreover, fillers constitute a moving target, in that their characteristics change with the stage of language acquisition that is being passed through.

To date, therefore, there has been no unified approach to describing fillers, whether motivated by theory or by data. With more and more researchers reporting fillers in more and more languages, it seems time to attempt three goals: (1) to review what we now know about fillers, including the major types that have been observed and the major functions for which learners seem to use them; (2) to pull

Table 6.1.1 Characteristics of fillers at different stages of development.

	Phonological	*Functional*	*Morphological*	*Production*

Premorphology	Full syllable
	Limited set of
	  vowels
	No/few
	  consonants
		Prosodic
		  extender
		Not lexically
		  selective
			–	Phonological
				  extension of
				  item it is
				  attached to

Protomorphology	Some match to
	  set of
	  morphemes
	  in this
	  position
		Rhythmic
		  placeholder
		Lexically
		  selective
		Idiosyncratic
			Morphological
			  placeholder
			May be
			  amalgamated
				Variable and
				  effortful

Full morphemes	Match target
	  within
	  articulatory
	  ability
		Approaching
		  adult
			Split into
			  subclasses
			Systematic
				Becoming
				  automatized

together from the literature a reasonably unified set of criteria for identifying them; and (3) to suggest a conceptual approach that will promote their further study.

A moving target: developmental changes and criteria for recognition

Because the very nature of fillers changes with development, we need some kind of developmental framework within which to address them. For the purposes of this note I will adapt one from Wolfgang Dressler. In his project to compare the acquisition of morphology across some two dozen languages, (Dressler & Karpf, 1995; Dressler & Dziubalska-Kolaczyk, 1997; Kilani-Schoch, de Marco, Christofidou, Vassilakou, Vollman & Dressler, 1997) he proposes a distinction between PRE-MORPHOLOGY, PROTOMORPHOLOGY, and MORPHOLOGY proper. To complicate things further, the particular dimensions along which fillers have been observed to vary also change as language develops. Table 6.1.1 summarizes these changes with reference to Dressler's stages, which will be described below.

The changing nature of these characteristics makes it difficult to identify a common set of criteria that can be used to identify fillers at different stages. One purpose of this note is to propose such a set of criteria. An important influence on my thinking here has been the work of Veneziano & Sinclair (2000), who are the first researchers I know of to tackle head-on the elusive and changing roles of fillers in developing grammar. In their analyses of the early language productions of a girl learning French, they ask an important [and] ingenious set of questions about the distribution of fillers, and their possible sources in the adult language. One of their concerns is whether it is possible for researchers to differentiate between fillers that are only motivated by phonology and fillers that are truly protomorphemic.

Premorphology

During this stage children produce utterances that contain more than one unit, but there is no evidence that such combinations are systematic. They include reduplications, truncations, and sporadic combinations, as well as the addition of fillers (Dressler & Dziubalska-Kolaczyk, 1997, p. 383). All of these operations are quite 'local', in the sense that a child may base a single formation on some recently heard form but does not extend it more widely. Dressler thus considers these operations 'extragrammatical', and believes them to be guided by general cognitive principles such as 'minimal-grouping, figure-ground distinction, transparency, indexicality, iconicity, and inclusion' (Kilani Schoch *et al.*, 1997, p. 4) rather than by 'a separate, distinct grammatical module' (Dressler & Karpf, 1995, p. 100). I suggest that the routine kinds of language that occur within specific interactive verbal routines tend to encourage and support premorphological productions.

Premorphological (or phonological) fillers are devoid of meaning. Most of those that have been reported seem to consist of full syllables, i.e. V or CV^2. Because [at] this unsystematic stage the researchers can not identify distributional correlates, and hence no (proto)syntactic functions, early fillers have sometimes been considered to be 'phonological extensions' to glossable lexical items; their function has been proposed to be one of building an articulatory bridge from one[-]word to two[-]word utterances. Within filler syllables at this stage, the inventory of vowels that a child produces reflects phonology rather than morphology. For instance, in French the final vowel of an open-class lexical item is the most prominent, and hence the most salient. Veneziano & Sinclair (2000) found that the set of vowels included in the early fillers produced by their subject reflected the set of all pre-final vowels in the input, whether part of the same word or part of a preceding grammatical morpheme. In this sense they corresponded with purely phonological rather than morphosyntactic attributes of the input. Eventually their subject shifted to replicating just the vowels of the grammatical morphemes that typically preceded the target lexical items. This is the sort of contrast which can help researchers differentiate premorphology from protomorphology.

One function underlying production of these early fillers seems to be preservation of the number of syllables in and/or the prosodic rhythm of the target (Peters, 1977; Klein, 1978, 1981; Peters, 1983; Echols & Newport, 1992; Echols, 1993; Peters, 1993; Scarpa, 1993; Peters, 1997; Veneziano & Sinclair, 2000). For example, between 1;7 and 1;9 Peters' subject, Seth, variably 'prefixed' open-class lexical items with unglossable syllables: tape ~ ŋ tap; hot ~ ə hot (Peters & Menn, 1993), in the process making them sound more like full phrases.

Recognition criteria. Most importantly, these forms are not readily mappable onto target adult morphemes, have no systematic morphosyntactic function (however idiosyncratic), and may be restricted to full syllables – although the possibility of purely consonantal fillers cannot yet be dismissed. In hindsight, once an individual child has moved past this stage, her premorphological fillers may be seen to have served as an utterance-planning bridge from one-word to two-word utterances and/or served a rhythmic function, enabling the child to achieve the gestalt of a full adult sentence. Thus, the ultimate decision about the status of a given child's early fillers must be made *post hoc*: if they just disappear, they were purely phonological;

if they evolve continuously into identifiable morphemes they were (or became) protomorphemic.

Protomorphology

During this stage a system of morphological grammar is starting to develop. Formerly unanalysed units are being analysed, and combinations begin to be extended to more than one form, but they are so limited in productivity that Dressler *et al.* are only comfortable attributing them to quite form-specific 'proto-rules'. It seems to me that Braine's 'positional associate patterns', such as *all clean*, *all done*, *all dry*, *all gone*, *all through*, *all wet* (Braine, 1976, p. 9), are examples of this limited kind of productivity. As Braine's term suggests, children are becoming increasingly aware of 'positions' within an utterance, the contents of which are either stable or variable. Kilani-Schoch *et al.* (1997) note that this stage seems to be characterized by 'blind alleys' in which individual children temporarily pursue paths that do not lead neatly to the adult system. An example of such a blind alley is Daniel's evident hypothesis that the {Z} suffixes in English were phonologically rather than morphologically governed (Peters & Menn 1993).[3]

Protomorphological fillers are beginning to show some of the distributional and phonological attributes of adult functors, (Peters & Menn, 1993; Peters, 1995, 1997). Although they increasingly manifest the distributions of identifiable classes of target morphemes (e.g. protodeterminers, proto prepositions, [proto]auxiliaries), these classes still seem to be internally undifferentiated (e.g. *a* has not yet been distinguished from *the*, or *can* from *will*). At the same time linear position may begin to play a noticeable role, in that fillers in different syntactic positions (e.g. in front of nouns or in front of verbs) may become increasingly distinguished on phonological grounds. For example, English protodeterminers may tend to begin with stops, while protoauxiliaries may include a nasal (Peters, 1993, 1999, 2001). It seems as if some children are trying to develop an 'item and slot' grammar.

What makes it difficult to talk about the role of 'position' is its dual nature: on the one hand it plays a role in phonology, on the other it plays a role in morphosyntax. Grammatical morphemes, whether bound or free, tend to be unstressed; as a result they participate in the rhythm of an utterance, in that they fall on the weaker beats. At the same time, grammatical morphemes have characteristic morphosyntactic positions, e.g. the determiner comes first in an English noun phrase. As utterances get longer and include more than one open-class item, position and rhythm begin to interact, particularly for those children who seem to be concerned with conveying the prosodic gestalt of a target utterance (Peters, 1977; Klein, 1978, 1981; Simonsen, 1993; Peters, 1997; Veneziano & Sinclair, 2000). For example, Seth produced utterances such as *m pick ə f[l]owers*, and Simonsen's Norwegian subject Nora produced some very rhythmical sentences studded with unglossable vowels: *hun /e/ datt /e/ den /ɛ/ sengen* 'she [?] fell [out-of] that [?] bed'.

A new kind of incompletely analysed production that may appear at the protomorphological stage comprises functor-like units which contain more than one syllable and which are based on frequent chunkings of adult morphemes. (In English one finds forms such as *umma* 'I'm gonna', *unna* 'I wanna' or *didja* 'did you'.)

At first they are rote-memorized and hence unsegmented; for this reason MacWhinney (1978) called them AMALGAMS. Like monosyllabic protomorphemes, they incorporate aspects of adult morphosyntax that are not yet productive in the learner's grammar (Peters, 1977, 1983), and they are used in functor-like ways[4] (e.g. as protomodals (Peters, 1996, 1999, 2001)). Before these multisyllabic amalgams are fully analysed into their adult components, they may go through stages of partial analysis in which fillers again appear (Peters & Menn, 1993; Peters, 1996).

Recognition criteria. Protomorphological fillers are beginning to take on some of the characteristics of adult functors, both distributionally and phonologically. Individual fillers may be associated with classes of target morphemes (e.g. protodeterminers, protoauxiliaries), but these classes are not yet internally differentiated. Fillers in different syntactic positions are becoming increasingly distinguishable on phonological grounds, although some protomorphological fillers may be multisyllabic amalgams modelled on frequently occurring clumps of target functors (e.g. *umma*, *didja*).

(Full) morphology

This stage begins when combinations become systematic enough that we feel comfortable calling them 'rule-like'. Depending on their relative weight in the language being learned, the inflectional, derivational, and compounding subsystems of morphology also become recognizable. Fully morphosyntactic forms have split into subclasses, with distinct functions and with distributional patterns which roughly match those of adult functional categories. Although these classes are not yet fully fleshed out, they can now be said to be systematic.

Recognition criteria. The phonological form must match that of an adult target well enough to identify it without much question; their distribution must match that of the identified adult target without 'too many errors'[5]; they seem to be used for much the same function as the adult target; their production is becoming increasingly fluent, suggesting their relegation to a separate (sub)section of the grammar, which is characterized by reasonably independent rapid automatic processing.

Theoretical considerations

Throughout my research on fillers I have assume[d] that their appearance is evidence of partial learning about grammatical categories. This is clearly a constructivist view which interprets a child's increasing ability to produce these hard-to-identify bits of speech as a sign of development-in-progress along several simultaneous fronts – phonological, distributional, lexical, pragmatic, and syntactic. The assumption is that children must construct their grammatical categories on the basis of gradual learning of phonological, distributional, and functional information embedded in the input.

A contrasting view is a more syntactic one based on the assumption that at any given point in development, children either do or do not 'have' the functional categories that underlie adult syntax. These categories may 'mature', or they may be 'available' from the beginning, but it is not believed that learners construct them for themselves. Maturationists, such as Radford (1990) or Lust (1994) believe that before functional categories have become available to learners, they can play no role in syntactic development; hence fillers are not evidence of protosyntax. Others, such as Pinker (1984), Gerken (1996) or Lleó & Demuth (1999), espouse a 'weak-continuity' position which holds that at least some functional categories are innate and available from the earliest stages of linguistic development; these researchers are more inclined to interpret early fillers as evidence for very early 'knowledge' of these categories.

To summarize one of the more extreme views, Radford (1990) proposes three stages which, although they focus on different attributes, can roughly be equated with Dressler's and my own. (The following outline relies heavily on O'Grady (1997, 340–342).)

1. Pregrammatical stage (generally before 1;8): [U]tterances consist of single 'words' which show no evidence of syntactic categorization (e.g. into nouns, verbs, etc.)[.] Although Radford does not discuss unsystematic combinations, including those with fillers, this stage seems closest to what we have been calling premorphology.

2. Lexical stage: Radford notes that at around 1;8 children begin to produce combinations of words which show some evidence of underlying patterns. These combinatorial patterns (which I take to be similar to Braine's limited scope patterns) are seen as evidence of categorization at the lexical level (nouns, verbs, adjectives . . .). Although such fillers as appear at this stage are somewhat systematic, my guess is that Radford would interpret their appearance as insufficient evidence for fullblown functional categories, which he proposes 'mature' several months later. I identify this stage with protomorphology.

[3]. Functional stage: Finally, somewhere around 2;0 children produce utterances in which functional categories such as determiners and 'inflections' can be identified on the basis of their structural properties. Radford's 1990 position is that these categories have now 'matured'. This is the equivalent of our morphosyntactic stage.

Whichever interpretation ultimately turns out to be 'true', I think we must continue to try to understand what children are doing when they produce fillers of different types. To do this we need to understand the sorts of roles which fillers play in early grammars, including possibly helping bootstrap awareness of particular grammatical constructs or constraints. Such an approach requires adopting a child-centred, rather than adult-centred view of the developing 'grammar'. We can ask perceptual questions such as: what might this language sound like to learners at differing stages of acquisition? What attributes are most salient? What are the relative roles of phonetics, prosody, and recognizable 'words' in allowing the learner to segment the speech stream? We can ask questions about production such as: Does the metrical structure of the target language foster the production of some prosodic structures over others (e.g. 1-syllable vs. 2-syllable vs. multisyllable)? More particularly, as suggested by Lleó and Demuth (1999): What is the role of the metrical structure of syntactic phrases (e.g. noun phrases) in the early production of the grammatical morphemes (e.g. determiners) involved in that type of phrase? We can also ask functional questions such as: What is this learner using language for at this stage of development, i.e. what kinds of functions do particular fillers seem to be fulfilling for this child at this time? Are there identifiable pressures (social, cognitive, or other) that might lead her to try to grammaticize particular bits of language?

A range of theoretical positions can thus be taken *vis à vis* fillers. The most obvious dichotomy is a phonological-grammatical one, which I state as positions I and II. Position I, which was adopted by most of the field until relatively recently, seems to have been based in the widespread structuralist assumption of a rather strict 'layering' of language (phonology is distinct from morphosyntax is distinct from lexicon). It is the recent 'cross-stratal' efforts of a number of the researchers mentioned in this Note that has brought awareness that these phonological phenomena may in fact not always be unrelated to the development of morphosyntax, along with a shift to Position II.

I. Fillers are purely phonological elements

Position: Fillers are an EVANESCENT PHENOMENON which appears in the early language productions of SOME children learning SOME languages. It is likely that they are influenced by prosodic patterns in the input as well as by the output style of the particular learner. Although observed in a range of languages, they have no connection to the development of the grammar of the adult language.

Evidence would be: A. They do not clearly correspond to any functional category/ies in the adult language. B. They just disappear. Moreover, there is a hiatus between the disappearance of fillers in a particular position and the identifiable appearance of the most closely related target category. Some fillers indeed seem to be of this variety, as witness the purely phonological fillers noted by Veneziano & Sinclair.

II. Fillers are early grammatical elements

Position: Fillers are phonological evidence of a language learner's early awareness of (some) adult functional categories. Precursors of categories such as determiners and 'inflections' may appear as early as the late one-word stage. Some children learning some languages may find it (prosodically/phonologically) preferable to produce syllabic traces of such categories rather than bare nouns or verbs.

Evidence would be: Structural continuity with the development of an identifiable target adult category.

Position II can be further subdivided into a NATIVIST VIEW (IIa) and a CONSTRUCTIVIST VIEW (IIb):

IIa. Fillers are evidence of innate syntactic elements

Position: Fillers are phonological evidence of the early availability to language learners of (some) adult functional categories. For those categories which are present from the beginning, they will still have to develop in language-specific ways (phonology, morphosyntax) as well as cognitively.

Possible evidence: Adult-like syntactic properties are present *from the beginning*.

Questions: Is there an identifiable range of functional categories in a given language which can appear first as fillers? *All of them? Only certain 'easy' ones?*

IIb.   Fillers are evidence of syntactic elements under construction

Position: Fillers are phonological evidence that the learner is in the process of constructing a grammatical/functional slot on the basis of the input. In this view all learners must construct such slots, although not all produce evidence of the process in the form of 'syllabic traces'. Development that must take place within each slot includes further specification of phonological, morphological, and syntactic properties.

Possible evidence: A. Although there is some early correspondence with the properties of an identifiable adult grammatical position, both phonological and morphosyntactic attributes are incomplete. B. The contents of this position differentiate gradually to allow for the range of adult forms that occur there. For example, protodeterminers differentiate into articles and demonstratives, or protomodals differentiate into auxiliaries, modals, and quasi-modals.

Questions: When fillers do appear which are recognizably proto-grammatical, how gradual is the development of target-like attributes? Is the evidence more consistent with innate syntactic categories (position II-S) or with construction (II-C)?

Open questions

Some of the things that we still do not know about fillers are summarized in the following developmental questions.

The role of 'position'. When and to what extent is it meaningful to say that fillers are reflexes of incompletely perceived positional slots? We noted above the dual nature of 'position', for linguists as well as for learners, comprising both a linear, physical aspect which plays a role in the rhythm of a language, and a morphosyntactic aspect which helps the listener identify word classes (e.g. the functional category that precedes a noun rather than a verb, or the kind of inflection that attaches to a noun rather than a verb). In learning their language children surely note the linear physical characteristics of the positions of unstressed syllables long before they sort out the phonological and morphosyntactic properties of what typically fills these positions. I have speculated that the marking of position with some phonological material can serve as a 'holding tank' for the accumulation of further phonological and functional information which can serve as a basis for further analysis and differentiation (Peters 1996, 1999, 2001). Mariscal (1997) suggests that positions may also contribute to the discovery of the morphosyntactic properties of accompanying open-class items; e.g. in Spanish, gender agreement on nouns may be bootstrapped by prior discovery of differences in preceding articles, differences which are then noticed in the rhyming concords on the nouns.

Across languages. Are fillers more prevalent in some languages than others? Can we identify constellations of attributes (rhythmic and other) that might lead children to begin producing fillers? (See Peters 1997 for a first try at this.)

Within a language. Holding language constant, it would be useful to have quantitative information about the fate of fillers that are produced. To what extent are they 'blind alleys' that disappear without a trace? To what extent do they evolve into word-onsets? To what extent do they evolve into closed-class items?

Developmental changes. When phonological fillers evolve into (proto)-morphological fillers, how closely can we identify the point at which this happens? What criteria should we use? Are there systematic relationships between holophrases and fillers? between fillers and formulaic speech? between fillers and amalgams? Virginia Valian (personal communication, July 1999) also asks how changes from prosody to syntax happen: construction? abstraction? triggering? interaction of perception with production? What evidence is there?

Developmental disorders. To what extent are fillers implicated in the phonological and morphological development of children with Specific Language Impairment?

I hope that this review clarifies some of the issues regarding this relatively robust phenomenon and provides a more unified framework for their future study.

Notes

1   Thanks to Katsura Aoyama, Catherine Kawahata, and William O'Grady for comments on earlier drafts.
2   It can be argued that sometimes they take the form of single-consonant suffixes, as with Daniel's use of [s/z] (Peters & Menn, 1993). In fact, I wonder whether such segmental fillers may not have been systematically overlooked in the data, on account of their low salience to researchers.
3   The evidence is that he added a sibilant to the end of a word on a phonological rather than a morphological basis: i.e. regularly when the word was a non-reduplicated two-syllable word ending in /r/, or having a medial coronal and ending in /i/, and variably to certain other words – regardless of whether they were plural, possessive, or in a context allowing a following contracted auxiliary or copula.
4   It is possible that researchers tend to classify one-syllable functors (e.g. articles) as 'fillers', but multisyllabic 'functor-chunks' (such as *wanna*, *gonna*, *didja*) as amalgams, overlooking the unitary-functor-like ways in which a child uses them.
5   Brown's '90% criterion' (1973) seems too strict. Certainly it is much stricter than needed to be able to say that a child is clearly 'working on' a particular class of morphemes. Furthermore, far from signalling that a child doesn't 'know' a morpheme at all, the commission of 'overgeneralization errors' suggests awareness of a morpheme and allocation of attention to it.

Nina Hyams

UNDERSPECIFICATION AND MODULARITY IN EARLY SYNTAX
A formalist perspective on language acquisition

1. Introduction: modularity and language development

ONE OF THE MOST STRIKING aspects of early language is the apparent optionality of various functional elements, such as pronouns, verbal inflection, and determiners. These elements, and the syntactic categories that contain them, constitute the syntactic frame of the sentence, providing a skeleton for the "meatier", more meaningful lexical categories. The functional categories have a clear pragmatic function as well; they are "anchor points" at which the sentence is fixed in discourse. For example, tense marking fixes the event time of the verb relative to discourse time (past or present); determiners and pronouns introduce either familiar or novel entities. The early stage of language development (what is traditionally referred to as *telegraphic speech* — Brown & Bellugi 1964) thus provides a fertile ground upon which to explore the development of both the grammatical and pragmatic components of language. We can try to determine the growth rates of the different components, the different roles they play, and the ways in which they interact. The approach to language development that I will outline presupposes a *modular view*, that is, the view that the development of language — like language in the mature speaker — involves a number of autonomous cognitive domains which may interact in various ways. Indeed, I will show that only under a modular view, which separates grammar from pragmatics and, hence, form from function, can we account for the basic properties of early language.

1998, reprinted with permission from M. Darnell, E. Moravcsik, F. Newmeyer, M. Noonan and K. Wheatley (eds), *Functionalism and Formalism in Linguistics*, vol. I: *General Papers*, Amsterdam, John Benjamins, pp. 387–413.

I will begin by reviewing a range of cross-linguistic empirical evidence supporting the view that "telegraphic" children have a rich and complex syntax, and hence that the omission of functional elements cannot be due to a lack of grammatical knowledge. I will then outline a theory of *functional underspecification* which accounts for the optionality in the early grammar. I will then briefly consider two possible functionalist accounts and show that they do not account for the grammatical patterns that we find during the telegraphic stage. I will make a similar point with respect to inductivist accounts such as the competition model (Bates & MacWhinney 1987). Finally, I will briefly discuss the implications of underspecification for the logical problem of language acquisition.

2. Optionality in early morphosyntax

2.1 The facts

Let me begin by providing some examples of the various omissions in early language that we are concerned with. These are given in (1) through (3). In (1) we find examples in which the verb lacks finite inflection. These are commonly referred to as *root infinitives*, following a suggestion of Rizzi (1994). In the languages which have an overt infinitival affix, such as Dutch, German, French, the child's root infinitives bear this affix as in (1a–d). English infinitives are not overtly marked, but as observed by Wexler (1994), English-speaking children also produce root infinitives, and these take the form of the verbal stem, as in (1e, f).

(1)   a.   *Papa schoenen wassen.*   (Dutch, Weverink 1989)
            Daddy shoes wash:INF
            'Daddy doesn't wash [the] shoes.'

      b.   *Thorstn das haben.*   (German, Wexler 1994)
            Thorstn that have:INF
            'Thorstn doesn't have that.'

      c.   *Pas manger la poupée.*
            not eat:INF the doll
            'The doll doesn't eat.'

      d.   *Michel dormir.*   (French, Pierce 1992)
            Michel sleep:INF
            'Michael sleeps.'   (English, Radford 1990)

      e.   Mommy eat cookie.

      f.   Man drive truck.

This early stage is also characterized by the omission of other functional elements, determiners as in (2), and subject pronouns, as in (3).

(2)   a.   Man drive truck.   (Radford 1990)

      b.   Hayley draw boat.

    c.   *Niekje ook boot maken.*   (Dutch, Schaeffer 1994)
        Niekje also boat make:INF
        'Niekje also makes the boat'

    d.   *Nur eisenbahn   moegen wir.*   (German, Becker 1995)
        only train   like:INF we
        'We like only the train'

(3) a.   Want more apple.   (Bloom *et al.* 1975)

    b.   *Veux   pas lolo.*   (French, Pierce 1992)
        want:1SG   not water
        '(I) don't want water'

    c.   *Kan niet slapen   op een schaap.*   (Dutch, de Haan & Tuijnman 1988)
        can not sleep:INF on a   sheep
        '(I) cannot sleep on a sheep.'

    d.   *a Matratze   schlafen.*   (German, Becker 1995)
         mattress   sleep:INF
        '(he) sleeps on the mattress'

It is important to note that during the early period sentences such as those in (1) through (3) alternate freely with more adult-like sentences containing functional

Table 6.2.1 Frequency of root infinitives in child languages (based on Sano and Hyams 1994).

	Child	Age	% RIs	% finite
French	Nathalie	1;9–2;3	49%	51%
(Pierce 1992)	Philippe*	1;9–2;6	20%	80%
	Daniel	1;8–1;11	43%	57%
English	Eve*	1;6–1;10	78%	22%
	Adam*	2;3–3;0	81%	19%
	Nina*	2;4–2;5	75%	25%
Swedish	Freja	1;11–2;0	38%	62%
(Platzack 1992;	Tor	1;11–2;2	56%	44%
Guasti 1994)	Embla	1;8–1;10	61%	39%
German	S	2;1	46%	54%
(Weissenborn, from		2;2	40%	60%
Guasti 1994)				
Dutch	Laura	1;8–2;1	36%	63%
(Weverink 1989)	Tobias	1;10–1;11	36%	63%
(Haegeman 1995)	Fedra	1;10–2;1	26%	74%
	Hein*	2;4–3;1	16%	84%
Icelandic	Birna	2;0–2;03	36%	64%
(Sigurjonsdottir p.c.)				

Note: *data available on CHILDES, MacWhinney & Snow (1985); Adam, Eve, Nina: Brown (1973); Philippe corpus: Suppes, [Smith] & Leveille (1973); Hein corpus: Elbers & Wijnen (1992).

Table 6.2.2 Percentage of missing and pronominal subjects
(adapted from Hyams and Wexler 1993).

	Missing	*Pronominal*
Adam	41%	38%
Eve	26%	46%

Table 6.2.3 Missing vs. overt determiners in early English.

	% Missing det	*% Overt det*	*Total n*
Adam	52%	48%	123
Nina	80%	20%	119

Table 6.2.4 Missing vs. overt determiners in early Italian (adapted from Pizzuto and Caselli 1992).

	% Missing det	*% Overt det*	*Total n*
Claudia (1;4–2;4)	22%	78%	694
Francesco (1;5–2;10)	40%	60%	677
Marco (1;5–3;0)	36%	64%	364

Table 6.2.5 Missing vs. overt determiners in early German.

	% Missing det	*% Overt det*	*Total n*
Wolfgang (2;9)	81%	19%	33
Johanna (2;9)	89%	11%	9
Philip (2;5)	89%	11%	18

elements. Tables 6.2.1 through 6.2.5 give some relevant statistics. First, we see that RIs (root infinitives) alternate with finite verbs. Table 6.2.1 reports the percentages of RIs and finite verbs in a number of different child languages.

Second, null subjects alternate with pronominal subjects. Hyams and Wexler (1993) report the rate of null vs. pronominal subjects for Adam and Eve, two English-speaking children (Brown 1973; CHILDES (The Child Language Data Exchange System), MacWhinney & Snow 1985). These figures are given in Table 6.2.2.

Although the determiner system in early language has been less widely studied than either inflection or null subjects, the available results show that determiners are optional in English and other languages. Table 6.2.3 shows the relevant figures for Adam and Nina.

Bare Ns alternate with nominals containing determiners in other languages as well. Table 6.2.4 reports the results of a study by Pizzuto and Caselli (1992) of three Italian-speaking children. Table 6.2.5 gives some figures for three German-speaking

Table 6.2.6 Missing vs. overt determiners in early Dutch (from Schaeffer 1994).

	% Missing det	% Overt det	Total n
Laura (1;9–3;4)	58%	42%	33

children studied by Becker (1995), and Table 6.2.6 has some figures for early Dutch (Niek corpus: Elbers & Wijnen 1992; Laura corpus: CHILDES, MacWhinney & Snow 1985).

2.2 Parameter-setting

The fact that these functional elements occur a significant percentage of the time means that their omission in other instances cannot be due to a lack of grammatical knowledge. In fact, one of the most important generalizations to emerge from the past decade of cross-linguistic acquisition research is that children develop language-specific morphosyntactic knowledge at a very early age. This is also clearly shown by the fact that the parameters of Universal Grammar, which are tied to functional categories, are set quickly and without error (see Hyams 1993, 1996 for discussion).

Consider, for example, the verb-raising parameter. In French and other languages, finite verbs raise to a functional position above negation and hence the verb precedes the negative marker *pas* in the sentence. Infinitives, in contrast, do not undergo verb raising and hence follow negation, as illustrated in the sentence in (4) (cf. Pollock 1989).

(4) *Verb-raising Parameter*

　　a.　*Je ne　vais pas.*
　　　　I　　go NEG
　　　　'I don't go'

　　b.　*Pas être　　heureux　est la condition humaine.*
　　　　NEG to be　happy　　is the human condition
　　　　'Not to be happy is the human condition'

Pierce (1989, 1992) and others have shown that French-speaking children correctly position finite and non-finite verbs relative to negation and do so from the earliest multi-word utterances (cf. also Meisel 1990b; Verrips & Weissenborn 1992). Some examples of children's finite and non-finite negative utterances are given in (5), and Table 6.2.7 shows the form-by-position interactions obtained by Pierce (1992). What we see is that finite verbs occur overwhelmingly before negation, while non-finite verbs occur following negation.

(5)　[+*finite*]　　　　　　　　　　　　　[–*finite*]

　　Elle a **pas** *la bouche.*　　　　　　**Pas** *la poupée*　　*dormir.*
　　she has not a mouth　　　　　　　　not the doll　　　sleep:INF
　　'She does not have a mouth'

Veux **pas** *lolo*.
(I) want not water
'I don't want water'

Pas *manger   la poupée*.
not eat:INF   the doll

Marche **pas**.
(she) walks not
'She doe[s] not walk'

Pas *casser*.
not break:INF

Ça tourne **pas**.
that turns not
'That does not turn'

Pas *tomber bébé*.
not fall:INF baby

(Pierce 1992)

Table 6.2.7 Form-by-position correlations in early French.

	+*finite*	−*finite*
pas verb	6	118
verb *pas*	121	1

Similar results show up in children acquiring verb second (V2) languages, such as Dutch and German. In the V2 languages, finite verbs are raised to second position (i.e. C) as in (6a), while non-finite forms do not undergo the verb-second rule and remain in sentence final position, as in (6b,c).

(6)   a.   *Johan besucht oft seine Eltern*
           John visits often his   parents
           'John often visits his parents'

      b.   *Johan wird oft   seine Eltern   besuchen*
           John will often   his parents   visit:INF
           'John will often visit his parents'

      c.   *Johan hat mir   empfohlen   den Kurs zu belegen*.
           Johan has to-me   recommended   the class to take:INF
           'John recommended to me to take the course'

German-speaking children set the V2 parameter at a very early age. In the various corpora that have been examined, there seems to be no period during which German- and Dutch-speaking children fail to reliably raise finite verbs. Table 6.2.8, from Poeppel and Wexler (1993), gives the form-by-position interactions for a German-speaking child, Andreas (age 2;1). Similar results are reported in numerous other studies of German (Becker 1995; Boser *et al.* 1992; Clahsen 1991; Meisel 1990b; Rohrbacher and Vainikka 1994; Verrips and Weissenborn 1992), and Dutch (Haan 1986; Jordens 1990; Weverink 1989).

     A third parameter to consider is the null subject parameter. In earlier work (Hyams 1983, 1986), I proposed that children acquiring non-pro-drop languages such as English, go through an initial stage in which they have the [+null subject]

Table 6.2.8 Form-by-position correlations in early German
(from Poeppel & Wexler 1993).

	+*finite*	−*finite*
V2	197	6
Verb final	11	37

setting along the null subject parameter. On this view, early English, Dutch, German and so on are like an adult pro-drop language, such as Italian. As we will see shortly, however, the distribution of null subjects in these early languages is rather different from that of a real pro-drop language, suggesting that English-speaking children do not have Italian-like null subjects, but something else. Contrary to my earlier claims, the null subject parameter seems to be set quickly and correctly by children acquiring pro-drop and non-pro-drop languages alike (Valian 1991).

2.3 Agreement

We now have a wide range of cross-linguistic evidence pointing towards the same conclusion — children have very early knowledge of the morphosyntactic requirements of the target language. We are left then with the question of why they sometimes fail to express functional elements in obligatory environments, as in the examples in (1)–(3). With regard to the root infinitive phenomenon, a possible explanation is that they have not yet learned the specific agreeing forms of the verbs. However, this hypothesis cannot be right. A number of studies investigating the early use of agreement in different languages have shown that (non-finite forms apart) children respect agreement requirements at a very early age. Agreement errors are not a robust phenomenon in early language. [. . .] Table 6.2.9 summarizes the results of various studies of subject–verb agreement, or SPEC(ifier)-head agreement, as it is referred to within recent linguistic theory.

Given that children use agreeing forms of the verb with a high degree of accuracy, it cannot be the case that root infinitives arise from a lack of knowledge of the specifier–head agreement requirement or of the specific forms themselves. [. . .]

2.4 Agreement between missing elements

There is more to be said, however, about agreement and the apparent optionality of these functional elements. Hoekstra, Hyams and Becker (1996) note that it is not entirely correct to say that the root infinitive phenomenon is optional. In fact, what we see is that the morphological expression of verbal finiteness is largely contingent on the properties of the subject. More specifically, a number of studies have shown that for children acquiring non-pro-drop languages, the vast majority of infinitive sentences occur with null subjects, whereas finite sentences most often have overt subjects. These results are summarized in Table 6.2.10.

Averaging across children and languages, approximately 83% of root infinitives occur with null subjects. This is to be contrasted with finite clauses, which have only about 24% null subjects. These results underscore the point made earlier

Table 6.2.9 Subject–verb agreement errors in early language.

Child	Language	Age	n	% errors	
Simone	German	1;7–2;8	1732	1 %	(Clahsen and [Penke] 1992)
Martina*	Italian	1;8–2;7	478	1.6 %	
Diana*	Italian	1;10–2;6	610	1.5 %	
Guglielmo*	Italian	2;2–2;7	201	3.3 %	(Guasti 1994)
CHILDES*	English	1;6–4;1	1352	.02%	(Harris & Wexler 1995)
Claudia	Italian	1;4–2;4	1410	3 %	(Pizzuto & Caselli 1992)
Francesco	Italian	1;5–2;10	1264	2 %	
Marco	Italian	1;5–3;0	415	4 %	(Torrens 1992)
Marti*	Cat/Span	1;9–2;5	178	.56%	
Josep*	Cat/Span	1;9–2;6	136	3 %	
Guillem*	Catalan	1;9–2;6	129	2.3 %	
Gisela*	Catalan	1;10–2;6	81	1.2 %	

Note: *data available on CHILDES, MacWhinney & Snow (1985); Martina, Guglielmo, Diana corpora: Cipriani *et al.* (1991); Marti, Josep, Guillem, Gisela corpora: Serra & Sòlé (1992).

concerning the rapid setting of parameters. Children acquiring non-pro-drop languages are not speaking an Italian-like null subject language. Their null subjects are not licensed by rich agreement, but rather occur predominantly with verbs that are not specified for the relevant agreement features.

The data in Table 6.2.10 do not distinguish between different types of overt subjects, however. Hoekstra, Hyams and Becker (1996) hypothesized that there would also be a correlation between finiteness on the verb and the presence or absence of the determiner in subject nominals, that is, between the properties expressed in (1) and (2). We proposed an analysis according to which "finiteness" is a property of both the verbal and nominal domains. In the verbal domain, finiteness is realized as tense or agreement morphology on the verb; in the nominal domain, finiteness is expressed by definiteness or plurality. Null subjects and bare Ns are non-finite; subjects with determiners or plural marking are finite. Since children respect agreement requirements, we predicted that there would be agreement regarding the specification of finiteness as well. Specifically, we made the predictions in (7).

(7)   a. The lexical subject of a root infinitive will be a "bare" noun phrase, i.e., no determiner, no number marking (e.g. *dog*). [. . .]

   b. Finite verbs will occur with finite DP subjects, i.e., DPs with a determiner (e.g. *the boy*).

   c. Plural subjects (which are also finite) will occur with finite verbs.

These predictions were tested in English and German child language. For English, we relied on the corpora of Adam and Nina (Brown 1973; CHILDES, MacWhinney

Table 6.2.10 Finiteness and subject type.

	finite			non-finite			
	overt	null	total n	overt	null	total n	
Dutch							
Hein 2;3–3;1*	68%	32%	3768	15%	85%	721	(Haegeman 1995)
Flemish							
Maarten 1;11*	75%	25%	92	11%	89%	100	(Krämer 1993)
German							
Simone 1;8–4;1	80%	20%	3636	11%	89%	2477	(Behrens 1993)
Andreas 2;1*	92%	8%	220	32%	68%	68	(Krämer 1993)
French							
Nathalie 1;9–2;3	70%	30%	299	27%	73%	180	(Krämer 1993)
Philippe 2;1–2;6	74%	26%	705	7%	93%	164	(Krämer 1993)

NB: for French only preverbal subjects were counted.

Note: *data from CHILDES, MacWhinney & Snow (1985); Philippe corpus: Suppes, Smith & Leveille (1973); Hein, Maarten corpora: Elbers & Wijnen (1992); Simone corpus: Miller (1976); Nathalie corpus: Lightbown (1977).

Table 6.2.11 Subject data.

Child	# of files	Age	Language
Adam	11	2;3–3;7	English
Nina	7	2;4–2;10	English
Philip	1	2;9	German
Sophie	1	2;5	German
Wolfgang	2	2;5	German
Johanna	1	2;5	German

Table 6.2.12 Finite and non-finite verbs in German-speaking children.

	RI	Finite verb
Philip	17	23
Sophie	5	42
Wolfgang	30	70
Johanna	13	14

and Snow 1985). The German data were collected by Becker (1995). The number of files examined and the age of each child is given in Table 6.2.11.

All of the children in our study were squarely within the root infinitive stage, which is to say that in each of the transcripts examined we found an alternation between finite and non-finite verbs, though the proportions varied from file to file. The number of finite and non-finite verbs at each data point is given in Tables

Table 6.2.13 Finite and non-finite verbs: Adam.

File	RIs	Finite verbs
08	17	3
10	48	6
12	8	5
14	14	5
20	10	10
22	15	14
24	9	10
28	18	15
30	25	35
32	18	37
34	3	18

Table 6.2.14 Finite and non-finite verbs: Nina.

File	RIs	Finite verbs
22	4	1
28	23	17
30	18	11
31	33	9
32	4	8
33	5	26
36	2	9

6.2.12–6.2.14. For the German-speaking children (cf. Table 6.2.12), we considered all sentences containing unambiguously finite or non-finite verbs. For the English-speaking children, Adam (cf. Table 6.2.13) and Nina (cf. Table 6.2.14), we considered only sentences with 3rd person singular subjects, either overt or null. For the null subject sentences, we used only those where the identity of the subject could be unambiguously inferred from context.

Tables 6.2.15 and 6.2.16 show the distribution of subject types across non-finite and finite clauses for Adam and Nina. For this purpose, we looked only at subjects with a common noun. Proper names and overt pronouns were excluded since their status is ambiguous within our theory. [. . .] In Tables 6.2.15 and 6.2.16 the category *finite verbs* includes finite lexical verbs and finite forms of the verb *be*, and the category of *non-finite verbs* includes root infinitives and cases in which *be* is missing, as in *sun shining, teddy hungry*. [. . .]

Adam's data in Table 6.2.15 provide clear confirmation of the predictions in (7a, b). Overt determiners occur overwhelmingly with finite verbs, while non-finite verbs occur with bare Ns. When the subject is underspecified with respect to finiteness, the verb is also underspecified.

The results for Nina, in Table 6.2.16, are more split; finite verbs behave as predicted, occurring roughly 92% of the time with overt determiners, that is, prediction (7b) is confirmed. With respect to prediction (7a) however, there are

Table 6.2.15 Definiteness and finiteness: Adam.

	Finite verbs	Non-finite verbs
Overt determiner	53	2
Null determiner	4	39

Table 6.2.16 Definiteness and finiteness: Nina.

	Finite verbs	Non-finite verbs
Overt determiner	34	12
Null determiner	3	9

too many overt determiners in root infinitives. This may be an effect of the smaller sample size. But it is also possible that we are seeing a grammatical effect. Our suggestion at this point is that Nina's 12 finite nominals that occur with root infinitives, as well as Adam's two examples, are not in subject position, but are rather dislocated constituents which bind a null subject. If the dislocation status of these DPs can be established, then these examples would fall out as a special case of the root infinitive-null subject correlation. I will not attempt to provide a full justification for the proposal here, but note that there is substantial support for a dislocation analysis. [. . .]

Note that the data in Tables 6.2.15 and 6.2.16 come from several files extending over a wide age range (at least in the case of Adam). It might be objected that this method of data presentation obscures some important developmental change, for example, an early stage in which Adam produces only root infinitives, which occur with bare Ns, and then a later stage in which Adam uses only finite verbs, which occur with full DPs. However, as noted in the introduction and illustrated in Tables 6.2.13 and 6.2.14, the RI-finite verbs alternation exists in each transcript examined for both Nina and Adam.

The English results just reviewed were replicated in the German corpora we examined. However, the German data examined are rather limited, consisting of only one or two files per child, so that conclusions here should be regarded as tentative. We first looked at the number of overt vs. null determiners in finite and non-finite sentences. The figures are presented in Table 6.2.17. In German child language, as well, we find the predicted correlation between finiteness of the verb and overt subject determiners. [. . .]

It is important to reiterate that we examined only one transcript for Philip, Sophie and Johanna, and two for Wolfgang. Hence, it is not the case that the data in Table 6.2.17 represent more than one stage, which would obscure possible developmental differences. For example, we cannot interpret these data as showing that the children went through an early stage in which they produced only root infinitives with bare N subjects and then a second stage at which they produced only finite verbs and full DPs. However, if we did have developmental data which showed

Table 6.2.17 Definiteness and finiteness in early
German.

	Finite verbs	Non-finite verbs
Overt determiner	9	2
Null determiner	1	11

Table 6.2.18 Finiteness and plural subjects in early
German.

	Finite (V2)	Non-finite (verb final)
Plural subjects	22	1
Non-plural subjects	46	43

Table 6.2.19 Different subject types in RIs in German (adapted from Clahsen, Eisenbeiss and
Penke 1996).

Child	Full DP	Bare N	Null
Simone	0	28%	72%
Mathias	0	58%	42%
Annelie	0	0	100%
Hannah	0	10%	90%

this stage-like progression, it would still be consistent with the theory we have outlined thus far, which predicts a correlation between finiteness in VP and finiteness in DP.

Fortuitously, the German data provide us with a further test of our hypothesis that is not available in English, viz. prediction (7c), that plural subjects will occur only with finite verbs. This prediction cannot be tested in English because there is no difference in either form or position between a plural finite verb form and an infinitive, viz. *The boys go*. In German, on the other hand, even though by and large the form of the plural inflected verb is identical to the form of the infinitive, viz. *machen* 'make', there is a positional difference: a plural inflected verb occurs in second position, while an infinitive occurs in clause-final position. Table 6.2.18 shows the relative distributions of plural and non-plural subjects across finite and non-finite verbs.

These data provide very strong confirmation of the prediction in (7c): with only a single counterexample, plural subjects occur with finite verbs, while non-plural subjects show an even distribution across finite and non-finite constructions (since we have not separated out different DP types for this count). However, additional support comes from a study by Clahsen *et al.* (1996), who also investigated the relationship between subjects and root infinitives under somewhat different assumptions. The relevant data are given in Table 6.2.19. The four children in their study failed to produce a single finite DP in RIs. (Note that Clahsen *et al.*'s 'bare N' category includes bare Ns, pronouns and proper names.)

In summary, the data just reviewed reveal a rich and complex syntax underlying the earliest multi-word utterances. Children quickly set parameters such as V2, V to I, and pro-drop, and they adhere to general principles such as Spec-head agreement, even where the particular agreement patterns are not given in the input, as in the case of the root infinitive/non-finite subject correlations. Nevertheless, the language in (1)–(3) is not adult-like. So the question which remains is why children use root infinitives, null subjects and bare Ns, while adult speakers of the relevant languages do not.

3. The underspecification hypothesis: a modular account

To address this question, let us take as a point of departure the observation that functional categories not only provide the syntactic skeleton of the sentence, but they are also the points at which the sentence is anchored into a larger discourse representation. Finite morphology on the verb is responsible for temporal specificity; that is, it places the event or state denoted by the verb at a specific interval of time relative to speech time; definite determiners and pronouns pick out *familiar* entities, that is, discourse referents. Thus, the child's omission of functional elements has implications for both the developing morphosyntax and pragmatics.

Hyams (1996) and Hoekstra and Hyams (1995) offer a modular account of the optionality of these elements, which tries to capture the intuition that functional elements stand at the interface of these two domains. Ignoring many technical details, what we propose is that the functional heads, specifically T(ense) and D(et), are pronominal in nature. The idea that Tense is pronominal was originally proposed in Partee (1973). As pronouns, they must have their reference fixed. In principle, this can be done in one of two ways, either grammatically, through binding to an operator, or pragmatically, through a direct discourse interpretation. This distinction corresponds roughly to the anaphoric vs. (co-)referential use of overt pronouns.

Again, ignoring details, we propose that the morphological specification of functional heads, such as Number and Person, allows a chain or a binding relation to be established between T and a deictic operator in the C-domain, as schematized in (8a). The temporal reference of T (*past, present*) is thus grammatically determined through binding, in the manner of a pronominal variable similar to what was proposed by Guéron and Hoekstra (1989, 1995) and Enç (1987). On this view, finiteness is the morphosyntactic reflex of tense binding. A similar structure would exist for nominal phrases, as in (8b), and the value of D would be determined by a chain linking D to an operator in DP. Definiteness and plurality, for example, are the morphosyntactic reflexes of a D-chain.

(8)   a. $[_{CP}$ OP . . .Per. . .Num. . . T $[_{VP}$ V $]]$

      b. $[_{DP}$ OP . . .Per. . .Num. . . D $[_{NP}$ N$]]$

There is a second option, which is for T (and D) to be interpreted directly in discourse. In this case, there is no operator-variable binding, hence no expression of finiteness, and the functional head receives its value in the manner of a free pronoun. It is this deictic option that is illustrated by the examples in (1)–(3). Our proposal is then, that finiteness does not need to be expressed in the early grammar because children can make use of a pragmatic option for interpreting functional heads (now understood as pronominals) — an option which is blocked in the adult grammar.

In the adult grammar, in contrast, T and D (and pronominals, more generally) must be assigned a value grammatically, that is, through binding; hence finiteness is required. Root infinitives, null subjects and bare Ns are excluded. There does not seem to be the deictic option, at least not in the languages under consideration. We propose that this follows from a general pragmatic principle, first formulated by Reinhart (1983), and later by Grodzinsky and Reinhart (1993), according to which the pragmatic (that is, non-anaphoric) option is blocked unless it yields an interpretation which is distinguishable from the binding option. Reinhart and Grodzinsky's principle is given in (9), though we leave open at this point the exact formulation that we would adopt.

(9)   **Rule I** (Grodzinsky and Reinhart 1993)

NP A cannot co-refer with NP B if replacing A with C, C a variable bound by B, yields an indistinguishable interpretation.

In other words, all else being equal, a pronominal is to be interpreted anaphorically. Thus, on Reinhart's account, the sentence in (10a) in which *him* refers to *John*, is blocked because there exists a bound variable alternative, as in (10b).

(10) a.   *John* fooled *him*.

      b.   John fooled himself.

Chien and Wexler (1990) and Grodzinsky and Reinhart (1993) have argued that Reinhart's pragmatic principle does not operate in young children; thus, children allow co-reference between *John* and *him* in sentences such as (10a). Our proposal is that the optionality of finiteness in early language results from a similar pragmatic insufficiency. Finiteness becomes obligatory when the relevant pragmatic principle develops. Thus, RIs, null subjects, and bare Ns are possible in the child's language, but not in the adult's because of the availability of a direct discourse construal of functional heads, which we take to be pronominal in nature.

4. Possible functionalist accounts

In the account just offered, we explain certain salient properties of early language, as well as adult-child differences, by appealing, on the one hand, to a specific principle of Universal Grammar, e.g. Specifier-head agreement (shared by children and adults), and, on the other, to a general principle of pragmatics, Reinhart's rule (which children lack). The fact that we see a staggered development in these two domains provides nice support for the modular approach. This might be a case in which language development offers an insight into the organization of the language faculty which is masked in the mature system. However, we might argue that these properties arise not from any formal constraints on the developing grammar and its interaction with pragmatics, but rather as a response to pressures imposed by communicative needs. There are at least two hypotheses which we might consider. The first I will call the *different functions hypothesis* and the second *the informativeness hypothesis*, based on ideas of Greenfield and Smith (1976). Finally, I will also consider a performance limitations account of the sort proposed in Bloom (1990). We will see that these accounts all make the wrong predictions with respect to the omission of functional elements.

4.1 *Different functions hypothesis*

According to the *different functions hypothesis*, finite and non-finite forms would alternate in early grammar because the child needs to signal different intentions and does so by associating each form with a different communicative function. Krämer (1993), in fact, claims that children's root infinitives often have a desiderative reading. For example, the sentence in (11) would mean that Maarten (the child) wants his mother to come pick him up.

(11) *Mama   komen*.
     Mommy   come:INF
     (= Marten (child) wants Mommy to come pick him up)

Krämer's claim that RIs have a modal reading is based on the spontaneous speech data of three Dutch-speaking children. However, Krämer did not examine finite clauses to see if they too could have the same desiderative meaning. Hence, her results do not readily allow us to determine whether there is a difference in function between finite and non-finite clauses. Wijnen (1995) has results which bear on this question. He compared children's interpretations of finite verbs and root infinitives using a picture matching task. The picture showed either an ongoing activity, corresponding to a declarative reading, or it depicted a future or wished-for event, corresponding to a modal reading. Table 6.2.20 reports Wijnen's results for Dutch- and English-speaking children.

Dutch children showed some difference in interpretation between finite verbs and root infinitives, allowing a modal reading for infinitives 39% of the time as

Table 6.2.20 Percentages of ongoing-activity interpretations (from Wijnen 1995).

	Finite		Non-finite	
	declarative	*modal*	*declarative*	*modal*
Dutch	92%	8%	61%	39%
English	95%	5%	95%	5%

against 8% for finite verbs. This is consistent with Krämer's observations. However, most often, 61% of the time, Dutch children assigned a descriptive reading to infinitives, that is, a reading which is indistinguishable from the finite verbs. For English-speaking children, the result is more dramatic; there was no difference whatsoever in the interpretations assigned to finite and non-finite root verbs. Note that this is precisely what we expect under the modular view, where children lack the pragmatic rule which blocks the indistinguishable non-finite option. However, these results do not support the hypothesis that children associate different functions with finite and non-finite verbs, and hence cast doubt on the proposal that finite/non-finite alternation arises out of a communicative need.

A further problem with the different functions hypothesis, as I have formulated it, is that although it is not implausible a priori that finite and non-finite forms would have different interpretations for children, the form–function relation would still not explain the morphosyntactic correlations that we observe during this stage. For what functional reason would a root infinitive need to occur with a null or bare nominal subject? Here we have a pure syntactic effect.

4.2 Informativeness

This same problem arises in a perspicuous way if we formulate an account of the optionality of functional elements in terms of informativeness. The *informativeness hypothesis* holds that children use their limited expressive capacity to encode those aspects of a situation which are most informative, or alternatively, that children omit information which is predictable or recoverable from context. An account along this line has been proposed for the null subject property of early English (cf. Greenfield & Smith 1976), and under somewhat different assumptions (Bloom 1990). Hyams and Wexler (1993) showed that an informativeness account fails to explain various properties of early null subjects, in particular, why null subjects alternate with pronouns which, by definition, encode contextually redundant information. A further problem, however, is that *the informativeness hypothesis* — like *the different functions hypothesis* — fails to account for the grammatical correlations discussed earlier. If children are attempting to make their utterances maximally informative given limited resources, we would expect them to omit agreement morphology on the verb when the subject is fully specified. This is not what we find, however. Rather, children omit finite morphology when the subject is unspecified (either null or determinerless), making the utterance maximally uninformative, and conversely, they redundantly mark the verb when the subject is specified.

The grammatical correlations we find also argue against a performance-limitations account of the sort proposed by P. Bloom (1990), in which children omit subjects to conserve limited resources necessary for the production and planning of the rest of the sentence (cf. also Valian, Hoeffner & Aubrey 1996). In looking at null subjects in early English, Bloom found an inverse relation between the "heaviness" of the subject and the length of the VP in terms of words, as in (12).

(12) **Length of VP (words) as a function of subject "heaviness"**
      (Bloom 1990)
      Null subject > pronoun > name

By Bloom's measure, null subject sentences had the longest VPs, pronominal subjects had shorter VPs, and name subjects had shorter VPs still. Bloom argued that the more elaborated subjects took up limited processing resources, leaving less available for the planning and production of the VP. If this were the case, we would expect null subject sentences to have the "heavier" inflected verbs while subjects containing determiners should occur with "lighter" non-finite verbs. But in fact, the results show just the opposite, that null subjects and "bare" Ns occur with uninflected verbs while "heavy" determiner-N subjects occur with finitely specified verbs, as schematized in (13).

(13) **Length of VP (morphemes) as a function of subject "heaviness"**
      (Hoekstra, Hyams and Becker 1996)
      Det N > Null subject/bare N

5. Concluding remarks: the logical problem of language acquisition

Let me conclude by saying a few words about the *logical problem of language acquisition* (LPLA), which provides the conceptual foundation for the formalist approach to language development. The debate over 'the poverty of the stimulus' often centers around the question of how children retreat from (morphological) over-generalization, i.e., why they give up *goed* in favor of *went* in the absence of direct negative evidence (cf. [the work of] MacWhinney [. . .]). However, what is most interesting about overgeneralization — the application of an otherwise general rule to a domain which is precluded in the adult grammar — is where it fails to occur. While we often find overgeneralization of morphology and other "accidental" properties of a language, children do not seem to overgeneralize rules whose domain of application is restricted by general principles of grammar. For example, in an elicited production task, English-speaking children will produce *wanna*-contraction in object questions, such as (14a), but they do not generalize this rule to subject questions, where it would be ungrammatical, as in (14b) (Crain and Thornton 1990).

(14) a. *Who do you wanna beat?*

      b. **Who do you wanna win?*

The impossibility of *wanna*-contraction in (14b) follows from a principle of Universal Grammar (UG) which blocks contraction across the trace of a moved constituent.

We see a similar effect with respect to the development of functional structure and the underspecification of functional categories. Children do not generalize the subject properties or positional properties of finite clauses to non-finite clauses. Rather, the morphological and positional requirements of these different clause types fall out from formal principles of grammar. Learning mechanisms, such as uniqueness, blocking, indirect negative evidence (Lasnik 1989) and connectionist-type models such as the MacWhinney and Bates (1989) competition model, which rely heavily on the corrective power of the input, can account for retreat from overgeneralization, but they do not explain the *absence* of overgeneralization in specific domains. Rather, the explanation lies in UG itself — child grammars, like adult grammars, are subject to universal formal constraints.

Acknowledgements

Research for this paper was supported by a UCLA Faculty Senate Grant. I am grateful to Teun Hoekstra for discussion.

Brian MacWhinney

EMERGENT LANGUAGE

IF YOU SPEND SOME TIME watching the checkout lines at a supermarket, you quickly find that the number of people queued up in each line is
roughly the same. At peak times, you may find five or six people in a line waiting
to check out. At slower times, lines have only two or three waiting. There is no
fixed rule governing this pattern. Instead, the rule that equalizes the number of
shoppers in the various lines emerges from other basic facts about the goals and
behavior of shoppers and supermarket managers. This simple idea of emergence
through constraint satisfaction is currently being invoked as a central explanatory
mechanism in many areas of cognitive science and neuroscience.

Given the often effortless nature of language use, the idea of viewing verbal
behavior as an emergent process seems particularly attractive. We can observe
speakers carrying on conversations on cellular phones while driving their cars in
rush hour traffic, and we can find accomplished seamstresses creating elaborate
embroidery while conversing fluently. It is not only adult language processing that
seems effortless; language learning in children also appears natural and painless.

Despite these appearances, when linguists look at language learning and processing, they find complex rules, categories, and symbols. How can we reconcile
these divergent perceptions? One possible reconciliation calls into question the
extent to which language learning and processing actually function in obedience to
an explicit set of formal rules. According to this new view of language learning and
processing, the behaviors that we tend to characterize in terms of rules and symbols

1998, reprinted with permission from M. Darnell, E. Moravcsik, F. Newmeyer, M. Noonan and K.
Wheatley (eds), *Functionalism and Formalism in Linguistics*, vol. I: *General Papers*, Amsterdam, John
Benjamins, pp. 361–86.

are in fact emergent patterns that arise from the interactions of other less complex or more stable underlying systems. I will refer to this new viewpoint on language learning and processing as "emergentism".

Proponents of functional linguistics have often spoken of grammar as an emergent property of features of discourse (Du Bois 1987; Hopper & Thompson 1984), contrasting their functional analysis with formalist approaches to grammar. The idea that grammar can emerge from discourse is fundamental to the debate between functionalism and formalism in linguistics and psycholinguistics. However, the emergence of grammar from discourse is only one aspect of a much broader emergentist vision of the shape of human language. The shape of human language is also tightly governed by the physiology of the vocal apparatus, the nature of the auditory system, and the development and decay of the many cognitive systems that manage the processing of language. When we consider these various additional constraints on the emergent shape of language, we reach a broader characterization than that offered in functionalist accounts that look only at discourse pressures.

Emergentist accounts have been formulated for a wide variety of linguistic phenomena, ranging from segmental inventories, stress patterns, phonotactic constraints, morphophonological alternations, lexical structures, pidginization, second language learning, historical change, on-line phrase attachment, and rhetorical structures. Formalisms that have been used to analyze the emergent nature of these forms include connectionist networks, dynamic systems theory, neuronal differentiation models, classifier systems, production-system architectures, Bayesian models, Optimality Theory, and corpora studies.

The basic notion underlying emergentism is simple enough. Consider the hexagonal shape of the cells in a honeycomb. There is nothing in the genetic makeup of the honey bee that determines that each cell in the honeycomb should take on the form of a hexagon. However, when circles are packed together, it turns out that packing distance is minimized when each circle has six neighbors. This same principle also applies in three dimensions to spheres. When the fluid in these six neighboring honey cells is tightly compressed against its neighbors, a hexagonal shape emerges. No rules are needed to control the shape of each individual cell of the honeycomb; instead this form emerges from the interaction of hundreds of small units. Nature is replete with examples of this type of formal emergence. The form of beaches and mountain ridges, the geometry of snowflakes and crystals, the appearance of *fata morgana*, and the movement of the jet stream in the air and the Gulf Stream in the sea — all of these patterns arise from interactions of physical principles with constraints imposed by physical bodies. Even in the biological world, much of our somatic form is emergent, whether it be the patterns of stripes on the tiger, the formation of teeth into a uniform bite, the structuring of enzymes to catalyze organic reactions, or our patterns of fingerprints and hair formations.

1. Basic assumptions

In this paper, we will explore three levels of emergent linguistic structure. The first level involves the acquisition of basic lexical structures in small areas of cortex called "local maps". The second level involves the interaction between lexical structures in terms of "lexical groups". The third level involves the processing of syntactic information across longer neural distances in "functional neural circuits". We will examine how linguistic form emerges from the interaction of these three levels of neurolinguistic processing.

2. Principles of neural networks

Connectionist models are implemented in terms of artificial neural networks. Neural networks that are able to learn from input are known as "adaptive neural networks". The architecture of an adaptive neural network can be specified in terms of eight design features:

1. *Units.* The basic components of the network are a number of simple elements called variously "neurons", "units", "cells", or "nodes". In Figure 6.3.1, the units are labeled with letters such as "x_1".

2. *Connections.* Neurons or pools of neurons are connected by a set of pathways which are typically called "connections". In most models, these connections are unidirectional, going from a "sending" unit to a "receiving" unit. This unidirectionality reflects the fact that neural connections also operate in only one direction. The only information conveyed across connections is activation information. No signals or codes are passed. In Figure 6.3.1, the connection between units x_1 and y_1 is marked with a thick line.

3. *Patterns of connectivity.* Neurons are typically grouped into pools or layers. Connections can operate within or between layers. In some models, there are no within-layer connections; in others all units in a given layer are interconnected. Units or layers can be further divided into three classes:

    a. *Input units* which represent signals from earlier networks. These are marked as "x" units in Figure 6.3.1.
    b. *Output units* which represent the choices or decisions made by the network. These are marked as "z" units in Figure 6.3.1.
    c. *Hidden units* which represent additional units juxtaposed between input and output for the purposes of computing more complex, nonlinear relations. These are marked as "y" units in Figure 6.3.1.

4. *Weights.* Each connection has a numerical weight that is designed to represent the degree to which it can convey activation from the sending unit to the receiving unit. Learning is achieved by changing the weights on connections. For example, the weight on the connection between x_1 and y_1 is given as .54 in Figure 6.3.1.

5. *Net inputs.* The total amount of input from a sending neuron to a receiving neuron is determined by multiplying the weights on each connection to the receiving unit times the activation of the sending neuron. This "net input" to the receiving unit is the sum of all such inputs from sending neurons. In Figure 6.3.1, the net input to y_1 is .76, if we assume that the activation of x_1 and x_2 are both at "1" and the x_1y_1 weight is .54 and the x_2y_1 weight is .22.

6. *Activation functions.* Each unit has a level of activation. These activation levels can vary continuously between "0" and "1". In order to determine a new

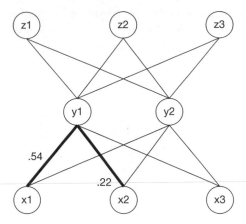

Figure 6.3.1 A sample adaptive neural network.

activation level, activation functions are applied to the net input. Functions that "squash" high values can be used to make sure that all new activations stay in the range of "0" to "1".

7. *Thresholds and biases.* Although activations can take on any value between "0" and "1", often thresholds and bias functions are used to force units to be either fully "on" or fully "off".

8. *A learning rule.* The basic goal of training is to bring the neural net into a state where it can take a given input and produce the correct output. To do this, a learning rule is used to change the weights on the connections. Supervised learning rules need to rely on the presence of a target output as the model for this changing of weights. Unsupervised learning rules do not rely on targets and correction, but use the structure of the input as their guide to learning.

All connectionist networks share this common language of units, connections, weights, and learning rules. However, architectures differ markedly both in their detailed patterns of connectivity and in the specific rules used for activation and learning. For excellent, readable introductions to the theory and practice of neural network modeling, the reader may wish to consult Bechtel and Abrahamsen (1991) or Fausett (1994). For a mathematically more advanced treatment, see Hertz, Krogh, and Palmer (1991).

3. Local lexical maps

Nothing is more basic to language than the learning of new words. The child's first word often appears toward the beginning of the second year of life. But word learning is not a sudden process. Rather, it depends on a whole range of experiences and activities in which the child participates during the first year of life. Some of these experiences involve producing non-conventional sounds through babbling. Another type of experience involves listening to the cadences and phonetic forms of the words used by the adult community. Still another type of experience involves the slow development of thinking about the various categories of objects and events in the natural world. All of these activities and experiences are prerequisites to the learning of the first words. About two or three months before the first productive words are produced, we find some evidence that the child has begun to acquire a passive comprehension of a few of the most common words of the language. For example, the 14-month-old who has not yet produced the first word, may show an understanding of the word "dog" by turning to a picture of a dog, rather than a picture of a cat, when the word "dog" is uttered. It is difficult to measure the exact size of this comprehension vocabulary in the weeks preceding the first productive word, but it is perhaps no more than 20 words in size.

During this early period of auditory learning, the child starts to form associations between certain auditory patterns and particular meaningful interpretations. In older models of lexical learning, the process of associating a sound with a meaning involved the trivial formation of a single link. For example, in Morton's (1970) Logogen Model, the learning of a new word requires nothing more than the linking up of one already available pattern or cluster to another. The idea that auditory and semantic patterns form coherent clusters seems to reflect real facts about the infant's cognition. On the semantic level, one could argue (Mervis 1984) that the child's previous experience with dogs has served to promote the consolidation of the concept of a "dog". On the phonological level, it also appears that repeated exposure to the consistent pattern of "dog" also leads to the emergence of a consolidated phonological pattern.

The self-organizing feature map (SOFM) framework of Kohonen (1982) and Miikkulainen (1990) provides us with a way of characterizing these early processes of semantic and phonological consolidation. In the framework of SOFM models, word learning can be viewed as involving the development of maps in which individual patterns can be stored and retrieved reliably. Three types of local maps are involved in word learning: auditory maps, meaning maps, and articulatory maps. Each of these three maps uses the same learning algorithm. Figure 6.3.2 illustrates the activation of a particular node in an auditory map.

The input to this feature map involves a large number of auditory phonological features taken from separate domains such as sibilance, formant transition direction, formant duration, formant frequency, stop click timing, and others. These are schematically represented as "auditory features" at the bottom of Figure 6.3.2. For the purposes of computational modeling, the multidimensional space is compressed onto a 2-D topological space.

What makes this mapping process self-organizing is the fact that there is no pre-established pattern for these mappings and no preordained relation between particular nodes and particular feature patterns. The SOFM algorithm decides which node on the map should be the "winner" for a particular input pattern. At first, the weights on the map are set to small random values. When the first input comes in, the random setting of these weights makes it so that, by chance, some particular node is the one that is maximally responsive to the current input pattern. That node then decrements the activation levels on the other nodes. This decrementation takes on the form of a "Mexican hat" or sombrero. Right around the winner, related nodes are not decremented as much as are more distant nodes. Because of the architecture

Auditory lexicon

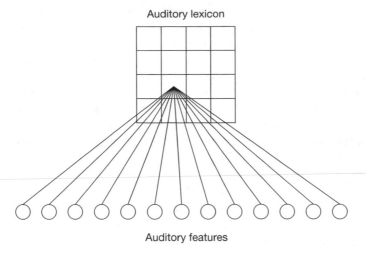

Auditory features

Figure 6.3.2 A self-organizing feature map for storing auditory patterns.

of the relation between the input and the grid, nodes that are nearby in the map come to respond to similar input patterns. For example, words that begin with similar initial segments will tend to be assigned to neighboring units in the map. The Mexican hat shape obeyed by the competitive interactions in the SOFM conforms closely to known facts about lateral inhibition and the redistribution of syntactic resources (Kohonen 1982) in cortical tissue. The actual computational implementation of this framework uses a computationally efficient algorithm that is faithful to these biological principles (Miikkulainen 1990).

This system works well to encode large numbers of patterns. In one sample simulation, we found that a 100 × 100 network with 10 000 nodes can learn up to 6 000 phonological patterns with an error rate of less than 1%. In this implementation, we used eight floating-point numbers to generate the input. At the beginning of learning, the first input vector of eight numbers led by chance to somewhat stronger activation on one of the 10 000 cells. This one slightly more active cell then inhibits the activation of its competitors, according to the Mexican hat function. As a result of this pattern of activation and inhibition, inputs that are close in feature space end up activating cells in similar regions of the map. Once a cell has won a particular competition, its activation is negatively dampened to prevent it from winning for all of the inputs. Then, on the next trial, another cell has a chance to win in the competition for the next sound-meaning input pattern. This process repeats until all 6 000 sound-meaning patterns have developed some "specialist" cell in the feature map. During this process, the dynamics of self-organization make it so that items with shared features end up in similar regions of the feature map.

We tracked the development of the feature map by computing the average radius of the individual items. After learning the first 700 words, the average radius of each word was 70 cells; after 3 000 words, the radius was 8; after 5 000 words the radius was 3; and after 6 000 words the radius was only 1.5 cells. Clearly, there is not much room for new lexical items in a feature map with 10 000 cells that has already learned 6 000 items. However, there is good reason to think that the

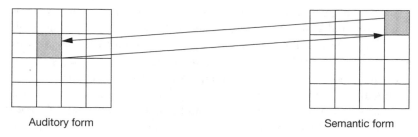

Figure 6.3.3 A bidirectional sound–meaning association in a feature map.

enormous number of cells in the human brain makes it so that the size of the initial feature map is not an important limiting constraint on the learning of the lexicon by real children. We have found that there is no clear upper limit on the ability of the SOFM to acquire more items, when it is given a larger dimensionality.

3.1 Using maps for retrieval

In order to model additional aspects of lexical structure, the basic SOFM architecture must be supplemented by additional connections. Miikkulainen (1990) did this by training reciprocal connections on two maps using Hebbian learning. Figure 6.3.3 illustrates the relations of these two maps. In this figure, a particular auditory form is associated with a particular semantic form or meaning.

Since neuronal connections can only fire in a single direction, training has to be conducted separately in each direction. In our simulations, learning begins with the consolidation of both the auditory and semantic maps according to the SOFM competitive learning algorithm. Once patterns are established on the two basic maps, Hebbian learning strengthens connections between units that are coactive on the sound map and the meaning map. This training is intended to represent the actual process of word learning, during which the child hears a word at the same time some meaningful aspect of the environment is being focused upon.

This proposed model is oversimplified in terms of both structure and process. In structural terms, additional maps are needed to represent additional aspects of lexical knowledge. In addition to the two maps given in Figure 6.3.3, there must be a map that encodes output phonological form, since the child must not only associate an auditory form to a semantic form, but must also associate the auditory form to an articulatory form and an articulatory form to the semantic form. Later, when the child learns to read and spell, there will also be maps for orthographic and visual forms. In processing terms, the SOFM given in Figure 6.3.3 fails to express important aspects of the serial structure of auditory and articulatory patterns. Later, we will discuss a lexical learning model developed by Gupta and MacWhinney (1997) that deals in a more explicit way with issues of serial ordering.

3.2 Articulatory scaffolding

The relation between a pattern in the auditory map and a pattern in the semantic map is essentially arbitrary. There is nothing about the phonological shape of /kæt/

that corresponds in some patterned way to the meaning "cat". However, the relation between auditory and articulatory forms is far more systematic. Once an adult has been exposed to a new auditory form, the corresponding articulatory form is extremely easy to produce. When we hear someone say that their last name is "Tomingo" we can quickly reproduce that name, even after only one trial.

For the child, the mapping from a new auditory form to an articulatory form is a bit more difficult, but it is still the case that audition serves to "scaffold" articulation. What this means is that the auditory form remains an active target as we attempt to match the form in articulation. By then listening to our articulation, we can verify the match of our output to the target auditory form. This allows us to correct errors and to set up an excitatory feedback loop between the two forms that stabilizes the new articulatory shape. Gupta and MacWhinney (1997) show how the development of this correspondence is based primarily on the mapping of correspondences between auditory fragments and articulatory fragments. In the simplest case, these fragments are syllables. For example, once the child has learned how to produce the syllable /go/ of "go", this auditory–articulatory correspondence is available for use in any new word. Even individual segments can be extracted through analysis. Some of this learning occurs during late babbling, but it is consolidated with the first words. Over time, the links between auditory and articulatory forms become more extensive.

3.3 Prosody and time

Both the auditory and the articulatory maps must be structured to deal effectively with multisyllabic patterns. In order to process multisyllabic words, the input to the basic lexical map needs to derive from preprocessing by a SOFM which identifies individual syllables. This map stores a large number of identifiable syllabic forms such as /ba/, /kɪb/, and /ʊv/, as well as subsyllabic forms such as /s/ or /n/. The input to this SOFM arrives in a sequential way, but each syllable is processed as a separate temporal chunk. This is easy to do on the level of the syllable, because there are many cues that tell whether a segment is in the position of the onset, the nucleus, or the coda. Because most coarticulation effects occur within the syllable, this is an effective way of dealing with low-level context effects. The syllabic processor operates repeatedly through the word to encode a series of activations of syllables.

The functioning of this syllabic map is supplemented by a process that associates particular syllabic vectors with additional prosodic information. This processor attends not to the segmental forms in the speech wave, but to the overall prosodic structure. Prosodic information works in terms of the system of metrical feet to encode the status of a given syllable as being in an iambic or trochaic foot and being either a strong or weak syllable. It is the union of these prosodic features with the basic segmental syllabic features which then serve as input to the auditory lexical SOFM. In a word like "banana" the syllabic processor operates repeatedly to encode three syllables. However, without the additional metrical information, these three encodings could be perceived as the patterns "nabana" or "nanaba", as well as "banana". In order to uniquely encode "banana", the first syllable /ba/ must be coded as a first foot weak beat, the second syllable /na/ must be coded as the strong beat and the final /na/ must be coded as the second foot weak beat. Thus, the complete input to the lexical map includes both segmental and prosodic information. It is this complete merged pattern which is then associated to the semantic pattern to specify emergent lexical items.

3.4 Acquiring inflectional markers

The local lexical map can be used to acquire not only stems such as "dog" or "jump" but also affixes such as the plural suffix or the past tense suffix. Stems can be learned directly. However, in order to model the learning of affixes, we need to examine an additional process called "masking" (Burgess 1995; Burgess & Hitch 1992; Carpenter, Grossberg, & Reynolds 1991; Cohen & Grossberg 1987; Grossberg 1987). Let us use the learning of the English past tense suffix to illustrate how masking works.

1. The net learns a set of present tense verbs, along with the corresponding past tense forms. We can refer to this initial phase of learning as "rote" learning. These rote-learned forms include regular pairs such as "jump–jumped" and "want–wanted", as well as irregulars such as "run–ran" and "take–took".
2. The network then learns a new present tense such as "push" for which the corresponding past tense form has not yet been learned.
3. Then the child hears the word "pushed" with the auditory form /pʊʃ/ and the semantic pattern "push + past". On the auditory map, the node corresponding to /pʊʃ/ is the closest match. On the semantic map, the node corresponding to "push + present" is the closest match.
4. A pattern of bidirectional activation is established between the two maps. It is this bidirectional activation that supports the process of "masking". Masking works to drain activation from nodes and features that are coactive in the two maps. In the current example, the features of the stem on both maps are all masked out, leaving the feature "past tense" as unmasked on the semantic map and the features corresponding to the final /ɪd/ as unmasked on the auditory map.
5. The unmasked phonology is then associated with the unmasked semantics through the same type of Hebbian learning that is used to produce the basic rote-learning of new lexical forms.

This implements in a neurally plausible way the process of morphological extraction by analysis. In the terms of MacWhinney (1978), affix analysis involves associating the "unexpressed" with the "uncomprehended". This approach to the problem of learning the English past tense solves two problems faced by earlier nonlexical models. First, the model succeeds in capturing both rote lexicalization and combinatorial lexicalization within a single connectionist model. Rote forms are picked up directly on the feature map. Combinatorial forms are created by the isolation of the suffix through masking and the use of masking in production.

Second, having learned to comprehend the past tense in a productive way, the child can then learn the association between the auditory pattern and an articulatory representation. This occurs when the child tries to produce the new form. The activation of a semantic pattern leads to the activation of an auditory pattern which then sets up a temporary excitatory feedback loop to the articulatory map. During the process of scaffolding, the auditory form remains active as we attempt to match the form in articulation. By then listening to our articulation, we can verify the match, correct errors, and set up an excitatory feedback loop between the two forms that stabilizes the new articulatory shape. As we noted earlier, the process of developing a match between the auditory and articulatory forms proceeds syllable by syllable by relying on prosody to encode the temporal properties of successive syllables.

3.5 Inflectional marking and the logical problem

In the network we have been discussing, a single lexical feature map can produce both a rote form like "went" and a productive form like "*goed". The fact that both can be produced in the same lexical feature map allows us to begin work on a general solution to the "logical problem of language acquisition" (Baker & McCarthy 1981; Gleitman 1990; Gleitman, Newport & Gleitman 1984; Morgan & Travis 1989; Pinker 1984; Pinker 1989; Wexler & Culicover 1980). In the case of the competition between "went" and "*goed", we expect "went" to become solidified over time because of its repeated occurrence in the input. The form "*goed", on the other hand, is supported only by the presence of the -ed form. Figure 6.3.4 illustrates this competition.

This particular competition is an example of what Baker and McCarthy (1981) calls a "benign exception to the logical problem". The exception is considered benign because the child can learn to block overgeneralization by assuming that there is basically only one way of saying "went". This Uniqueness Constraint is thought to distinguish benign and non-benign exceptions to the logical problem. However, from the viewpoint of the Competition Model account we are constructing here, all exceptions are benign.

The basic idea here is that, when a child overgeneralizes and produces "*goed", the system itself contains a mechanism that will eventually force recovery. In cases

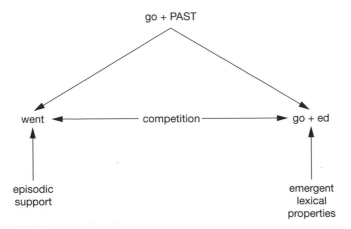

Figure 6.3.4 Competition between episodic and combinatorial knowledge.

of overgeneralization, alternative expressions compete for the same meaning. One of these forms receives episodic support from the actual linguistic input. This episodic support grows slowly over time. The other form arises productively from the operation of analogistic pressures. When episodic support does not agree with these analogistic pressures, the episodic support eventually comes to dominate and the child recovers from the overgeneralization. This is done without negative evidence, solely on the basis of positive support for the form receiving episodic confirmation.

4. Lexical groups

The second level of linguistic structure we will discuss is the level of the lexical group. The formation of Level 2 lexical groups is an emergent process that depends on the existence of a Level 1 substrate of lexical items organized into SOFMs. The force that drives the emergence of lexical groups and their related syntactic properties is the linking of words into morphological and syntactic combinations. We can refer to the properties that emerge in this way as "emergent lexical properties". In this section, we will review some of these emergent properties.

4.1 Inflectional morphology and lexical groups

Having acquired productive use of inflectional morphology, the child can begin to learn how to combine inflections with stems. The emergentist approach to language acquisition holds that the patterns governing these combinations emerge from information implicit in the lexical map. To illustrate how this works, let us take as an example the network model of German gender learning developed by MacWhinney, Leinbach, Taraban, and McDonald (1989). This network is designed to model how German children learn how to select one of the six different forms of the German definite article: "der", "die", "das", "des", "dem", or "den". Which of the six forms of the article should be used to modify a given noun in German depends on three additional features of the noun: its gender (masculine, feminine, or neuter), its number (singular or plural), and its role within the sentence (subject, possessor, direct object, prepositional object, or indirect object). To make matters worse, assignment of nouns to gender categories is often quite nonintuitive. For example, the word for "fork" is feminine, the word for "spoon" is masculine, and the word for "knife" is neuter.

Although these relations are indeed complex, MacWhinney *et al.* show that it is possible to construct a neural network that learns the German system from the available cues. The MacWhinney *et al.* model, like most current connectionist models, involves a level of input units, a level of hidden units, and a level of output units (Figure 6.3.5). Each of these levels or layers contains a number of discrete units or nodes. For example, in the MacWhinney *et al.* model, the 35 units within the input level represent features of the noun that is to be modified by the article. Each of the two hidden unit levels includes multiple units that represent combinations of these input-level features. The six output units represent the six forms of the German definite article.

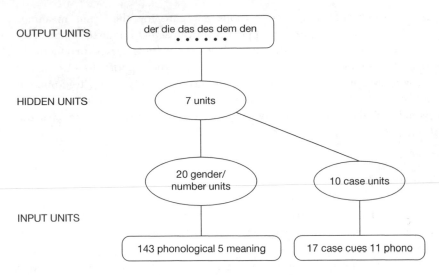

OUTPUT UNITS

der die das des dem den
• • • • • •

HIDDEN UNITS

7 units

20 gender/
number units

10 case units

INPUT UNITS

143 phonological 5 meaning

17 case cues 11 phono

Figure 6.3.5 A back propagation model for German declension.

This network successfully learned its input corpus and displayed a good ability to generalize gender assignment to new nouns. It was also able to take a nominal form presented in one case and use it to predict a form in another case. The over-generalization patterns the model produced matched up well with those produced by children. Despite its successes, this model and a similar model for English (MacWhinney & Leinbach 1991) faced certain basic problems. These problems all arose from the fact that the model assigned no privileged role to words as lexical items. Instead, all learning was based on an input composed of phonological patterns. A clear example of this type of problem arises in the case of the sound /rɪŋ/ which represents three different verb meanings (to "ring" a bell, to "wring" out the clothes, and to "ring" the city with troops). The past tense forms of these verbs will be "rang", "wrung", and "ringed" depending on the meaning of the stem. By itself, the back propagation net cannot distinguish homophonic relations of this type. However, when a Level 2 back propagation network is joined to a Level 1 SOFM, homophony is no longer a problem, because the various homophonic meanings of "ring" are now representationally distinct in terms of the input that the SOFM can provide to the back propagation network. The reason for this is simply that the lexical SOFM contains semantic information which can be passed on to promote disambiguation in the back propagation network.

Gupta and MacWhinney (1992) showed how the addition of lexical information to the back propagation network for German leads to improved performance. Because the Gupta and MacWhinney model combines two different architectures, inflectional formations can be produced in several different ways. First, the SOFM can generate both regular and irregular forms by rote. Second, because the SOFM includes affixes along with stems, regular affixation can be produced through combination. Third, the pattern generalization processes found in the back propagation network can help produce irregularizations. For example, the past tense forms "wrung" and "rang" could be produced either directly by rote or by generalization using the back propagation network.

4.2 Argument frame induction from lexical groups

The strategy of linking a Level 2 back propagation network to the Level 1 lexical SOFM also helps us account for the learning of syntactic patterns. The Competition Model (MacWhinney 1988) has consistently emphasized the role of lexical argument ("valency" or "dependency") relations as the basic controllers of syntactic structure. This analysis was grounded originally on the theories of Lexical Functional Grammar (LFG) (Bresnan 1982) and Head-driven Phrase Structure Grammar (HPSG) (Pollard & Sag 1994) that developed during the early 1980s. The role of lexical predicates in determining syntactic structure is now widely accepted. However, there is still no agreement regarding the ways in which children learn to attach argument frames to lexical items or groups of lexical items. Non-connectionist proposals regarding this learning can be found in Brent (1994), MacWhinney (1988), and Pinker (1984). Within a connectionist framework, the major attempts to deal with syntactic processing include Elman (1990). McClelland and Kawamoto (1986), Miikkulainen (1993), and St John (1992). However, none of these accounts comes to grips with the relation between argument frames and specific lexical items.

We know that the induction of argument relations must occur in parallel with the process of learning new words. To illustrate this process, consider an example in which the child already knows the words "Mommy" and "Daddy", but does not know the word "like". Given this state of lexical knowledge, the sentence "Daddy likes Mommy" would be represented in this way:

d a d i		l aɪ k s		m a m i
Daddy	|	unknown	|	Mommy

For the first and third phonological stretches, there are lexical items that match. These strings and the semantics they represent are masked. The unknown stretch is not masked and therefore stimulates lexical learning of the new word "likes". The core of the learning for "likes" is the association of the sound /laɪk/ with the meaning "like". In addition to this basic Level 1 lexical association, the child must also construct additional links to Level 2 argument relations. At first these patterns are grounded on a few lexical items. However, these Level 2 patterns quickly generalize to apply to lexical groups. The initial lexical argument frame for the word "likes" is:

    arg1: preposed, "Daddy", experiencer
    arg2: postposed, "Mommy", experience

Further exposures to sentences such as "Daddy likes pancakes" or "Billy likes turtles" will soon generalize the dependency frame for "likes" to:

    arg1: preposed, experiencer
    arg2: postposed, experience

No theoretical weight is placed on the notion of "experiencer" or "experience" and different learners may conceptualize this role in different ways.

Adjectives typically have only one argument. Prepositions have two — one for the object of the preposition and a second for the head of the prepositional phrase. Verbs can have as many as three arguments. For each lexical item, we can refer to these arguments as arg1, arg2, and arg3. When a group of words share a common set of semantic relations with a particular argument, they form a lexical group argument frame, or, more succinctly, a "group frame". For example, words like "send" or "promise" share the syntactic property of permitting a double object construction as in "Tim promised Mary the book". Pinker (1989) and others have argued that there are a variety of semantic cues which work together to decide which verbs allow this type of double object construction.

4.3 Relations between Level 1 and Level 2

Level 1 information is stored in SOFMs and Level 2 information is organized into back propagation networks dependent on Level 1 information. Figure 6.3.6 illustrates the overall shape of these relations. Activation of a specific lexical item on Level 1 induces argument frame information on Level 2. However, this item-specific information also leads to further activation on Level 2 for group frames. In other words, lexical items that have similar meanings will tend to activate similar group frames.

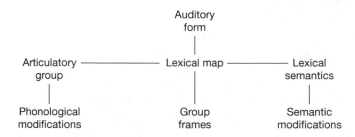

Figure 6.3.6 Relations between Level 1 lexical forms and Level 2 lexical groups.

4.4 Argument frames and the logical problem

Children often produce double object overgeneralizations such as "I recommended him the book". Bowerman (1988) and Pinker (1989) argue that, because children do not receive or process negative evidence correcting these errors, the process of recovery constitutes a difficult case of the logical problem of language acquisition. However, in the Competition Model framework, this learning is just as "benign" as recovery from errors such as "*goed" which were discussed earlier. Figure 6.3.7 illustrates the situation.

In this case, the child receives episodic support for the construction "X recommends Y to Z". However, there is also analogistic pressure from the argument frame of words such as "send" or "promise" for the double object argument frame "X recommends Z Y". Because the verb "recommend" shares many semantic features with transfer verbs such as "give" and "offer", it becomes attracted by that lexical

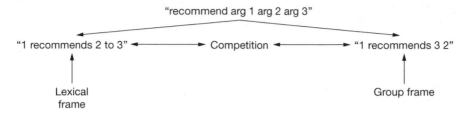

Figure 6.3.7 Competition between a lexical frame and a group frame.

group and is subject to group frame effects. In the case of "recommend", the double object frame is incorrect and receives no episodic support. Over time, the continuing growth of positive episodic support for the prepositional dative form will lead to a decrease in overgeneralizations of the double object form, without any need to invoke negative evidence. Thus, a competitive system of this type learns on the basis of positive evidence.

Perhaps the most complicated form of argument frame competition arises when there are two semantically similar lexical groups with alternative argument patterns. For example, verbs like "pour" or "dump" have a frame in which arg2 is the thing transferred and arg3 is the goal. Thus, we say "Tim poured water into the tub." Another group of verbs like "fill" or "cover" has a frame in which arg2 is the goal and arg3 is the thing transferred. Thus, we say "Tim covered the lawn with gypsum." [See Figure 6.3.8.]

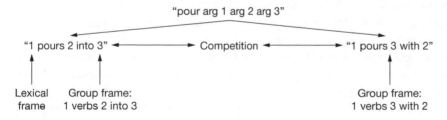

Figure 6.3.8 Competition between a lexical frame and two group frames.

4.5 Sentence interpretation

In addition to the Level 2 networks for phonological and syntactic modification, Figure 6.3.7 includes a Level 2 system for semantic modification. This system works to adapt meanings when words are linked together. Because connectionist systems are constraint satisfaction systems, rather than rule systems, they can deal with partial violations in the combinations of words. Consider a combination like "another sand". Typically, the word "another" requires a count noun and "sand" is a mass noun. However, when the listener is confronted with this particular combination, it is still possible to retrieve an interpretation by treating "sand" as a count noun. This can be done by thinking of bags of sand, types of sand, alternative meanings of the word "sand", or even the act of applying sandpaper to something. MacWhinney (1989) talks about these semantic extension effects in terms of a process of "pushy polysemy".

5. Functional neural circuits

The third level of neurolinguistic structure is the level of the functional neural circuit. This level requires the integration of information across large distances in the cerebral cortex. A prototypical example of a functional neural circuit is the phonological rehearsal loop that supports verbal short-term memory (Gathercole & Baddeley 1993; Gupta & MacWhinney 1994). Recent work with neural imaging (Grasby *et al.* 1993; Paulesu, Frith & Frackowiak 1993) indicates that this loop is based on the coparticipation of auditory processing areas in the superior temporal gyrus, attentional regions in the frontal cortex, and articulatory areas in the motor cortex. Similar posterior-frontal functional neural circuits have also been identified in visual processing.

Unlike Level 1 and Level 2 processing, the type of processing that requires the use of functional neural circuits can place severe demands on attentional resources. As long as sentence processing can emerge from Level 2 use of argument frame structures, a minimal demand is placed on additional attentional resources. As each predicate is linked to its several arguments, the listener shifts focus away from the individual lexical items onto the emerging sentence interpretation (Gernsbacher 1990; MacWhinney 1977). In effect, every word that is linked to the growing interpretation is "masked" in Level 1 lexical maps. This type of local processing is highly automatic and essentially effortless. However, some syntactic structures place a heavy demand on working memory. For example, in a sentence such as "The dog the cow the pig chased kicked barked", the listener cannot construct interpretations by linking each word to its neighbor. Instead the string of three nouns and three verbs have to be stored in unassociated form in working memory, while the listener attempts to find meaningful clusters. Sentences of this type, while technically grammatical, are notoriously difficult to process. Accumulations of unattached nouns in relative clauses are a well-known problem for speakers of SOV languages such as Hungarian (MacWhinney & Pléh 1988) and Japanese (Hakuta 1981).

5.1 Conservatism, functional circuits, and the logical problem

The Competition Model emphasizes the extent to which lexical competition can solve the logical problem of language acquisition. However, there are certain complex syntactic structures for which the lexical solution is more questionable. For example, O'Grady (1987) notes that children learn positive contexts for *wh*-movement in this order:

(1)   What did the little girl hit _____ with the block today?
(2)   What did the boy play with _____ behind his mother?
(3)   What did the boy read a story about _____ this morning?

Although one might be able to formulate a lexical basis for the processing of these *wh*-movement patterns, it is more likely that they involve a form of sentence memory that relies rather more on functional neural circuits and less on lexically-organized information. What is interesting is the fact that, precisely in these non-lexical contexts, children's tendency toward conservatism seems to be maximized. Children are never presented with contexts such as (4):

(4)   *What did the boy with _____ read a story this morning?

Because children approach the learning of these contexts conservatively, they seldom make overgeneralizations of this type and seldom attempt *wh*-movement in this particular context. The general principle seems to be that overgeneralization occurs primarily with Level 2 argument frame patterns and not with Level 3 long-distance movement patterns. For Level 3 patterns, the attentional and computational difficulties involved lead children to adopt a conservative approach that minimizes the role of overgeneralization. This is not to say that overgeneralization of long-distance movement never occurs. However, numerically speaking, it is much rarer than argument frame overgeneralization. Because of this conservativism, attribution of language acquisition to innate knowledge of conditions blocking subjacency violations seems unmotivated.

Summary

At this point, it may be useful to summarize the core assumptions being made in this account of language emergence:

1.   The model assumes an auditory processing mechanism that can extract information regarding the onset, nucleus, and coda elements of individual syllables.
2.   The information from the syllabic processor is supplemented by information from the prosodic processor which marks the position of each syllable in terms of feet and beats.
3.   Auditory and semantic information about words is encoded in a self-organizing feature map.
4.   Associations between sound and meaning are formed through Hebbian learning.
5.   Auditory information can be used to scaffold the construction of an articulatory representation. This is done in terms of syllables and prosodic structures.
6.   Masking in lexical recognition provides the support for the extraction of new affixes.
7.   Changes in stems and affixes can be controlled through a system of modifications using the back propagation algorithm.
8.   Sentence interpretation requires the linking of words in terms of argument structures. These structures are learned through frame generalization in back propagation networks which receive input form the lexical map.

9.   The processing of complex syntactic structures and lists of words requires the
      involvement of functional neural circuits including frontal attentional
      processing and temporal lobe verbal memory and rehearsal.

In this model of language development, the first commitment that the brain makes
is to the encoding of auditory, articulatory, and lexical information in localized
maps. After this information is consolidated, back propagation systems develop to
fine-tune the interactions of lexical items, and functional neural circuits control
capacity-intensive aspects of sentence processing.

   Although the developments we have discussed lead to a great complexity of
patterns and constructions, the underlying elements of feature maps, masking, argument frames, and rehearsal loops from which these patterns emerge are themselves
cognitively basic structures grounded in fundamental properties of neural structure
and functioning. Some aspects of these structures are probably basic to all of
mammalian cognition. However, the great elaboration of lexical structures that we
find in human language point to the extensive elaboration of earlier structures during
the million years of human evolution. Most recently, the overlay of functional neural
circuits between areas such as the frontal attentional areas and the temporal auditory areas has led to further species-specific advances in the capacity for learning
and using language. Moreover, the specific elaboration of lexical feature maps also
appears to be a specifically human adaptation. Although this model tends to emphasize the cognitive adaptations involved in supporting language processing, it would
be a mistake to ignore the important changes in social structure and interpersonal
subjectivity that have also supported the evolution of human language. Hopefully,
continuing rapid advances in our understanding of brain function and structure will
allow us to soon begin to understand how these emotional and social underpinnings
support the computational and cognitive structures we have discussed here.

   These biological and cognitive aspects of an emergentist account of human
language will eventually need to be related to the equally important social and
discourse pressures that control the shape of grammar and the lexicon. Together,
these various emergentist visions allow us to construct a new view of human
language that goes beyond the simple debate between functionalism and formalism
and emphasizes the interplay of alternative streams, mechanisms, and processes of
emergence.

Part 7

Bilingualism and Cross-cultural Comparisons

INTRODUCTION

S LOBIN (1973A) SAW THE possibility of constructing interesting arguments on the basis of data from research by Mikeš (1967). Mikeš had studied some young children acquiring two languages simultaneously. The languages were Hungarian and Serbo-Croatian, belonging to two different language families. Hungarian locative constructions (an example in translation would be 'in the drawer') are clearly marked through the choice of one out of a number of regular suffixes. But Serbo-Croatian locatives use a preposition and a suffix together, the suffix chosen from a set of suffixes which also encode other distinctions and exhibit quite a lot of irregular patterning. There is no reason to think that some languages are overall more complicated than others, but every language seems to have some tricky corners and some easy sections. There were times in the young bilingual children's development when their Hungarian locative expressions were correct, but they were making grammatical errors in Serbo-Croatian while talking about the same situations. Difficulty over understanding what it is for one thing to be located relative to another appeared not to be the explanation for immature Serbo-Croatian when talking about location, because the same children's Hungarian descriptions of similar situations showed that they could think the relevant thoughts. It seemed that cognition could develop ahead of language, and children's learning of how to put their thoughts into words then depended on the simplicity or complexity of the ways offered by individual languages for encoding particular kinds of thought. (The introductions to Parts 2 and 6 of the *Reader* also contain discussion of relations between language acquisition and cognition.)

Questions can be raised about the validity of the conclusions. Mikeš had studied only a small number of children and Slobin (1973a) did not present information about the balance between their two languages, nor on how often and in what ways the children heard adults talking about location in each of the languages; nor had comprehension been considered. However, Slobin had drawn attention to the potential of cross-linguistic comparisons in bilingual situations, the union of the two topic areas represented in the present part of the *Reader*. See Nicoladis (2002) for a recent example of this genre, with a substantial sample of children, and tabs kept on both input frequency and the balance between the child's two languages. Bilingual acquisition has long been a valued branch of child language research (e.g. Ronjat 1913; Leopold 1939–49; De Houwer 1990). Part of the foundation of modern cross-linguistic language acquisition research is a collection of major articles edited by Slobin into a series of books on the subject (1985–97).

Bilingualism

Romaine (1992: 126) surmises that about half of the world's population is **bilingual**. Bilingual people and situations differ on a number of dimensions. Chapter 7.1, the survey article by Romaine reproduced in the *Reader*, deals with **simultaneous bilingualism**. This term applies to the availability from birth (or soon afterwards) of adequate opportunities to acquire two languages. As the child gets older the judgement of bilingualism is increasingly based on levels achieved in the two languages rather than on availability of the languages in the child's immediate environment. How much of an opportunity is adequate? Barbara Pearson, summarising impressions from her bilingualism research, estimated that children exposed to a language for less than 20 per cent of their waking hours during the first three years of life, do not develop into speakers of that language, whereas they do with exposure of 25 per cent or more (see Pearson *et al.* 1997).

A child with adequate exposure to two languages from the start is, in effect, growing up with two first languages. **Sequential bilingualism** is the label for bilingualism achieved through the learning of another language only after the establishment in early childhood of a single first language. Sequential bilingualism is a goal in many education systems and it is the central topic in **SLA** (second language acquisition)[1] studies. SLA is beyond the scope of the *Reader*, but some important issues that have been focused on in the study of early simultaneous bilingualism can be set in context through a short consideration of the 'bilingual paradox', a term used by Petitto *et al.* (2001: 454) to describe the apparently contradictory thinking of some parents and educational planners.

The 'bilingual paradox' is seen when people who believe that children are particularly adept at language acquisition during early childhood nonetheless feel that experience of other languages should be withheld until later childhood. Illustrative data come in an appendix to an international comparison of language education (Dickson and Cumming 1996: 131), which shows, for 26 different education systems, the age that the majority of children start taking classes in English as a second or foreign language. At the time of the survey, the average age – across these countries – for beginning to study English at school was 9.8 years (SD = 2.0 years). In 16 of these education systems, German is taken as a second or foreign language by large enough numbers of students to justify the tabling of figures. For German the average starting age is 11.6 years (SD = 2.0 years). Why is English started at a younger age than German, on average? The answer is surely to be found in the global usefulness, allure and power of English (see Crystal 1997). Many millions of people with first languages other than English think it very important that they or their children should be taught English.

Another question suggests itself: if English is so important, then, given the widespread acceptance that young children are particularly good at language learning, why is the learning of English (or whatever second or foreign language is favoured) not generally begun at, say, 5 or 6 years old or even earlier? One reason is practical: in many countries there probably would not be enough trained infant school or early primary school teachers with adequate foreign language competence. A second reason is a common assumption that the first language should be properly established before another language is attempted; prevalent fears being that first language acquisition could be delayed and mental confusion induced through the child making a start in two languages at once.

Related to these concerns, one strand of research is concerned with whether acquisition is delayed in simultaneous bilinguals. Another is whether simultaneous bilinguals, in some early period of their development, have a single **fused** system for their two languages, instead of separate systems. If bilingual children do begin with a fused system it might be taken as confirming the feared confusion mentioned at the end of the previous paragraph.

The phenomenon of **code-switching** also strikes some people as symptomatic of confusion. In code-switching, bilinguals talking to other people who are bilingual in the same two languages will, in the course of a single conversation, change from speaking one of their languages to speaking the other (and such changes can occur back and forth repeatedly). Code-switching within a sentence — rather than between sentences — is sometimes called **code-mixing**, or just **mixing**. For example, Dewaele (2000) reports that at 21 months his daughter (who was growing up as a speaker of three languages), talking about her toy mother duck, asserted 'Maman petit canard spreken Nederlands', where the italicised part is in French and the rest is in Dutch (meaning 'Mother duck speak Dutch'). Monolingual outsiders listening to bilingual code-switching can find it disconcerting. However, adult bilinguals usually take into account the capabilities of their conversation partners and refrain from switching when talking to people who know only one of the languages.

Studies of simultaneous childhood bilingualism have examined not only whether there is code-switching in the early years, but also the age at which children begin to show sensitivity to the capabilities of their listeners, and the extent to which early code-mixing is grammatically systematic rather than haphazard. Pairs of words that are translation equivalents across young children's two languages are also of interest, because there have been suggestions that monolinguals shun synonyms in their early years; and a fused system might be similar in relevant respects to monolingual language competence. (In the introduction to Part 3 of the *Reader*, see discussion of 'mutual exclusivity', the subject of Merriman and Stevenson's paper (Chapter 3.2).)

Petitto *et al.* (2001) is a recent paper addressing these issues. Their investigation, of six simultaneous bilinguals representing two different pairs of languages, did not detect any delay and does not support the idea of a fused stage in simultaneous bilingualism. As regards code-switching, the children showed sensitivity to the language repertoires of their interlocutors and a grammatical basis – instead of randomness – when they mixed languages within single utterances. Perhaps fusion occurs in other children or perhaps it can be uncovered by different research methods, but Petitto *et al.* made a good attempt and did not find it.

An interesting result from the study by Petitto *et al.* (2001) highlights the informative potential of cross-linguistic comparisons, which will be considered next in this introduction. Petitto *et al.* compared the acquisition of two spoken languages (French and English) with the acquisition of a spoken language and the sign language of Quebec's Deaf community (French and Langue des Signes Québécoise (LSQ)). The language of many words spoken by the youngest of the French-English bilingual children could not be determined. For example the researchers could not decide whether the child's *ba* 'banana' represented an English word (*banana*) or a French word (*banane*), or both (2001: 472). Fully 42 per cent of the utterances recorded from this child between the ages of 12½ months and 20½ months were indeterminate in this way (2001: 482). The other two French–English bilinguals, who were older, also produced language-indeterminate words, though fewer of them. Does the difficulty of allocating these words to a language indicate a degree of vocabulary fusion in the children? It probably merely points to pronunciation (and perhaps transcriptional) difficulties, because there were no language-indeterminate words at all in the transcripts of the comparison group of three French–LSQ bilinguals. The visual and auditory modes are sufficiently different for there to be no difficulty over deciding whether a form belongs to the sign language or the spoken language.

Cross-linguistic comparisons in language acquisition

What happens in language acquisition depends on some or all of the following four factors, acting both separately and via interrelationships, such as the obvious dependence of (b–d) on (a) and their likely influence back on (a) over millennia:

a   human nature
b   features of the languages being acquired
c   the input and interaction offered by people in the environment that a child grows up in
d   ways of thinking.

Comparisons of situations in which some aspects of (a–d) vary while others remain constant are the basis for many attempts to understand how children acquire language. As Gopnik (Chapter 7.2) points out, there are obvious ethical reasons why experiments that interfere with children's language acquisition are not conducted.

However, language differences and cultural differences in the ways that adults and older children tend to converse with young children mean that many combinations occur in life anyway. These invite study by child language researchers. Researchers who study atypical language development at times compare children who are genetically exceptional (a) and/or atypical cognitively (d). The focus in the present introduction, however, is on studies involving comparisons of the (b) and (c) kind.

In Chapter 3.3 Bowerman reasons that language-specific features (b) are involved over and above innateness (a). Her evidence is in the form of coincidences between the semantic encoding of directed motion in Korean and English and in patterns found in, respectively, Korean- and English-acquiring children's utterances expressing directed motion. Gopnik (Chapter 7.2), also recounting findings from comparisons of children growing up as speakers of either Korean or English, reports differences in the paths (not the endpoints reached) that children follow during cognitive development (d) and language development. She seeks to relate these to differences in what adults characteristically talk to young children about in the two language communities (c), differential emphases which she suggests might, in part, stem from language differences (b). The fact that both language differences (b) and discourse patterns (c) are involved in these comparisons across the same two languages points to the intricate nature of argumentation in cross-linguistic research.

Fee (Chapter 5.2) and Hyams (Chapter 6.2) adduce data from language differences (b) to argue for general principles of language, possibly reflecting a human language faculty (a) (see the introductions to Parts 5 and 6 of the *Reader*, for additional discussion). Fee uses comparisons of early words in English and Hungarian child language to advance the case for an overarching account of syllable structure. Hyams supports a view on universals of syntactic development with evidence from the acquisition of nine European languages.

Peters (Chapter 6.1) mentions a dozen languages in her attempt to summarise and organise what is known about apparently meaningless but possibly developmentally interesting 'filler' syllables. She tabulates some patterns of acquisition and suggests that they relate, at least in part, to differences between languages (b), particularly as regards rhythmic structure.

Other articles in the *Reader* that cite cross-linguistic data are: Coates (Chapter 1.2) and MacWhinney (Chapter 6.3).

When we consider differences in the experiences that children have of people using language (factor (c), in the list above) useful cross-community comparisons can be made within a single language. A classic paper by Heath (1982) illustrates this. She wrote about three English-speaking communities, all in the south-eastern United States. The three communities differed in the practices they followed for introducing young children to books and Heath argues that this led to the children being rather differently prepared for participation in school learning. Aspects of communicative competence developed differently in the three communities, despite their shared language (see the introduction to Part 1 for more on communicative competence).

The papers

Towards the end of **Suzanne Romaine**'s survey of simultaneous bilingualism (Chapter 7.1), she deals with comparisons relating to different inputs, similar to those considered in the previous subsection of this introduction. When cross-linguistic comparisons are made in bilingual acquisition studies, an important control has been added: the same child is involved both times, so the innate contribution of the child is not a factor making for different outcomes. Consider Romaine's account of De Houwer's (1990) finding that her bilingual daughter, for a period, used simple past forms in English (such *jumped, fell*) but not present perfect forms (such as *have jumped, have fallen*), while, during the same period, doing almost the opposite with the corresponding Dutch forms, where she used present perfects most of the time. The explanation is that the simple past is more often used in adult English whereas the present perfect is the common way of talking about the past in Dutch. Note that this is a different outcome from one discussed at the beginning of the present introduction. Slobin's (1973a) interpretation of Mikeš's bilingual data offered linguistic complexity as an explanation for different ages of appearance of constructions in the two languages of bilinguals. However, in the Dutch–English case, we would have to say that the present perfect forms are linguistically more complex (because they require an extra word) but it seems that frequency of use overrode linguistic complexity. Romaine's classification (near the beginning of Chapter 7.1) of bilingualism into six different subspecies is an important step towards understanding how, not only family, but nation and society can affect the language acquisition of individual children.

Though simultaneous bilinguals start with two first languages, it is often the case that one of the languages becomes the **dominant** (or preferred language) of the child, and the importance of the other language can diminish. In part this depends on the amount of exposure the child gets to each of the languages, but another important influence on which language becomes dominant for the child is the amount of use and support the community provides for each of the languages. In characterising the six bilingual environments Romaine is careful to state the relationship between home languages and the language(s) with wider currency. (See the introduction to Part 1 for more discussion of language acquisition's social matrix.)

The question in one of Romaine's subheadings – 'Is a bilingual the sum of two monolinguals?' – is not just about arithmetic. It extends to education policy and fairness. The article by Petitto *et al.* (2001), mentioned earlier in this introduction, shows that in terms of vocabulary counts and the ages at which some important early milestones were reached, the children whom they studied could be argued to be numerically equal to two monolinguals each. This is not always so. For instance, bilingual children arriving at schools where the dominant school language happened not to be their dominant language have been tested in the school language and found to be below par. On this sort of basis, bilingualism has sometimes been asserted to be bad for intellectual development. Bilingualism is also, occasionally, inappropriately discussed under the heading of atypical language development.

Half the world does it, so it is not atypical and it certainly is not an impairment. When fair assessments are done, a reasonable question to raise is the one heading a section of Chapter 7.1: 'Is there cognitive advantage to bilingualism?'

Useful sources for further reading on bilingualism are Li (2000) and Oller and Eilers (2002).

In Chapter 7.2, **Alison Gopnik** discusses the **theory theory**, which offers the following metaphor for cognitive development: coming to understand the world amounts to acquiring and refining a theory about it. The theory simply is that the child's mental representation of everything is like a theory, and modification over time of the child's representation is similar to the way scientific theories change. In Gopnik's words: 'The idea is both that the types of knowledge that are acquired in childhood are theory-like, and that the processes by which they are acquired are analogous to processes of theory formation and revision in science'. This is not to say that all children are scientists like Marie Curie, Alexander Fleming or Rosalind Franklin. In fact, Gopnik suggests that average children are more like science students, who do not have to discover everything for themselves thanks to having teachers to tell them about existing theories and arrange demonstrations in which relevant observations can be made. Thus individual students get up to speed faster than science as a whole did in history, but they also pick up the biases of the particular schools of science they are trained in. As with science students, adult talk helps children discover their society's favoured theories of reality.

Gopnik reports on her investigations of three linguistic achievements and three cognitive developments that seem to arrive in pairs somewhere around the middle of the second year:

- words for disappearance – object permanence
- words for success and failure – solving means–end problems with sudden 'insight' (e.g. how to use a rake to get something that is out of reach)
- a spurt in vocabulary – ability to do exhaustive sorting into categories.

Though close in, time there does not seem to be tight linkage from any one pair to either of the other pairs, which Gopnik would have expected if all of these developments were a manifestation of a single underlying cognitive advance. Instead, she suggests that closeness within pairs and the imprecise time synchrony between them look like three separate areas of 'theory' being worked out by children.

Gopnik also presents cross-linguistic comparisons. In both longitudinal and cross-sectional studies, children growing up as speakers of English tended to have the vocabulary spurt earlier and they were usually more advanced on categorisation, relative to Korean children, but the Korean children led on success and failure words and means–end insight. She suggests that this is relatable to Korean parents talking more about actions, whereas the English-speaking parents talked more about objects. Gopnik sees the influence of language on children's 'theorising' becoming prominent from the age of around 18 months. It is interesting that Bowerman and Choi (2001: 477), who also did cross-linguistic comparisons between Korean and English (concerning a different area: expression of spatial relations, *in, on, off,* etc.) found evidence of language-specific influences 'from as early as the one-word stage'. They were able to look for earlier influences because they included comprehension testing in their investigation.

Benjamin Lee Whorf (1956), mentioned in the title of Gopnik's paper, studied Native American languages and was impressed by how different they were from what he called 'Standard Average European' languages. He went on to surmise that speakers might be influenced by their languages into particular modes of thought. The strongest form of this hypothesis is **linguistic determinism**: the idea that each language is a straitjacket forcing its users to think in ways determined by the language's structural characteristics. Gopnik is not a linguistic determinist. Instead she sees 'reality checks' as eventually ensuring that all children converge on rather similar 'theories'. She is merely claiming that different sequences and emphases during the course of personal theory development are influenced by the linguistic community children are reared in. Bowerman and Choi, in the paper mentioned above, restrict their claim to the impingement of language differences on how children learn to talk; whether and how children's thinking might be affected by this is a matter for separate investigation (2001: 477).

Note

1   See Lam (2001) and Nunan (2001) for introductions to the field of second language acquisition.

Suzanne Romaine

BILINGUAL LANGUAGE
DEVELOPMENT

Introduction

MOST OF THE RESEARCH ON children's language acquisition has
been concerned with monolinguals rather than bilinguals, despite the
predominance of bilingualism in the world's population. Moreover, most of it deals
with the acquisition of English (see however, Slobin, 1985[–1997]), and is largely
biased towards middle class children. In principle, the acquisition of bilingual
competence is no different from monolingual acquisition. Nevertheless, given the
diversity of the contexts in which children acquire language(s), it is not easy to
extrapolate from the available studies, what the "normal" sequence of development
might be for a child growing up in very different circumstances from those which
have been studied. It is therefore not yet clear what constitutes "delay" or "abnor-
mality" as far as bilingual acquisition is concerned. Investigators face the difficult
issue of how to decide whether utterances deviating from adult monolingual norms
reflect errors or are simply transitional stages in the normal development of bilingual competence.

The available literature on children's bilingualism is also fraught with methodological problems and does not yet provide a solid basis for answering decisively
many of the important questions one would like most to have answers to, e.g. to
what extent are the bilingual's two languages differentiated both at the conceptual
and linguistic levels; to what extent does bilingual acquisition parallel monolingual
acquisition; is it the case that a feature or category acquired from one language acts

1999, reprinted with permission from M. Barrett (ed.), *The Development of Language*, Hove: Psychology
Press, pp. 251–75.

as a booster to its acquisition in the other; and is there a cognitive advantage to bilingualism?

[. . .]

Types of childhood bilingualism

[. . .]

There are [. . .] possibilities for bringing up children bilingually which have been described in the literature and still others which occur but have not been studied systematically. Following Harding and Riley (1986, pp. 47–8), I have classified the main types of early childhood bilingualism which have been studied into five categories, depending on factors such as the native language of the parents, the language of the community at large and the parents' strategy in speaking to the child.

I have also listed some of the available studies of particular languages to be discussed in the course of this chapter (for a more detailed discussion see Romaine, 1995, chapter 5). I have given each of the five types a brief descriptive name based on some aspect of the strategy employed by the parents. In addition, I have included a sixth type, not mentioned by Harding and Riley, because their aim is mainly to give advice on the most successful methods of raising children bilingually. As will be seen later, the sixth strategy leads (arguably) to more mixing and interference than the other types, but it is nevertheless probably the most frequently occurring context for "natural" bilingual acquisition in multilingual societies. Unfortunately, it has also been the least systematically studied and most researchers treat mixing as a stage in the child's development which must be overcome if the child is to be a "true" bilingual.

Six types of childhood bilingualism

Type 1: "One-person-one-language"

> Parents: The parents have different native languages with each having some
>   degree of competence in the other's language.
> Community: The language of one of the parents is the dominant language of
>   the community.
> Strategy: The parents each speak their own language to the child from birth.

Some studies and the languages in each of mother, father, and the community, respectively: Ronjat (1913; German, French, French); Leopold (1939–49; English, German, English); Taeschner (1983; German, Italian, Italian); De Houwer (1990; English, Dutch, Dutch); Döpke (1992; German, English, English).

Type 2: "Non-dominant home language"/"one language-one-environment"

> Parents: The parents have different native languages.
> Community: The language of one of the parents is the dominant language of
>   the community.

Strategy: Both parents speak the non-dominant language to the child, who is fully exposed to the dominant language only when outside the home, and in particular in nursery school.

A study, and the languages of mother, father, and the community, respectively: Fantini (1985; Spanish, English, English).

Type 3: "Non-dominant home language without community support"

Parents: The parents share the same native language.
Community: The dominant language is not that of the parents.
Strategy: The parents speak their own language to the child.

A study, and the languages of mother, father, and the community, respectively: Oksaar (1977; Estonian, Estonian, Swedish/German).

Type 4: "Double non-dominant home language without community support"

Parents: The parents have different native languages.
Community: The dominant language is different from either of the parents' languages.
Strategy: The parents each speak their own language to the child from birth.

A study, and the languages of mother, father, and the community, respectively: Hoffman (1985; German, Spanish, English).

Type 5: "Non-native parents"

Parents: The parents share the same native language.
Community: The dominant language is the same as that of the parents.
Strategy: One of the parents always addresses the child in a language which is not his/her native language.

Some studies and the languages of mother, father, and the community, respectively: Saunders (1982/1988; English, English (German), English); Döpke (1992; English, English (German), English).

Type 6: "Mixed languages"

Parents: The parents are bilingual.
Community: Sectors of community may also be bilingual.
Strategy: Parents code-switch and mix languages.

Some studies, and the languages of mother, father, and the community respectively: Tabouret-Keller (1962; French/German, French/German, French/German); Smith (1935; English, English, Chinese); Burling (1959; English, English, Garo).

Similarities and differences in the types of bilingualism

Each of the types has something in common with the others. For example, in Types 1 and 2, the parents have different languages and the language of one is the dominant language of the community. What distinguishes them is the strategy used to address the child. In Type 1 the child is exposed systematically to both languages at home, while in Type 2, exposure to the community language is generally later and outside the home. In Type 4 the parents also have different native languages, but neither one is the same as the dominant language. Here the child gets exposed to its parents' two languages in the home and introduced to the community language later outside the home. In this case the outcome is a trilingual child. In Types 3 and 5 the parents share the same language, but in one case (3), the language of the parents is not the community language, and in the other, one of the parents addresses the child in a language which is not native to him/her.

Type 6 is perhaps a more common category than it might seem to be on the basis of its representation in the literature. In other words, multilingual communities are in the majority in the world's population so many children grow up in cases where individual and societal multilingualism coincide. There are a number of reasons why this kind of acquisition is not proportionately reflected in the literature on childhood bilingualism. The main one is that a great many of the studies have been done by parents educated as linguists, i.e. middle class professionals, investigating their own children's development.[1] Thus, the majority of detailed longitudinal studies deal with so-called "additive" bilingualism among privileged children, whose acquisition of a second language does not threaten or undermine the development of the other language (see discussion on any cognitive advantages to bilingualism at the end of the chapter).

Strictly speaking, Smith's and Burling's studies probably do not come under the heading of Type 6. Or perhaps Type 6 conflates what are really two different situations. I have included them here, however, because they represent cases where the child is exposed to two languages in the home in an apparently unsystematic fashion. Thus, the notion of "strategy" is misleading in all the Type 6 cases since no deliberate attempt was made to address the child in this fashion. In the case of Smith's study, the child had input in Chinese from nurses and playmates and input from parents in English. In Burling's case there was a Garo-speaking nurse and Burling himself, a native English speaker, reports that he also sometimes spoke in Garo (a Tibeto-Burman language) to his son.

A very common outcome of the "one-person-one-language" method was a child who could understand the languages of both parents, but spoke only the language of the community in which they lived. Sociolinguistic studies of *minority* languages have shown that it is usually very difficult for children to acquire active command of a minority language, where that language does not receive support from the community. This is especially the case if there is only one parent in the home speaking this language. In such circumstances the child can use the other language, but generally does not. There are, however, some success stories. Saunders (1982/1988), for example, has described in detail how he managed to bring his children up bilingually in German and English in Australia, even though neither he nor his wife are native speakers of German. Similarly, the comparatively greater success of one boy (Keith) out of the six English/German bilingual children whom Döpke (1992) studied in Australia is noteworthy since the father, like Saunders, was not a native speaker and he provided virtually all of Keith's German input. Other successes include those of Kielhöfer and Jonekeit (1983) with French and German in Germany, and Taeschner (1983) with German and Italian in Italy. However, it should be pointed out that in all these cases the minority language was not stigmatised, and the children came from an advantaged background.

As I will argue later, both Saunders' and Döpke's studies underline the fact that quality of input is more important than the amount. Both studies also attest the positive role that fathers can play in their children's language development, particularly in the transmission of a minority language.

In my discussion of some of the studies of these six types of childhood bilingualism, I will highlight only some of the major developments noted by the researchers. Often it is not possible to compare exactly the same phenomena across the different cases due to differences in methods and aims of the studies. Further in this chapter I will take a more detailed look at some of the issues arising from this research, e.g. cross-linguistic influence and code-switching.

There are obviously also many other factors I will discuss later which affect the outcome in each case. Among these are amount and kind of exposure to each language, parents' consistency in language choice, attitudes towards bilingualism on the part of children and parents, and the individual personalities of children and parents.

Theoretical issues in childhood bilingualism

Among the issues I will consider here are whether there are discernible stages in bilingual acquisition which parallel those of monolingual acquisition. A number of scenarios are possible:

1. Each language develops independently as it would in a monolingual child.
2. The acquisition of both languages is delayed by comparison to monolingual acquisition.
3. The child prefers or is dominant in one of the languages, and the acquisition of the dominant language determines the development of constructions and categories which are matched in both systems.
4. The two languages develop differently with respect to different types of constructions and categories.

I will examine evidence in the domains of vocabulary, phonology, and syntax. [. . .]

Is a bilingual the sum of two monolinguals?

There has been a tendency to regard bilingual competence as the sum of the acquisition of monolingual competence in each of the two languages rather than as a unitary system which allows the pooling of resources across two languages.

Researchers have often noted that bilingual children lag behind monolinguals in terms of vocabulary development (Doyle, Champagne, & Segalowitz, 1978). In an early study Smith (1949) tested Hawai'i children of Chinese ancestry in both English and Chinese. She found that the scores of these children on vocabulary development were below the monolingual norms. However, when the scores from the two languages were combined, the children compared favourably with monolinguals. Nevertheless, she (1949, p. 309) concluded that it would be unwise to start children in a second language unnecessarily during the preschool years, unless they were of superior linguistic ability.

Another example is Fantini's son Mario, who was first tested in English on the Peabody Picture Vocabulary Test when he was 4 years and 9 months and dominant in Spanish. He ranked only in the 29th percentile according to the established norms for monolingual English speakers. A day or so later he was tested in Spanish and his raw score doubled. However, in subsequent formal testing in English at school Mario compared favourably with his monolingual peers (Fantini 1985, p. 186).

Saunders tested his children's ability in the two languages at various stages. The boys scored well on tests for both German and English vocabulary. At age 5 years and 5 months Frank scored in the 75th percentile and Thomas in the 93rd in English vocabulary. Thomas at age 7 years and 3 months scored in the 98th percentile. Thomas's German was, however, consistently more accurate than Frank's. Saunders reports (1982, p. 162) that at age 5 years and 5 months Frank knew 144 out of 200 items in German and 135 out of 200 in English. At the same age Thomas knew more in both languages (155 in German and 145 in English). In both cases the boys knew slightly more German than English words. Even at 7 years and 3 months Thomas still knew more German than English words, which Saunders says is striking in view of the fact that there was a 3:1 balance in favour of English in the boys' input.

It is more revealing, however, to look at the boys' total vocabulary across the two languages since a bilingual's total vocabulary may exceed that of a monolingual child. This is the case for Thomas and Frank. Frank knew 163 out of 200 items in at least one of the languages. This is a higher score than he obtained in either of the languages tested individually. Thomas knew 169 out of 200 items in at least one language, which is also a higher score than either of the ones for the languages assessed individually.

These results serve to underline a point which is now increasingly made in the study of bilingual proficiency. It does not make much sense to assess bilinguals as if they were two monolinguals since it is unlikely that a bilingual will have the same experiences in both languages. For instance, Thomas at age 5 years and 5 months did not know the English term *soldering*, but knew its German equivalent.

The development of the bilingual lexicon

Most researchers have found that at any particular stage there are more words in a given language without equivalents in the other language than there are with equivalents. Taeschner (1983, p. 29) kept a detailed record of her daughters' production of equivalents for individual lexemes and for grammatical categories (see also Vihman, 1985). The girls began using equivalent vocabulary items around the end of the first year. Between the ages of 2 and 3, roughly one-third of the vocabulary items in the girls' lexicons were equivalents and two-third were new acquisitions. She (1983, p. 54) says that it is therefore problematic to compare the bilingual's acquisition of the lexicon with that of the monolingual child. The bilingual child's capacity to produce new words is split between the two languages. The child deals with this by giving priority to new words at the expense of equivalents. Thus, by using the total lexicon available at any given time, she is able to speak both languages and to denote the same number of new concepts as the monolingual child.

Taeschner (1983, p. 23) stresses the importance of bilingual children's acquisition of synonyms. Children learn the German word *Baum* in one context and the word *tree* in another. Words which may function as equivalents for adults do not necessarily do so for children. One of her daughters used German *da* for things that were present and visible, and Italian *la* (both of which mean "there") for things that were not present and not visible. Leopold's daughter Hildegard knew both *please* and *bitte*, but used the English words in formal situations, while the German one was used in familiar contexts.

Bilingual children also face the problem of apparent equivalents in the two languages which have different semantic extensions. Imedadze (1967) found that a bilingual Georgian/Russian child used the Georgian word *ball* to denote a toy, a radish, and stone spheres at the park entrance and then transferred these same denotations to the Russian equivalent.

The fact that bilingual children do not have twice the number of words in their vocabulary as monolinguals does not impair their ability to communicate. Doyle et al. (1978) came to this conclusion after examining 22 bilingual and 22 monolingual children between the ages of 42 months and five years, seven months. They found that the monolinguals had a greater number of words than the bilinguals did in their dominant language, but that the verbal fluency of the bilinguals was greatly superior to that of the monolinguals. This was measured in terms of ability to tell stories and by the number of concepts expressed by each child per story (see under the final heading of this chapter for further evidence of the superiority of bilinguals).

As with monolingual acquisition, there is considerable variability among children in the rate of vocabulary acquisition. For example, Fantini (1985, p. 142) comments that at the end of his second year Mario used only 21 words compared to Hildegard's 337. By age 3, however, he had a productive lexicon of 503 words.

The development of bilingual phonology

During the first two years, Hildegard evidently did not confuse the sounds of English and German. Leopold said that the deviations from adult norms were not due to interference between the languages, but to more general processes of simplification and substitution that are systematically found in the speech of monolingual children (see also Saunders 1982, p. 201). By comparison. Ronjat (1913) observed that his son Louis had mastered the phonemes of both languages at 3 years and 5 months, which represents a slight lag in terms of the norms for monolingual children. Leopold, however, admits that English and German are too similar to decide which language the child's early vocalisations belong to. It is impossible to tell whether Hildegard had separate phonological systems before the age of two.

Mario's Spanish sound system was the first to be established and accordingly his earliest English words, which were acquired later than Spanish, were given Spanish pronunciations. This phonological interference gradually decreased, although some residual problems remained until the fifth year. By contrast, English phonology exerted practically no influence on Mario's Spanish. Fantini (1985, p. 180) reports that at age 5, Mario's phonemic inventory was normal for both languages.

The development of bilingual syntax

As far as syntactic and morphological development is concerned, there are also conflicting reports on the degree of separateness of the systems being acquired. Saunders (1982, p. 47) found that both his sons tended to keep the syntactic systems separate. Only certain types of syntactic constructions posed some difficulty. Frank, for example, differentiated the word order rules in English and German in his use of the first past tenses he learned. Occasionally, however, he used the English pattern in his German utterances. Leopold's daughter and Taeschner's daughters had some difficulty with word order too. An example of one of these word order "errors" is: *Du hast vergessen das* [You have forgotten that]. The correct German should be: *Du hast das vergessen*, where the (pronominal) object, *das*, occurs between the auxiliary, *hast*, and the past participle, *vergessen*, or is "embraciated" by the two verbal elements. Frank's speech during this stage, however, always showed the correct placement of the verb at the end, when the first verbal element was a modal auxiliary.

Taeschner claims that her two daughters initially developed a single syntactic system which was applied to the lexicons of both Italian and German. Meisel (1989, p. 16) has, however, pointed out that her evidence is not altogether consistent with the three stage hypothesis. It is really only Lisa whose behaviour is consistent with the claim that there is a single syntactic system and Italian was clearly Lisa's dominant language.

Taeschner (1983, p. 164) found that although her girls acquired Italian word order in the same way and order as Italian monolinguals, their development in German was only partially the same as that of monolinguals. They did not immediately use the correct word order for subordinate clauses. Yet their word order strategy was not simply transferred from Italian, but reflected simply the ordering which would have been used if the two clauses had stood on their own.

Meisel's (1986, 1990a) data from French/German bilinguals indicated that not all bilingual children use this strategy. He (1986, p. 146) found that children who were acquiring French and German simultaneously used predominantly SVO word order, a pattern which is common to both languages, but not the preferred order for monolingual children acquiring either French or German. Monolingual French children more frequently placed the subject at the end, while German children put the verb in final position (see, however Meisel, 1990a, p. 285 for further details). Because the bilingual children learned very early to distinguish the word order regularities of the two languages, Meisel (1986, p. 170) concluded that bilinguals used grammatical means of expression earlier than monolinguals, although they acquire them in the same way. The use of SVO word order may, however, be the outcome of two factors, one of which is the overlap between the two languages with respect to this ordering. The other may be a universal preference for SVO order.

In other cases researchers have reported that the order of acquisition of grammatical categories reflected their difficulty as indicated by factors such as the perceptual salience and regularity of the linguistic means used to mark them. For example, Hungarian/Serbo-Croat bilingual children use locative case relations in Hungarian earlier than in Serbo-Croat (see Mikeš, 1967). In Hungarian the locative is encoded by means of a noun inflection. In Serbo-Croat it is marked by both noun inflection and preposition. Monolingual speakers of Serbo-Croat also acquire the locative relatively late (in comparison with Hungarian speakers).

Cross-linguistic influence

While virtually all researchers report some degree of cross-linguistic influence in bilingual acquisition, there is a great deal of variation in the amount reported at various stages, depending on the child's acquisition pattern. Researchers have also used a number of different terms defined in different ways to describe this influence, e.g. mixing, interference, borrowing, and code-switching. Volterra and Taeschner (1978), for example, use the term "mixing" to refer to the application of the same syntactic rules to two lexicons, while Redlinger and Park (1980) apply it to indiscriminate combinations of elements from each language. Genesee (1989), however, defines it as an interaction between the child's developing language systems (see also Genesee et al., 1995). Meisel (1995) proposes that the term "mixing" be restricted to errors in language choice on the part of a child already possessing two grammatical systems and fusion to refer to the inability to separate two grammatical systems. Fusion is the result of insufficient competence. Code-switching (i.e. alternation between two languages) can only occur then, according to Meisel, once there are two distinct grammatical systems in place.

Fantini (1985, pp. 127, 168) prefers to speak of a gradual process of separation rather than interference in cases where the languages appear fused from the beginning. What has been called interference may be a reflection of incomplete acquisition. Thus, in the case of his son Mario, he does not speak of interference until after the stage where the child began to use the languages separately, i.e. at 32 months. Imedadze (1967) found that separation occurred as early as 20 months for a Russian/Georgian bilingual child. Yet, many other researchers suggest that children younger than 3 years of age have not yet differentiated their languages. It would appear that at different stages in the developmental process and depending on various social circumstances, e.g. amount of mixing in the input, various components of the child's linguistic system go through periods of fusion and separation.

Bergman (1976), for example, attributed the use of mixed possessive forms to the child's exposure to a context in which a clear distinction was not maintained between Spanish and English. Although the child, Mary, was able to use correct forms in Spanish and English, she also produced forms like: es annie's libro ("it's Annie's book") and es de papa's ("It's Papa's"). (Compare Spanish: es el libro de Annie/es de Papa.) Bergman noticed that the mother of some of Mary's playmates used possessives like these. When Bergman asked her if she had used them often, she said that she had picked them up from her children. Thus, the mother's input was probably reinforcing the children's use of mixed forms, although it is not clear whether the mother was the original model. Bergman attributed interference to input rather than to the child's failure to differentiate the two codes.

It is not clear, however, that this was the only contributing factor. From the earliest stage Mary, unlike, for example, the Taeschner girls, kept the constructions separate in both languages and then went through a period of mixing before finally using each morpheme correctly in its respective language. Other studies of Spanish/English bilingualism in the United States have reported mixing in the child's input, but no evidence of an abnormal rate of linguistic development (see Huerta, 1977; Padilla & Liebman, 1975).

Gawlitzek-Maiwald and Tracy (1995) observed mixed utterances such as *ich hab gemade you much better* ("I have made you much better") in the speech of Hannah, a German/English bilingual at age 28 months, and *Esther du cutst dein toe* ("Esther you cut your toe") at age 32 months. Taeschner (1983, p. 131) too found instances of word internal mixing. Lisa between 28 months and 36 months, for example, used the German prefix *aus-* with Italian verbs, as in *Giulia hat ausbevuto?* "Has Giulia drunk everything?" (Compare German: *Hat Giulia ausgetrunken?*). Both girls also used the German past participle prefix *ge-* with Italian verbs, as in *lo ho gevinto*, "I have won." [< German *ge-* + Italian *vinto* "won"].

Such examples violate one of the major constraints operative in adult code-switching, namely, the free morpheme constraint proposed by Sankoff and Poplack (1981). This predicts that a switch may not occur between a bound morpheme and a lexical form unless the lexical form has been phonologically integrated into the language of the morpheme. To take an example from Spanish/English bilingual speech, this constraint would predict that *flipeando* "flipping" would be permissible, but that **catcheando* would not be, because *catch* has not been integrated into the phonology of Spanish, and therefore cannot take the Spanish progressive suffix *-eando*.

Petersen (1988), who found word internal mixing of this type in her study of Thea, a Danish/English bilingual child at age 38 months, attributed it to the fact that the girl was English-dominant. She found that Danish lexical morphemes could co-occur with either English or Danish grammatical morphemes, but Danish grammatical morphemes could co-occur only with Danish lexical morphemes. English grammatical morphemes, however, could co-occur with either Danish or English lexical morphemes. Thus, Danish *vask* "wash" could combine with the English suffix *-ing* to produce a mixed verb from *vasking* "washing". Combinations such as *her dukke* "her doll" are also grammatical, but forms like **liver* "lives", which combine English *live* with the Danish present tense verb suffix *-(e)r*, are not. Similarly, *wateret* "the water", which combines an English word with the Danish suffixed definite article *-et*, and *min bed* "my bed", a combination of Danish possessive pronoun and an English noun, are ungrammatical.

This means that of the four logically possible word types shown below which might occur through the free mixing of English and Danish grammatical and lexical morphemes, only the first three are permitted to occur. Petersen (1988, p. 486) found that the second type accounted for just under one-third of her data (28.5%). Half of the child's utterances were in English. Although the lexical morphemes were almost evenly divided between the two languages, there were many more instances of English grammatical morphemes. Over three-quarters of the grammatical categories Petersen examined contained English grammatical morphemes, while only 21% contained Danish ones:

Type 1   monolingual combinations of English grammatical morphemes and lexemes

Type 2   bilingual combinations of English grammatical morphemes plus Danish lexemes

Type 3   monolingual combinations of Danish grammatical morphemes and lexemes

Type 4   bilingual combinations of Danish grammatical morphemes and English lexemes

Lanza's (1992) study of Siri, a bilingual Norwegian/English girl, found a pattern of mixing different from that of Petersen's Thea. Siri used English lexical morphemes with Norwegian grammatical morphemes, e.g. *jeg eat* "I eat" (i.e. Petersen's Type 4), but Norwegian lexical morphemes did not occur with English grammatical morphemes, e.g. **I spiser* (i.e. Petersen's Type 2).

Petersen claims more generally that in utterances containing morpheme level code-switching, the encoding of grammatical morphemes in one of the languages is an indication of that language's dominance. This hypothesis requires testing with a larger sample of bilingual children. Thea represents somewhat of a special case like many of the other children whose development I have discussed in this chapter. She was always addressed in Danish by her parents and was never exposed to individuals who code-switched. Siri, on the other hand, was brought up in Norway with the "one-person-one-language" strategy. Her father spoke to her in Norwegian and her mother, in English. Lanza (1992) notes that the directionality of Siri's mixing, which is the mirror-image of Thea's, indicates Siri's dominance in Norwegian. She relied on Norwegian grammatical structure when communicating in English, but not on English grammatical structure when communicating in Norwegian. Siri also mixed more when speaking with her mother. Her mixing with her father was mainly lexical (discussed later on).

Nevertheless, Petersen's hypothesis would make the wrong prediction in a number of other cases. Burling's (1959) comment that Garo was his son's first language suggests dominance in Garo. Yet he found word level mixing of all four possible types. His son assimilated English vocabulary into Garo and used Garo endings on English words, as in the following example: *mami laitko tunonaha* "Mommy turned on the light". The roots of every word are English, but the suffixes *-ko* "direct object marker", and *-aha* "past tense", word order and phonology are Garo. Later when English sentences appeared, the boy borrowed Garo words into them and gave them English inflections. Petersen's hypothesis would predict that if the child were Garo-dominant, he would not use Garo words with English grammatical morphemes.

[. . .]

Researchers have since recognised the importance of looking at mixed utterances as a separate category. Gawlitzek-Maiwald and Tracy (1995) observed that Hannah's unmixed utterances followed the paths of development observed in monolingual children. That is, she fell within the normal range with respect to MLU for age, types of structures produced, and the sequence of emergence of structures.

Evidence for differentiation or fusion

It is often difficult to decide what counts as evidence for differentiation or fusion, with different studies counting different phenomena. Taeschner (1983), for instance, bases her decision on whether the child makes appropriate sociolinguistic choices. Does she speak the "right" language to the "right" person? This is a distinct issue, however, from whether the child has one or two linguistic systems. Part of the problem is the familiar one of what we can infer about competence from performance. Genesee (1989, p. 189) argues that in order to maintain the one language system hypothesis one would need to show that bilingual children could use items from both languages indiscriminately in all contexts. However, even if a young child at the two or three word stage of development produces mixed utterances, it may mean only that the child is drawing on his or her total communicative repertoire in order to be understood. Some children, such as De Houwer's (1990) Dutch/ English bilingual, Kate, showed no significant change over time either in address patterns or in her use of mixed utterances. From the outset, Kate tended to use English with English speakers and Dutch with Dutch speakers. In fact, De Houwer argues that no language dominance can be discerned. Nor in her view can mixed utterances be used to determine whether two languages are separate or fused. The problem in comparing studies is compounded by lack of consistency in defining terms such as switching, mixing, etc. as well as by lack of adequate studies of first language acquisition by monolingual children for comparison.

Some researchers consider the child to be "truly bilingual" only at the stage where there is separation of the two systems (Arnberg & Arnberg, 1985, p. 21). Leopold, for example, says that Hildegard was not really bilingual during the first two years. Some studies have found a reduction in the use of mixed forms after the point at which separation is alleged to have occurred (Redlinger & Park, 1980), while others have reported an increase (see Vihman, 1985, p. 316). However, since Redlinger and Park's study followed the children' development for only 9 months between the ages of 2 to 3, the decrease in mixing may reflect simply an increase in the number of lexical equivalents. In some cases it is not clear whether there are two separate languages to be acquired because the adults to whom the child is exposed always use a code-mixed variety. Redlinger and Park found more mixing in the speech of a child who had mixed input from adults. For this reason, language mixing *per se* is not a valid measure for determining whether the child lacks awareness of the two languages. Lexical mixing, in particular, may decline over time as the child's vocabulary increases thus lessening the need for borrowing from one language when speaking the other.

As far as Arnberg and Arnberg (1992) are concerned, awareness of the two languages as distinct plays a crucial role in deciding the issue of differentiation. However, as McLaughlin (1984) points out, the argument that bilingual children separate the languages when they are aware there are two systems is circular unless some criterion is provided for assessing what is meant by awareness other than that children separate the languages. Arnberg and Arnberg asked a sample of bilingual children to name pictures in each of the two languages on separate occasions. They also asked parents to rate their children on a scale of awareness. In addition, they collected a half-hour speech sample from the children to measure the percentage of mixed utterances. On the basis of their performance on the picture naming task, the children were grouped into categories of "aware" and "non-aware". The mean score for language mixing in the aware group was 1.7% and 12.3% for the non-aware group. There were no differences related to age or level of linguistic development as assessed by MLU and other measures.

Arnberg and Arnberg (1992) attribute differences in awareness primarily to social factors, such as patterns of exposure to the two languages and the extent to which parents drew attention to the two languages by offering children prompts such as "Mommy says", "how does Daddy say it?", and translations such as, "in Swedish that's called". Some parents reported they never spoke about the languages in this way, while one family had signs attached to common objects in the home with the words for each object in both languages.

Separate development

Evidence has recently been mounting in favour of the separate development hypothesis, although as yet, this needs more extensive testing with acquisition of languages which are very different typologically. De Houwer (1990), who has argued strongly in favour of separate development from birth, looked at two very similar languages, Dutch and English. Despite the obvious extensive similarities between Dutch and English, there are some clear differences, e.g. Dutch grammatical vs. English "natural" gender, and word order, where Dutch is more like German than English. De Houwer found that in both these areas and indeed with regard to the development of other areas of the grammar, Kate kept the two language systems separate. Her use of both gender systems was language specific from the start. There was also no influence from one language to the other in the verb phrase. De Houwer proposed a principle of morphological language stability, which predicts that when children acquire two languages simultaneously from birth using the one-person-one-language method, bound morphemes belong to the main language of the utterance from the beginning. Morphemes do not travel from one language to another.

Input and social context as factors affecting rate and order of acquisition

Quantity of input

More studies need to be done to determine the extent to which differential distribution of a form in the child's input has an effect on the emergence of a structure. A suggestive case can be found by comparing children's acquisition of the ergative in Samoan and Kaluli, a Papua New Guinean language. Kaluli children acquire ergative case marking quite early (i.e. at 26 months) according to Schieffelin (1981), while Samoan children do not learn it until relatively late (i.e. after 4 years) according to Ochs (1982). If linguistic and cognitive factors take precedence over other ones, then we would expect Samoan children to acquire ergative case marking no less early than Kaluli children since the category is encoded in both languages in a transparent and uniform manner. In Ochs's (1982, p. 78) view, however, the reason for "delayed acquisition" is social. Ergative case marking is not distributed equally throughout the Samoan community. It is more typical of men's than women's speech. Furthermore, it rarely appears in the speech of family members within the household, where women and older siblings are the child's primary socialising agents.

Ochs's findings certainly have far-reaching implications for developmental psycholinguistic studies which attempt to explain the order of acquisition of various structures in terms of purely cognitive and innate principles. Many of those who have argued for a link between complexity and order of emergence have not taken account of the fact that social context is an important mediator in this process. In De Houwer's study (1990, p. 234) the use of tense forms cannot be explained in terms of complexity. In English Kate used exclusively the simple past, while in Dutch she used mainly the present perfect, a form which could be said to be more complex than the English past. The simple past is, however, more frequently used in English than in Dutch, so it appears Kate is following the most frequent forms in her input.

Those aspects of language structure which are more specifically determined by or related to aspects of social structure will obviously be affected by exposure to the social contexts in which input for these features is present in sufficient amounts to trigger acquisition. One area in which this can be clearly seen is in the acquisition of the so-called T/V distinction. Languages like German, Spanish and French require the speaker to make socially appropriate choices between the second person singular vs. plural form of the personal pronoun (compare German *Du/Sie*, French *tu/vous*, Spanish *tu/usted*) depending on factors such as the social status of the addressee and the intimacy of the relationship between speaker and addressee. The stage at which these distinctions are acquired varies even for monolingual speakers (see Romaine, 1984, p. 142). Rural Hungarian children, for example, learn the system of address later than urban children because the rural child's network includes mainly family members and peers with whom the familiar pronouns are used. The formal pronouns are not used until a later stage (Hollos, 1977).

Similar factors can be seen to work in the case of some of the bilingual children under discussion here. Although Fantini's son Mario showed sensitivity to social distinctions at a very early age, even at age 10 he did not consistently employ the *tu/usted* distinction in Spanish (Fantini, 1985, pp. 110–11). Similarly, the Saunders' boys rarely used the more polite German form *Sie*. They scarcely heard it in the speech of others and needed only the more familiar form with their father. In addition, the familiar form is more frequently used in the Australian German-speaking community than in Germany (Saunders, 1982, p. 205).

Taeschner unfortunately does not comment on her daughters' acquisition of the pronominal address system, which might be expected to proceed differently for various reasons. For one thing, both German and Italian have similar systems. In the case of the Saunders' children and Mario, however, German and Spanish, which do have such systems, were being acquired along with another language, namely English, which did not. In both cases English was the language of the society at large, and the main language of schooling. Thus, the fact that English did not make such a distinction, coupled with the fact that the distinction did not receive support in the home context, could have had an effect on rate of acquisition.

[. . .]

Interactional styles

Other aspects of parents' interactional styles can make a difference too. Parents have differed in the extent to which they have adhered strictly to the one-person-one-language principle. Siri's Norwegian-speaking father, for instance, accepted replies from her in English, while her mother adopted a monolingual English strategy with her. Leopold and Ronjat did not supply vocabulary requested by their children in the other language, while Fantini and Saunders freely gave translations and supplied words when they thought the children needed them.

Döpke's (1992, p. 62) study of the varying degrees of language competence achieved by six German/English bilingual children in Australia stresses the importance of both these points. She concludes that there are two main factors which create a necessity for the child to become bilingual: One is the parents' consistency of choice of language and the other is their insistence that the child respects the "one-parent-one-language" principle. The children who achieved the highest degree of proficiency in German were Keith and Fiona. Both sets of parents were most consistent in their language choice and also most insistent that the child speak German when spoken to by the German-speaking parent. As I noted above, Keith's success was all the more remarkable given that all the odds were against him. Not only did he have a non-native speaking father, but his primary care-giver, his mother, was the non-German speaking parent. Even though Keith's father tried to provide contact with other German-speaking people and a variety of different language media, Fiona had a naturally much richer language environment. She had German-speaking relatives who came for long visits as well as the most contact with German-speaking friends of the family. Fiona also later made several trips to Austria, while Keith never visited a German-speaking country.

Attitudes

Attitudes of the extended family, the school, and society at large are also important. Even children within the same family can react differently to the attitudes of outsiders. One of Saunders' sons, Frank, ignored covert or overt disapproval of German and spoke to his father in that language wherever they were or whoever was present. Thomas, however, was much more sensitive and was reluctant to speak German at certain stages. For example, at 40 months he did not want to speak to his father in German in the environment of the English-speaking kindergarten. Frank, however, showed no such inhibition. When Thomas began primary school, the presence of other bilingual children encouraged him and he aligned himself with them (Saunders, 1982, p. 134). Both boys have expressed the desire to pass German on to their own children. Saunders' daughter Katrina at age 40 months reacted adversely at first when the family went to Hamburg for 6 months. She would not speak German to any adults but her father during the whole of her stay. Although she was able to interact in German with children at kindergarten, she did not speak to the teacher.

Saunders (1982, p. 114) notes that he was warned by a doctor just after Thomas's third birthday that speaking two languages was too great a burden and was inhibiting his acquisition of English. He advised the family to address him only in English. This assessment was made after a 15-minute examination in which Thomas's failure to perform well was attributed to his bilingualism, rather than to shyness or other factors in the testing situation. Similarly, Mario's English pronunciation attracted the attention of a teacher who wanted to send him for speech therapy. She was unaware that he spoke another language at home and was still Spanish-dominant when he entered kindergarten. His parents, however, resisted this attempt at remediation. Only two years later, however, his teacher expressed surprise when she found out that he spoke Spanish at home. His ability in Spanish and English thereafter continued without interruption to the extent that native speakers of Spanish and English never perceived Mario as anything other than a native speaker of their respective languages.

Many professionals such as speech therapists view normal language mixing as harmful and are therefore liable to give advice to parents which is not in keeping with the realities of normal bilingual development in bilingual communities elsewhere. Beliefs about bilingualism causing stuttering and delayed onset of language are also widespread, despite lack of evidence for them. Harding and Riley (1986, p. 126) write bluntly in their advice to parents: "It makes as much sense to ask your doctor for advice about bilingualism as it would to ask him about your car".

Is there cognitive advantage to bilingualism?

Contrary to the prevailing view in the first half of this century that bilingualism had a negative effect on children's intellectual development (see Hakuta, 1986 for further discussion), both Ronjat and Leopold believed that bilingualism did not disadvantage their children. Leopold in fact emphasised that there was some positive advantage in bilingualism. He said that Hildegard came to separate word from referent at an early stage and was aware of the arbitrary nature of the relationship through using two languages. Monolingual children are not aware of this until a later stage in their development.

Meisel (1990a, pp. 17–18) suggests that bilingual children exhibit less variation than monolinguals in their acquisition. Thus, the task of "cracking" the codes of two different language systems simultaneously enhances the child's awareness of grammatical categories and helps rather than hinders learners. He found, for example, that both bilingual German/French and monolingual German children go through an initial stage in which all inflection is lacking. However, this stage ends earlier for the bilingual than monolingual children. Compare this positive statement with Karniol's (1992) unsubstantiated claim that stuttering is prevalent in bilinguals due to the syntactic overload imposed by processing and producing two languages (see Paradis & Lebrun, 1984 for counter evidence).

The alleged advantages and disadvantages of bilingualism have been generally assessed with reference to their impact on intelligence, itself a controversial concept. Martin-Jones and Romaine (1985) have discussed the ways in which negative and erroneous ideas about bilingual children's language development become "received wisdom" in educational circles and are passed on uncritically.

In a series of studies done by Bialystock (1987, 1991, 1992), bilinguals were more advanced than monolinguals in specific uses of language applied to certain types of problems. She says (1987, p. 138) that bilingual children were notably more advanced when they were required to separate out individual words from meaningful sentences, focus on only the form or meaning of a word under highly distracting conditions, and reassign a familiar name to a different object. Each of these tasks requires selective attention to words or their features and the performance of some operation on that isolated component, e.g. counting the number of words in a sentence. The ability to attend selectively to units of language such as words and their boundaries and to apply specific processes to them is an integral part of using language for advanced and specialised purposes such as literacy. Bialystock says that the seemingly diverse range of tasks on which bilinguals are superior to monolinguals are all dependent on high levels of selective attention, which is a central mechanism of cognitive performance.

These kinds of general abilities to manipulate language as a formal system have sometimes been referred to as "metalinguistic" skills, or in other words, the use of language to talk about or reflect on language. They allow an individual to step back, so to speak, from the comprehension or production of language to analyse its form. Such skills are believed to be helpful in learning how to read and necessary for advanced uses of oral and literate language in school (Bialystock, 1991). Schooling in general increases an awareness of language as an object in and of itself (Romaine, 1984). Metalinguistic problems demand a high level of selective attention, such as when a child is asked what the sun and moon would be called if they switched names. In order to separate the word from its meaning children must attend selectively in an unusual way. Translation is also another example of a metalinguistic task. Many bilingual children are habitual and skilled translators.

Yet bilingualism is still in many quarters seen as a stigma and a hindrance to children's intellectual development, and cited as a reason for children's failure in school. It is no accident that many of the alleged negative consequences emerge in cases where children are socially disadvantaged, e.g. the children of migrant workers in various parts of the European community, or among the Chicano population in California. Most of the studies demonstrating positive advantage have looked at bilinguals who were equally proficient in both languages and given every opportunity to develop that proficiency.

There are many different ways and contexts in which children become bilingual, and not surprisingly, many different outcomes. It is too early to compare with any confidence the outcomes of monolingual and bilingual acquisition.

Note

1   This is a well-established research practice in the study of first language acquisition too.

Alison Gopnik

THEORIES, LANGUAGE, AND CULTURE
Whorf without wincing

IF THERE IS ONE CLEAR CONCLUSION to be drawn from this volume [i.e. Bowerman and Levinson 2001] it is that, after decades of obloquy, Benjamin Whorf is back. Of course, Whorf never really went away in the popular imagination or in the wilder reaches of the post-modern humanities. In serious cognitive psychology and cognitive science, though, that very fact reinforced the sense that Whorfian ideas were disreputable, not to say crackpot. In contrast to this scornful tradition, many of the chapters in this volume, both empirically and conceptually, seriously explore the possibility that the language we hear can have strong effects on the ways that we understand the world.

Aside from the sociology there were more serious reasons why cognitive science rejected Whorf. There were obvious empirical objections to his work. More broadly, Whorf presupposed a relativist, indeed a wildly relativist, and anti-realist ontology. In contrast, cognitive science is realist and anti-relativist almost by definition. "Cognition" refers to the way that we learn about the world around us in an at least roughly veridical way, and the assumption of cognitive science is that there are general procedures all human beings use to do so. Since the late 1960s psycholinguistics has built on this cognitive foundation.

In this chapter, I will outline an approach to the idea that language restructures cognition that is congruent with the wider insights of cognitive science rather than in conflict with them. I will suggest that one recently influential theory of cognitive development, what I will call the "theory theory", offers an interesting and novel account of the relation between language and thought. The theory proposes

2001, reprinted with permission from M. Bowerman and S.C. Levinson (eds), *Language Acquisition and Conceptual Development*, Cambridge: Cambridge University Press, pp. 45–69.

that cognitive development is analogous to processes of theory formation and change in science. The analogy to science suggests an interactive relation between language and cognition that is not like either the classical Whorfian or anti-Whorfian views. I will also present data from extensive empirical studies of the relation between language and cognition that support this view. In particular, I will present data from cross-linguistic studies comparing English and Korean which show that particular kinds of linguistic input can influence cognitive development. I will suggest that the analogy to conceptual change in science gives us a new way of characterizing these effects of language on cognition. We can combine Whorfian ideas with the insights of contemporary cognitive science.

1 The theory theory

Recently, an increasing number of cognitive developmentalists have employed the model of scientific theory change to explain cognitive development. The idea is both that the types of knowledge that are acquired in childhood are theory-like, and that the processes by which they are acquired are analogous to processes of theory formation and revision in science. This model of development has been applied to a wide range of areas of children's knowledge, including their understanding of the physical world, the biological world, and the psychological world (Karmiloff-Smith & Inhelder 1974; Karmiloff-Smith 1988; Gopnik 1984, 1988; Carey 1985, 1988; Wellman 1985, 1990; Keil 1987, 1989; Perner 1991; Gelman & Wellman 1991; Gopnik & Wellman 1992; 1994; Wellman & Gelman 1992). We have argued that these theory formation processes are deep and fundamental. There may be innate theories and the process of theory change and revision begins even in infancy (Gopnik & Meltzoff 1997).

We might think of the theory-formation view as a view about the characteristic representations that children employ in understanding the world and the characteristic rules they use to manipulate those representations. The thesis of the "theory theory" is that the rules and representations of infancy and childhood are similar to the rules and representations that are involved in scientific progress. There are several features, on this view, that are characteristic of theories and that differentiate theories from other types of cognitive structures.

First, theories have distinctive structural characteristics. Theories postulate abstract entities related to one another in complex and coherent ways. Causal attribution plays an important role in theories: theories are essentially accounts of the underlying causal structure of the world. As a consequence theories have distinctive functional features as well. They generate characteristically wide-ranging and unexpected predictions about evidence. Theories support both deductive and inductive inferences. They allow you to make constrained predictions about new events. Knowing that two animals are members of the same species, for example, allows you to make quite specific and new predictions about the properties of those animals. Theories also have strong interpretive effects. They lead to selections, interpretations, and sometimes misinterpretations of evidence. Finally, theories provide explanations of evidence.

Perhaps most importantly and distinctively of all, however, theories change. These changes are caused by external evidence, particularly, though not exclusively, counter-evidence to the theory. Often the initial reaction to evidence is simply a kind of denial – the theorizer ignores the counter-evidence. Eventually, however, enough counter-evidence accumulates to force revisions, and, eventually, even more radical changes in the theory. Simple falsification, however, is often not itself enough to generate theory change. An alternative theory must be available. The alternative theory often seems to come by borrowing ideas from other parts of the theory or from theories of other domains. For example, Darwin takes the idea of artificial selection, which was widely appreciated and understood, and applies it to natural processes of species change. (For detailed discussion see Gopnik & Wellman 1994; Gopnik & Meltzoff 1997.) These dynamic aspects of theories will be most important in considering the relation between language and thought.

[. . .]

In my work, I have also applied the theory theory to cognitive developments in infancy, particularly to several striking cognitive changes that take place in late infancy (Gopnik 1988; Gopnik & Meltzoff 1997). During the period between about fifteen and twenty-one months, there appear to be significant changes in children's understanding of several basic domains, including their understanding of object appearances, of actions and goals, and of object categories. These changes are reflected in changes in the ways that these infants solve problems and act on objects.

Piaget originally observed some of these changes. He characterized them as manifestations of a single stage change, from early sensorimotor representations to a new "symbolic" type of representation. This new type of representation was a prerequisite for the emergence of language. Piaget's account of this transition is plainly incorrect. Many of the "symbolic capacities" Piaget identified, such as language use and deferred imitation, turn out, empirically, to be in place well before these other cognitive changes take place. Moreover, and more generally, recent work on infancy suggests that such abstract representations must be in place much earlier in infancy to underpin a variety of kinds of early knowledge. Finally, many studies suggest that the various types of changes in the broad period of late infancy are not correlated with one another. Although, on average, the abilities emerge at around the same age, there can be considerable independence among them.

I have argued that these changes can be more helpfully construed as theory changes. They involve fundamental and yet quite abstract and complex aspects of children's understanding of the world. These include children's understanding of the way that we perceive (or fail to perceive) objects, the way that our actions fulfill (or fail to fulfill) our goals, and the way that we divide the world into "natural kind" categories. These changes are manifested in changes in the ways that children search for hidden objects (in "object permanence" tasks), design solutions to problems (in "means–end" tasks), and spontaneously sort and classify objects.

Changes in infants' underlying conceptions of these domains have quite wide-reaching implications: a variety of the infant's predictions and interpretations of evidence seem to shift together in a theory-like way. For example, at about eighteen months infants make a new set of predictions about a wide range of object disappearances, disappearances about which they made inaccurate predictions at fifteen months. These predictions seem to depend on a quite general conception of the way that objects can be perceived or can fail to be perceived. Similarly, infants begin consistently to make a wide range of new predictions about the causal properties of objects in this period, and use these predictions to guide their actions on the objects. Finally, children at this age develop new classification and categorization behaviors which may be the first sign of some understanding of "natural kinds." (See Gopnik & Meltzoff 1997, for detailed discussion.) Moreover, these changes are reflected in children's language. Early words do not just pick out some set of perceptual or functional features, nor do they simply encode social routines. Instead, they may, and often do, pick out events with quite different superficial features but similar underlying causal structure.

These changes also have some of the characteristic dynamic features of theory change. The two-year-old's conception of these domains appears to be qualitatively different from that of the one-year-old, and yet at the same time seems to follow logically from the failures of the earlier account. Children also seem to engage in extensive experimentation in these problem domains in this period.

2 Language, culture, and theorizing

How do language and culture fit into this picture of the child as theorizer? What role would the child's linguistic and cultural experience, and social life more generally, play in cognitive development on this view?

There is a classic opposition between two contrasting views of the relation between language and thought. On the one hand there is the Piagetian view which argues that cognitive and conceptual development are the driving force behind language development. On this account semantic development depends upon and reflects earlier conceptual development.

In spite of the ideological divides between Chomskyans and Piagetians, a similar view has been widespread in the Chomskyan tradition. The neo-Chomskyan position differs from the classical Piagetian position in two important respects. First, neo-Chomskyans tend to see cognitive structure itself as innate rather than constructed or developed. Second, and more significantly, they see cognition as a necessary but not sufficient condition for semantic development. On this position merely having a cognitive representation of the world does not determine one's semantic representations. Further rules are necessary to determine which aspects of the cognitive representation should be encoded linguistically.

For example, Pinker argues that children learn the semantic structure of their particular language by linking the cognitive representations of relevant contexts to the relevant syntactic structures, a process he calls "semantic bootstrapping" (Pinker 1989). Landau & Jackendoff (1993) suggest that semantic structures encode innate and universal representations that are determined by the perceptual system. Perhaps the most influential view of this sort in the literature on lexical acquisition comes from the work of Markman and her colleagues. Markman has proposed that there are quite general linguistic constraints on children's interpretation of early words. These constraints influence, even determine, children's decisions about which concepts those words encode (Markman 1989). The assumption behind the "constraints" view, however, is that these constraints are additions to basic conceptual structure. The child's conceptual system is capable of multiple construals of the world, and the constraints determine which of those construals will be encoded linguistically.

In contrast, Whorf (1956) and Vygotsky (1962) both advanced a view that was closer to what we might now call "social constructivism." On their view, much of cognitive development could be seen as the internalization of concepts that were provided by relevant adults in the society, particularly through the medium of language. Whorf emphasized the role of the particular syntactic structures of particular languages. The implication was that these structures embodied particular conceptual structures which were transmitted to speakers of the language. Vygotsky emphasized the particular distinctive pragmatic characteristics of the language parents produced in the course of their interaction with children, what we might now call "motherese." Again, however, the implication was that these linguistic interactions shaped children's cognitive development as well as their semantic development. More recently a number of researchers have been reviving both neo-Whorfian and neo-Vygotskyan ideas about this sort of influence of language on cognition.

The theory theory is often perceived as a theory that deemphasizes the role of language, culture, and social life in cognitive development, and so as a theory that would endorse the idea that cognition precedes language. Critiques of the theory theory often make the assumption that seeing the child as "little scientist" means seeing the child as a cognitive isolate, a recluse. This is not, of course, what children really are like, but then it is also not what scientists really are like. Both theoretically and empirically, the theory theory is very congruent with a stronger, more interactionist view of the relation between language and thought. In fact, we have argued that the model of theory change in science provides us with a particularly perspicuous way of understanding such interactions between cognitive and linguistic development. The view that emerges is different from either of the classical opposing views.

On this view, we can think of the child as analogous to a physics student, or perhaps to a "normal" scientist hearing about a new theoretical possibility from a scientific innovator. Consider the acquisition of scientific terms like *entropy* in these circumstances. Developing an understanding of such words and the ability to use them appropriately is one sign, often the most relevant sign, of theory formation. We pay attention to words like *entropy* because they are relevant to the scientific problems we are trying to solve. At the same time, however, learning the words is an important part of learning the concepts. At the simplest level, hearing the same word across a variety of contexts may lead us to see similarities in those contexts that we might not otherwise have considered. Hearing the professor say *entropy* both when she discusses randomness and when she discusses heat may lead us to link these otherwise disparate phenomena, and this linkage itself has implications for other aspects of our understanding of physics. At a more sophisticated level, *entropy* gains its meaning from its connections to a number of other concepts in a complex, coherent theoretical structure. Most of us acquire this structure largely through the medium of language.

Neither the Piagetian/Chomskyan prerequisites view nor the classical Whorf/Vygotsky interactionist view seem to capture the character of this sort of semantic change in science. In such cases we do not say either that conceptual development precedes semantic development or vice versa. It is not simply that we have an innate repertoire of concepts, including "entropy," and are merely waiting to map the correct term onto that concept. But it is also not that we are simply mindlessly matching our linguistic behavior to that of our teacher, and that our cognition is shaped accordingly. Rather the two types of developments, learning the word and learning the related concept, appear to go hand in hand, with each type facilitating the other.

3 Developmental relations between language and cognition

Starting in the late 1980s, we have conducted a series of studies examining the empirical relations between linguistic and cognitive development in 15- to 21-month-old children. The results of these studies support the "theory-like" interactionist approach I have just outlined. Particular cognitive developments and related semantic developments appear to be closely linked, but one area does not seem to be a prerequisite for the other. Our earliest studies looked at the cognitive developments between 15 and 21 months that we described earlier as theory changes: object permanence and means–ends developments. These changes in problem-solving behavior turn out to be related to the emergence of "relational" words like *gone* and *uh-oh*. More recently we have examined the relations between children's spontaneous categorization and their development of a naming spurt. In a series of intensive longitudinal studies, we recorded children's spontaneous language development in detail using both a maternal questionnaire and video recordings, and also recorded children's performance on a variety of nonlinguistic cognitive tasks.

We found a relation between the development of words for disappearance, like *gone*, and the development of high-level object permanence abilities, a finding also replicated in other studies (Corrigan 1978; McCune-Nicolich 1981; Gopnik 1982, 1984; Gopnik & Meltzoff 1984, 1986; Tomasello & Farrar 1984, 1986). Within a week or two of the time children showed the highest-level object search behaviors in the laboratory, their mothers, quite independently, recorded that they had begun to say words like *allgone*.

We discovered another independent relation between words encoding success and failure, such as *there* and *uh-oh*, and the development of means–ends abilities, in particular the ability to solve certain problems with "insight," immediately and without a period of trial and error (Gopnik & Meltzoff 1984, 1986). Again within a week or two of our first observation of these behaviors in the laboratory, mothers independently reported the emergence of these words.

Finally, we found a relation between the naming spurt and children's spontaneous classification – in particular, the ability to sort objects exhaustively into many categories. This finding has been replicated by Mervis & Bertrand, both in normally developing children and in children with Down's syndrome (Gopnik & Meltzoff 1987, 1992; Mervis & Bertrand 1994). In addition, we have replicated and confirmed all these longitudinal studies with data from cross-sectional studies with a larger number of subjects (Gopnik & Meltzoff 1986, 1992).

All three of these specific relations between semantic and cognitive developments have some similar characteristics. All three take place on average at about
the same time, around 18 months. All three involve particular semantic developments, the development of words with specific types of meanings, rather than
involving structural developments, such as the ability to use words or combine
them. Most significantly, in all three cases, the linguistic developments and the
nonlinguistic cognitive abilities appear to emerge at about the same time, within a
few weeks of one another in our longitudinal studies.

However, the three conceptual domains – knowledge about our perception of
objects, reflected in "object permanence," knowledge about desires and actions, and
knowledge about object categories – are strikingly independent of each other. Some
individual children acquire *gone* and related nonlinguistic object permanence abilities
months before they acquire "success/failure" words and related means–ends
abilities. Other children reverse this pattern. Moreover, while there are strong
relations between the ages at which the semantic developments emerge and those
at which the related cognitive developments emerge, the cross-relations do not
hold: object permanence is not linked to success/failure words and means–ends
development is not linked to disappearance words. The same pattern holds for
means–ends development and the naming spurt. Specifically, there are relatively
small temporal gaps between the related cognitive and semantic developments, the
two developments literally appearing at almost the same time in longitudinal studies.
There are much larger gaps between the unrelated developments. Individual children begin to say the words and develop the related abilities at about the same time.

Similarly, in cross-sectional studies, eighteen-month-olds who solve object
permanence tasks are more likely to say *gone* than children who do not solve these
tasks. They are not more likely to say *uh-oh*. Eighteen-month-old children who solve
means–ends tasks are not more likely to say *gone* than children who do not (Gopnik
& Meltzoff 1986). Thus there are also specific correlations between linguistic and
cognitive abilities in cross-sectional samples.

Rather than being the result of some more general relation between linguistic
and cognitive abilities, these relations appear to involve quite specific links between
particular conceptual developments and related semantic developments. These
results are among very few empirical demonstrations of a close and specific relation
between language and nonlinguistic cognition in this period (or in any other).

The specificity of these results strongly suggests that a conceptual change
underlies both types of development, the nonlinguistic cognitive changes and the
emergence of new words. By themselves either the linguistic or the cognitive
changes might be due to many general developmental changes. For example, the
words might emerge because of changes in general linguistic or phonological abilities, or the changes in problem-solving behavior might be the result of increased
mnemonic or motor abilities. Indeed such proposals have been made in the literature. The close and specific relations between the semantic and cognitive
developments are, however, very difficult to explain on these views. To explain
these developments we need to postulate some underlying causal factor, some
change in the child's mind, that is common to both the emergence of *gone* and the
development of object permanence problem-solving, but is not common to either

the emergence of *uh-oh* or the development of means–ends skill. A conceptual change, of the sort we see in theory change, seems the best candidate.

Notice that the fact that the two developments emerge at the same time provides particularly strong evidence for a causal relation between these particular linguistic and cognitive abilities. The correlational cross-sectional evidence shows that children who had developed the linguistic abilities tended to have developed the related cognitive ability. However, it might be that some earlier linguistic or cognitive development was responsible for the later developments, and the apparent relation between the specific cognitive and linguistic developments at eighteen months was due to these earlier relations. Of course, this would still imply that there were specific links between cognitive and linguistic developments, but they might not be the links we have identified. However, the fact that the two developments emerge at almost the same time would be difficult to explain on this view.

These relations don't fit neatly with either of the classical pictures of the relations between language and thought. Eighteen-month-olds do not simply encode every aspect of their cognitive representation of a context. They also do not encode the aspects of cognitive representation that are most fundamental to the grammar of the adult language, as the neo-Chomskyan views would suggest.

On the other hand, children also do not simply match the patterns in the speech they hear. The children's uses of such relational words as *gone* and *uh-oh* to encode concepts of disappearance and failure are often strikingly different from the uses of these words in the language the children hear. Children apply *gone*, for example, to a very wide range of cases in which an object is not visible to them, from turning over a piece of paper, to putting a block in a box, to turning away from an object. However, they never use *gone* to refer to the fact that an object is invisible to someone else. In fact, in some of our studies children would select a word to encode these concepts on the basis of just one or two salient uses. For example, one little girl used *come off* to refer to all cases of failure and Bowerman reports a similar use of *heavy* (Bowerman 1978).

These children choose to encode the concepts that are at the frontiers of their cognitive development, the concepts that are central to the theories that are currently under construction. In fact, there are interesting parallels between the kinds of cognitive developments that seem to occur between fifteen and twenty-one months and the kinds of concepts expressed most frequently in early language in the same period. Object appearances, actions, and kinds, as well as spatial relations, are all areas of great cognitive significance to children of this age. These are also the notions that are most likely to be encoded in early language.

So we have shown that linguistic development and related conceptual changes are closely linked. This concurrent development suggests a picture like the picture of our acquisition of scientific terms like *entropy*, where semantic and conceptual changes also seem to be closely linked. But we also said that hearing about "entropy" might itself be a cause of the conceptual change. Is this also true in childhood? Could linguistic input itself be a factor in theory change?

The fact that, in our longitudinal studies, the semantic and conceptual developments occurred in close temporal concert suggested that the interaction might go in both directions. The changes in problem-solving occurred at about the same time as the linked linguistic changes, and sometimes the linguistic changes preceded the changes in problem-solving. This temporal pattern raises the possibility that language was causally implicated in the conceptual change. Moreover, some studies suggest that providing infants with linguistic (or nonlinguistic) labels for objects in the laboratory makes them more likely to categorize those objects (Roberts & Jacob 1991; Waxman 1991; Baldwin & Moses 1994). Neither of these finding by itself demonstrates, however, that language is implicated in the kinds of theory changes we have described here.

4 Crosslinguistic studies

How could we further test the interactionist hypothesis that language may restructure and influence cognition? As always in developmental psychology, the crucial experiments are immoral or impossible: we could not experimentally alter children's linguistic environment and observe the effects on their problem-solving. We could, however, see whether naturally occurring variations in linguistic input are related to different patterns of cognitive development. Both Bowerman (1989) and Slobin (1982) have suggested that morphological and syntactic differences in different languages might make certain conceptual distinctions particularly salient. In collaboration with Professor Soonja Choi at San Diego State University, I have been investigating the relations between language and cognition in Korean-speakers (Gopnik & Choi 1990, 1995; Choi & Gopnik 1995; Gopnik, Choi, & Baumberger 1996).

English has a highly analytic structure, with relatively little reliance on morphological variation. Moreover, nouns are generally obligatory in English sentences. In contrast, Korean and Japanese, languages with similar structures, have a very rich verb morphology, depend on different verb endings to make important semantic distinctions, and are verb-final. Pragmatic rules in Korean and Japanese allow massive noun ellipsis, particularly in informal conversation where the objects that are referred to are present (Clancy 1985). Parental speech in these languages, which occurs in precisely such a setting, often consists of highly inflected verbs with few nouns, very much in contrast to North American English parental speech. As will be shown, we have found that Korean-speaking mothers consistently used fewer nouns than English-speaking mothers, and Fernald & Morikawa (1993) report a similar pattern for Japanese-speaking mothers.

There is also some evidence that there are differences in the very early language of Korean- and Japanese- vs English-speaking children. A number of investigators have noted that Korean- and Japanese-speaking children use verb morphology productively earlier than English-speaking children, but use fewer and less varied names (Tanouye 1979; Clancy 1985; Choi 1986, 1991; Rispoli 1987; Fernald & Morikawa 1993; Choi & Gopnik 1995. Au et al. 1994 did not detect such a difference but there are a number of methodological reasons for this (see Gopnik et al. 1996)). Given the relations between language and cognition in English speakers we might predict that Korean speakers would be advanced in their understanding of actions, concepts encoded by verbs, and delayed in their understanding of object kinds, concepts encoded by nouns. These both seem to be important areas of conceptual change between fifteen and twenty-one months.

Gopnik & Choi (1990) studied the linguistic and cognitive development of five Korean-speaking children in an intensive longitudinal study. The results suggested that both the emergence of a naming explosion and the development of exhaustive categorization were indeed particularly delayed in Korean-speaking children relative to the children in a comparable English-speaking sample. In a second longitudinal study (Gopnik & Choi 1995; Gopnik et al. 1996), we tested a larger sample of Korean-speaking children. In each testing session children received both the cognitive tasks that we used in our earlier studies of English-speakers and an extensive language questionnaire specifically designed for Korean. Children received means–ends tasks that required the use of insight (such as using a rake to pull a distant object towards them), and spontaneous categorization tasks (such as sorting a set of different objects into groups). There was a significant difference between the Korean and English speakers' performance on the categorization tasks. The Korean speakers were significantly delayed on this measure compared to the English speakers. Similarly, there was a significant difference between Korean and English speakers' performance in the development of a naming explosion: Korean speakers were also delayed on this measure.

Importantly, however, the opposite pattern held for the development of means–ends abilities and success/failure words. Korean-speaking children were significantly advanced in both these areas of development compared to the English speakers.

In a second cross-sectional study we again compared the cognitive performance of eighteen Korean-speaking children and thirty English speakers (Gopnik et al. 1996). The results confirmed those in the longitudinal studies. The Korean speakers were significantly worse on categorization tasks than the English speakers: only 11% of the Korean children passed the task while 47% of the English speakers did. In contrast, 89% of the Korean speakers passed the means–ends task while only 60% of the English speakers did.

Moreover, we also collected data comparing the speech of these Korean-speaking mothers to the speech of English-speaking mothers. At the start and end of each testing session in the cross-sectional study, the mothers were asked to play and talk with their children for five minutes in one of two semi-structured sessions, either "reading" picture books or playing with a toy house. We then analyzed the mothers' use of nouns and verbs. Korean-speaking mothers consistently used more words that were relevant to actions than English speakers, they used more referential verbs – that is, verbs that refer clearly to actions – and in a pragmatic analysis they also used more activity-oriented utterances than English speakers. In contrast, English-speaking mothers used more nouns, more referential nouns and more naming-oriented utterances. The specific patterns of relations suggest that these differences in linguistic input may be responsible for the children's different patterns of cognitive development.

Precisely which aspects of the input are influential is still unclear. Crosslinguistic studies suggest that some languages which syntactically permit noun omission, like Italian, pattern differently than other languages, like Mandarin Chinese. Mandarin children, like Korean children, use verbs as early and as frequently as nouns, while Italian children do not. Our findings also suggest that it is not simply the presence or absence of nouns and verbs in the input that is important but the way that they are used in speech to children (see Caselli, Bates, Casadio, & Fenson 1995; Gopnik *et al.* 1996; Tardif 1996; Tardif, Gelman, & Xu 1999, for discussion).

5 Language as evidence

How might we conceptualize these effects of linguistic input on cognitive development? The classic Whorfian interpretation of these findings might be that the syntactic differences between English and Korean determine a basic difference, a kind of incommensurability, in the ways that English and Korean speakers conceptualize actions and objects. The behaviors of the children reflect this type of incommensurability. The English-speaking children conceive of the world in fundamentally different ways than the Korean speakers.

This view seems to us far too strong, both too strong in general, and too strong, in particular, when applied to our data. After all, in our studies both Korean and English children eventually seemed to converge on similar understandings of both actions and objects. At least, both groups of children came to share the same problem-solving abilities, and presumably the same conceptions of the world underlying those abilities, by the time they were two or three. On the theory view, the reason they did so was because these conceptions were accurate, or, at least, they accounted for the vast majority of the evidence that was available to the children in the most economical way. The differences lay more in the timing and the route by which children converged on the solutions than in the solutions themselves.

An alternative way of understanding these differences is that the different patterns of linguistic input in the two languages provided children with different patterns of evidence that were relevant to the cognitive problems the children attempted to solve. Recall that a crucial aspect of the theory theory is the idea that patterns of evidence cause theory formation and change. In principle, quite different patterns of cognitive development could take place, and quite different theories could be developed, if children were exposed to different patterns of evidence. The usual common, even universal, patterns of development stem from the fact that, for the problems children try to solve, the patterns of evidence are not typically very variable. The disappearances of objects or the relations between means and ends will generally be apparent in all the evidence the infant collects, and that evidence will be ubiquitous.

But once language enters the picture this uniformity and ubiquity will change. In infancy children are always acquiring evidence directly from their observations of the environment. Cultural patterns may have some effect, even at this point: children who are exposed to different types of objects may develop certain theories before others. Still, these cultural effects will largely be swamped by the uniform and ubiquitous behavior of objects, behavior that infants can easily observe.

At about eighteen months, however, children have a powerful new source of evidence about the structure of the world. As soon as children become members of the linguistic community they will acquire much, indeed most, of the evidence they use in theory formation through the medium of language. By the time they reach the stage of adult science, only a tiny portion of evidence will come from direct observation. The use of linguistic evidence is a double-edged sword. On the one hand, it gives children access to a vast store of information that has been accumulated by other people at other times. This includes information about far-off times and places that the child could not directly observe. On the other hand, it also raises the possibility that there will be wide variation in the kinds of evidence that individual children will receive. In fact, different children might receive conflicting evidence through the medium of language, depending on the beliefs of their adult informants. At the stage of adult science, this becomes a thorny problem, which requires a great deal of social infrastructure for its solution.

These effects of linguistic evidence on theory formation may range from relatively weak to quite strong. Simply using language at all in a context can be a powerful way of drawing children's attention to that context. At 18 months, or even earlier, infants already seem to recognize that language can be an important source of information about the world and to attend to events that are linguistically marked. In the case of Korean more language seems to be produced in action contexts than in object contexts, while the opposite pattern holds for English. At the simplest level a child who is paying more attention to actions than to objects might well have a more advanced understanding of that domain.

Moreover, the patterns of lexical use across contexts can draw children's attention to particular evidential patterns. The use of a single common name for a wide variety of objects, for example, may present the child with *prima facie* evidence that there is some common underlying nature to those objects. Moreover, such behaviors may suggest to the children that other inductive predictions about the objects will follow from their common name. Objects with the same name will also share other properties. In fact, there is good evidence that by 2½ or 3 children do make these assumptions. Linguistic similarities lead children to assume that there will be other similarities between objects. In fact, linguistic similarities play a more powerful role in determining children's inductions than other perceptual similarities between objects (Gelman & Markman 1986; Gelman & Coley 1991).

More generally, the very fact of naming itself, the fact that all objects are named, might lead children to notice, in general, that objects belong in categories. I have suggested that this may be the explanation for the link between the naming spurt and exhaustive categorization. The relevant fact about both these behaviors is that *all* objects, not just particularly salient or important objects, are named or classified. In the naming spurt, children provide, and search for, names for everything they see. In exhaustive categorization they spontaneously place all the objects they see into groups. The naming behaviors of mothers may prompt the children to make this more general inference that all objects have names and belong in kinds, as well as to make the particular inference that objects with the same name belong to the same kind. This may be particularly likely when mothers themselves are constantly naming a wide variety of objects, often for no apparent reason. This was the sort of behavior we saw particularly frequently in our English-speaking mothers.

Conversely, Korean mothers' emphasis on verbs may lead infants to attend to actions and relations. We know much less about children's developing understanding of actions and relations than about their understanding of objects (perhaps partly because most psychologists speak English!). The Korean mothers are also more likely to mark similarities between actions and relations than the English mothers, and this behavior may lead children to make further inferences about these events. Some suggestive evidence along these lines comes from the work of Choi & Bowerman (1991) on early spatial verbs in Korean. Korean spatial verbs mark different distinctions than spatial prepositions in English. For example, Korean verbs make distinctions between loose and tight fit rather than between containment and support. The Korean children show similar patterns in their use of these words from an early age. The theory theory would suggest that these children might also show distinctive nonlinguistic patterns of inference about spatial relations that reflect these linguistic patterns. If such effects do exist they might be analogous to the effects that Gelman found in the domain of objects. Just as children assume that giving the same name to two objects means that they share a common nature, so they may make similar assumptions about marking two spatial events with the same verb.

More general effects might also be found. Just as the English-speaking children may have been prompted to the discovery that *all* objects belong in kinds, so Korean-speaking children may be prompted to similarly general discoveries about actions and relations, such as the fact that *all* actions may succeed or fail. Korean verbs mark the success or failure of actions in a particularly clear and perspicuous way. We have argued that this more general understanding of the nature of actions is reflected in the changes in children's performance on means–ends tasks, particularly the emergence of "insightful" problem-solving. These changes involve a very wide variety of particular actions and events. The cognitive changes appear to have less to do with the child's understanding of particular events (such as their understanding of tight and loose fit or support and containment) than with their understanding of how actions lead to events in general (see Gopnik & Meltzoff 1997). In our studies, these linguistic and cognitive developments are closely related.

Our studies have been concerned with lexical rather than syntactic and morphological acquisition. We might speculate, however, that as children come to understand syntax and morphology, and begin to appreciate the propositional structure of language, language might play another and still stronger role in theory formation. One important element in theory change is the accumulation of patterns of evidence and counter-evidence. The kinds of linguistic effects I have discussed so far seem to reflect the way that children use language as a source of evidence. But another important factor in theory change is the availability of alternative theoretical models to the currently held models. As I mentioned earlier these alternative models may come from many sources.

Once we have complex syntax and morphology, language itself may be an important medium for passing on alternative theoretical models to children. Adults may not only pass on the relevant evidence to children, they may also provide the child with alternative theoretical models more directly, by representing them syntactically. Again, the fact that the theory the child will converge on is available in the adult language in this way may partly explain why the child's cognitive development is relatively swift – at least, in comparison to the slow and painful development of theories in science. As I mentioned earlier, in this regard the child may be more like a science student than a scientist *per se*.

This last possibility begins to sound more like the strong Whorfian alternative I initially rejected. The important difference, however, is that I think that the child is driven by considerations of veridicality, of predictive accuracy and explanatory adequacy, throughout development. Children will only consider novel patterns of evidence if they are congruent with other information in the world. The fact that objects have the same name *does*, in fact, correlate with other inductive generalizations about the objects. It is a good inductive strategy to predict that a new object that is described as a *cat* will have the same properties as familiar objects that are also called *cat*. Similarly, the general fact that all objects have names does correlate with the nonlinguistic fact that all objects belong in kinds, [. . .] so that this inductive strategy can be applied quite generally and productively. On my view purely arbitrary linguistic generalizations, generalizations that did not lead to good predictions or explanations in this way, would be rejected or reshaped.

Similarly, on this view, an alternative theory that was presented linguistically would only be accepted if it was relatively congruent with the child's previous theories and current evidence. If this is not the case the child may simply fail to make the new theory his own. (At one point I asked my six-year-old if he knew why the moon changed its shape. He replied with a surprisingly polished recital of the scientific story, only to add at the end: "Actually, I don't know why it changes at all, this is just what my big brother told me." Further discussion showed that this was quite true.)

More frequently, the theory the adults present will be modified and restructured to be more explanatorily adequate from the child's point of view. I mentioned examples of this kind of restructuring of input in our own work on children's use of "relational" words — for example, the use of *come off* to mean failure. Similar examples abound and many are offered in other chapters in this book [i.e. Bowerman and Levinson 2001], particularly in the work of Eve Clark and Melissa Bowerman. A particularly elegant example comes from Carolyn Mervis' work on child-basic categories (Mervis, Mervis, Johnson, & Bertrand 1992). In her studies, for example, young children used *money* only to refer to coins rather than bills. The adult use points to the underlying theoretical similarity of these objects in our "folk" (and for that matter our scientific) economics. But young children have no way of beginning to understand or evaluate this type of theoretical structure. Instead they restructure the adult usage to fit their own theories of the world more closely.

One might, in this way, be a kind of Whorfian in one's recognition of a strong effect of language on cognition and yet reject the anti-realism and relativism that seems to accompany the Whorfian position. Children do pay attention to the particularities of the adult language, and these particularities do affect the child's conception of the world. They do so, however, because they feed into universal mechanisms for understanding the world, particularly mechanisms for theory formation and change.

[A section on 'theories, language, and relativity in adults' has been edited out of the version of this article reprinted here. Eds]

Note

This research was supported by National Science Foundation Grant DBS9213959. I am grateful to Andrew Meltzoff, Dan Slobin, and the contributors to this volume [i.e. Bowerman and Levinson 2001] for ideas and comments.

Appendix
About statistical analysis

THESE NOTES ARE INTENDED for readers unfamiliar with statistical analysis. The hope is that talking around a small selection of relevant concepts will make the statistical statements that appear in some of the papers in the *Reader* less intimidating. For those who want to know more there are courses, or they could read a beginner text, for example Coolidge (2000), and then go on to a more comprehensive manual such as Howell (1996) or Cramer and Howitt (2002). Some people's learning styles might be catered for by the 'tutorial' and 'help' files in a computer statistics package.

The appendix introduces the following terms, in the order set out in this list. Commonly used abbreviations are given in parentheses.

sample
population
mean, or average (M)
variability
range
standard deviation (SD)
standard error
significance
t-test
probability (p)
analysis of variance (ANOVA)
Wilcoxon test
Mann-Whitney test

chi-square test (χ^2)
contingency
correlation
Pearson correlation coefficient (r)
Spearman's *rho*
causality

Statistical analysis is concerned with interpreting information in numerical form: measurements (such as how many words there are in a child's utterance) or counts (such as how many of a child's sentences in a transcript lack a grammatical subject). A central issue for statisticians is the assessment of how confident we can be about estimating, on the basis of numbers that derive from study of a **sample**, what the numbers would be for some larger collection that the sample is thought to represent. The larger collection is called a **population**, though it does not have to consist of people. It could be middle-class, monolingual English-speaking toddlers in the US. But it could be all the utterances spoken by a particular child from, say, age 24 months to age 25 months (many of which might never have been recorded).

If all the items in a sample were exact duplicates, like the products coming off a simple assembly line, then we could be rather confident that ones we haven't seen yet are going to be the same. However, humans aren't like that. Human performances almost always evince variability. A toddler who, on average, speaks in three-word utterances, will often produce utterances one or two words in length and will sometimes produce utterances longer than three words, perhaps occasionally managing an eight-worder. Where there is lots of variability it is less easy to be confident about generalising from a sample to the population.

Graphs and other visual displays are valuable tools for making sense of numerical information. They are often used for initial exploration of the patterns in a set of data and some of them may be reproduced in the eventual published work. If statistical summaries in an article are hard to grasp, a degree of understanding can often come from studying any visual presentations there are of the data.

An obvious way of beginning to summarise the numbers that come from a sample is to say what the **average** (or **mean**, often symbolised by *M*) is. Because of variability, however, it is important also to indicate the extent that the numbers fluctuate on either side of the average. The mean of 2 and 3 and 1 and 2 and 2 and 2 is 2 (because 2 + 3 + 1 + 2 + 2 + 2 divided by 6 equals 2), but the mean of a more variable set of numbers, e.g. 0 and 0 and 4 and 1 and 3 and 4 is also 2; so just indicating the average is not enough. The extent of **variability**, or spread, around the central figure should also be quantified. Merriman and Stevenson (Chapter 3.2) take a step in this direction when they report the **range** (lowest and highest observed values) of 45 to 668 around the average vocabulary score of 381, for the 32 children in their experiment.

But even knowing that the child credited with the smallest vocabulary had 45 words and the top scorer had 668 does not tell us how much variability there was among the other 30. Were they clustered close to the mean of 381 or did their vocabulary totals vary widely? What is needed is a kind of average of the amount by which each of the 32 children strayed on one side or the other of the mean. The **standard deviation** is the most common way of stating this kind of 'average of departures from the average'. It is not calculated in the same way as an ordinary average, but involves squaring and the taking of a square root. Statistical packages are readily available to compute standard deviations, and introductory books will explain how it is done and why. (At various points in Chapter 3.2, Merriman and Stevenson report standard deviations, e.g. for the means in Table 3.2.1.)

An approximation for making some sense of a reported standard deviation (or *SD* as it is often abbreviated) can be illustrated with an example from Chapter 4.2 (Swan). She states that Ross, the child in her study, averaged 3.4 novel word types per month with an SD of 3.1 words. Subtract the SD from the mean and remember the answer (3.4 − 3.1 = 0.3). Add the SD to the mean and remember that answer too (3.4 + 3.1 = 6.5). These two answers give a band 0.3–6.5, from one SD below the mean to one SD above the mean. That band (two standard deviations wide, with the mean in the middle of it) is interesting because, generally, when it is appropriate to report SD values (technically, when the distribution is roughly symmetrical), the band from 1 SD below to 1 SD above the mean encompasses roughly two-thirds of the sample. Swan sampled Ross's productions in 36 different months. Two-thirds of 36 is 24 months. Thus in a large majority of months – around 24 of the months – Ross innovated between 0.3 words and 6.5 words. (He couldn't very well have innovated .3 or .5 of a word; so it would be better to say that he innovated between no words and seven words in two-thirds of the months.) When he innovated 14 words in one particular month he was going well beyond the band of 0–7, but that was unusual, and calculation of the SD gives Swan a way of indicating just how unusual it was.

Getting an indication of the scores for two-thirds of the sample in this way (by calculating the 2SD-wide band around the mean, by subtracting one SD from the mean and adding one SD to the mean) is not exact and not guaranteed to be true every time, but it is often close enough to be worth calculating when the SD is given for a mean that is of some interest to you.

Most statistics textbooks explain how – provided the data are a random sample from the population – the SD together with the number of observations determines a **standard error** of the mean, an indication of how close the sample mean might be to the population mean that is being estimated on the basis of the sample. This is the main reason why standard deviations are so often presented in journal articles. They indicate how confident we can be about inferences based on averages from samples.

In Coates' survey of the acquisition of gender-differentiated language (Chapter 1.2) she quite often says whether or not a difference between the speech of females and males was found to be **significant**. Several – not all – of the differences that she refers to are differences between averages. The way the significance of some of those differences between means was assessed can be illustrated by examining a comparison between two averages presented by Merriman and Stevenson (Chapter 3.2).

In Merriman and Stevenson's experiment, 32 two-year-olds were asked to indicate all of the bears in an array of pictures that included two atypical exemplars,
a bear with a long neck and one with oversized feet and a funny tail. In other trials
they performed the same task in relation to arrays of spoons, horses and cars.
Beforehand the children heard a story in which one of the atypical exemplars was
repeatedly labelled with a competing name. Of great interest to Merriman and
Stevenson was whether the competing label would make the children reluctant to
select that specific atypical exemplar. (In the case of the bear pictures, prior
labelling of one of the pictured animals as a *mave* would perhaps suggest to the
children that it could not be a bear.) The relevant result was that atypical exemplars that had been given a competing label were selected by the children, on
average, only 1.25 times in four trials. By comparison, atypical exemplars that had
not been given a competing label were selected on average in 1.84 out of four trials.
Is the difference between the two means, 1.25 and 1.84, one that deserves attention; is it significant? A test of significance called the **t-test** is commonly used to
assess the significance of differences between two means.

Concentrated pondering alone cannot answer the question of whether 0.59
(which is the difference between the means of 1.25 and 1.84) is impressively big.
Variability within the sample has to be brought into consideration. If the standard
deviations associated with the two means are small, showing that children's performances clustered closely around each of the two means, then the difference is worth
paying attention to. If the standard deviations are large, showing a big spread in
performances up and down from each of the means, then the difference is less
impressive.

Merriman and Stevenson report the results of a matched sample t-test which
indicates that the difference between the two means is significant. This t-test divides
the difference between means by the standard error (which, as mentioned above,
depends on the standard deviation, i.e. reflects variability in the sample). The
purpose of doing a division is to calibrate the difference in relation to the variability: big variability divided into the difference yields a small number, but if the
variability is small it won't reduce the size of the difference so much when divided
into it. The result of this division is known as *t* and, in statistics books and computer
software, there are tables for looking up whether or not a calculated value of t is
significant.

The verdict from the table comes as a **probability** (usually abbreviated to *p*).
For the difference between the means of 1.25 and 1.84, Merriman and Stevenson
report that $p < .02$ (i.e. p is less than two per cent). In significance testing, *small*
values of p are significant. The usual convention in statistics is to treat a result as
significant if p is less than five per cent (i.e. $p < .05$). It is small values of p that
are significant because this is the theoretical *probability of a result as impressive
as the one under test being found by chance alone*. Thus, in the light of the amount
of variability in their sample, the difference that Merriman and Stevenson found,
of 0.59 between the two means, would be expected to occur by chance alone on
fewer than 2 per cent of the occasions when that experiment is performed. They
did it once and got the result. You can believe that it was a fluke, but (given how

rarely it could have come about by chance) most researchers in this field would treat it as a significant finding.

Finding statistically significant results is not the goal of research. Statistical analysis is a merely a tool used in research, and interpretation of statistically significant results should always be tempered by asking whether they make sense and are of relevance.

There are other tests, besides the t-test, for the significance of differences between means. **Analysis of variance** (abbreviation: ANOVA), also used by Merriman and Stevenson, compares more than two means simultaneously. ANOVA makes it possible to 'unpack' multidimensional interrelationships. The **Wilcoxon** Signed Rank test and the **Mann-Whitney** test, both employed by Richards and Malvern (Chapter 2.3), are substitutes for the t-test, suitable for use with small samples and in other cases when a t-test may be inapplicable.

A different kind of significance test, the **chi-square test** (abbreviated as χ^2), is used when the information from the sample comes in the form of counts of how children (or sentences, or consonants, etc.) were found to be divided between different categories. For instance a table reproduced by Coates (Chapter 1.2) indicates that 10 girls (out of a sample of 12) used predominantly a standard pronunciation for the suffix -ing and only 2 of the girls more often had a non-standard pronunciation for -ing. The 12 boys in the same study divided differently: only 5 used predominantly the standard pronunciation; the other 7 pronounced the suffix in a non-standard way on the majority of occasions. Coates does not give details, but when chi-square is calculated for the data and looked up in a chi-square table, the result turns out to be significant ($p < .05$, which indicates that a split as disparate as this would be expected to occur less than 5 per cent of the time if chance alone was responsible). The observed difference would only rarely be likely to occur by chance. When something rare is observed we usually sit up and pay attention; so it was reasonable for the researcher, who carried out the investigation just once and yet found this difference between girls and boys, to regard it as significant. The significant chi-square result points to a **contingency** between the two splits, which is to say that gender and standardness of pronunciation were significantly linked in this sample, for at least this one suffix. (Notice that 'Girls 10/2, Boys 5/7' is not a statement about averages, nor do standard deviations enter the picture; so the t-test has no role in this case.) Quite a few of the tables in Hyams (Chapter 6.2) are of a kind suitable for testing with chi-square.

The final statistical concept to be outlined here is **correlation**, the extent to which paired sets of numbers mirror each other. For example, the average length of utterances tends to be longer for older children than for younger ones: utterance length and age are correlated. The following is a small imaginary (but plausible) dataset for six children, with their ages given in months and the mean length of each child's utterances shown under the heading *MLU*.

Age	MLU
15	1.6
16	1.7

16	2.1
17	2.0
18	2.2
18	2.0

The tendency for these two measures to go in tandem is shown by the youngest child here (15 months old) having the shortest mean length of utterance (1.6), one of the two 18-month-olds having the longest MLU (2.2) and children intermediate in age (16 months and 17 months) having MLUs intermediate between the lowest and the highest. It is also clear that the two columns of numbers are not in 'lockstep', for instance one of the two 16-month-olds has a higher MLU than the child of 17 months and one of the 18-month-olds. The correlation (full name: Pearson correlation coefficient (usual shorthand symbol r)) calculated for these six pairs of numbers is 0.75.

The highest possible value a **correlation coefficient** can reach is 1, which would indicate that the two columns of numbers were absolutely in tandem, something virtually never seen in statistics relating to human behaviour and cognition. A correlation of 0 signifies that there is no (linear) relationship between the paired numbers. The closer a correlation coefficient is to zero, the smaller the relationship between the paired numbers; the further from zero, the stronger the relationship. A correlation of 0.75 would point to quite a lot of predictability between Age and MLU. To understand what is meant by predictability in this context, imagine covering up a number in the MLU column and persuading a cooperative person to study the other numbers in the table and guess at the hidden one. A reasonably numerate person should be able to come close to a right answer.

The significance of a correlation is an indication of how likely or unlikely it is that a coefficient that far from zero could come about by chance alone, e.g. from randomly stacking a lottery's winning numbers into two columns. Again, there is a table to consult for the significance of a correlation coefficient after it has been calculated. For $r = 0.75$ on six pairs of numbers (the imaginary data above), the table gives $.05 < p < .10$, which is to say that, if you are working from such a small dataset as only six pairs of numbers, then by chance alone correlations as far from zero as .75 can be expected somewhere between 5 per cent and 10 per cent of the time. Ten per cent of the time is not often, but it is not all that rare either. As pointed out earlier, the conventional maximum for 'rare enough to be regarded as significant' is 5 per cent. This result is not in that category. It is very important to understand that a result which fails to reach significance is *not* one that has somehow been proved to be insignificant. There definitely is a moderately-sized relationship between MLU and age, but a sample as small as only six children is not enough of a basis for establishing this.

Correlation coefficients can be negative too. A positive correlation coefficient is always somewhere between zero and +1. The coefficient of a negative correlation lies between zero and −1. Richards and Malvern (Chapter 2.3) recount a study from the literature that reported a negative correlation between MLU and TTR (the ratio of word types to word tokens, a measure that has been offered as a possible way of indicating richness in vocabulary use). This surprising result – an inverse relationship (longer MLUs go with less rich word choice; richer word usage with shorter MLUs) – is one of the arguments that Richards and Malvern put forward against TTR as a valid measure of vocabulary diversity.

Richards and Malvern give a coefficient called **Spearman's** *rho* for some of their results. This is a correlation coefficient too; however, it is calculated not on the raw numbers but on their ranks, each of the two columns being treated like a 'league table' with the positions 1st, 2nd, 3rd, etc. going into the calculations. This ignores the distances between adjacent values in each column, and has the desirable consequence that the outcome is not unduly affected by extreme scores.

An important general point to note is that correlations are not an assurance of causality. (**Causality** is the matter of what made what happen; what caused a state of affairs to come about.) A significant correlation between two sets of measurements, e.g. between some aspect of older and younger siblings' interactional style, could indicate that the older siblings influence the younger ones, but there are other possibilities too: personality traits of the younger ones might elicit particular interaction patterns from their elders; there could be causality going both ways; or there might be no causal relation between the two, with the correlation perhaps arising on account of the sibling children imitating adults in the family. Food for thought on such issues can be found in Chapter 1.1 (Lieven) and the related part of the introduction to Part 1 of the *Reader* (though Lieven does not report correlations and was not investigating relationships between siblings). In a thorough discussion, Richards (1994) shows just how difficult it can be to determine whether correlations between, on the one hand, adaptations that adults make when speaking to young children and, on the other, various aspects of the children's language development imply a causal role for the adult modifications.

Finding significant correlations raises the possibility of causality, but it takes a theory to supply the causal links. An illustration of this is Gopnik's discussion, within the framework of what she calls 'theory theory' (Chapter 7.2), of a correlation between a frequently reported mid second-year vocabulary 'spurt' and the cognitive development of exhaustive categorization (an ability to sort things into piles without leaving any items unsorted). She suggests that both developments might be prompted by a strong predilection of mothers – in Gopnik's studies, particularly the English-speaking mothers – to name objects when interacting with their children, leading the latter to make the discovery that every object has a name. For researchers, a theoretical proposal such as this is an incentive to think of consequences that should follow if the theory is right, and then to try to discover whether or not those predictions hold true.

References

Acker, J., Bery, K. and Esseveld, J. (1983) 'Objectivity and truth: problems in doing feminist research', *Women's Studies International Forum*, 6: 423–35.

Alderson, P. (1993) *Children's Consent to Surgery*, Buckingham: Open University Press.

—— (1995) *Listening to Children: children, ethics and social research*, Ilford: Barnardo's.

Ament, W. (1899) *Die Entwicklung von Sprechen und Denken beim Kinder*, Leipzig: Ernst Wunderlich.

Anglin, J. (1993) 'Vocabulary development: a morphological analysis', *Monographs of the Society for Research in Child Development*, 58, serial no. 238.

Arnberg, L.N. and Arnberg, P.W. (1985) 'The relation between code differentiation and language mixing in bilingual three to four year old children', *Bilingual Review*, 12: 20–32.

—— and —— (1992) 'Language awareness and language separation in the young bilingual child', in R.J. Harris (ed.), *Cognitive Processing in Bilinguals*, Amsterdam: North-Holland.

Aske, J. (1989) 'Path predicates in English and Spanish: a closer look', *Proceedings, Berkeley Linguistics Society*, 15: 1–14.

Au, T.K. and Glusman, M. (1990) 'The principle of mutual exclusivity in word learning: to honor or not to honor?', *Child Development*, 61: 1474–90.

—— , Dapretto, M. and Song, Y.K. (1994) 'Input vs constraints: early word acquisition in Korean and English', *Journal of Memory and Language*, 33: 567–82.

Augustine (1952) *The Great Books*, vol. 18, *The Confessions of St Augustine*, Chicago: Encyclopedia Britannica.

Axia, G. (1996) 'How to persuade mum to buy a toy', *First Language*, 16: 301–17.

Baker, C.L. and McCarthy, J.J. (eds) (1981) *The Logical Problem of Language Acquisition*, Cambridge, MA: MIT Press.

Balassa, J. (1893) 'A gyermek nyelvének fejlodése', *Nyelvtudomámanyi Közlemények*, 23: 60–73, 129–44.

Baldwin, D.A. and Moses, L.J. (1994) 'Early understanding of referential intent and attentional focus: evidence from language and emotion', in C. Lewis and P. Mitchell (eds), *Origins of a Theory of Mind*, Hillsdale, NJ: Erlbaum.

Banigan, R.L. and Mervis, C.B. (1988) 'Role of adult input in young children's category evolution: 2. An experimental study', *Journal of Child Language*, 15: 493–504.

Barrett, M. (1986) 'Early semantic representations and early word usage', in S.A. Kuczaj and W. Wannenmacher (eds), *Concept Development and the Development of Word Meaning*, Berlin: Springer.

—— (1996) 'Early lexical development', in P. Fletcher and B. MacWhinney (eds), *The Handbook of Child Language*, Oxford: Blackwell.

—— (1999a) 'An introduction to the nature of language and to the central themes and issues in the study of language development', in M. Barrett (ed.), *The Development of Language*, Hove: The Psychology Press.

—— (ed.) (1999b) *The Development of Language*, Hove: The Psychology Press.

——, Harris, M. and Chasin, J. (1991) 'Early lexical development and maternal speech: a comparison of children's initial and subsequent uses', *Journal of Child Language*, 18: 21–40.

Bates, E. (1975) 'The development of conversational skills in 2, 3 and 4 year olds', *Pragmatics Microfiche*, 1.5, Cambridge University.

—— (1976) *Language and Context: the acquisition of pragmatics*, New York: Academic Press.

—— (1979) *The Emergence of Symbols: cognition and communication in Infancy*, New York: Academic Press.

—— (1999) 'Language and the infant brain', *The Journal of Communication Disorders*, 32: 195–205.

—— and Goodman, J.C. (1999) 'On the emergence of grammar from the lexicon', in B. MacWhinney (ed.), *The Emergence of Language*, Mahwah, NJ: Erlbaum.

—— and MacWhinney, B. (1987) 'Competition, variation and learning', in B. MacWhinney (ed.), *Mechanisms of Language Learning*, Hillsdale, NJ: Erlbaum.

—— and —— (1989) 'Functionalism and the competition model', in B. MacWhinney and E. Bates (eds), *The Crosslinguistic Study of Sentence Processing*, New York: Cambridge University Press.

——, Benigni, L., Bretherton, I., Camaioni, L. and Volterra, V. (1979) *The Emergence of Symbols: cognition and communication in infancy*, New York: Academic Press.

——, Bretherton, I. and Snyder, L. (1988) *From First Words to Grammar: individual differences and dissociable mechanisms*, Cambridge: Cambridge University Press.

——, Dale, P.S. and Thal, D. (1995) 'Individual differences and their implications for theories of language development', in P. Fletcher and B. MacWhinney (eds), *The Handbook of Child Language*, Oxford: Blackwell.

Bechtel, W. and Abrahamsen, A. (1991) *Connectionism and the Mind: an introduction to parallel processing in networks*, Cambridge, MA: Blackwell.

Becker, J. (1994) ' "Sneak-shoes", "sworders", and "nose-beards": a case study of lexical innovations', *First Language*, 14: 195–211.

Becker, M. (1995) 'Acquisition of syntax in child German: verb finiteness and verb placement', Senior Honors thesis, Wellesley College, MA.

Beckwith, R., Tinker, E. and Bloom, L. (1989) 'The acquisition of non-basic sentences', paper presented at the Boston University Conference on Language Development, Boston.

Behrens, H. (1993) 'Temporal reference in German child language', doctoral dissertation, University of Amsterdam.

Benedict, H. (1977) 'Language comprehension in the 10–16-month-old infant', unpublished Ph.D. thesis, Yale University.

—— (1979) 'Early lexical development: comprehension and production', *Journal of Child Language*, 6: 183–200.

Bergman, C.R. (1976) 'Interference vs independent development in infant bilingualism', in G. Keller, R. Teschner and S. Viera (eds), *Bilingualism in the Bicentennial and Beyond*, New York: Bilingual Press.

Berko, J. (1958) 'The child's learning of English morphology', *Word*, 14: 150–77.

Berlin, B. and Kay, P. (1969) *Basic Color Terms: their universality and evolution*, Los Angeles: University of California Press.

Berman, R.A. (1986) 'A crosslinguistic perspective: morphology and syntax', in P. Fletcher and M. Garman (eds), *Language Acquisition: studies in first language development*, 2nd edn, Cambridge: Cambridge University Press.

—— and Slobin, D.I. (eds) (1994) *Relating Events in Narrative: a crosslinguistic developmental study*, Hillsdale, NJ: Erlbaum.

Bernhardt, B. and Stoel-Gammon, C. (1996) 'Underspecification and markedness in normal and disordered phonological development', in J. Gilbert and C. Johnson (eds), *Children's Language*, vol. 9, Hillsdale, NJ: Erlbaum.

Bernstein Ratner, N., Rooney, B. and MacWhinney, B. (1996) 'Analysis of stuttering using CHILDES and CLAN', *Clinical Linguistics and Phonetics*, 10: 169–87.

Bialystock, E. (1987) 'Words as things: development of word concept by bilingual children', *Studies in Second Language Acquisition*, 9: 133–40.

—— (1991) 'Metalinguistic dimensions of bilingual language proficiency', in E. Bialystock (ed.), *Language Processing in Bilingual Children*, Cambridge: Cambridge University Press.

—— (1992) 'Selective attention in cognitive processing: the bilingual edge', in R.J. Harris (ed.), *Cognitive Processing in Bilinguals*, Amsterdam: North-Holland.

Bleile, K. (1991) *Child Phonology: a book of exercises for students*, San Diego: Singular Publishing Group.

Blevins, J. (1995) 'The syllable in phonological theory', in J.A. Goldsmith (ed.), *The Handbook of Phonological Theory*, Cambridge, MA: Blackwell.

Bloom, L. (1970) *Language Development: form and function in emerging grammars*, Cambridge, MA: MIT Press.

—— (1973) *One Word at a Time: the use of single-word utterances before syntax*, The Hague: Mouton.

—— (1981) 'The importance of language for language development: linguistic determinism in the 1980s', *Annals of the New York Academy of Sciences*, 379: 160–71.

——, Hood, L. and Lightbown, P. (1974) 'Imitation in language development: if, when and why', *Cognitive Psychology*, 6: 380–420.

——, Lightbown, P. and Hood, L. (1975) 'Structure and Variation in Child Language', *Monograph for the Society for Research in Child Development*, 40, 2.

——, Margulis, C., Tinker, E. and Fujita, N. (1996) 'Early conversations and word learning: contributions from child and adult', *Child Development*, 67: 3154–75.

Bloom, P. (1990) 'Subjectless sentences in child language', *Linguistic Inquiry*, 21: 491–504.

—— (1994) 'Possible names: the role of syntax–semantics mappings in the acquisition of nominals', *Lingua*, 92: 297–329.

—— (2000) *How Children Learn the Meanings of Words*, Cambridge, MA: MIT Press.

—— (2001) 'Roots of word learning', in M. Bowerman and S.C. Levinson (eds), *Language Acquisition and Conceptual Development*, Cambridge: Cambridge University Press.

BMA, GMSC, HEA, Brook Advisory Centres, FPA and RCGP (1993) *Confidentiality and People under 16*, London: HEA.

Bornstein, M. and Haynes, O.M. (1998) 'Vocabulary competence in early childhood: measurement, latent construct, and predictive validity', *Child Development*, 69: 654–71.

Boser, K., Lust, B., Santelmann, L. and Whitman, J. (1992) 'Theoretical significance of auxiliaries in early child German', paper presented at the Boston University Child Language Conference, October, 1991.

Bowerman, M. (1973) *Early Syntactic Development: a crosslinguistic study, with special reference to Finnish*, Cambridge: Cambridge University Press.

—— (1978) 'The acquisition of word meaning: an investigation into some current conflicts', in N. Waterson and C. Snow (eds), *The Development of Communication*, New York: John Wiley.

—— (1982a) 'Evaluating competing linguistic models with language acquisition data: implications of developmental errors with causative verbs', *Quaderni de Semantica*, 3: 5–66.

—— (1982b) 'Reorganizational processes in lexical and syntactic development', in E. Wanner and L.R. Gleitman (eds), *Language Acquisition: the state of the art*, Cambridge: Cambridge University Press.

—— (1982c) 'Starting to talk worse: clues to language acquisition from children's late speech errors', in S. Strauss (ed.), *U-shaped Behavioural Growth*, New York: Academic Press.

—— (1985) 'What shapes children's grammars?', in D.I. Slobin (ed.), *The Crosslinguistic Study of Language Acquisition*, vol. 2, *Theoretical Issues*, Hillsdale, NJ: Erlbaum.

—— (1988) 'The "no negative evidence" problem', in J. Hawkins (ed.), *Explaining Language Universals*, London: Blackwell.

—— (1989) 'Learning a semantic system: what role do cognitive dispositions play?', in M.L. Rice and R.L. Schiefelbusch (eds), *The Teachability of Language*, Baltimore, MD: Paul H. Brooks.

—— (1996) 'The origins of children's spatial semantic categories: cognitive vs linguistic determinants', in J.J. Gumperz and S.C. Levinson (eds), *Rethinking Linguistic Relativity*, Cambridge: Cambridge University Press.

—— and Choi, S. (2001) 'Shaping meanings for language: universal and language-specific in the acquisition of spatial semantic categories', in M. Bowerman and S.C. Levinson (eds), *Language Acquisition and Conceptual Development*, Cambridge: Cambridge University Press.

Braine, M.D.S. (1963) 'The ontogeny of English phrase structure: the first phase', *Language*, 39: 1–13.

—— (1976) 'Children's first word combinations', *Monographs of the Society for Research in Child Development*, 41, serial no. 164.

—— (1987) 'What is learned in acquiring word classes – a step toward an acquisition theory', in B. MacWhinney (ed.), *Mechanisms of Language Acquisition*, Hillsdale, NJ: Erlbaum.

Brent, M. (1994) 'Surface cues and robust inference as a basis for the early acquisition of subcategorization frames', *Lingua*, 92: 433–70.

Bresnan, J. (ed.) (1982) *The Mental Representation of Grammatical Relations*, Cambridge, MA: MIT Press.

Broselow, E. (1982) 'On the interaction of stress and epenthesis', *Glossa*, 16: 115–32.

Brown, R. (1957) 'Linguistic determinism and the part of speech', *Journal of Abnormal and Social Psychology*, 55: 1–5.

—— (1973) *A First Language: the early stages*, Cambridge, MA: Harvard University Press.

—— and Bellugi, U. (1964) 'Three processes in the child's acquisition of syntax', in E. Lenneberg (ed.), *New Directions in the Study of Language*, Cambridge, MA: MIT Press.

—— and Fraser, C. (1963) 'The acquisition of syntax', in C. Cofer and B. Musgrave (eds), *Verbal Behavior and Learning*, New York: McGraw-Hill.

—— , Cazden, C. and Bellugi, U. (1969) 'The child's grammar from I to III', in J. Hill (ed.), *Minnesota Symposia on Child Psychology 2*, Minneapolis: University of Minnesota Press.

Bruner, J. (1974) 'Organisation of early skilled action', in M. Richards (ed.), *The Integration of a Child into a Social World*, London: Cambridge University Press.

—— (1975) 'The ontogenesis of speech acts', *Journal of Child Language*, 2: 1–19.

—— (1983) *Child's Talk: learning to use language*, Oxford: Oxford University Press.

Burgess, N. (1995) 'A solvable connectionist model of immediate recall of ordered lists', in G. Tesauro, D. Touretzky and J. Alspector (eds), *Neural Information Processing Systems 7*, San Mateo, CA: Morgan Kaufmann.

—— and Hitch, G. (1992) 'Toward a network model of the articulatory loop', *Journal of Memory and Language*, 31: 429–60.

Burling, R. (1959) 'Language development of a Garo and English speaking child', *Word*, 15: 45–68; reprinted in A. Bar-Adon and W. Leopold (eds) (1971) *Child Language: a book of readings*, Englewood Cliffs, NJ: Prentice Hall.

Bushnell, E.W. and Maratsos, M.P. (1984) 'Spooning and basketing: children's dealing with accidental gaps in the lexicon', *Child Development*, 55: 893–902.

Butterworth, G. (1989) 'Events and encounters in infant perception', in A. Slater and G. Bremner (eds), *Infant Development*, London: Erlbaum.

Bybee, J.L. and Slobin, D.I. (1988) 'Rules and schemas in the development and use of the English past tense', *Language*, 58: 265–89.

Cambridge, P. (1993) 'Taking account of user choice in community care', in P. Alderson (ed.), *Disabled People and Consent to Medical Treatment and Research*, London: SSRU.

Carey, S. (1978) 'The child as word learner', in M. Halle, J. Bresnan and G.A. Miller (eds), *Linguistic Theory and Psychological Reality*, Cambridge, MA: MIT Press.

—— (1985) *Conceptual Change in Childhood*, Cambridge, MA: Bradford/MIT Press.

—— (1988) 'Conceptual differences between children and adults', *Mind and Language*, 3: 167–81.

Carpenter, G., Grossberg, S. and Reynolds, J. (1991) 'ARTMAP: supervised real-time learning and classification of nonstationary data by a self-organizing neural network', *Neural Networks*, 4: 565–88.

Carroll, J.B. (1964) *Language and Thought*, Englewood Cliffs, NJ: Prentice Hall.

Case, R. (1992) 'Neo-Piagetian theories of intellectual development', in H. Beilin and P.B. Pufall (eds), *Piaget's Theory: prospects and possibilities*, Hillsdale, NJ: Erlbaum.

Caselli, M.C., Bates, E., Casadio, P. and Fenson, J. (1995) 'A cross-linguistic study of early lexical development', *Cognitive Development*, 10: 159–99.

Cassell, J. (1982) 'Harms, benefits, wrongs and rights in fieldwork', in J. Sieber (ed.), *The Ethics of Social Research: fieldwork, regulation and publication*, New York: Springer.

Cazden, C.B. (1968) 'The acquisition of noun and verb inflections', *Child Development*, 39: 433–48.

Chaney, C. (1989) 'I pledge a legiance to the flag: three studies in word segmentation', *Applied Psycholinguistics*, 10: 261–82.

Chen, Y.S. and Leimkuhler, F.F. (1989) 'A type-token identity in the Simon-Yule model of text', *Journal of the American Society for Information Science*, 40: 45–53.

Chiat, S. (1989) 'The relation between prosodic structure, syllabification, and segmental realization: evidence from a child with fricative stopping', *Clinical Linguistics and Phonetics*, 3: 223–42.

Chien, Y.-C. and Wexler, K. (1990) 'Children's knowledge of locality conditions in binding as evidence for the modularity of syntax', *Language Acquisition*, 1: 225–95.

Choi, S. (1986) 'A pragmatic analysis of sentence-ending morphemes in Korean children', paper presented at the Linguistic Society of America, New York, December.

—— (1991) 'Early acquisition of epistemic meanings in Korean: a study of sentence-ending suffixes in the spontaneous speech of three children', *First Language*, 11: 93–119.

—— and Bowerman, M. (1991) 'Learning to express motion events in English and Korean: the influence of language-specific lexicalization patterns', *Cognition*, 41: 83–121.

—— and Gopnik, A. (1995) 'Early acquisition of verbs in Korean: a crosslinguistic study', *Journal of Child Language*, 22: 497–529.

Chomsky, N. (1959) 'Review of *Verbal Behavior* by B.F. Skinner', *Language*, 35: 26–58.

—— (1965) *Aspects of the Theory of Syntax*, Cambridge, MA: MIT Press.

—— (1968) *Language and Mind*, New York: Harcourt Brace Jovanovich.

—— (1981) *Lectures on Government and Binding*, Dordrecht: Foris.

—— (1986) *Knowledge of Language: its nature, origins and use*, New York: Praeger.

—— (1995) *The Minimalist Program*, Cambridge, MA: MIT Press.

—— and Halle, M. (1968) *The Sound Pattern of English*, New York: Harper and Row.

Cipriani, P., Chilosi, A.M., Bottari, P. and Pfanner, L. (1991) *L'acquisizione della Morphosintassi: fasi e processi*, Padova: Unipress.

Clahsen, H. (1991) 'Constraints on parameter setting: a grammatical analysis of some acquisition stages in German child language', *Language Acquisition*, 1: 361–91.

—— and Penke, M. (1992) 'The acquisition of agreement morphology and its syntactic consequences: new evidence on German child language from the Simone corpus', in J. Meisel (ed.), *The Acquisition of Verb Placement*, Dordrecht: Kluwer.

——, Eisenbeiss, S. and Penke, M. (1996) 'Lexical learning in early syntactic development', in H. Clahsen (ed.), *Generative Perspectives on Language Acquisition*, Amsterdam: John Benjamins.

Clancy, P. (1985) 'The acquisition of Japanese', in D.I. Slobin (ed.), *The Crosslinguistic Study of Language Acquisition*, vol. 1, *The Data*, Hillsdale, NJ: Erlbaum.

Clark, E.V. (1973) 'What's in a word? On the child's acquisition of semantics in his first language', in T.E. Moore (ed.), *Cognitive Development and the Acquisition of Language*, New York: Academic Press.

—— (1982) 'The young word maker: a case study of innovations in the child's lexicon', in E. Wanner and L.R. Gleitman (eds), *Language Acquisition: the state of the art*, Cambridge: Cambridge University Press.

—— (1983) 'Meanings and concepts', in J.H. Flavell and E.M. Markman (eds), P.H. Mussen (Series ed.) *Handbook of Child Psychology*, vol. 3, *Cognitive Development*, New York: Wiley.

—— (1987) 'The principle of contrast: a constraint on language acquisition', in B. MacWhinney (ed.), *Mechanisms of Language Acquisition*, Hillsdale, NJ: Erlbaum.

—— (1991) 'Acquisitional principles in lexical development', in S. Gelman and J. Byrnes (eds), *Perspectives on Language and Thought*, New York: Cambridge University Press.

—— (1993) *The Lexicon in Acquisition*, New York: Cambridge University Press.

—— and Berman, R.A. (1984) 'Structure and use in the acquisition of word formation', *Language*, 60: 542–90.

—— and Hecht, B.F. (1982) 'Learning to coin agent and instrument nouns', *Cognition*, 12: 1–24.

——, Gelman, S.A. and Lane, N.M. (1985) 'Compound nouns and category structure in young children', *Child Development*, 56: 84–94.

Clarke-Stewart, A. (1973) 'Interactions between mothers and their young children: characteristics and consequences', *Monographs of the Society for Research in Child Development*, 153, 38 (6–7).

Coates, J. (1993) *Women, Men and Language*, London: Longman.

Cohen, D. (2002) *How the Child's Mind Develops*, London: Routledge.

Cohen, M. and Grossberg, S. (1987) 'Masking fields: a massively parallel neural architecture for learning, recognizing, and predicting multiple groupings of patterned data', *Applied Optics*, 26: 1866–91.

Coolidge, F.L. (2000) *Statistics: a gentle introduction*, London: Sage.

Corrigan, R. (1978) 'Language development as related to stage 6 object permanence development', *Journal of Child Language*, 5: 173–89.

Corsaro, W. and Rizzo, T. (1990) 'Disputes in the peer culture of American and Italian nursery-school children', in A. Grimshaw (ed.), *Conflict Talk*, Cambridge: Cambridge University Press.

Crain, S. and Thornton, R. (1990) 'Levels of representation in child grammar', paper presented at the 13th GLOW Conference, Cambridge, UK.

Cramer, D. and Howitt, D. (2002) *An Introduction to Statistics in Psychology*, 2nd edn, London: Prentice Hall.

Cross, T.G. (1978) 'Mothers' speech and its association with rate of linguistic development in young children', in N. Waterson and C. Snow (eds), *The Development of Communication*, Chichester: Wiley.

Crystal, D. (1997) *English as a Global Language*, Cambridge: Cambridge University Press.

Dabrowska, E. (2001) 'Discriminating between constructivist and nativist positons: fillers as evidence of generalization', *Journal of Child Language*, 28: 243–45.

Dale, P. (1976) *Language Development*, 2nd edn, New York: Holt Rinehart and Winston.

——— , Bates, E., Reznick, S. and Morisset, C. (1989) 'The validity of a parent report instrument of child language at twenty months', *Journal of Child Language*, 16: 239–49.

Darwin, C. (1877) 'A biographical sketch of an infant', *Mind*, 2: 292–4.

Davies, I., Corbett, G., McGurk, H. and Jerrett, D. (1994) 'A developmental study of the acquisition of colour terms in Setswana', *Journal of Child Language*, 21: 693–712.

Davis, B. and MacNeilage, P.F. (1995) 'The articulatory basis of babbling', *Journal of Speech and Hearing Research*, 38: 1199–211.

De Houwer, A. (1990) *The Acquisition of Two Languages from Birth: a case study*, Cambridge: Cambridge University Press.

Demuth, K. (1995) 'The prosodic structure of early words', in J. Morgan and K. Demuth (eds), *From Signal to Syntax: bootstrapping from speech to grammar in early acquisition*, Hillsdale, NJ: Erlbaum.

——— and Fee, E.J. (1995) 'Minimal prosodic words in early phonological development', manuscript, Brown University and Dalhousie University.

Dewaele, J.-M. (2000) 'Trilingual first language acquisition: exploration of a linguistic «miracle»', *La Chouette* (Birkbeck College, London University), 31: 41–5.

Dickson, P. and Cumming, A. (1996) *Profiles of Language Education in 25 Countries: overview of phase 1 of the IEA Language Education Study*, Slough: NFER.

Döpke, S. (1992) *One Parent, One Language: an interactional approach*, Amsterdam: John Benjamins.

Dore, J. (1975) 'Holophrases, speech acts and language universals', *Journal of Child Language*, 2: 21–40.

——— (1985) 'Holophrases revisited: their 'logical' development from dialogue', in M.D. Barrett (ed.), *Children's Single-Word Speech*, Chichester: Wiley.

——— , Franklin, M.B., Miller, R.T. and Ramer, A.L.H. (1976) 'Transitional phenomena in early language acquisition', *Journal of Child Language*, 3: 13–19.

Dorval, B. (1990) *Conversational Organisation and its Development*, Norwood, NJ: Ablex.

Doyle, A., Champagne, M. and Segalowitz, N. (1978) 'Some issues on the assessment of linguistic consequences of early bilingualism', in M. Paradis (ed.), *Aspects of Bilingualism*, Columbia, SC: Hornbeam Press.

Dressler, W.U. and Dziubalska-Kolaczyk, K. (1997) 'Contributions from the acquisition of Polish phonology and morphology to theoretical linguistics', in S. Eliasson and E.H. Jahr (eds), *Language and its Ecology: essays in memory of Einar Haugen*, New York: Mouton de Gruyter.

——— and Karpf, A. (1995) 'The theoretical relevance of pre- and protomorphology in language acquisition', in G. Booij and J.V. Marle (eds), *Yearbook of Morphology 1994*, Dordrecht: Kluwer Academic Publishers.

Dromi, E. (1987) *Early Lexical Development*, Cambridge: Cambridge University Press.

Du Bois, J. (1987) 'The discourse basis of ergativity', *Language*, 63: 805–56.

Echols, C.H. (1993) 'A perceptually-based model of children's earliest productions', *Cognition*, 46: 245–96.

——— and Newport, E.L. (1992) 'The role of stress and position in determining first words', *Language Acquisition*, 2: 189–220.

Edelsky, C. (1976) 'The acquisition of communicative competence: recognition of linguistic correlates of sex roles', *Merrill-Palmer Quarterly*, 22: 47–59.

Eder, D. (1990) 'Serious and playful disputes: variation in conflict talk among female adolescents', in A. Grimshaw (ed.), *Conflict Talk*, Cambridge: Cambridge University Press.

Edwards, J.A. (1992) 'Computer methods in child language research: four principles for the use of archived data', *Journal of Child Language*, 19: 435–58.

Edwards, J.R. (1979) 'Social class differences and the identification of sex in children's speech', *Journal of Child Language*, 6: 121–7.

Eisikovits, E. (1987) 'Sex differences in inter-group and intra-group interaction among adolescents', in A. Pauwels (ed.), *Women and Language in Australian and New Zealand Society*, Sydney: Australian Professional Publications.

—— (1988) 'Girl-talk/boy-talk: sex differences in adolescent speech', in P. Collins and D. Blair (eds), *Australian English*, Queensland: University of Queensland Press.

Elbers, F. and Wijnen, F. (1992) 'Effort, production, skill and language learning', in C. Ferguson, L. Menn, and C. Stoel-Gammon (eds), *Phonological Development: models, research, implications*, Parkton, MD: York Press.

Elman, J.L. (1990) 'Finding structure in time', *Cognitive Science*, 14: 179–211.

Ely, R. and Gleason, J.B. (1995) 'Socialisation across contexts', in P. Fletcher and B. MacWhinney (eds), *The Handbook of Child Language*, Oxford: Blackwell.

Enç, M. (1987) 'Binding conditions for tense', *Linguistic Inquiry*, 18: 633–57.

Endrei, G. (1913) 'Adalékok hangalaki jellemzöi a gyemeknyelvben', *A Gyermek*, 7: 441–66, 524–6.

Erickson, F. (1990) 'The social construction of discourse coherence in a family dinner table conversation', in B. Dorval (ed.), *Conversational Organisation and its Development*, Norwood, NJ: Ablex.

Evey, J.A. and Merriman, W.E. (1996) *The Prevalence and the Weakness of an Early Name Mapping Preference*, manuscript under review.

Faden, R. and Beauchamp, T. (1986) *A History and Theory of Informed Consent*, New York: Oxford University Press.

Fantini, A. (1985) *Language Acquisition of a Bilingual Child: a sociolinguistic perspective*, San Diego, CA: College Hill Press.

Fausett, L. (1994) *Fundamentals of Neural Networks*, Englewood Cliffs, NJ: Prentice Hall.

Fee, E.J. (1992) 'Exploring the minimal word in early phonological acquisition', *Proceedings of the 1992 Annual Conference of the Canadian Linguistic Association*, Toronto: Toronto Working Papers in Linguistics.

Feldman, H., Goldin-Meadow, S. and Gleitman, L.R. (1978) 'Beyond Herodotus: the creation of language by linguistically deprived deaf children', in A. Lock (ed.), *Action, Symbol and Gesture: the emergence of language*, New York: Academic Press.

Fenson, L., Dale, P.S., Reznick, J.S., Thal, D., Bates, E., Hartung, J.P., Pethick, S. and Reilly, J.S. (1993) *The MacArthur Communicative Development Inventories: user's guide and technical manual*, San Diego: Singular Publishing Group.

——, Dale, P.S., Reznick, J.S., Bates, E., Thal, D. and Pethick, S. (1994) 'Variability in early communicative development', *Monographs of the Society for Research in Child Development*, 59, serial no. 242.

Fernald, A. and Morikawa, H. (1993) 'Common themes and cultural variations in Japanese and American mother's speech to infants', *Child Development*, 64: 637–56.

Fichtelius, A., Johansson, I. and Nordin, K. (1980) 'Three investigations of sex-associated speech variation in day school', in C. Kramarae (ed.), *The Voices and Words of Women and Men*, Oxford: Pergamon Press.

Fikkert, P. (1994) 'On the acquisition of prosodic structure', dissertation, University of Leiden.

Fischer, J.L. (1964) 'Social influences on the choice of a linguistic variant', in D. Hymes (ed.), *Language in Culture and Society*, New York: Harper International.

Fisher, C., Gleitman, H., and Gleitman, L.R. (1991) 'Relationships between verb meanings and their syntactic structures', *Cognitive Psychology*, 23: 331–92.

—— , Hall, D.G., Rakowitz, S. and Gleitman, L.R. (1994) 'When it is better to receive than to give: structural and conceptual cues to verb meaning', *Lingua*, 92: 333–75.

Fletcher, P. (1985) *A Child's Learning of English*, Oxford: Blackwell.

—— and Garman, M. (1986) *Language Acquisition*, 2nd edn, Cambridge: Cambridge University Press.

—— and MacWhinney, B. (eds) (1995) *The Handbook of Child Language*, Oxford: Blackwell.

Fodor, J.A. (1983) *Modularity of Mind*, Cambridge, MA: MIT Press.

Foster, S. (1990) *The Communicative Competence of Young Children*, London: Longman.

Fowler, A.E., Gelman, R. and Gleitman, L.R. (1994) 'The course of language learning in children with Down Syndrome: longitudinal and language level comparisons with young normally developing children', in H. Tager-Flusberg (ed.), *Constraints on Language Acquisition: studies of atypical children*, Hillsdale, NJ: Elrbaum.

Fowles, B. and Glanz, M. (1977) 'Competence and talent in verbal riddle comprehension', *Journal of Child Language*, 4: 433–452.

French, P. and Woll, B. (1981) 'Context, meaning and strategy in parent–child conversation', in G. Wells (ed.), *Learning Through Interaction*, Cambridge: Cambridge University Press.

Gallaway, C. and Richards, B.J. (eds) (1994) *Input and Interaction in Language Acquisition*, Cambridge: Cambridge University Press.

Garton, A. and Pratt, C. (1998) *Learning to be Literate*, Oxford: Blackwell.

Gathercole, V. and Baddeley, A. (1993) *Working Memory and Language*, Hillsdale, NJ: Erlbaum.

Gawlitzek-Maiwald, I. and Tracy, R. (1995) 'Bilingual bootstrapping', *Linguistics*, 34: 901–26.

Gelman, S.A. and Coley, J.D. (1991) 'Language and categorization: the acquisition of natural kind terms', in S.A. Gelman and J.P. Byrnes (eds), *Perspectives on Language and Thought: interrelations in development*, Cambridge: Cambridge University Press.

—— and Markman, E. (1986) 'Categories and induction in young children', *Cognition*, 23: 183–209.

—— and Taylor, M. (1984) 'How two-year-old children interpret proper and common names for unfamiliar objects', *Child Development*, 55: 1535–40.

—— and Wellman, H.M. (1991) 'Insides and essence: early understandings of the non-obvious', *Cognition*, 38: 213–44.

—— , Wilcox, S.A. and Clark, E.V. (1989) 'Conceptual and lexical hierarchies in young children', *Cognitive Development*, 4: 309–26.

Genesee, F. (1989) 'Early bilingual language development: one language or two?' *Journal of Child Language*, 16: 161–79.

—— , Nicoladis, E. and Paradis, J. (1995) 'Language differentiation in early bilingual development', *Journal of Child Language*, 22: 611–31.

Gentner, D. (1978) 'On relational meaning: the acquisition of verb meaning', *Child Development*, 49: 988–98.

—— (1982) 'Why nouns are learned before verbs: linguistic relativity versus natural partitioning', in S. Kuczaj (ed.), *Language Development,* vol. 2, *Language, Thought, and Culture*, Hillsdale, NJ: Erlbaum.

Gerken, L. (1987) 'Telegraphic speaking does not imply telegraphic listening', *Stanford Papers and Reports in Child Language Development*, 26: 48–55.

—— (1994) 'A metrical template account of children's weak syllable omissions from multi-syllabic words', *Journal of Child Language*, 21: 565–84.

—— (1996) 'Phonological and distributional information in syntax acquisition', in J.L. Morgan and K. Demuth (eds), *Signal to Syntax: bootstrapping from speech to grammar in early acquisition*, Mahwah, NJ: Erlbaum.

——— , Landau, B. and Remez, R. (1990) 'Function morphemes in young children's speech perception and production', *Developmental Psychology*, 26: 204–16.

Gernsbacher, M.A. (1990) *Language Comprehension as Structure Building*, Hillsdale, NJ: Erlbaum.

Gierut, J.A., Cho, M-H. and Dinnsen, D. (1993) 'Geometric accounts of consonant-vowel interactions in developing systems', *Clinical Linguistics and Phonetics*, 7: 219–36.

Gillette, J., Gleitman, H., Gleitman, L. and Lederer, A. (1999) 'Human simulations of vocabulary learning', *Cognition*, 73: 135–76.

Gillis, S. (1990) 'Why nouns before verbs? Language structures and use provide an answer', paper presented at the 5th International Congress for the Study of Child Language, Budapest.

Gleason, J.B. (1980) 'The acquisition of social speech routines and politeness formulas', in H. Giles, W.P. Robinson and P.M. Smith (eds), *Language: social psychological perspectives*, Oxford: Pergamon Press.

Gleitman, L.R. (1990) 'The structural sources of verb meanings', *Language Acquisition*, 1: 3–55.

——— and Gleitman, H. (1992) 'A picture is worth a thousand words, but that's the problem: the role of syntax in vocabulary acquisition', *Current Directions in Psychological Science*, 1: 31–5.

——— , Newport, E.L. and Gleitman, H. (1984) 'The current status of the motherese hypothesis', *Journal of Child Language*, 11: 43–79.

Goldfield, B.A. and Reznick, J.S. (1990) 'Early lexical acquisition: rate, content, and the vocabulary spurt', *Journal of Child Language*, 17: 171–83.

Goldin-Meadow, S. and Feldman, H. (1977) 'The development of language-like communication without a language model', *Science*, 197: 401–3.

Goldsmith, J.A. (1976) 'An overview of autosegmental phonology', *Linguistic Analysis*, 2: 23–68.

——— (1995) *The Handbook of Phonological Theory*, Oxford: Blackwell.

——— (ed.) (1999) *Phonological Theory: the essential readings*, Oxford: Blackwell.

Golinkoff, R.M., Hirsh-Pasek, K., Bailey, L. and Wenger, N. (1992) 'Young children and adults use lexical principles to learn new nouns', *Developmental Psychology*, 28: 99–108.

——— , Mervis, C.B. and Hirsh-Pasek, K. (1994) 'Early object labels: the case for a developmental lexical principles framework', *Journal of Child Language*, 21: 125–55.

Goodwin, M.H. (1980) 'Directive-response speech sequences in girls' and boys' task activities', in S. McConnell-Ginet, R. Borker and N. Furman (eds), *Women and Language in Literature and Society*, New York: Praeger.

——— (1988) 'Cooperation and competition across girls' play activities', in A.D. Todd and S. Fisher (eds), *Gender and Discourse: the power of talk*, Norwood, NJ: Ablex.

——— (1990) *He-said-she-said: talk as social organisation among black children*, Bloomington: Indiana University Press.

——— and Goodwin, C. (1987) 'Children's arguing', in S. Philips, S. Steele and C. Tanz (eds), *Language, Gender and Sex in Comparative Perspective*, Cambridge: Cambridge University Press.

Gopnik, A. (1982) 'Words and plans: early language and the development of intelligent action', *Journal of Child Language*, 9: 303–8.

——— (1984) 'Conceptual and semantic change in scientists and children: why there are no semantic universals', *Linguistics*, 20: 163–79.

——— (1988) 'Conceptual and semantic development as theory change', *Mind and Language*, 3: 197–217.

——— and Choi, S. (1990) 'Do linguistic differences lead to cognitive differences? A cross-linguistic study of semantic and cognitive development,' *First Language*, 10: 199–215.

——— and ——— (1995) 'Names, relational words and cognitive development in English and Korean speakers: nouns are not always learned before verbs', in M. Tomasello and

W.E. Merriman (eds), *Beyond Names for Things: young children's acquisition of verbs*, Hillsdale, NJ: Erlbaum.

—— and Meltzoff, A. (1984) 'Semantic and cognitive development in 15- to 21-month-old children', *Journal of Child Language*, 11: 495–513.

—— and —— (1986) 'Relations between semantic and cognitive development in the one-word stage: the specificity hypothesis', *Child Development*, 57: 1040–53.

—— and —— (1987) 'The development of categorization in the second year and its relation to other cognitive and linguistic developments', *Child Development*, 58: 1523–31.

—— and —— (1992) 'Categorization and naming: basic-level sorting in eighteen-month-olds and its relation to language', *Child Development*, 63: 1091–103.

—— and —— (1997) *Words, Thoughts and Theories*, Cambridge, MA: Bradford/MIT Press.

—— and Wellman, H. (1992) 'Why the child's theory of mind really is a theory', *Mind and Language*, 7: 145–72.

—— and —— (1994) 'The "theory theory" ', in L. Hirschfield and S. Gelman (eds), *Mapping the Mind: domain specificity in culture and cognition*, New York: Cambridge University Press.

——, Choi, S. and Baumberger, T. (1996) 'Cross-linguistic differences in early semantic and cognitive development', *Cognitive Development*, 11: 197–227.

Gosy, M. (1978) 'Szavak és toldalékok hangalaki jellemzöi a gyemeknyelvben', *Hungarian Papers in Phonetics*, 2: 90–8.

Graddol, D. and Swann, J. (1989) *Gender Voices*, Oxford: Blackwell.

Grasby, P.M., Frith, C.D., Friston, K.J., Bench, C., Frackowiak, R.S.J. and Dolan, R.J. (1993) 'Functional mapping of brain areas implicated in auditory-verbal memory function', *Brain,* 116: 1–20.

Greenfield, P. and Smith, J. (1976) *The Structure of Communication in Early Language Development*, New York: Academic Press.

Greif, E.B. (1980) 'Sex differences in parent–child conversations', in C. Kramarae (ed.), *The Voices and Words of Women and Men*, Oxford: Pergamon Press.

Grice, H.P. (1975) 'Logic and conversation', in P. Cole, and J. Morgan (eds), *Syntax and Semantics,* vol. 3, *Speech Acts*, New York: Academic Press.

Griffiths, P. (1986) 'Early vocabulary', in P. Fletcher and M. Garman (eds), *Language Acquisition*, 2nd edn, Cambridge: Cambridge University Press.

——, Atkinson, M. and Huxley, R. (1974) 'Project report', *Journal of Child Language*, 1: 157–8.

Grimshaw, J. (1981) 'Form, function and the language acquisition device', in C.L. Baker and J. McCarthy (eds), *The Logical Problem of Language Acquisition*, Cambridge, MA: MIT Press.

—— (1990) *Argument Structure: Linguistic Inquiry Monograph 18*, Cambridge, MA: MIT Press.

Grodzinsky, Y. and Reinhart, T. (1993) 'The innateness of binding and coreference', *Linguistic Inquiry,* 24: 69–102.

Grossberg, S. (1987) 'Competitive learning: from interactive activation to adaptive resonance', *Cognitive Science*, 11: 23–63.

Guasti, M.T. (1994) 'Verb syntax in Italian child grammar', *Language Acquisition*, 3: 1–40.

Guéron, J. and Hoekstra, T. (1989) 'T-Chains and constituent structure of auxiliaries', in A. Cardinaletti, G. Cinque and G. Giusti (eds), *Constituent Structure: papers from the Venice GLOW*, Dordrecht: Foris.

—— and —— (1995) 'The temporal interpretation of predication', in A. Cardinaletti and M.T. Guasti (eds), *Syntax and Semantics 28: small clauses*, New York: Academic Press.

Guiraud, P. (1960) *Problèmes et Méthodes de la Statistique Linguistique*, Dordrecht: D. Reidel.

Gunzi, S. (1993) 'Early language comprehension and production', unpublished Ph.D. thesis, University of London.

Gupta, P. and MacWhinney, B. (1992) 'Integrating category acquisition with inflectional marking: a model of the German nominal system', *Proceedings of the Fourteenth Annual Conference of the Cognitive Science Society*, Hillsdale, NJ: Erlbaum.

—— and —— (1994) 'Is the articulatory loop articulatory or auditory? Re-examining the effects of concurrent articulation on immediate serial recall', *Journal of Memory and Language*, 33: 63–88.

—— and —— (1997) 'Vocabulary acquisition and verbal short-term memory: computational and neural bases', *Brain and Language*, 59: 267–333.

Gutfreund, M., Harrison, M. and Wells, C.G. (1989) *Bristol Language Development Scales*, Windsor: NFER-Nelson.

Gvozdev, A.N. (1949) *Formirovaniye u Rebenka Grammaticheskogo Stroya*, Moscow: Akademija Pedagogika Nauk RSFSR.

Haan, G. de (1986) 'A theory-bound approach to the acquisition of verb placement in Dutch', paper presented at the Workshop Universals in Child Language, Heidelberg University, February.

—— and Tuijnman, K. (1988) 'Missing subjects and objects in child grammar', in P. Jordens and J. Lalleman (eds), *Language Development*, Dordrecht: Foris.

Haas, A. (1978) 'Sex-associated features of spoken language by four-, eight-, and twelve-year-old boys and girls', paper given at the 9th World Congress of Sociology, Uppsala, Sweden, 14–19 August.

Haegeman, L. (1995) 'Root infinitives, tense and truncated structures', *Language Acquisition*, 4: 205–55.

Hakuta, K. (1981) 'Grammatical description versus configurational arrangement in language acquisition: the case of relative clauses in Japanese', *Cognition*, 9: 197–236.

—— (1986) *Mirror of Language: the debate on bilingualism*, New York: Basic Books.

Halliday, M.A.K. (1975) *Learning How to Mean*, London: Edward Arnold.

Hamilton, A, Plunkett, K. and Schafer, G. (2000) 'Infant vocabulary development assessed with a British CDI', *Journal of Child Language*, 27: 689–705.

Hampson, E. (1998) 'Spatial reasoning in children with congenital adrenal hyperplasia due to 21-hydroxylase deficiency', *Developmental Neuropsychology*, 14: 299–320.

Harding, E. and Riley, P. (1986) *The Bilingual Family: a handbook for parents*, Cambridge: Cambridge University Press.

Harris, M. (1992) *Language Experience and Early Language Development: from input to uptake*, Hove: Erlbaum.

—— and Chasin, J. (1993) 'Developing patterns in children's early comprehension vocabularies', in J. Clibbens and B. Pendleton (eds), *Proceedings of the 1993 Child Language Seminar*, Plymouth: University of Plymouth.

——, Jones, D. and Grant, J. (1984/5) 'The social-interactional context of maternal speech to children: an explanation for the event-bound nature of early word use?', *First Language*, 5: 89–100.

——, ——, Brookes, S. and Grant, J. (1986) 'Relations between the non-verbal context of maternal speech and rate of language development', *British Journal of Developmental Psychology*, 4: 261–8.

——, Barrett, M., Jones, D. and Brookes, S. (1988) 'Linguistic input and early word meaning', *Journal of Child Language*, 15: 77–94.

Harris, T. and Wexler, K. (1995) 'The optional infinitive stage in child English: evidence from negation', in H. Clahsen (ed.), *Generative Approaches to First and Second Language Acquisition*, Amsterdam: John Benjamins.

Hasan, R. and Cloran, C. (1990) 'A sociolinguistic interpretation of everyday talk between mothers and children', in M.A.K. Halliday, J. Gibbons and H. Nicholas (eds), *Learning, Keeping and Using Language: selected papers from the 8th World Congress of Applied Linguistics*, Amsterdam: John Benjamins.

Hayes, B. (1989) 'Compensatory lengthening in moraic phonology', *Linguistic Inquiry*, 20: 253–306.

Heath, S.B. (1982) 'What no bedtime story means: narrative skills at home and school', *Language in Society*, 11: 49–76.

Herdan, G. (1960) *Type-Token Mathematics: a textbook of mathematical linguistics*, The Hague: Mouton.

Hertz, J., Krogh, A. and Palmer, R. (1991) *Introduction to the Theory of Neural Computation*, New York: Addison-Wesley.

Hess, C.W., Sefton, K.M. and Landry, R.G. (1986) 'Sample size and type-token ratios for oral language of preschool children', *Journal of Speech and Hearing Research*, 29: 129–34.

Hickey, T. (1993) 'Identifying formulas in first language acquisition', *Journal of Child Language*, 20: 27–41.

Hirsh-Pasek, K. and Golinkoff, R.M. (1996a) 'The intermodal preferential looking paradigm: a window onto emerging language comprehension', in D. McDaniel, C. McKee and H.S. Cairns (eds), *Methods for Assessing Children's Syntax*, Cambridge, MA: MIT Press.

—— and —— (1996b) *The Origins of Grammar*, Cambridge, MA: MIT Press.

Hoek, D., Ingram, D. and Gibson, D. (1986) 'Some possible causes of children's early word overextensions', *Journal of Child Language*, 13: 477–94.

Hoekstra, T. and Hyams, N. (1995) 'The syntax and interpretation of dropped categories in child language: a unified account', *Proceedings of WCCFL XIV*, CSIL, Stanford University.

——, —— and Becker, M. (1996) 'The role of the specifier and finiteness in early grammar', paper presented at the Conference on Specifiers, University of York, UK.

Hoffman, C. (1985) 'Language acquisition in two trilingual children', *Journal of Multilingual and Multicultural Development*, 6: 479–95.

Hollingshead, A. (1975) 'Four Factor Index of Social Status', unpublished manuscript, Yale University.

Hollos, M. (1977) 'Comprehension and use of social rules in pronoun selection by Hungarian children', in S. Ervin-Tripp and C. Mitchell-Kernan (eds), *Child Discourse*, New York: Academic Press.

Hopper, P.J. and Thompson, S.A. (1984) 'The discourse basis for lexical categories in universal grammar', *Language*, 60: 703–52.

Howell, D.C. (1996) *Statistical Methods for Psychology*, 4th edn, New York: Wadsworth.

Huerta, A. (1977) 'The acquisition of bilingualism: a code-switching approach', *Sociolinguistic Working Paper*, 39: 1–33.

Hutchinson, J.E. (1986) 'Children's sensitivity to the contrastive use of object category terms', *Papers and Reports on Child Language Development*, 25: 49–55.

Hyams, N. (1983) 'The acquisition of parametrized grammars', doctoral dissertation, CUNY.

—— (1986) *Language Acquisition and the Theory of Parameters*, Dordrecht: Reidel.

—— (1993) 'An overview of null subjects', talk presented at the TECS Workshop 'Crosslinguistic Studies on Language Acquisition', SISSA, Trieste, Italy.

—— (1996) 'The underspecification of functional categories in early grammar', in H. Clahsen (ed.), *Generative Approaches to First and Second Language Acquisition*, Amsterdam: John Benjamins.

—— and Wexler, K. (1993) 'On the grammatical basis of null subject in child language', *Linguistic Inquiry*, 24: 421–59.

Hymes, D.H. (1972) 'On communicative competence', in J.B. Pride and J. Holmes (eds), *Sociolinguistics*, Harmondsworth: Penguin.

Imedadze, N.V. (1967) 'On the psychological nature of child speech formation under conditions of exposure to two languages', *International Journal of Psychology*, 2: 129–32.

Ingram, D. (1976) *Phonological Disability in Children*, London: Edward Arnold.

—— (1989) *First Language Acquisition*, Cambridge: Cambridge University Press.

—— (2002) 'The measurement of whole-word productions', *Journal of Child Language*, 29: 713–33.

—— and Le Normand, M.-T. (1996) 'A diary study on the acquisition of Middle French: a preliminary report on the early language acquisition of Louis XIII', in A. Stringfellow, D. Cahana-Amitay, E. Hughes and A. Zukowski (eds), *Proceedings of the 20th Annual Boston University Conference on Language Development*, vol. 1, Somerville, MA: Cascadilla Press.

Jacoby, L.L. and Craik, F.I.M. (1979) 'Effects of elaboration of processing at encoding and retrieval: trace distinctiveness and recovery of initial context', in L.S. Cermak and F.I.M. Craik (eds), *Levels of Processing in Human Memory*, Hillsdale, NJ: Erlbaum.

Jensen, J. (1991) 'Vowel laxing and vowel reduction in English', *Proceedings of the 1991 Annual Conference of the Canadian Linguistic Association*, Toronto: Toronto Working Papers in Linguistics.

Johnson, C.E. (1999) 'What you see is what you get: the importance of transcription for interpreting children's morphosyntactic development', in L. Menn and N.B. Ratner (eds), *Methods for Studying Language Production*, Mahwah, NJ: Erlbaum.

Johnston, J.R. (1985) 'Cognitive prerequisites: the evidence from children learning English', in D.I. Slobin (ed.), *The Crosslinguistic Study of Language Acquisition*, vol. 2, *Theoretical Issues*, Hillsdale, NJ: Erlbaum.

Jordens, P. (1990) 'The acquisition of verb placement in Dutch and German', *Linguistics*, 28: 1407–48.

Kail, R. (1991) 'Developmental change in speed of processing during childhood and adolescence', *Psychological Bulletin*, 109: 490–501.

Karmiloff-Smith, A. (1979) *A Functional Approach to Child Language*, Cambridge: Cambridge University Press.

—— (1988) 'The child is a theoretician, not an inductivist', *Mind and Language*, 3: 183–97.

—— (1992) *Beyond Modularity: a developmental perspective on cognitive science*, Cambridge, MA: MIT Press.

—— and Inhelder, B. (1974) 'If you want to get ahead, get a theory', *Cognition*, 3: 195–212.

——, Grant, J., Berthoud, I., Davies, M., Howlin, P. and Udwin, O. (1997) 'Language and Williams Syndrome: how intact is "intact"?', *Child Development*, 68: 246–262.

Karniol, R. (1992) 'Stuttering out of bilingualism', *First Language*, 12: 255–83.

Katz, N., Baker, E. and Macnamara, J. (1974) 'What's a name? On the child's acquisition of proper and common nouns', *Child Development*, 45: 469–73.

Keenan, E.O. and Klein, E. (1974) 'Coherency in children's discourse', paper presented at the summer meeting of the Linguistic Society of America, Amherst, Massachusetts, July.

Keil, F.C. (1987) 'Conceptual development and category structure', in U. Neisser (ed.), *Concepts and Conceptual Development*, New York: Cambridge University Press.

—— (1989) *Concepts, Kinds, and Cognitive Development*, Cambridge, MA: Bradford/MIT Press.

Kennedy, I. (1988) *Treat Me Right*, Oxford: Clarendon Press.

Kenyeres, E. (1926) *A Gyermek Elsö Szavai es a Szófajók Föllépése* [The child's first words and the appearance of parts of speech], Budapest: Kisdednevelés.

Kerswill, P. and Williams, A. (2000) 'Creating a New Town koine: children and language change in Milton Keynes', *Language in Society*, 29: 65–115.

Kielhöfer, B. and Jonekeit, S. (1983) *Zweisprachige Kindererziehung*, Tübingen: Stauffenberg.

Kilani-Schoch, M., de Marco, A., Christofidou, A., Vassilakou, M., Vollman, R. and Dressler, W.U. (1997) 'On the demarcation of phases in early morphology acquisition in four languages', *Poznan Studies in Contemporary Linguistics*, 33.

Kimura, D. (1992) 'Sex differences in the brain', *Scientific American*, 267: 118–25.

—— (1996) 'Sex, sexual orientation and sex hormones influence human cognitive function', *Current Opinion in Neurobiology*, 6: 259–63.

Klee, T. (1992) 'Developmental and diagnostic characteristics of quantitative measures of children's language production', *Topics in Language Disorders*, 12: 28–41.

Klein, H. (1978) *The Relationship Between Perceptual Strategies and Production Strategies in Learning the Phonology of Early Lexical Items*, Bloomington, IN: Indiana University Linguistics Club.

—— (1981) 'Early perceptual strategies for the replication of consonants from polysyllabic lexical models', *Journal of Speech and Hearing Research*, 24: 535–51.

Kohonen, T. (1982) 'Self-organized formation of topologically correct feature maps', *Biological Cybernetics*, 43: 59–69.

Krämer, I. (1993) 'The licensing of subjects in early child language', in C. Phillips (ed.), *Papers on Case and Agreement II*, MIT Working Papers in Linguistics, 19: 197–212.

Kuczaj, S.A., II (1977) 'The acquisition of regular and irregular past tense forms', *Journal of Verbal Learning and Verbal Behavior*, 16: 589–600.

—— (1978) 'Children's judgments of grammatical and ungrammatical irregular past-tense verbs', *Child Development*, 49: 319–26.

Labov, W. (1972) *Language in the Inner City*, Philadelphia: University of Pennsylvania Press.

Lam, A. (2001) 'Bilingualism', in R. Carter and D. Nunan (eds), *The Cambridge Guide to Teaching English to Speakers of Other Languages*, Cambridge: Cambridge University Press.

Landau, B. and Gleitman, L.R. (1985) *Language and Experience: evidence from the blind child*, Cambridge, MA: Harvard University Press.

—— and Jackendoff, R. (1993) ' "What" and "where" in spatial language and spatial cognition', *Behavioral and Brain Sciences*, 16: 217–55.

——, Smith, L.B. and Jones, S.S. (1992) 'Syntactic context and the shape bias in children's and adults' lexical learning', *Journal of Memory and Language*, 31: 807–25.

Lange, T.E. (1992) 'Hybrid connectionist models: temporary bridges over the gap between the symbolic and subsymbolic', in J. Dinsmore (ed.), *The Symbolic and Connectionist Paradigms*, Hillsdale, NJ: Erlbaum.

Lanza, E. (1992) 'Can bilingual two year olds switch?', *Journal of Child Language*, 19: 633–58.

Lasnik, H. (1989) 'On certain substitutes for negative data', in R. Mathews and W. Demopoulos (eds), *Learnability and Linguistic Theory*, Dordrecht: Kluwer.

Lederer, A., Gleitman, L.R. and Gleitman, H. (1995) 'Verbs of a feather flock together: semantic information in the structure of maternal speech', in M. Tomasello and W.E. Merriman (eds), *Beyond Names for Things: young children's acquisition of verbs*, Mahwah, NJ: Erlbaum.

Leech, G., Rayson, P. and Wilson, A. (2001) *Word Frequencies in Written and Spoken English*, Harlow: Pearson Education.

Lenneberg, E. (1967) *Biological Foundations of Language*, New York: Wiley.

Leonard, L.B., Miller, C. and Gerber, E. (1999) 'Grammatical morphology and the lexicon in children with specific language impairment', *Journal of Speech, Language and Hearing Research*, 42: 678–89.

Leopold, W. (1939) *Speech Development of a Bilingual Child: a linguist's record*, vol. 1, *Vocabulary Growth in the First Two Years*, Evanston, IL: Northwestern University Press.

—— (1947) *Speech Development of a Bilingual Child: a linguist's record*, vol. 2, *Sound-learning in the First Two Years,* Evanston, IL: Northwestern University Press.

—— (1949a) *Speech Development of a Bilingual Child: a linguist's record*, vol. 3, *Grammar and General Problems in the First Two Years*, Evanston, IL: Northwestern University Press.

—— (1949b) *Speech Development of a Bilingual Child: a linguist's record*, vol. 4, *Diary from Age 2*, Evanston, IL: Northwestern University Press.

Levelt, C.C. (1996) 'Consonant-vowel interactions in early child language', in E.V. Clark (ed.), *Proceedings of the 30th Annual Child Language Forum*, Stanford: CSLI.

Levin, B. (1993) *English Verb Classes and Alternations: a preliminary investigation*, Chicago: University of Chicago Press.

Li, W. (ed.) (2000) *The Bilingualism Reader*, London: Routledge.

Liebermann, P. (1967) *Intonation, Perception and Language*, Cambridge, MA: MIT Press.

Lightbown, P. (1977) *Consistency and Variation in the Acquisition of French*, doctoral dissertation, Columbia University.

Liittschwager, J.C. and Markman, E.M. (1994) 'Sixteen- and 24-month-olds' use of mutual exclusivity as a default assumption in second-label learning', *Developmental Psychology*, 30: 955–68.

LIPPS Group (2000) 'The LIDES Coding Manual: a document for preparing and analyzing language interaction data', *Journal of Bilingualism*, 4 (whole no. 2).

Lleó, C. and Demuth, K. (1999) 'Prosodic constraints on the emergence of grammatical morphemes: crosslinguistics evidence from Germanic and Romance languages, in A. Greenhill, H. Littlefield and C. Tano (eds), *Proceedings of the 23rd Annual Boston University Conference on Language Development*, Somerville, MA: Cascadilla Press.

Local, J. (1982) 'Modelling intonational variability in children's speech', in S. Romaine (ed.), *Sociolinguistic Variation in Speech Communities*, London: Edward Arnold.

Locke, J. (1690/1964) *An Essay Concerning Human Understanding*, Cleveland: Meridian Books.

Low, A.A. (1931) 'A case of agrammatism in the English language', *Archives of Neurology and Psychiatry*, 25: 556–97.

Lucariello, J. (1987) 'Concept formation and its relation to word learning and use in the second year', *Journal of Child Language*, 14: 309–32.

Lust, B. (1994) 'Functional projection of CP and phrase structure parameterization: an argument for the strong continuity hypothesis', in B. Lust, M. Suñer and J. Whitman (eds), *Syntactic Theory and First Language Acquisition*, vol. 1, Hillsdale, NJ: Erlbaum.

—— (1999) 'Universal grammar', in W. Ritchie and T.J. Bhatia (eds), *Handbook of Child Language Acquisition*, New York: Academic Press.

Lyons, J. (1968) *Introduction to Theoretical Linguistics*, Cambridge: Cambridge University Press.

Macaulay, R.K.S. (1978) 'Variation and consistency in Glaswegian English', in P. Trudgill (ed.), *Sociolinguistic Patterns in British English*, London: Edward Arnold.

McCarthy, J. and Prince, A. (1986) 'Prosodic morphology', manuscript, University of Massachusetts and Brandeis University.

—— and —— (1995) 'Prosodic morphology', in J.A. Goldsmith (ed.), *The Handbook of Phonological Theory*, Cambridge, MA: Blackwell.

McClelland, J.L. and Kawamoto, A. (1986) 'Mechanisms of sentence processing: assigning roles to constituents', in J.L. McClelland and D.E. Rumelhart (eds), *Parallel Distributed Processing*, Cambridge, MA: MIT Press.

Maccoby, E.E. and Jacklin, C.N. (1974) *The Psychology of Sex Differences*, Stanford: Stanford University Press.

McCormick, R. (1982) *How Brave a New World? Dilemmas in bioethics*, Washington, DC: Georgetown University Press.

McCune-Nicolich, L. (1981) 'The cognitive bases of relational words in the single-word period', *Journal of Child Language*, 8: 15–34.

McDaniel, D., McKee, C. and Cairns, H.S. (eds) (1996) *Methods for Assessing Children's Syntax*, Cambridge, MA: MIT Press.

McEvoy, S. and Dodd, B. (1992) 'The communication abilities of 2- to 4-year-old twins', *European Journal of Disorders of Communication*, 27: 73–87.

McKee, G., Malvern, D. and Richards, B.J. (2000) 'Measuring vocabulary diversity using dedicated software', *Literary and Linguistic Computing*, 15: 323–38.

Macken, M.A. (1979) 'Development reorganization of phonology: a hierarchy of basic units of acquisition', *Lingua*, 49: 11–49.

McLaughlin, B. (1984) 'Early bilingualism: methodological and theoretical issues', in M. Paradis and Y. Lebrun (eds), *Early Bilingualism and Child Development*, Lisse: Swets and Zeitlinger.

Macnamara, J. (1982) *Names for Things: a study of human learning*, Cambridge, MA: MIT Press.

McTear, M. (1985) *Children's Conversation*, Oxford: Blackwell.

MacWhinney, B. (1977) 'Starting points', *Language*, 53: 152–68.

—— (1978) 'The acquisition of morphophonology', *Monographs of the Society for Research in Child Development*, 43, (whole no. 1): 1–123.

—— (1988) 'Competition and teachability', in R. Schiefelbusch and M. Rice (eds), *The Teachability of Language*, New York: Cambridge University Press.

—— (1989) 'Competition and lexical categorization', in R. Corrigan, F. Eckman and M. Noonan (eds), *Linguistic Categorization*, New York: John Benjamins.

—— (2000) *The CHILDES Project: tools for analyzing talk*, 3rd edn, Mahwah, NJ: Erlbaum.

—— and Bates, E. (1989) *The Crosslinguistic Study of Sentence Processing*, New York: Cambridge University Press.

—— and Leinbach, J. (1991) 'Implementations are not conceptualizations: revising the verb learning model', *Cognition*, 29: 121–57.

—— and Pléh, C. (1988) 'The processing of restrictive relative clauses in Hungarian', *Cognition*, 29: 95–141.

—— and Snow, C.E. (1985) 'The Child Language Data Exchange System', *Journal of Child Language*, 12: 271–96.

—— and —— (1990) 'The Child Language Data Exchange System: an update', *Journal of Child Language*, 17: 457–72.

——, Leinbach, J., Taraban, R. and McDonald, J.L. (1989) 'Language learning: cues or rules?', *Journal of Memory and Language*, 28: 255–77.

Maltz, D.N. and Borker, R.A. (1982) 'A cultural approach to male–female miscommunication', in J. Gumperz (ed.), *Language and Social Identity*, Cambridge: Cambridge University Press.

Malvern, D.D. and Richards, B.J. (1997) 'A new measure of lexical diversity', in A. Ryan and A. Wray (eds), *Evolving Models of Language*, Clevedon: Multilingual Matters.

—— and —— (2000) 'Validation of a new measure of lexical diversity: a pilot study', in M. Beers, B. van den Bogaerde, G. Bol, J. de Jong and C. Rooijmans (eds), *From Sound to Sentence: studies on first language acquisition*, University of Groningen: Centre for Language and Cognition.

Maratsos, M. and Chalkley, M.A. (1980) 'The internal language of children's syntax: the ontogenesis and representation of syntactic categories', in K. Nelson (ed.), *Children's Language*, vol. 2, New York: Gardner Press.

Marazita, J. and Merriman, W.E. (1994) 'Preschoolers' lexical novelty monitoring ability and their tendency to map novel names onto novel objects', paper presented at the biennial Conference on Human Development, Pittsburgh, April.

Marcus, G.F., Pinker, S., Ullman, M., Hollander, M., Rosen, T.J. and Xu, F. (1992) 'Overregularization in language acquisition', *Monographs of the Society for Research in Child Development*, 57, serial no. 228.

Mariscal, S. (1997) 'El processo de grammaticalización de las categorias nominales en Español', doctoral dissertation, Universidad Autonoma de Madrid.

Markman, E.M. (1989) *Categorization and Naming in Children: problems of induction*, Cambridge, MA: MIT Press.

—— (1992) 'Constraints on word learning: speculations about their nature, origins, and domain specificity', in M.R. Gunnar and M.P. Maratsos (eds), *Modularity and Constraints in Language and Cognition*, *Minnesota Symposium on Child Psychology*, Hillsdale, NJ: Erlbaum.

—— and Wachtel, G.F. (1988) 'Children's use of mutual exclusivity to constrain the meanings of words', *Cognitive Psychology*, 20: 121–57.

Martin-Jones, M. and Romaine, S. (1985) 'Semilingualism: a half-baked theory of communicative competence', *Applied Linguistics*, 6: 105–17.

Masur, E.F. (1982) 'Mothers' responses to infants' object-related gestures: influences on lexical development', *Journal of Child Language*, 9: 23–30.

Matsumoto, Y. (1993) 'Japanese numeral classifiers: a study of semantic categories and lexical organization', *Linguistics*, 31: 667–713.

Matthews, P. (2001) *A Short History of Structural Linguistics*, Cambridge: Cambridge University Press.

Maybin, J. (1996) 'Story voices: the use of reported speech in 10–12-year-olds' spontaneous narratives', *Current Issues in Language and Society*, 3: 36–48.

Maynard, D. (1986) 'Offering and soliciting collaboration in multi-party disputes among children (and other humans)', *Human Studies*, 9: 261–85.

Meditch, A. (1975) 'The development of sex-specific patterns in young children', *Anthropological Linguistics*, 17: 421–33.

Meggyes, K. (1971) *Egy Kétéves Gyermek Nyelvi Rendszere*, Budapest: Akadémiai Kiadó.

Meisel, J. (1986) 'Word order and case marking in early child language. Evidence from simultaneous acquisition of two first languages: French and German', *Linguistics*, 24: 123–83.

—— (1989) 'Early differentiation of languages in bilingual children', in K. Hyltenstam and L. Obler (eds), *Bilingualism Across the Lifespan: aspects of acquisition, maturity, and loss*, Cambridge: Cambridge University Press.

—— (1990a) 'Grammatical development in the simultaneous acquisition of two first languages', in J. Meisel (ed.), *Two First Languages: early grammatical development in bilingual children*, Dordrecht: Foris.

—— (1990b) 'Inflection, subjects and subject-verb agreement', in J. Meisel (ed.), *Two First Languages: early grammatical development in bilingual children*, Dordrecht: Foris.

—— (1995) 'Code-switching in young bilingual children: the acquisition of grammatical constraints', *Studies in Second Language Acquisition*, 16: 413–39.

Meltzoff, A.N. (1999) 'Origins of theory of mind, cognition and communication', *Journal of Communication Disorders*, 32: 251–69.

Ménard, N. (1983) *Mesure de la Richesse Lexicale*, Geneva: Slatkine.

Menn, L. (1971) 'Phonotactic rules in beginning speech', *Lingua*, 26: 225–51.

—— (1983) 'Development of articulatory, phonetic, and phonological capabilities', in B. Butterworth (ed.), *Language Production*, vol. 2, London: Academic Press.

—— and Ratner, N.B. (eds) (1999) *Methods for Studying Language Production*, Mahwah, NJ: Erlbaum.

Merriman, W.E. (1986) 'Some reasons for the occurrence and eventual correction of children's naming errors', *Child Development*, 57: 942–52.

—— (1991) 'The mutual exclusivity bias in children's word learning: a reply to Woodward and Markman', *Developmental Review*, 11: 164–91.

—— and Bowman, L.L. (1989) 'The mutual exclusivity bias in children's word learning', *Monographs of the Society for Research in Child Development*, 54, serial no. 220.

—— and Kutlesic, V. (1993) 'Bilingual and monolingual children's use of two lexical acquisition heuristics', *Applied Psycholinguistics*, 14: 229–49.

—— and Marazita, J.M. (1995) 'The effect of hearing similar-sounding words on two-year-olds' disambiguation of novel noun reference', *Developmental Psychology*, 31: 973–84.

—— and Schuster, J.M. (1991) 'Young children's disambiguation of object name reference', *Child Development*, 62: 1288–301.

——, Marazita, J. and Jarvis, L.H. (1993a) 'On learning two names for the same thing: the impact of mutual exclusivity violation on two-year-olds' attention and learning', paper presented at the biennial meeting of the Society for Research in Child Development, New Orleans.

——, —— and —— (1993b) 'Four-year-olds' disambiguation of action and object word reference', *Journal of Experimental Child Psychology*, 56: 412–30.

——, —— and —— (1995) 'Children's disposition to map new words onto new referents', in M. Tomasello and W.E. Merriman (eds), *Beyond Names for Things: young children's acquisition of verbs*, Hillsdale, NJ: Erlbaum.

Mervis, C.B. (1984) 'Early lexical development: the contributions of mother and child', in C. Sophian (ed.), *Origins of Cognitive Skills*, Hillsdale, NJ: Erlbaum.

—— (1987) 'Child-basic object categories and early lexical development', in U. Neisser (ed.), *Concepts and Conceptual Development: ecological and intellectual factors in categorization*, Cambridge: Cambridge University Press.

—— and Bertrand, J. (1994) 'Acquisition of the novel name-nameless category (N3C) principle', *Child Development*, 65: 1646–62.

——, Mervis, C.A., Johnson, K. and Bertrand, J. (1992) 'Studying early lexical development: the value of the systematic diary method', in C. Rovee-Collier and L. Lipsitt (eds), *Advances in Infancy Research*, vol. 7, Norwood, NJ: Ablex.

Michéa, R. (1969) *Répétition et Variété dans l'Emploi des Mots*, Bulletin de la Sociéte de Linguistique de Paris.

Miikkulainen, R. (1990) 'A distributed feature map model of the lexicon', *Proceedings of the 12th Annual Conference of the Cognitive Science Society*, Hillsdale, NJ: Erlbaum.

—— (1993) *Subsymbolic Natural Language Processing*, Cambridge, MA: MIT Press.

Mikeš, M. (1967) 'Acquisition des catégoires grammaticales dans le language de l'enfant', *Enfance*, 20: 289–98.

Miller, J.F. (1981) *Assessing Language Production: experimental procedures*, London: Arnold.

—— (1991) 'Quantifying productive language disorders', in J.F. Miller (ed.), *Research on Child Language Disorders: a decade of progress*, Austin, TX: Pro-Ed.

—— and Chapman, R. (1983) *SALT: systematic analysis of language transcripts, user's manual*, Madison, WI: University of Wisconsin Press.

Miller, M.H. (1976) *Zur Logik der Frühkindlichen Sprachentwicklung* [On the Logic of Early Language Development], Stuttgart: Klett.

Miller, P., Danaher, D. and Forbes, D. (1986) 'Sex-related strategies for coping with interpersonal conflict in children aged five and seven', *Developmental Psychology*, 22: 543–8.

Moerk, E. (1983) *The Mother of Eve as a First Language Teacher*, Norwood, NJ: Ablex.

Morgan, G., Herman, R. and Woll, B. (2002) 'The development of complex verb constructions in British Sign Language', *Journal of Child Language*, 29: 655–75.

Morgan, J. and Travis, L. (1989) 'Limits on negative information in language input', *Journal of Child Language*, 16: 531–52.

Morton, J. (1970) 'A functional model for memory', in D.A. Norman (ed.), *Models of Human Memory*, New York: Academic Press.

Mulford, R.C. (1983) 'On the acquisition of derivational morphology in Icelandic: learning about -ari', *Islenskt mal og almenn malfraedi*, 5: 105–25.

Naigles, L.R. (1990) 'Children use syntax to learn verb meanings', *Journal of Child Language*, 17: 357–74.

—— and Hoff-Ginsberg, E. (1993) 'Input to verb learning: verb frame diversity in mother's speech predicts children's verb use', unpublished manuscript, Yale University.

Nelson, K. (1973a) 'Some evidence for the cognitive primacy of categorization and its functional basis', *Merrill-Palmer Quarterly*, 19: 21–39.

—— (1973b) 'Structure and strategy in learning to talk', *Monographs of the Society for Research in Child Development*, 149, 38 (1–2).

—— (1988) 'Constraints on word learning?', *Cognitive Development*, 3: 221–46.

—— and Lucariello, J. (1985) 'The development of meaning in first words', in M. Barrett (ed.), *Children's Single-Word Speech*, Chichester: Wiley.

Nespor, M. and Vogel, I. (1986) *Prosodic Phonology*, Dordrecht: Foris.

Newmeyer, F.J. (1998) *Language Form and Language Function*, Cambridge, MA: MIT Press.

Nicoladis, E. (2002) 'What's the difference between "toilet paper" and "paper toilet"? French–English bilingual children's crosslinguistic transfer in compound nouns', *Journal of Child Language*, 29: 843–63.

Ninio, A. (1980) 'Ostensive definition in vocabulary teaching', *Journal of Child Language,* 7: 565–74.

Nunan, D. (2001) 'Second language acquisition', in R. Carter and D. Nunan (eds), *The Cambridge Guide to Teaching English to Speakers of Other Languages*, Cambridge: Cambridge University Press.

Ochs, E. (1982) 'Talking to children in Western Samoa', *Language in Society*, 11: 77–105.

—— and Schieffelin, B.B. (eds) (1979) *Developmental Pragmatics*, New York: Academic Press.

—— and —— (1983) *Acquiring Conversational Competence*, London: Routledge and Kegan Paul.

—— and —— (1984) 'Language acquisition and socialization: three developmental stories', in R. Shweder and R. Levine (eds), *Culture Theory: essays in mind, self and emotion*, New York: Cambridge University Press.

O'Grady, W. (1987) *Principles of Grammar and Learning*, Chicago: Chicago University Press.

—— (1997) *Syntactic Development*, Chicago: University of Chicago Press.

Oksaar, E. (1977) 'On becoming trilingual', in C. Molony (ed.), *Deutsch im Kontakt mit Anderen Sprachen*, Kronberg: Scriptor.

Oller, D.K. and Eilers, R.E. (eds) (2002) *Language and Literacy in Bilingual Children*, Clevedon: Multilingual Matters.

Padilla, A.M. and Liebman, E. (1975) 'Language acquisition in the bilingual child', *Bilingual Review*, 2: 34–55.

Paradis, M. and Lebrun, Y. (eds) (1984) *Early Bilingualism and Child Development*, Lisse: Swets and Zeitlinger.

Parrish, M. (1996) 'Alan Lomax: documenting folk music of the world', *Sing Out! The Folk Song Magazine*, 40: 30–9.

Partee, B. (1973) 'Some structural analogies between tenses and pronouns in English', *The Journal of Philosophy*, 70: 1–28.

Paulesu, E., Frith, C.D. and Frackowiak, R.S.J. (1993) 'The neural correlates of the verbal component of working memory', *Nature*, 362: 342–45.

Pearson, B.Z., Fernández, S., Lewedag, V. and Oller, D.K. (1997) 'Input factors in lexical learning of bilingual infants (aged 10 to 30 months)', *Applied Psycholinguistics*, 18: 41–58.

Perkins, M. (1983) *Modal Expressions in English*, London: Frances Pinter.

Perner, J. (1991) *Understanding the Representational Mind*, Cambridge, MA: Bradford/MIT Press.

Peters, A.M. (1977) 'Language learning strategies: does the whole equal the sum of the parts?', *Language*, 53: 560–73.

—— (1983) *The Units of Language Acquisition*, New York: Cambridge University Press.

—— (1986) 'Early syntax', in P. Fletcher and M. Garman (eds), *Language Acquisition*, 2nd edn, New York: Cambridge University Press.

—— (1993) 'The interdependence of social, cognitive and linguistic development: evidence from a visually-impaired child, in H. Tager-Flusberg (ed.), *Constraints on Language Acquisition: studies of atypical children*, Hillsdale, NJ: Erlbaum.

—— (1995) 'Strategies in the acquisition of syntax', in P. Fletcher and B. MacWhinney (eds), *The Handbook of Child Language*, Oxford: Blackwell.

—— (1996) 'The emergence of catenatives from filler syllables', paper presented at conference on Approaches to Bootstrapping in Early Language Development, Berlin, September.

—— (1997) 'Language typology, prosody and the acquisition of grammatical morphemes', in D.I. Slobin (ed.), *The Crosslinguistic Study of Language Acquistion*, Hillsdale, NJ: Erlbaum.

—— (1999) 'The emergence of so-called 'functional categories' in English: a case study of auxiliaries, modals and quasi-modals', in S.J. Hwang and A. Lommel (eds), *LACUS Forum XXV*, Fullerton, CA: Linguistic Association of Canada and the United States.

—— (2001) 'From prosody to grammar in English: the differentiation of catenatives, modals, and auxiliaries from a single protomorpheme', in J. Weissenborn and B. Höhle (eds), *Approaches to Bootstrapping: phonological, lexical syntactic and neurophysiological aspects of early language acquisition*, vol. 2, Amsterdam: John Benjamins.

—— and Menn, L. (1993) 'False starts and filler syllables: ways to learn grammatical morphemes', *Language*, 69: 742–77.

Petersen, J. (1988) 'Word internal code-switching constraints in a bilingual child's grammar', *Linguistics*, 26: 479–94.

Petitto, L.A., Katerelos, K., Levy, B.G., Gauna, K., Tétreault, K. and Ferraro, V. (2001) 'Bilingual signed and spoken language acquisition from birth: implications for the mechanisms underlying early bilingual language acquisition', *Journal of Child Language*, 28: 453–96.

Piaget, J. (1954; 1st edn 1937) *The Construction of Reality in the Child*, New York: Basic Books.

—— and Inhelder, B. (1969) *The Psychology of the Child*, London: Routledge and Kegan Paul.

Pick, A. (1913) *Die Agrammatischer Sprachstörungen*, Berlin: Springer-Verlag.

Pierce, A. (1989) 'On the emergence of syntax: a cross-linguistic study', doctoral dissertation, MIT.

—— (1992) *Language Acquisition and Syntactic Theory: a comparative analysis of French and English child grammars*, Dordrecht: Kluwer.

Pine, J.M., Lieven, E.V.M. and Rowland, C. (1997) 'Stylistic variation at the "single-word" stage: relations between maternal speech characteristics and children's vocabulary composition and usage', *Child Development*, 68(5): 807–19.

Pinker, S. (1984) *Language Learnability and Language Development*, Cambridge, MA: Harvard University Press.

—— (1989) *Learnability and Cognition: the acquisition of argument structure*, Cambridge, MA: MIT Press.

—— and Prince, A. (1988) 'On language and connectionism: analysis of a parallel distributed processing model of language acquisition', *Cognition*, 28: 73–193.

Pizzini, F. (1991) 'Communication hierarchies in humour: gender differences in the obstetrical/gynaecological setting', *Discourse and Society*, 2: 477–88.

Pizzutto, E. and Caselli, M.C. (1992) 'The acquisition of Italian morphology: implications for models of language development', *Journal of Child Language*, 19: 491–558.

Platzack, C. (1992) 'Functional categories and early Swedish', in J. Meisel (ed.), *The Acquisition of Verb Placement*, Dordrecht: Kluwer.

Plunkett, K. (1995) 'Connectionist approaches to language acquisition', in P. Fletcher and B. MacWhinney (eds), *The Handbook of Child Language*, Oxford: Blackwell.

—— and Marchman, V.A. (1993) 'From rote learning to system building: acquiring verb morphology in children and connectionist nets', *Cognition*, 48: 21–69.

—— and Schaffer, G. (1999) 'Early speech perception and word learning', in M. Barrett (ed.), *The Development of Language*, Philadelphia, PA: Psychology Press.

—— , Sinha, C., Moller, M.F. and Strandsby, O. (1992) 'Symbol grounding or the emergence of symbols? Vocabulary growth in children and a connectionist net', *Connection Science*, 4: 293–312.

Poeppel, D. and Wexler, K. (1993) 'The full competence hypothesis of clause structure', *Language*, 69: 1–33.

Pollard, C. and Sag, I. (1994) *Head-driven Phrase Structure Grammar*, Chicago: Chicago University Press.

Pollock, J.-Y. (1989) 'Verb movement, Universal Grammar, and the structure of IP', *Linguistic Inquiry*, 20: 365–424.

Preyer, W. (1882) *Die Seele des Kindes*, Leipzig: Grieben's.

Quine, W. (1960) *Word and Object*, Cambridge, MA: Harvard University Press.

Quirk, R., Greenbaum, S., Leech, G. and Svartvik, J. (1985) *A Comprehensive Grammar of the English Language*, London: Longman.

Radford, A. (1990) *Syntactic Theory and the Acquisition of English Syntax*, Oxford: Blackwell.

Ramsey, P. (1976) 'The enforcement of morals: nontherapeutic research on children', *Hastings Centre Report*, 6: 23–30.

Redlinger, W. and Park, T.-Z. (1980) 'Language mixing in young bilinguals', *Journal of Child Language*, 7: 337–52.

Reinhart, T. (1983) *Anaphora and Semantic Interpretation*, Chicago: University of Chicago Press.

Remick, H. (1976) 'Maternal speech to children during language acquisition', in W. von Raffler-Engel and Y. Lebrun (eds), *Baby Talk and Infant Speech*, Amsterdam: Swets and Zeitlinger.

Rescorla, L.A. (1976) *Concept Formation in Word Learning*, unpublished doctoral dissertation, Yale University.

Richards, B.J. (1987) 'Type/token ratios: what do they really tell us?' *Journal of Child Language*, 14: 201–9.

—— (1994) 'Child-directed speech and influences on language acquisition: methodology and interpretation', in C. Gallaway and B. Richards (eds), *Input and Interaction in Language Acquisition*, Cambridge: Cambridge University Press.

—— and Malvern, D.D. (1997) *Quantifying Lexical Diversity in the Study of Language Development*, Reading: The University of Reading, The New Bulmershe Papers.

Ringen, C.O. (1988) 'Transparency in Hungarian vowel harmony', *Phonology*, 5: 327–42.

Rispoli, M. (1987) 'The acquisition of the transitive and intransitive action verb categories in Japanese', *First Language*, 7: 183–200.

—— (1999) 'Functionalist accounts of first language acquisition', in W. Ritchie and T.J. Bhatia (eds), *Handbook of Child Language Acquisition*, New York: Academic Press.

Ritchie, W. and Bhatia, T.J. (1999) 'Child language acquisition: introduction foundations and overview', in W. Ritchie and T.J. Bhatia (eds), *Handbook of Child Language Acquisition*, New York: Academic Press.

Rivero, M., Gràcia, M. and Fernández-Viader, P. (1998) 'Including non-verbal communicative acts in the mean length of turn analysis using CHILDES', in A. Aksu Koç, E. Taylan, A. Özsoy and A. Küntay (eds), *Perspectives on Language Acquisition*, Istanbul: Bogaziçi University Press.

Rizzi, L. (1994) 'Early null subjects and root null subjects', in B. Schwartz and T. Hoekstra (eds), *Language Acquisition Studies in Generative Grammar*, Amsterdam: John Benjamins.

Roberts, K. and Jacob, M. (1991) 'Linguistic vs attentional influences on nonlinguistic categorization in 15-month-old infants', *Cognitive Development*, 6: 355–75.

Robson, C. (2001) *Real World Research: a resource for social scientists and practitioner-researchers*, 2nd edn, Oxford: Blackwell.

Rohrbacher, B. and Vainikka, A. (1994) 'On German verb syntax under age 2', IRCS Report 94–24.

Romaine, S. (1978) 'Postvocalic /r/ in Scottish English: sound change in progress?', in P. Trudgill (ed.), *Sociolinguistic Patterns in British English*, London: Edward Arnold.

—— (1984) *The Language of Children and Adolescents: the acquisition of communicative competence*, Oxford: Blackwell.

—— (1992) 'Bilingualism', in T. McArthur (ed.), *The Oxford Companion to the English Language*, Oxford: Oxford University Press.

—— (1995) *Bilingualism*, 2nd edn, Oxford: Blackwell.

Ronjat, J. (1913) *Le Développement du Langage Observé chez un Enfant Bilingue*, Paris: Champion.

Ruddy, M.G. and Bornstein, M.H. (1982) 'Cognitive correlates of infant attention and maternal stimulation over the first year of life', *Child Development*, 53: 183–8.

Ryan, J. (1974) 'Early language development: towards a communicational analysis', in M.P.M. Richards (ed.), *The Integration of a Child into a Social World*, Cambridge: Cambridge University Press.

Sachs, J. (1987) 'Preschool boys' and girls' language use in pretend play', in S. Phillips, S. Steele and C. Tanz (eds), *Language, Gender and Sex in Comparative Perspective*, Cambridge: Cambridge University Press.

—— , Brown, R. and Salerno, R. (1976) 'Adults' speech to children', in W. von Raffler-Engel and Y. Lebrun (eds), *Baby Talk and Infant Speech*, Amsterdam: Swets and Zeitlinger.

—— , Lieberman, P. and Erickson, D. (1973) 'Anatomical and cultural determinants of male and female speech', in R. Shuy and R. Fasold (eds), *Language Attitudes: current trends and prospects*, Washington, DC: Georgetown University Press.

Sacks, H., Schegloff, E. and Jefferson, G. (1974) 'A simplest systematics for the organisation of turn-taking in conversation', *Language*, 50: 696–735.

St John, M. (1992) 'The story gestalt: a model of knowledge-intensive processes in text comprehension', *Cognitive Science*, 16: 271–306.

Sankoff, D. and Poplack, S. (1981) 'A formal grammar for code-switching', *Papers in Linguistics*, 14: 3–46.

Sano, T. and Hyams, N. (1994) 'Agreement, finiteness, and the development of null arguments', *Proceedings of NELS 24*, Amherst: GLSA, 543–58.

Santelmann, L., Berk, S., Austin, J., Somashekar, S. and Lust, B. (2002) 'Continuity and development in the acquisition of inversion in yes/no questions: dissociating movement and inflection', *Journal of Child Language*, 29: 813–42.

Saunders, G. (1982) *Bilingual Children: guidance for the family*, Clevedon: Multilingual Matters.

—— (1988) *Bilingual Children: from birth to teens*, Clevedon: Multilingual Matters.

Scarpa, E. (1993) 'Filler-sounds and the acquisition of prosody: sound and syntax', paper presented at 6th International Conference for the Study of Child Language, Trieste.

Schaeffer, J. (1994) 'On the acquisition of scrambling in Dutch', *Proceedings of the Boston University Conference on Language Development*, I, Somerville, MA: Casadilla Press.

Schieffelin, B. (1981) 'A developmental study of pragmatic appropriateness of word order and case marking in Kaluli', in W. Deutsch (ed.), *The Child's Construction of Language*, New York: Academic Press.

—— (1990) *The Give and Take of Everyday Life: language socialisation of Kaluli children*, Cambridge: Cambridge University Press.

Schlesinger, I.M. (1971) 'Production of utterances and language acquisition', in D.I. Slobin (ed.), *The Ontogeny of Grammar*, New York: Academic Press.

Scollon, R. (1976) *Conversations with a One Year Old,* Honolulu: University of Hawaii Press.

Selkirk, E. (1984) *Phonology and Syntax: the relation between sound and structure*, Cambridge, MA: MIT Press.

Serra, M. and Sòlé, R. (1992) 'Language acquisition in Spanish and Catalan children, longitudinal study', Universidad de Barcelona.

Sheldon, A. (1990) 'Pickle fights: gendered talk in preschool disputes', *Discourse Processes*, 13: 5–31.

—— (1992) 'Conflict talk: sociolinguistic challenges to self-assertion and how young girls meet them', *Merrill-Palmer Quarterly*, 38: 95–117.

Shipman, V.C. (1971) 'Disadvantaged children and their first school experiences', Educational Testing Service Head Start Longitudinal Study.

Sichel, H.S. (1986) 'Word frequency distributions and type-token characteristics', *Mathematical Scientist*, 11: 45–72.

Simonsen, H.G. (1993) 'Models in the description of phonological acquisition', paper presented at 6th International Conference for the Study of Child Language, Trieste.

Skinner, B.F. (1957) *Verbal Behavior,* New York: Appleton-Century-Crofts.

Slater, A. (1989) 'Visual memory and perception in early infancy', in A. Slater and G. Bremner (eds), *Infant Development*, London: Erlbaum.

Slobin, D.I. (1973a) 'Cognitive prerequisites for the development of grammar', in C.A. Ferguson and D.I. Slobin (eds), *Studies of Child Language Development*, New York: Holt, Rinehart and Winston.

—— (1973b) 'Universals of grammatical development in children', in G.B. Flores D'Arcais and W.J.M. Levelt (eds), *Advances in Psycholinguistics*, Amsterdam: North-Holland.

—— (1982) 'Universal and particular in the acquisition of language', in E. Wanner and L.R. Gleitman (eds), *Language Acquisition: the state of the art*, New York: Cambridge University Press.

—— (1985) 'Crosslinguistic evidence for the language-making capacity', in D.I. Slobin (ed.), *The Crosslinguistic Study of Language Acquisition*, vol. 2, *Theoretical Issues*, Hillsdale, NJ: Erlbaum.

—— (ed.) (1985–97) *The Crosslinguistic Study of Language Acquisition*, 5 vols, Hillsdale/Mahwah, NJ: Erlbaum.

—— and Welsh, C.A. (1973) 'Elicited imitation as a research tool in developmental psycholinguistics', in C.A. Ferguson and D.I. Slobin (eds), *Studies in Child Language Development*, New York: Holt, Rinehart and Winston.

Smith, M.E. (1935) 'A study of the speech of eight bilingual children of the same family', *Child Development*, 6: 19–25.

—— (1949) 'Measurement of vocabularies of young bilingual children in both of the languages used', *Journal of Genetic Psychology*, 74: 305–10.

Smith, N.V. (1973) *The Acquisition of Phonology: a case study*, Cambridge: Cambridge University Press.

Smith, R.K. and Connolly, K. (1972) 'Patterns of play and social interaction in pre-school children', in N.B. Jones (ed.), *Ethological Studies of Child Behaviour*, Cambridge University Press.

Snow, C.E. (1975) 'The development of conversation between mothers and babies', *Pragmatics Microfiche*, 1.6 A2, Cambridge University.

—— (1977) 'Mothers' speech research: from input to interaction', in C.E. Snow and C.A. Ferguson (eds), *Talking to Children: language input and acquisition*, Cambridge: Cambridge University Press.

—— (1989) 'Imitativeness: a trait or a skill?' in G.E. Speidel and K.E. Nelson (eds), *The Many Faces of Imitation in Language Learning*, New York: Springer-Verlag.

—— (1995) 'Issues in the study of input: finetuning, universality, individual and developmental differences, and necessary causes', in P. Fletcher and B. MacWhinney (eds), *The Handbook of Child Language*, Oxford: Blackwell.

Soja, N.N. (1992) 'Perception, ontology and word meaning', *Cognition*, 45: 101–7.

Sokolov, J.L. and Snow, C. (eds) (1994) *Handbook of Research in Language Development Using CHILDES*, Hillsdale, NJ: Erlbaum.

Stanford Research Institute (1972) 'Follow-through pupil tests, parent interviews, and teacher questionnaires', Appendix C.

Stephany, U. (1986) 'Modality', in P. Fletcher and M. Garman (eds), *Language Acquisition: studies in first language development*, 2nd edn, Cambridge: Cambridge University Press.

Stern, C. and Stern, W. (1907) *Die Kindersprache*, Leipzig: Barth.

Stickler, K.R. (1987) *Guide to Analysis of Language Transcripts*, Eau Claire, WI: Thinking Publications.

Stoel-Gammon, C. (1983) 'Constraints on consonant-vowel sequences in early words', *Journal of Child Language*, 10: 455–58.

—— (1985) 'Phonetic inventories 15–24 months: a longitudinal study', *Journal of Speech and Hearing Research*, 28: 505–12.

—— (1993) 'Phonological characteristics of children's first words: the earliest stages', paper presented at the 6th International Congress for the Study of Child Language, Trieste, Italy, July.

—— (1994) 'Segments, syllables, and stress in child speech', Child Phonology Conference, Sun Valley, ID, May.

—— and Cooper, J. (1984) 'Patterns of early lexical and phonological development', *Journal of Child Language*, 11: 247–71.

—— and Stemberger, J. (1994) 'Consonant harmony and under-specification in child speech', in M. Yavas (ed.), *First and Second Language Phonology*, San Diego: Singular Publishing Group.

Streeck, J. (1986) 'Towards reciprocity: politics, rank and gender in the interaction of a group of schoolchildren', in J. Cook-Gumperz, W. Corsaro and J. Streeck (eds), *Children's Worlds and Children's Language*, Berlin: Mouton de Gruyter.

Suppes, P., Smith, R. and Leveille, M. (1973) 'The French syntax of a child's noun phrases', *Archives de Psychologie*, 42: 207–79.

Swann, J. (1989) 'Talk control: an illustration from the classroom of problems in analysing male dominance in education', in J. Coates and D. Cameron (eds), *Women in their Speech Communities*, London: Longman.

—— (1992) *Girls, Boys and Language*, Oxford: Blackwell.

Szuman, S. (1955) 'Rozwój treści słownika u dziece', *Studia Pedagogicane*, 2.

Tabouret-Keller, A. (1962) 'L'acquisition du language parlé chez un petit enfant en milieu bilingue', *Problèmes de Psycholinguistique*, 8: 205–19.

Taeschner, T. (1983) *The Sun is Feminine: a study on language acquisition in bilingual children*, Berlin: Springer.

Talmy, L. (1981) 'How language structures space', in H. Pick and L. Acredolo (eds), *Spatial Orientation: theory, research, and application*, New York: Plenum.

—— (1982) 'Borrowing semantic space: Yiddish verb prefixes between Germanic and Slavic', *Proceedings, Berkeley Linguistics Society*, 8: 231–50.

—— (1985) 'Lexicalization patterns: semantic structure in lexical forms', in T. Shopen (ed.), *Language Typology and Syntactic Description*, vol. 3, *Grammatical Categories and the Lexicon*, Cambridge: Cambridge University Press.

—— (1991) 'Path to realization: a typology of event conflation', *Proceedings, Berkeley Linguistics Society*, 17: 480–519.

Tannen, D. (1990a) 'Gender differences in conversational coherence: physical alignment and topical cohesion', in B. Dorval (ed.), *Conversational Organisation and its Development*, Norwood, NJ: Ablex.

—— (1990b) 'Gender differences in topical coherence: creating involvement in best friends' talk', *Discourse Processes*, 13: 73–90.

Tanouye, E.K. (1979) 'The acquisition of verbs in Japanese children', *Papers and Reports on Child Language Development*, 17: 49–56.

Tardif, T. (1996) 'Nouns are not always learned before verbs: evidence from Mandarin speakers' early vocabularies', *Developmental Psychology*, 32: 492–504.

——, Gelman, S.A. and Xu, F. (1999) 'Putting the "noun bias" in context: a comparison of English and Mandarin', *Child Development*, 70: 620–35.

Taylor, M. and Gelman, S.A. (1989) 'Incorporating new words into the lexicon: preliminary evidence for language hierarchies in two-year-old children', *Child Development*, 60: 625–36.

Templin, M. (1957) *Certain Language Skills in Children*, Minneapolis: University of Minnesota Press.

Thompson, G.H. and Thompson, J.R. (1915) 'Outlines of a method for the quantitative analysis of writing vocabularies', *British Journal of Psychology*, 8: 52–69.

Tomasello, M. (1992) *First Verbs: a case study of early grammatical development*, Cambridge: Cambridge University Press.

—— and Brooks, P.J. (1999) 'Early syntactic development', in M. Barrett (ed.), *The Development of Language*, Philadelphia, PA: Psychology Press.

—— and Farrar, J. (1984) 'Cognitive bases of lexical development: object permanence and relational words', *Journal of Child Language*, 11: 477–93.

—— and —— (1986) 'Object permanence and relational words: a lexical training study', *Journal of Child Language*, 13: 495–505.

—— and Kruger, A.C. (1992) 'Joint attention on actions: acquiring verbs in ostensive and non-ostensive contexts', *Journal of Child Language*, 19: 1–23.

Torrens, V. (1992) 'The acquisition of inflection in Catalan and Spanish', talk given at Psycholinguistics Lab, UCLA.

Tufte, E.F. (1983) *Visual Display of Quantitative Information*, Cheshire, CT: Graphics Press.

Tweedie, F.J. and Baayen, R.H. (1998) 'How variable may a constant be? Measures of lexical richness in perspective', *Computers and the Humanities*, 32: 323–52.

UNICEF (2003) (http://www.unicef.org/crc/crc.htm) Text of Article 12 of the Convention on the Rights of the Child, accessed on 6 February 2003.

Valian, V. (1991) 'Syntactic subjects in the early speech of American and Italian children', *Cognition*, 40: 21–81.

—— , Hoeffner, J. and Aubrey, S. (1996) 'Young children's imitation of sentence subjects: evidence of processing limitations', *Developmental Psychology*, 32: 153–64.

Velten, H.V. (1943) 'The growth of phonemic and lexical patterns in infant language', *Language*, 19: 218–92.

Veneziano, E. and Sinclair, H. (2000) 'The changing status of "filler syllables" on the way to grammatical morphemes', *Journal of Child Language* 27: 461–500.

Vermeer, A. (2000) 'Coming to grips with lexical richness in spontaneous speech data', *Language Testing*, 17: 65–83.

Vernon, T. (1980) *Gobbledegook*, London: NCC.

Verrips, M. and Weissenborn, J. (1992) 'Routes to verb placement in early German and French: the independence of finiteness and agreement', in J. Meisel (ed.), *The Acquisition of Verb Placement*, Dordrecht: Kluwer.

Vihman, M. (1985) 'Language differentiation by the bilingual infant', *Journal of Child Language*, 12: 297–324.

Vincent-Smith, L., Bricker, D. and Bricker, W. (1974) 'Acquisition of receptive vocabulary in the toddler-age child', *Child Development*, 45: 189–93.

Volterra, V. and Taeschner, T. (1978) 'The acquisition and development of language by bilingual children', *Journal of Child Language*, 5: 311–26.

Vygotsky, L.S. (1962) *Thought and Language*, New York: John Wiley and MIT Press.

—— (1978) *Mind in Society: the development of higher psychological processes*, Cambridge, MA: Harvard University Press.

Walters, J. (1981) 'Variation in the requesting behaviour of bilingual children', *International Journal of the Sociology of Language*, 27: 77–92.

Waterson, N. (1971) 'Child phonology: a prosodic view', *Journal of Linguistics*, 7: 179–211.

Watkins, R.V., Kelly, D.J., Harbers, H.M. and Hollis, W. (1995) 'Measuring children's lexical diversity: differentiating typical and impaired language learners', *Journal of Speech and Hearing Research*, 38: 1349–55.

Waxman, S.R. (1991) 'Convergences between semantic and conceptual organization in the preschool years', in J.P. Byrnes and S.A. Gelman (eds), *Perspectives on Language and Thought: interrelations in development*, Cambridge: Cambridge University Press.

—— and Senghas, A. (1992) 'Relations among word meanings in early lexical development', *Developmental Psychology*, 28: 862–73.

Weist, R.M. (1986) 'Tense and aspect', in P. Fletcher and M. Garman (eds), *Language Acquisition: studies in first language development*, 2nd edn, Cambridge: Cambridge University Press.

Wellman, H.M. (1985) 'The child's theory of mind: the development of conceptions of cognition', in S.R. Yussen (ed.), *The Growth of Reflection in Children*, Orlando: Academic Press.

—— (1990) *The Child's Theory of Mind*, Cambridge, MA: Bradford/MIT Press.

—— and Gelman, S.A. (1992) 'Cognitive development: foundational theories of core domains', *Annual Review of Psychology*, 43: 337–75.

Wells, C.G. (1979) 'Variation in child language', in V. Lee (ed.), *Language Development*, London: Croom Helm.

—— (ed.) (1981) *Learning Through Interaction*, Cambridge: Cambridge University Press.

—— (1985) *Language Development in the Pre-School Years*, Cambridge: Cambridge University Press.

—— (1986) 'Variation in child language', in P. Fletcher and M. Garman (eds), *Language Acquisition*, 2nd edn, Cambridge: Cambridge University Press.

Wernicke, C. (1874) *Die Aphasische Symptomenkomplex*, Breslau: Cohn and Weigart.

Weverink, M. (1989) 'The subject in relation to inflection in child language', thesis, University of Utrecht.

Wexler, K. (1994) 'Optional infinitives, head movement and the economy of derivation in child grammar', in D. Lightfoot and N. Hornstein (eds), *Verb Movement*, Cambridge: Cambridge University Press.

—— and Culicover, P. (1980) *Formal Principles of Language Acquisition*, Cambridge, MA: MIT Press.

Whorf, B.L. (1956) *Language, Thought, and Reality: selected writings of Benjamin Lee Whorf* (ed. J.B. Carroll), Cambridge, MA: MIT Press.

Wijnen, F. (1995) 'The meaning and structure of optional infinitives', thesis, University of Utrecht.

Woodward, A.L. and Markman, E.M. (1991) 'Constraints on learning as default assumptions: comments on Merriman and Bowman's "The mutual exclusivity bias in children's word learning"', *Developmental Review*, 14: 57–77.

Yule, G.U. (1944) *The Statistical Study of Literary Vocabulary*, Cambridge: Cambridge University Press.

Zwicky, A. (1971) 'In a manner of speaking', *Linguistic Inquiry*, 2: 223–33.

Index